I0539399

CLUSTERS OF WIDE-RANGING ESCAPADES

Written by James E. Diamond, PhD

Edited by Susan Sprague Diamond

© 2024 by James E. Diamond, PhD

All rights reserved. No part of this publication may be reproduced or transmitted in any form or by any means, electronic or mechanical, including photocopying, recording, or any other information storage and retrieval system, without the written permission of the author or publisher.

Printed in the United States of America

Published in Hellertown, PA

Library of Congress Control Number available upon request

ISBN 978-8-89420-022-4

For more information or to place bulk orders, contact the author or the publisher at Jennifer@BrightCommunications.net.

Bright
COMMUNICATIONS

Thank you, Susan! This book of narratives is dedicated to my dearest wife, Susan Sprague Diamond. My wonderful wife not only encouraged me to chronicle these life experiences in the form of narratives, but she dedicated innumerable hours to improving the composition of this book by using her incredible editorial skills to make the best better.

—James E. Diamond, PhD

From his start as a farm boy in Southwestern Pennsylvania who delivered his first calf at age twelve to the completion of his career as dean of agriculture and environmental sciences at Delaware Valley University, Jim Diamond has been a powerhouse of brains and achievement. Writing this book has been no exception. Age has not dimmed his memory or his keen observations of the world around him. This world has been wide, diverse and well-traveled.

Aren't we fortunate that he is willing and able to share some of his adventures in this book, which I happily edited with him. Unlike other authors, he welcomed and embraced criticisms, becoming a student once again as he honed his grammar and writing skills

In his own inimitable writing style, each subject has a prelude, photo or illustration, and a single-page story. Read them one at a time or as many as you care to enjoy in a single sitting. Each will give you a brief glimpse into the amazing life of James E. Diamond, PhD.

—Susan Sprague Diamond

TABLE OF CONTENTS

ABOUT THE AUTHOR

James E. Diamond, PhD, was born and raised on a beef cattle and sheep farm in Southwest Pennsylvania near a small village called Smithfield. He received the Bachelor of Science Degree in Animal Husbandry from Delaware Valley University in Doylestown, Pennsylvania, in 1961; Master's Degree in Education from Lehigh University in Bethlehem, Pennsylvania, in 1967; and Doctor of Philosophy Degree in Agricultural Education from the Pennsylvania State University, University Park, Pennsylvania, in 1981.

Dr. Diamond taught Animal Sciences for nearly ten years at both Delaware Valley University and Upper Bucks County Area Vocational Technical School while he and his late wife, Betty, raised registered Suffolk Sheep on their Cedar Brook Farm near Ottsville, Pennsylvania. During the spring months, Dr. Diamond was a professional sheep shearer who sheared sheep on farms in Eastern Pennsylvania. Joining the Peace Corps in 1971 was the beginning of Dr. Diamond's international career.

Before becoming the Dean of Agriculture and Environmental Sciences at Delaware Valley College, Dr. Diamond was an international Agricultural and Extension Education Consultant for the United Nations. He worked extensively with people in various agricultural endeavors in countries such as Albania, Bulgaria Cameroon, Tchad, China, England, Ethiopia, Mali, Swaziland, Tanzania, Democratic Republic of the Congo and other countries where he visited and studied. In addition, while an Assistant Professor of Agricultural and Extension Education for more than 14 years at the Pennsylvania State University, Dr. Diamond taught and worked with scores of international undergraduate and graduate students. He was a charter member and past secretary of the Association for International Agricultural and Extension Education, and he co-chaired its membership committee.

Dr. Diamond has published numerous professional refereed journal articles related to international agricultural and extension education. He has presented lectures at universities in several countries and authored extension publications for international extension officers. He is affiliated with a number of professional organizations, received several prestigious recognitions and is well known by international colleagues at universities, Ministries of Agriculture, Agricultural Schools and Agricultural Extension Training Centers in nations around the world. Because of Dr. Diamond's extensive agricultural, academic and international background, he felt a need to write short narratives as a way to put into perspective his life experiences.

Dr. Diamond does not profess to be a renowned author. However, his writings are a sincere attempt to express his inner feelings from the heart without shame or inhibitions. He published the first edition of *Poetry from the Heart* in 2012. In addition to writing poetry, Dr. Diamond has written a book titled *I Did What I Had to Do,* which captures the unique Peace Corps life Dr. and the late Mrs. Diamond experienced in Tchad, Africa.

THE AUTHOR'S INTERPRETATION OF NARRATIVES

The Power of a Narrative

Words make you think a thought.

A thought makes you feel the words.

A narrative makes you feel thoughtful words.

My Intention

My intention is to put on paper thoughts, experiences, feelings, opinions, reactions, lessons and memories in the form of narratives that publicly express hallmark components of my persona unashamed and without restraints.

My Request

When I can no longer speak, hear me through my narratives.

My Challenge

There is a lesson consciously and intentionally snuggled within each narrative. As readers read my narratives, I challenge them to find the embedded lesson(s) and ponder their intentions.

Narratives are a description of incidents, adventures, encounters or escapades experienced by the author.

NOTE: Where an asterisk is seen following a word, it refers the reader to its definition in the glossary found in back of this publication.

1

PRELUDE: While traveling in the Democratic Republic of Congo (aka Republic of Zaire), my late wife, Betty, and I had a layover for a couple days in the capital city of Kinshasa—a large city with a population of more than seven million people. Kinshasa was the place where all administrative decisions of importance were made. It was the center of the nation's political life, accommodating the office of the president and the executive and legislative councils. Located in the southwestern side of the country, Kinshasa was a port 320 miles from the Atlantic Ocean on the south bank of the Congo River. Betty and I decided to seek out Kinshasa's sights because we knew we might never visit this part of Africa again. I was inspired to write this narrative titled "African Art" for a variety of reasons. I was especially interested in seeing the *marché* (market, pronounced *mar-shay*) because I wanted to see where and how people purchased their food and what kinds of tropical fruits, vegetables and processed goods were available. Also the *marchè* might be a good place to find local artists with their creative arts such as paintings or carvings that could be of interest. What an enormous market we stumbled onto, which featured a plethora of tropical fruits, vegetables, processed foods, clothing and works of art.

AFRICAN ART

What a beautiful black-and-white oil painting of a fishing village along the Congo River. My camera could not have captured the beauty this oil painting displayed to me. (Photo by Jim Diamond of a black-and-white oil painting by an unknown artist near Kinshasa, Zaire, in May 1972)

2

AFRICAN ART

Our self-guided walking tour to explore the city of Kinshasa led us to the Zando Market (aka Grand Marché). WHOA! What a captivating, interesting marketing venue! Anything you needed could probably be found somewhere within the vastness of this extraordinary market. Commodities such as tropical fruits, vegetables, clothes, toys, food, bed sheets, shoes, kitchen utensils and anything else one needed for a comfortable existence in rural bush villages without electricity and running water. It was not the cleanest market, but cleaner than other markets we visited in other countries.

I admired the salesmanship of the vendors, who were very determined and persistent in selling their goods. Bartering was expected to be part of the pricing experience. One had to be patient because the vendors' aggressive salesmanship was persuasive and often untrustworthy. Their aggressiveness was nonstop and could border on harassment.

I like to visit markets because they tell me what kind of food crops are produced locally, what the people can afford to purchase, how vendors protect displayed foodstuffs from heat and insects and much more.

I was particularly interested in finding a piece of local art. Many so-called artists exhibited their works, but most could be considered unappealing—at least to me. For example, one vendor approached me and attempted to sell me copper wall hangings. I had no interest in buying them because he was asking way too much money. He was persistent and kept reducing his price. Finally, I made him a ridiculous offer for two wall hangings instead of one, and he said the four magic words, "Give me the money."

As Betty and I continued walking around the market carrying my two copper wall hangings, a gentleman walked up to me and displayed a gorgeous black-and-white oil painting of a fishing village along the Congo River. My camera could not have captured the beauty of that village as well as the artist did with his oil painting displayed before me. I learned that he had no canvas or easel! He improvised by painting on a white flour sack attached to a piece of plywood. I was so impressed with his work that I did not have the intestinal fortitude to barter a lower price for the painting. I knew his asking price was much higher than its actual value, but his talents were stellar, and I decided he should be paid his asking price as a reward for being so skillful. I paid him his asking price. He earned it!

That oil painting is my favorite, and it has been elegantly hanging in my home since September 1973. I would like to close this narrative by quoting an American landscape photographer and environmentalist who said, "You don't take a photograph; you make it." The work of that artist who painted that beautiful painting on a used white flour sack could not be replicated with the most expensive Canon camera.

PRELUDE: A handmade *piroque** is a shallow canoe-type boat made by hollowing a log. It can safely carry two or three passengers plus some cargo, such as mangoes, dead monkeys and fish. The *piroque* is powered with one or two paddles. A *piroque* is the main source of transportation for people living in the bush on or near the Congo River and its tributaries. One day, while my late with, Betty, and I were visiting our Peace Corps friends Sam and Joanne Samaduroff who were stationed in Mbandaka, Zaire (aka Democratic Republic of the Congo), we saw the Congo River flowing close by. I was inspired to write this narrative titled "Crossing the Congo River in a *Piroque*" because the river tantalized my thinking, imagination and fantasies. Earlier, Joanne had said she would just love to take a boat ride across the Congo River to see what was on the other side. Sam and Betty said that no way were they going to cross that river. I said to Joanne, "I too would like to cross the river just for the hell of it." Joanne and I had a phenomenal experience crossing the Congo River in this handmade *piroque* while Sam and Betty sat on the river bank watching us cross the river.

CROSSING THE CONGO RIVER IN A *PIROQUE*

Our handmade *piroque** is a shallow canoe-type vessel made by hollowing out a log. It can safely carry two or three passengers plus some cargo, such as mangoes, yams, dead monkeys and fish. The *piroque* is powered with one or two paddles. (Photo by Jim Diamond of our handmade *piroque* on the Congo River bank, Mbandaka, Zaire, in April 1972)

CROSSING THE CONGO RIVER IN A *PIROQUE*

Why did two Peace Corps volunteers cross the Congo River? Joanne had said she would love to take a boat ride across the Congo to see what was on the other side. I said I too would like to cross the river just for the hell of it. As I rode Sam's bicycle along the river's edge, I saw three men pulling their *piroque** onto the riverbank. I asked, "What would you charge to take two people across the river and back again?" He said, "Six Zaires each." (US $12.00) I said, "You wait right here until I fetch my friend." I excitedly entered the house and asked, "Joanne, I have two people waiting to take you and me across the Congo River; do you still want to go?" Joanne said, "You bet I want to go!" When we arrived at the river's edge, the two fishermen were waiting for us. At the very back of the *piroque's* bottom was a large hole so we had to sit toward the front of the *piroque* so our weight kept the back end high, preventing the *piroque* from taking on water and sinking. We pushed off and began the adventure of crossing the exotic and intriguing Congo River with Betty and Sam watching from the riverbank. From where we pushed off, the Congo River was more than a kilometer wide, very deep and heavily infested with crocodiles, hippopotamuses and huge catfish. Because of swiftly moving water, one could not row directly across the river without being pulled downriver by the current. The water flowed rapidly and caused a forceful eddy on each side of the river. To get to the other side, the fishermen paddled their *piroque* into the eddy and rowed upstream about five kilometers. Then we reversed our direction. We started to go downriver guiding the *piroque* out of the eddy into the swiftly flowing Congo River toward a point diagonally across the river. As we were crossing the river, we saw huge islands of water hyacinths, which broke away from tributaries upriver floating lickety-split downstream. During our adventurous ride across river, I kept my eye on that hole on the *piroque's* far end, making sure we were not taking on water. When we got to the other side, we were directly across from where we started.

On the other side, we saw small fishing villages set back from the riverbank. Fishermen sold fresh, dried and smoked fish daily for the Mbandaka food market. The huts were made of traditional mud brick, each with a grass-thatched roof with swirling streams of smoke meandering upward. Not far from each hut was a structure of bamboo poles to hang fish for drying and mud brick structures for smoking fish. We waved to the people as we passed by, and they joyfully waved back to us. That was Africa!

After satisfying our curiosity for seeing the other side of the river, Joanne and I decided to return to where we had set off. Again the two fishermen paddled their *piroque* into the eddy, paddled upstream, then again reversed our direction. We started downstream guiding the *piroque* diagonally toward our starting point. When we finally landed, yep, you guessed it: Betty and Sam were patiently waiting for us. Wow! Crossing the crocodile-infested Congo River in a hand-dug-out canoe with a huge open hole in the rear of the floor, with two fishermen using the power of an eddy to get us upstream so we could diagonally cross the river was a sensational, awesome experience. Being close to islands of water hyacinths rapidly floating down the Congo River, sensing the power of rapidly flowing water that bulged with huge catfish, seeing people on the other side eking a living by smoking fish and watching them joyfully wave back to us was mesmerizing. All of this and more just to see the other side. Now how many answers can you give for the opening question of this narrative: "Why did two Peace Corps volunteers cross the Congo River?" If you can name four or more reasons, you are a perceptive reader.

PRELUDE: On 1 May 1972, my late wife, Betty, and I arrived in Mbandaka, the Democratic Republic of the Congo (aka Zaire), a town on the equator, to visit dear friends Sam and Joanne Samaduroff, who were Peace Corps volunteers from Washington state. We had met while studying French together in St. Thomas, Virgin Islands. The Democratic Republic of the Congo, located in Central Africa, is bordered on the north by the Central African Republic and South Sudan, on the east by Uganda, on the southwest by Angola, and on the west by twenty-five miles of Atlantic coastline. I was inspired to write this narrative titled "Floating Market" because this was a once-in-a-lifetime experience. After nearly a month visiting our dear friends the Samaduroffs, it was time for Betty and me to say goodbye. We were scheduled to fly from Mbandaka to Kinshasa. Instead of flying, we opted to take a boat 1,000 kilometers down the Congo River to Kinshasa. The Congo River was navigable from Mbandaka to Kinshasa, the capitol of the Democratic Republic of the Congo (aka Zaire).

FLOATING MARKET ON CONGO RIVER

As the boat progressed down the river, more and more people from jungle villages would paddle upstream several kilometers to meet our boat in their *piroques** to do their marketing. Each village had its speciality or uniqueness. (Photo by Jim Diamond of *piroques* attached to a floating market on the Congo River in April 1972)

FLOATING MARKET ON CONGO RIVER

As our boat was cruising along the Congo River pushing six barges with thick jungle on both sides of the river, I was overwhelmed by the remoteness and density of the jungle. When I looked ahead, I suddenly saw scores of hand-dug-out canoes *(piroques*)* with several people standing up paddling the canoes toward us. They resembled attacking warriors! However, instead of bearing arms for an attack, the canoes were laden with all kinds of commercial commodities grown in, harvested from and made in the jungle to be sold to passengers on the boat and barges.

Because there were few if any railroads, roads, or landing strips, our boat was a lifeline that provided both a market and livelihood for hundreds of thousands of people living in jungle villages on each side of the Congo River and its tributaries. The canoes rowed to our boat and were tied to its side. There was a loud flurry of activity and commotion by the passengers on the boat, barges and people in the canoes. After the canoes were attached to the side of the boat, they would be bombarded by passengers throwing a rag or towel wrapped around a small stone or something heavy into a canoe containing, for example, a stalk of plantain. That meant that particular stalk of plantain was to be sold to the person who threw the rag. Passengers actually got into fights over who claimed what.

The goal of the people from the jungle villages in the canoes was to sell their commodities to passengers on the boat. Some boarded the boat or barges and purchased commodities from the passengers. While this flurry of haggling over price was taking place, our boat kept chugging along. When the boat approached the village from whence the people came, they would get back into their canoes, detach and paddle back to shore with their newly purchased commodities, money they earned selling their products, or both.

As the boat progressed down the river, more and more people from jungle villages would paddle upstream several kilometers to meet the boat and barges to do an encore of marketing. Each village had its specialty or uniqueness. One villager approached me with a carved ivory pipe with a cow-horn stem. Back then, I smoked a pipe, and I found that one to be attractive and different. However, I smoked it only twice—the first time and the last time. What a horrible-tasting pipe! When the tobacco was lit, it smelled and tasted like burnt horn. I still have that pipe, but I never smoked it again. But seeing it reminds me of how watching all of this flurry from the second deck of the boat was an interesting, entertaining, intriguing, colorful, cultural, spectacular, educational, comical, exciting experience.

I would like to close this narrative by saying a person who does not travel does not know the value of people in different societies. That experience gave us a greater appreciation and a different perspective of people's lifestyles in a society that was different than ours. As a citizen of the world, one must learn to understand, respect and appreciate the culture, traditions, foods, religions and lifestyles of people in societies that are drastically different from what we are accustomed to in Europe, North America, or Asia.

PRELUDE: Traveling to Yaounde, Cameroon, was a demanding experience. My purpose as a consultant was to plan and implement an International Farming Systems Research* (FSR) Conference funded by United States Agency for International Development (USAID). The idea behind the FSR concept was to research how African farm enterprises exist in rural areas. On-farm research with farming systems is a style of doing agricultural research assuming that changes would be adapted to the farmer's production circumstances. New farming systems development focused on building radically new systems without any previous research-based knowledge or information as guidelines. It was essentially a practical agricultural research program that had some merit but was not widely implemented.

A MISSION IN YAOUNDE, CAMEROON

The beautiful Congressional Palace was a perfect conference site. The entire facility was available to use for teaching Farming System Research concepts. Agricultural educators traveled from eight nations to study new crops, farm equipment, production practices and ideas and to discuss their adoption into new market areas. (Photo by Jim Diamond in the Congressional Palace during the International Farming Systems Research* Conference at Yaounde, Cameroon, Africa.)

A MISSION IN YAOUNDE, CAMEROON

Yaoundé is Cameroon's bustling capital city, where people speak either English or French. Cameroon is sometimes described as "Africa in miniature" because it exhibits all major climates and vegetation on the continent, including mountains, desert, rainforest, coastland and savanna* grassland. Cameroon's physical, climatic and vegetative features create a vulnerable lifestyle. Family farming could serve as an economic foundation for national growth and food security. However, Cameroon's biggest development challenge is food insecurity, as in other sub-Saharan nations. Our mission was to plan and implement an international conference designed for promoting a non-formal farming system for farmers known as Farming Systems Research* (FSR).

A four-day FSR Conference was planned for agricultural educators and/or government officers who traveled from eight nations to participate in the conference at the Congressional Palace, Yaoundé, Cameroon. The beautiful Congressional Palace was a perfect conference site! The entire facility was available to use for teaching Farming Systems Research concepts and demonstrating agricultural supplies and equipment companies' promotional exhibits. Agricultural educators and government officials from eight nations studied new crops, farm equipment, production practices and ideas and discussed their adoption into new market areas.

Agricultural research can be broadly defined as any research activity aimed at improving productivity and quality of crops genetically or through better plant protection, irrigation, storage methods, farm mechanization, efficient marketing and better management of resources. Outside the city limits where food crops were produced, affluence and quality of life were different. Cameroonian citizens and families in many sub-Saharan nations struggled to protect their integrity, dignity and pride because cyclic food became scant at times.

Farming systems research was based on a holistic consideration of farmers along with their plants and livestock, starting with the assumption that local systems consisted of mutually related elements that constitute a whole. Based upon the reaction I was not convinced Cameroonian government ministers would subsidize a different approach for educating farmers that lacked a research foundation. Furthermore, the officials from other countries seemed not to exhibit any enthusiasm toward the value of FSR. It appeared that they pretended to support FSR's concept without being sinister. To assure the Minister of Agriculture would attend and arrive at his scheduled time and give a speech during the conference, I wrote his speech. After arriving thirty minutes past his scheduled time, he gave his speech, then expeditiously departed. FSR concepts obviously would not comply with all governmental sectors, yet parts of the system would nicely conform where agricultural development visions prevailed. After all the long hours of planning and implementing such a stately event, the question remained, "Will agricultural educators and government officials promote FSR within their respective nations?"

PRELUDE: Working in the Federal Democratic Republic of Ethiopia in 1998 on a project funded by the United States Agency for International Development, my colleague Harry Burcalew, Director of Extension for the State of Washington, and I worked as a team in Ethiopia's capital, Addis Ababa, for a short period of time before we traveled some 200 miles south-southeast to the village of Agarfa. Our mission was to develop an agricultural education curriculum for a two-year formal diploma program at the Agarfa Multipurpose Agricultural Development Agents Training Center, located near the village of Agarfa, Bole Zone and Oromia Region.

After communism was denounced in Ethiopia, a more democratic form of government was installed to govern the country. Traditionally, as reported by the media to the Western world,

Ethiopia was perceived as an impoverished nation, scourged with starvation and plagued with disease that was aggravated by droughts. Television stations showed dying children unblinking despite flies walking across their eyes, exhibiting deplorable conditions to the Western conscience.

The new President of Ethiopia made a decree, "Ethiopia must be self-sufficient in food production within five years." "Self-sufficiency" was a politically correct word to use at the time. Self-sufficiency in food production was an attainable goal; however, to accomplish that goal, cadres of well-trained extension officers strategically placed throughout Ethiopia's hinterlands would be necessary to teach farmers how to make management decisions that affected their agricultural production and income.

I was inspired to write this narrative to encapsulate the appalling poverty-stricken lifestyles that existed in Ethiopia during that time in 1998.

PLEASE GIVE ME A GIFT!

We were taught when working overseas not to give money to beggars. As this girl passed by, she implored, "Please give me a gift! Please give me a gift!"(Photographer unknown)

PLEASE GIVE ME A GIFT!

I cannot find words that suitably describe my personal anguish of seeing so many beggars in Addis Ababa and outlying villages, desperately in need of food and medical attention. We were taught when working overseas not to give money to beggars. The domestic people were not proud that there were so many beggars within their midst. Giving money to beggars encouraged other people to become beggars as opposed to getting some type of employment. Nevertheless, beggars or not, they were frail, diseased human beings, who displayed agony in their eyes and scowling facial expressions. These were genuine symbols of destitute humans who had no hope. Yet we were instructed not to give to beggars.

One Sunday morning after breakfast, Harry and I went for a walk outside our hotel. As we walked, we came upon a church service with hundreds of people outside a completely filled Protestant church. We wanted to see what was happening but couldn't see over the people from our vantage point. We saw a low stone wall on the edge of the sidewalk. When Harry and I stepped up on the top of the stone wall, we were able to see over the people's heads.

A church service was being conducted across the street, but we couldn't hear anything or see the preacher inside the packed church. After a short time standing on the stone wall, a frail young girl who appeared to be about nine years old walked by, leading her blind mother with what appeared to be a broom handle. As the girl passed by, she said, "Please give me a gift. Please give me a gift." I ignored her as she slowly walked by, holding out her hand while her blind mother said something that I could not understand in a soft, woeful voice. A soiled cloth covered the blind mother's forehead, shoulders and back. They walked a short distance, then turned around and again walked past us. Slowly walking toward me, the young girl again looked at me with sorrowful eyes and her hand out saying, "Please give me a gift. Please give me a gift." Again, I ignored her. However, that time I heard a noise that sounded like a cough from the blind mother's back. I looked closer and thought, *Oh my God, a baby is strapped to her back.*

When I heard the baby's rasping cough, I couldn't take it any longer. I jumped off the wall, reached into my pocket and gave the girl a 20 CFA bill and all the loose coins I had. That should have been enough money for them to purchase a sufficient amount of food to eat decent meals for three to four days.

Later that evening at the hotel, when Harry and I were having dinner together, I said, "It's been said that confession is good for the soul."

Harry said, "Well, Jim, now what did you do?"

I said, "This morning while I was standing on that stone wall across the street from that church service and saw that little girl walk by with her blind mother, I weakened and gave the girl all the money from pockets. When I heard that little baby on the blind mother's back cough, I couldn't take it any longer."

Harry smiled and with a twinkle in his eye said, "Jim, I weakened, too!"

PRELUDE: The Bandiagara Escarpment in the Dogon country in the Republic of Mali is a sandstone cliff approximately 1,600 feet above sandy flatlands. Because of the archaeological, ethnological and geological characteristics of the area, the entire 125 miles of Bandiagara Escarpment in 1989 was listed in the UNESCO World Heritage List.

In January 1971, my late wife, Betty, and I were privileged to visit the Bandiagara Cliff, the land of the Dogon people, as part of our livestock study tour of Mali. I was inspired to write this narrative titled "Cliff Dwellers" because of the unique lifestyle of their society which survive in a harsh, dry environment with scant infertile soils.

CLIFF DWELLERS

A short distance away was a crevice in the rock whereby Dogon people made uneven stone steps to climb to the top of the escarpment. This raised garden of onions was surrounded by stone and filled with soil. Each day, water was carried up to the top on those uneven stone steps. (Photos by Jim Diamond of onion garden on top of cliff and Dogon house against the cliff in January 1973)

CLIFF DWELLERS

We visited a small village clustered with disorganized mud brick houses with flat roofs and some with cone-shaped straw roofs snuggled against the cliff. We were able to talk with a few Dogon people.

CLIFF DWELLERS

While visiting farmers and local officials on a one-month, intensive-study tour of North-Central and Southern Mali to determine if making grass silage for cattle, sheep, and goats was feasible, my late wife, Betty, and I sidelined one day to visit the Bandiagara Escarpment and a Dogon village. The Dogons were one of Africa's most isolated ethnic groups, who were virtually unheard of in the West until the early 1930s. Wow! What a captivating, interesting, fascinating life experience!

We drove along a solid limestone road on top of the escarpment, not far from its edge. At one point, we stopped, got out of the car and walked about 500 feet to the edge. What an awesome sight! We were looking straight down about 1,000 feet above the sandy plains below.

We got back into our vehicle and continued our journey on top of the escarpment to where there were several raised garden beds on top of the limestone. A short distance away was a crevice in the rock whereby Dogon people had made uneven stone steps to enable them to climb to the top of the escarpment. The raised gardens were surrounded by stone and soil that had been carried up those uneven stone steps in the crevice. They were growing onions at the time, and they had to carry containers full of water from a nearby stream up those steps.

After they harvested the onions, they pounded them in a mortar and pestle and rolled the crushed onions into balls to dry. Those balls were then stored for later use.

We climbed down those treacherous steps in the steep crevice to the bottom to a series of mud-walled homes amongst a few baobab trees and huge boulders. We visited a small village clustered with disorganized mud brick houses with flat roofs and some with cone-shaped straw roofs snuggled against the cliff. We were able to talk with a few Dogon people.

We saw a few sheep and watched a Dogon woman spin wool with a handheld spindle. The lady used a slender, rounded rod with tapered ends to hand spin and twist wool into yarn from grease wool.* That was the first time we saw this method of spinning. Betty asked the lady if she would teach her to spin with a spindle. The Dogon lady was astonished and overjoyed that Betty asked to teach her how to spin. What a delightful experience! The ladies were so appreciative to teach Betty, they gave her a spindle to take home.

After Betty's spinning lesson, we looked up to see what appeared to be cave openings in the side of the cliff. When I asked a Dogon about them, he told me it was a long-time Dogon tradition to bury their deceased in those caves. No one was permitted to reenter the caves.

I learned also that in the Dogon village, health clinics were scant. When they were sick, most people relied on monkey paws, beads and other fetishes provided by the village spiritual leader to try to heal.

I would like to end this narrative with a Dogon proverb that describes many unknowns about the Dogon society. It goes like this, "No one knows if a bird in flight has an egg in its belly."

PRELUDE: After the success of developing a method of feeding cattle grass silage from pit silos in Tchad, word spread across Tchad and also to neighboring countries in Central Africa and even as far away as Washington DC.

The Director of Livestock *(Directeur de Elevage)* from the Republic of Mali was in Washington, DC on official business. One of his meetings was with the Director of the Peace Corps. He had heard from someone in Washington DC about the pit silo project in Tchad and wanted to know if the Peace Corps would repeat that success in Mali.

In November 1972, I began getting telegrams from the Peace Corps Director in Mali and letters from Tchad's Director of Peace Corps wanting to know if I would travel to Mali to do a study to determine if it was feasible to dig pit silos and make grass silage for their oxen and dairy cattle.

In December 1972, my late wife, Betty, and I traveled to Njamina (Ft. Lamy) for an all-Peace-Corps-volunteer meeting and to meet with the Director to discuss traveling to Mali. After our deliberations, we agreed that Betty and I would travel to Mali for January 1973 to conduct a feasibility study of making grass silage throughout Mali and to ascertain the level of interest among farmers.

I was inspired to write this narrative titled "Pit Silo Treatise with Peace Corps/Mali" because I was quite pleased our work in Tchad now had an international reputation to help farmers have sufficient feedstuff for their oxen and dairy cattle.

PIT SILO TREATISE WITH PEACE CORPS/MALI

In my report, I recommended trial pit silos and silage be introduced in the Southern regions where there were several dairy cattle. (Photo by Jim Diamond of Africans chopping silage)

14

PIT SILO TREATISE WITH PEACE CORPS/MALI

After a long, tiring two-day flight from Tchad to Nigeria to Dahomey to Ivory Coast to the Republic of Mali, my late wife, Betty, and I finally reached our destination in Bamako. On the first day, we immediately established a plan of work, scheduling a series of meetings with Ministry of Agriculture officials, meeting Peace Corps volunteer Leslie Temelson, and choosing what regions in Mali would be appropriate for the study.

Leslie Temelson had a strong interest in getting involved with the pit silo project in Mali. We invited Leslie to join us at various points of our itinerary to enlighten him of our proposed efforts.

From Bamako we traveled north to Mopti, visiting local officials and farmers along the way. We talked with farmers, describing the definition and importance of silage and checking the depth of the water table in wells to make sure the water table would be below a pit. We asked the farmers what they fed their animals during the dry seasons, if the farmers were sedentary or migrated with their cattle, what kinds of crop residue they had access to (for example peanut vines, rice straw and maize* fodder), how many cows they milked, how many sheep or goats they owned, where they got water for their animals during the dry season and was the water potable? The answers to these questions and more helped us to form a mental picture of local conditions that would impact making silage.

Leslie Temelson extended his work in Mali for one year to become the Peace Corps' pit silo and silage expert. During the first year, an example of the reaction to the pit silo technique can be found in the *Cercle de Rangaba*. (A *cercle* is an area designating an administrative unit similar to a county. Only one pit silo was dug in that *cercle*.)

As a result of its success, the *Commandant de Cercle* proposed establishing a program whereby a pit silo be found in every major village within the *cercle* the following year.

The results of the experimental pit silos done in the zones showed a major impact on the dairy industry of Mali. Amazingly, cows fed on silage increased their milk productivity during the dry season.

At the end of the second year of the program, fifteen pit silo teams had dug and filled 525 pit silos. Almost all the pits yielded fresh green silage. The villagers who fed their cattle silage during the dry months noticed considerable change in their animals' weight and strength when compared to animals that didn't have silage to eat.

For example, oxen that were fed silage were able to plough in one day what it took oxen that were not fed silage three days to plough. Before silage was introduced, the oxen couldn't make it through a full day's work.

Kudus to Peace Corps volunteers for their success! The Peace Corps volunteers showed perseverance, persistence and patience—without ever really knowing how much headway was actually being made in helping farmers help themselves.

PRELUDE: While on a safari in Kruger National Park, South Africa, with my late wife, Betty, and our dear friends Katie and Barbara Graham, twice we sighted banded mongoose in semi-wooded environments. Mongooses are long, furry creatures with pointed faces and bushy tails. Contrary to popular belief, mongooses are not rodents. They are members of the Herpestidae family, which also includes civets and meerkats. A group of banded mongooses is called a troop. The banded mongoose is native only to African countries from the Sahara Desert to Southern Africa. They live in dens that were abandoned by other burrowing animals, although they do not spend more than three or four days in any one place. They are territorial critters that mark their territory with a scent they secrete. I was inspired to write this narrative titled "Banded Mongoose" because it was the first time we sighted this interesting nomadic critter.

BANDED MONGOOSE

Banded mongooses *(Mungos mungo)* have quite a long menu of prey to satisfy their varied diets, including snakes, ants, crickets, centipedes, termites, beetles, bird eggs, hares, fruit, frogs, caterpillars, grasshoppers, lizards, small rodents and occasionally small fruits. (Photo by Jim Diamond of a banded mongoose in Kruger National Park, South Africa, September 2015)

BANDED MONGOOSE

If you live in or have lived one or more countries of Southern Africa, you probably have seen or heard wild banded mongooses running around the neighborhood, countryside, or savannas.* They live in grasslands, savannas and open forests. I found it interesting to learn that banded mongooses are active during the day and sleep at night.

If you are quiet and non-disturbing, you can hear their constant "chatting" to each other throughout the day. They chatter to each other and combine discrete vocal units somewhat like vowel sounds and syllable combinations to possibly coordinate group movements and convey forage information and other important messages. We also learned that their name was derived from the highly visible dark bands that go down the entire length of their back.

Mongooses are very sociable and find safety in large numbers. Banded mongooses are easy prey for predators* such as wild dogs, jackals, hyenas, birds of prey and snakes. If mongooses can't find safety or shelter, they form a tight group with all their heads facing outward. An ideal home for banded mongooses is an old, abandoned termite mound. They never feel trapped in it and have plenty of air holes because termite mounds have many entrances and exits.

Banded mongooses have quite a long menu of prey to satisfy their varied diets, including snakes, ants, crickets, centipedes, termites, beetles, bird eggs, hares, frogs, caterpillars, grasshoppers, lizards, small rodents, nuts, roots, berries, seeds and occasionally small fruits. Once young pups are old enough to look for food themselves, they are individually cared for by an escort. This escort teaches the pup how to hunt and forage and keeps them safe.

Often one can see a banded mongoose eating ticks off a warthog. This symbiotic* relationship benefits both critters: The mongoose gets to eat while the warthog gets cleaned.

Banded mongooses are fearless hunters and attackers. They will stalk a victim and when close enough, pounce. Often they will follow their prey to its burrow and dig it out. A number of mongooses will attack and kill venomous snakes. They depend on speed and agility, darting at the head of the snake and cracking the skull with a powerful bite. Native Africans believe that the mongoose is immune to cobra venom. Zoologists claim that banded mongooses do have some resistance to the venom.

When scared, a mongoose bristles its fur stiffly to appear twice its size and make it more difficult for snakes to strike. They avoid being bitten by making quick, combative fighting moves.

I would like to close this narrative by quoting Shaun Singh Baldwin, a Canadian-American novelist of Indian descent who once said, "Fiction: It's like goading a mongoose and a cobra into battle and staying with them to see who wins." I'm not interested in reading about such violence or who wins the bloody battle.

PRELUDE: Bushbucks are a small African antelope normally found in forested, wooded, bushy regions in Kruger National Park, South Africa; Kenya, and other African regions. Their coloring is a reddish body with white spots near the hind flanks. Bushbucks live in a wide range of habitats, although they prefer forested or wooded regions close to a water source. They can live on mountain slopes as high as 13,120 feet in East Africa as well as in regions settled by humans. Their coloring, small size and standoffish behavior help them survive near human neighborhoods and in instinctive habitats. I was inspired to write this narrative because seldom does one observe this shy African antelope in most African regions. I was fortunate to stumble upon this bushbuck in the north central region of Kruger National Park, South Africa.

BUSHBUCK

At the moment of this writing, there are no serious threats to bushbuck *(Tragelaphus scriptus)* populations. However, some regions are experiencing habitat destruction due to agriculture and suburban development. *(*Photo by Jim Diamond of a bushbuck in Kruger National Park, South Africa, in 2013)

BUSHBUCK

Bushbucks exist in forty different countries from West Africa to Central Africa and from Northeastern Africa to Southern Africa. They even live on the small islands off the West coast.

Bushbucks are browsers. They eat a range of herbs and young leaves from shrubs, trees and farm crops. They are diurnal, which means they eat throughout the day and night; however, this might vary depending the bushbuck's age and gender and the season. Bushbucks have a keen sense of smell.

At the moment of this writing , there are no serious threats to bushbuck populations. However, some regions are experiencing habitat destruction due to agriculture and suburban development.

It's not unusual to find baboons and vervet monkeys hanging around bushbucks because they have learned that a bushbuck's bark means a predator* is near and it's time to flee. In return, bushbucks benefit from the primates' ability to detect predators lurking in trees. Leopards are the primary enemy of bushbucks, but lions, hyenas and crocodiles also prey on them.

I would like to close this narrative with an African proverb that goes like this: "The Earth is large enough for all to share, but mankind's heart is not large enough to care."

The moral of this proverb is why do wealthy, large-game hunters kill African animals just for fun and the prestige. I have no issue if an animal is killed for personal protection or a need for food, but I can't comprehend the rationale behind why wealthy wild game hunters (especially Europeans and Americans) kill wild animals just for the hell of it.

They seem to thrive on getting their picture taken next to or on the animal with their gun and sometimes their girlfriend. They spend thousands of dollars to get the heads mounted and shipped to their home to hang in their dens and brag about the dangers of the hunt. I prefer to and have been successful at shooting wild African animals with my EOS Canon camera.

PRELUDE: My late wife Betty, and I planned a safari to Kruger National Park, South Africa. We called them "Diamond Safari Tours: Where Travel Agents Can't Find!" Our safari guests included our longtime friends Bob and Linda DeRosa on their first trip to Africa and Bill and Jeff Lindley who had once lived in Africa. This exciting excursion took place from 21 September to 6 October 2013. Shortly after we arrived at Kruger National Park in mid-afternoon 23 September 2013, our anxieties were high so we went directly into the bush on our first safari. Then we went to the Abangane Guest Lodge to rest and have dinner after a long three-day trip from Pennsylvania. On the fourth day, we observed a horrendous hippopotamus fight. I was inspired to write this narrative titled "Hippopotamus Fight" because after thirty-eight visits over four years to Kruger National Park, that was my first observation of such a vicious fight.

HIPPOPOTAMUS FIGHT

Hippo *(Hippopotamus amphibius)* pods* normally have one dominant male that mates with a harem of about thirty females. Dominant hippos resolve issues by fighting, so the dominant male has earned his status by fighting, and he can be considered a warrior. (Photo by Jim Diamond of two hippos fighting in Kruger National Park, South Africa, on 24 September 2013)

HIPPOPOTAMUS FIGHT

During a safari, my late wife, Betty, our four friends and I experienced a once-in-a-lifetime happening. These rare moments of seeing two colossal hippos fighting trumped spotting lions, crocodiles, cape buffalos, leopards, rhinos, elephants and many, many other wild African animals and birds. Yes, the rare moments spent observing the big five—cape buffalo, rhino, lion, leopard and elephant—are unforgettable, but seeing that hippo fight was an extraordinary happening the DeRosas, Lindleys and Diamonds still remember with ecstasy.

On land, groups will forage wherever there is copious amounts of grassland. That day, we drove into a hide* overlooking a shallow water inlet where a pod of hippos was basking in the sun on the water's edge. We quietly sat on a bench in the hide for nearly an hour, watching and photographing animals that came to drink and birds flitting around. We all appreciated the beauty of the interesting wildlife scenario.

Because of the hour, it was about time for us to move on, but just as we were leaving the hide, all hell broke loose. A high-pitched hippo's squeal grabbed our attention.

We kept our distance because we knew that hippos kill more people in Africa than any other animal. Even crocodiles keep their distance from a savage hippo brawl.

We quickly learned that hippos are inordinately territorial and will not shy away from fighting a territorial intruder. Hippos are guardians of their watery turf, and such fights usually take place in their watery sphere of influence.

We watched as the male hippo fought off other males that were disrespecting his authority and invading his territory. To declare their dominance, the hippo opened its massive jaw to display its tusks (knife-like incisors) to scare off the would-be intruders. The male marked his territory with honking, grunting sounds. Male hippos will viciously protect their pod of females, and this hippo fight is what we observed. The larger, more vicious, dominant male hippo caused a bleeding wound on the smaller hippo. The splashing water subsided as the larger hippo chased its wounded opponent away from its pod.

I would like to end this narrative with a Luo proverb that goes like this: "Hunger pushes the hippopotamus out of the water."

PRELUDE: Ndebele people are any of several Bantu-speaking Africans who live primarily in Mpumalanga or Limpopo Provinces of South Africa. The Ndebele people are ancient offshoots of the Nguni-speaking peoples and began migrating to the Transvaal region in the seventeenth century. The Ndebele are well known for their magnificent craftsmanship, decorative homes, and distinctive and highly colorful dress style and ornamentation. Esther Mahlangu is an internationally known Ndebele painter and decorator. Ndebele art has always been important in identifying cultural characteristics of the Ndebele. Painting is done freehand, without prior layouts, rulers or squares. The designs are planned beforehand, which results in the characteristic symmetry, proportion and straight edges of Ndebele decorations. Ndebele women are responsible for painting the colorful, intricate patterns on the walls of their houses. I was inspired to write this narrative after visiting a Ndebele village and observing the astonishing artworks on their homes, the fencing around their homes and the decorative dresses proudly worn by the Ndebele women.

NDEBELE PEOPLE

Ndebele women traditionally adorn themselves with ornaments, each symbolizing her status in society. After marriage, dresses become increasingly elaborate and spectacular. (Photo by Jim Diamond of a Ndebele lady outside her village home in Mpumalanga Province, South Africa, in 1988)

22

NDEBELE PEOPLE

The majority of the Ndebele moved into Zimbabwe, although many of them stayed in South Africa in the area that became known as the Kwandebele homeland during the apartheid years. You will find them living there today.

Ndebele authority is vested in the tribal head (*ikozi*), assisted by an inner tribal council (*amaphakathi*). Wards (*izilindi*) are administered by ward heads. The residential unit of each family is called an *umuzi*. The umuzi usually is made up of a family head (*umnumzana*) with his wife and unmarried children. If an umuzi has more than one wife, the *umuzi* are divided into a right and a left half to accommodate the different wives. An *umuzi* sometimes grows into a more complex dwelling unit when the head's married sons and younger brothers join the household.

The staple food of the Ndebele people is corn (maize*), which is known as *isitshwala*. Maize cereals and sorghum with milk are commonly consumed by the Ndebele people. Even though corn is their favorite food, they also grow and consume a variety of fruits and vegetables.

Ancestral spirits are important in Ndebele religious life, and offerings and sacrifices are made to the ancestors for protection, health, and happiness. Ancestral spirits come back to the world in dreams, illnesses, and sometimes in the form of snakes. The Ndebele believe in the use of magic.

Traditionally, the Ndebele believe that illnesses are caused by external forces, such as spells or curses that are put on an individual. The power of a traditional healer is measured by his or her ability to defeat these forces with medicines or by throwing bones. Some present-day Ndebele still adhere to ancestral worship, but many have become Christians and belong to mainstream Christian churches or one of the many local Africanized churches.

Ndebele women traditionally adorn themselves with ornaments that symbolize her status in society. After marriage, their dresses became even more spectacular. Once a Ndebele wife's home is built, she wears copper and brass rings (*idzila*) around her arms, legs, and neck to symbolize her bond and faithfulness to her husband. She will only remove the rings after his death. The rings were believed to have strong ritual powers. Husbands provide their wives with rings, and the wealthier the husband, the more rings the wife would wear. It is no longer common for wives to wear these rings permanently.

In addition to the rings, married women also wear neck hoops made of grass *(isigolwani)* twisted into a coil and covered in beads, particularly for ceremonial occasions. *Isigolwani* are sometimes worn as neckpieces and as leg and arm bands by newlywed women whose husbands have not yet provided them with a home or by girls of marriageable age after the completion of their initiation ceremony.

I would like to close this narrative by quoting Ndebele artist Dr. Esther Nikwambi Mahlangu, who received her honorary doctorate from the University of Johannesburg, who said, "There has always been a fascination, demand, and admiration for art from Africa, and Ndebele paintings are the most significant styles of painting that still resembles original shapes and forms. Its colorful and abstract lends itself to incorporation into modern design." It is my passion to transfer this skill to the generations after me. I want them to learn where it comes from and why the Ndebele people paint their houses and monuments."

23

PRELUDE: One day during the middle of January 2015, I asked my late wife, Betty, "What do you want to do special on our fifty-fifth wedding anniversary?" She promptly responded, "I would like to see Kruger National Park in South Africa one more time!" I said, "Okay! Your wish is my command!" Immediately, I set about making travel plans to South Africa. Four of us would travel together, including two dear friends Barbara and Katie Graham who yearned to go. We planned our travels for late August and early September 2015, which would be our thirty-eighth visit to this beautiful, exciting park. Kruger National Park, located in northeastern South Africa, is a significant sanctuary of flora and fauna* larger than the state of New Jersey where wild African animals live in the way that God intended. After viewing wild African animals in their natural habitat, visits to zoos in metropolitan suburbs are anti-climactic and depressing. During our fourteen days in Kruger National Park, we observed forty-four species of wild animals, 111 species of wild birds, and eight species of wild reptiles. My purpose for writing this narrative titled "One More Time" was to renew and humbly describe incredible once-in-a-lifetime memories we experienced.

ONE MORE TIME!

Napoleon Hill once said, "The starting point of achievement is having a desire." In spite of Betty's age at eighty-six, she had a strong desire to experience the excitement and joy of seeing wildlife at Kruger National Park one more time. (Photo by Barbara Graham of Jim and Betty Diamond at Oliphant's Rest Camp, Kruger National Park, South Africa, in September 2015)

ONE MORE TIME!

Our mission was to focus on my late wife's desire to visit the unique wildlife refuge Kruger National Park (KNP), South Africa, one more time. Scheduling land and air travel, lodging, car rental, passports, travel insurance, meals, daily events, and many other details was a truly enjoyable chore. Finally, our departure date arrived, and four anxious travelers were ready to ride a stretch limousine to John F. Kennedy International Airport.

When we got to our South African Airline seats, we sat back and began to relax and enjoy the fifteen-hour flight to Johannesburg, South Africa. After a long flight and arrival at OR Tambo International Airport, we gathered our luggage and met a hotel shuttle driver who drove us to Gold Reef City Hotel.

The next day, we took a flight to Nelspruit where we rented a car and drove to KNP. Barbara and Katie were in disbelief. It was their first visit to Africa and the park. Many memories were rekindled for Betty and me because we had been in KNP many times.

Whether one entered the park through Crocodile Bridge Gate or any of the six additional gates into the park, the adrenalin-producing anticipation of seeing the big five—leopard, elephant, cape buffalo, lion, and rhinoceroses—immediately kicked in. All eyes pierced the grasses, tree branches, water holes, far-off open plains, shaded areas, and roadsides, looking for movement or the horizontal shape of an animal in the grass.

The first wild animal we saw was an impala. Katie went wild photographing her first wild African animal.

Late one evening driving toward our rest camp, Kate said, in her normal voice, "Leopard." It did not sink in with me, and I kept on driving. Then Katie loudly yelled, "I SAID LEOPARD!"

I stopped and backed up, and sure enough we saw a leopard resting on a branch after killing and partially eating a steenbok. What a thrilling experience!

In KNP, no one is permitted out of their vehicle except where designated. Even where it is permissible to disembark from one's vehicle, it is still dangerous. One must never let down one's guard.

As we slowly drove through the park, we observed a large number of animals and birds. During our fourteen-day wildlife expedition in KNP, we sighted lions, cheetahs (Betty's favorite cat), elephants, rhinos, cape buffalo, giraffes, baboons, kudus, impala, water bucks, vervet monkeys, crocodiles, hippos, warthogs, bush hogs, sables, zebras, and many other animals and birds.

PRELUDE: The common ostrich is indigenous to large areas of Africa. It is the largest bird on planet Earth. It is a flightless bird, but when frightened, it can run with sixteen-foot strides more than forty miles per hour. People are advised not to get close to or provoke an ostrich because they have a dangerous kick. An ostrich has a different but interesting anatomy. It has a large eight-compartment heart, eyes two inches in diameter that are larger than its brain, and three stomachs. I was inspired to write this narrative titled "Ostrich" because of their uniqueness and the excitement of observing them in the wild in national parks in Africa.

OSTRICH

While on numerous wildlife safaris in various South African national parks, we would occasionally sight a small flock of ostriches *(Struthio camelus)* in open bushlands. The males (cocks) have black feathers except for white blotches around their legs and brown feathers over the colaca.* (Photo by Jim Diamond of an ostrich in Kruger National Park, South Africa)

26

OSTRICH

While on numerous wildlife safaris in various South African national parks, we occasionally sighted a small flock of ostriches in open bushlands. The females (hens) have dull brown feathers except for white blotches.

In South Africa and some other countries, ostriches are grown on farms. Farm-raised ostriches are prized for their feathers to make feather dusters, skin for leather products such as belts and purses, and lean red meat.

Ostriches do not bury their heads in the sand. If an ostrich feels threatened, it will lie down and place its head on the ground. Because its head and neck are about the color of sand, from a distance it looks like its head is buried in the sand.

Ostriches fight predators* with their feet. They use a vicious, forward kick because that is the direction their legs bend.

Once in the Kingdom of eSwatini (Swaziland) at the King Mswati III International Airport (once known as Matsapha Airport), I saw approximately 100 young ostriches being confiscated by airport authorities. Poachers had been sending them to Texas via Mexico because the climate in Texas is conducive to raising ostriches on farms. The poachers were arrested and jailed. The eSwatini government then owned 100 young ostriches, and officials had to decide where to place them. They were ultimately transported to Hlane Royal National Park in eSwatini.

One day, we were sitting under a shelter at the Hlane campsite, eating sandwiches when suddenly fifteen to twenty of those young half-grown ostriches walked up to us, looking for a treat. Apparently, previous visitors gave them some nibbles, and the ostriches quickly learned to walk up to visitors like us, looking for a piece of sandwich. The bold ostriches walked close to us begging for a small bite. They were large enough to pose a threat to us with their feet if perturbed, so we chased them away so we could finish our lunch.

Although ostriches prefer plant foods such as roots, seeds, and leaves, on occasion they will also eat meat like locusts, lizards, small snakes, and rodents. Ostriches have a gizzard like a chicken. An ostrich gizzard is a thick-walled, muscular pouch for the initial grinding of food with small pebbles and grit before it enters the stomachs. Also, an ostrich will occasionally eat pebbles and sand to break down its food.

I would like to end this narrative with an African proverb that goes like this, "Even the ostrich, with its long neck and sharp eyes, cannot see what will happen in the future."

PRELUDE: Seeing an elephant in the wild in Africa causes a physical feeling of intense excitement that generates an adrenaline rush. Looking beyond the excitement, one must be careful and cautious not to get too close to African wildlife, especially elephants, hippopotamus, and cape buffalo. They can be dangerous! On one trip, we were staying at Letaba Rest Camp. Early that morning, we were driving a short distance on the main road H-16 when was a secondary road S-62 turned to the right. We decided to explore that road to see whatever animal we could find. Suddenly, in front of us an enormous elephant with huge tusks was slowly trudging toward us. This massive animal was considered to be one of the great tuskers in Kruger National Park. Seeing it was a once-in-a-lifetime experience to cherish. This experience inspired me to write this narrative poem titled "Spectacular Tusker."

SPECTACULAR TUSKER

Masthulele is one of the largest tuskers in Kruger National Park, with each of his tusks weighing in excess of 88 pounds (40 killigrams)! He was named by elephant researcher Dr. Ian Whyte, who chose the name to demonstrate the bull's passive character traits; it translates to the "quiet one." (Photo by Jim Diamond of one of Kruger National Park's largest tuskers near Letaba Rest Camp on road H-16 in Kruger National Park on 6 September 2015)

SPECTACULAR TUSKER

While on safari with dear friends Barbara and Katie Graham, my late wife, Betty, and I arrived at the rest camp late Saturday afternoon where we had reservations to stay overnight. Letaba Rest Camp is located in the north of Kruger National Park, fifty kilometers from Phalaborwa, the nearest entry gate to the park. After a grueling, exciting day observing twelve different animal species in the African bush, we were ready for a good night's rest.

Early Sunday morning 6 September 2015, we ate breakfast at the rest camp restaurant on a gorgeous, cloud-free, blue-sky morning before we began our drive into the bush. We decided to go on a morning safari then return for lunch and visit the elephant museum at the rest camp. We began our morning drive on the main road H-16 and shortly we came upon a secondary road S-62 that turned to the right. Just for the hell of it, we all agreed to explore this road for wild animals. After slowly driving a short distance, we four almost said in unison, "Oh my God! Look at the size of that massive elephant slowly trudging toward us!" Its huge tusks nearly touched the road. That was by far the largest elephant I have observed.

We returned to the rest camp to visit the Letaba Elephant Museum that covers elephant evolution, biology, behavior, ecology, and research. Furthermore, it showcased the ivory of eight of Kruger's greatest tuskers. We reported to the elephant hall curator our sighting of a colossal elephant within the hour. At first he seemed to indicate what we reported to be of no consequence until I showed him the photos I had on my camera. The look on his face was a "Kodak moment." That really got his attention, and he began to document the details of our sighting.

He informed us that the name of this elephant was Masthulele, meaning the "quiet one" because he was seldom seen. At the time of our sighting, according to the curator, Masthulele became a feature in the vicinity of the rest camp. The curator told us that Masthulele was a male with a thickened skin growth toward the narrowing section of the trunk, a golf-ball-sized scar tissue area at the top of the trunk, and an uneven scar next to his left tusk. His tusks were fairly symmetrical, with the left tusk curving slightly higher than the right.

In late 2016, mournfully Masthulele's carcass was found in the section between Giriyondo and Letaba. Reportedly, the likely cause of death was a bull fight near his regular stomping ground in autumn and spring. The carcass site was investigated by the Letaba Section Ranger, and no foul play was suspected. The tusker was estimated to have been between forty-nine and fifty years of age at the time of his death.

I would like to close this narrative poem by quoting an African proverb that goes like this, "When elephants fight, it's the grass that suffers." Even though the grass suffered in Masthulele's last fight, it was an honor to have seen Kruger National Park's largest elephant at the time, who was without doubt a prominent "Spectacular Tusker."

PRELUDE: Tchad is the fifth largest country in Africa, which is bordered on the north by Libya, on the east by Sudan, on the south by Central African Republic and on the west by Cameroon, Nigeria and Niger. As I write this narrative, sadly I have not had the opportunity to revisit Tchad during the forty-seven years since leaving in 1973 because the U.S. State Department considered Tchad extremely dangerous due to the risk of terrorism, kidnapping, unrest and violent crime. Security in Tchad is volatile, and hotspots include the country's East and near the borders with Libya, Sudan and the Central African Republic. Protests could quickly turn violent. I was inspired to write this narrative titled "African Throwing Knife" because I purchased this one from the village blacksmith and kept it handy for personal safety. It is believed that this knife originated in Southern Tchad.

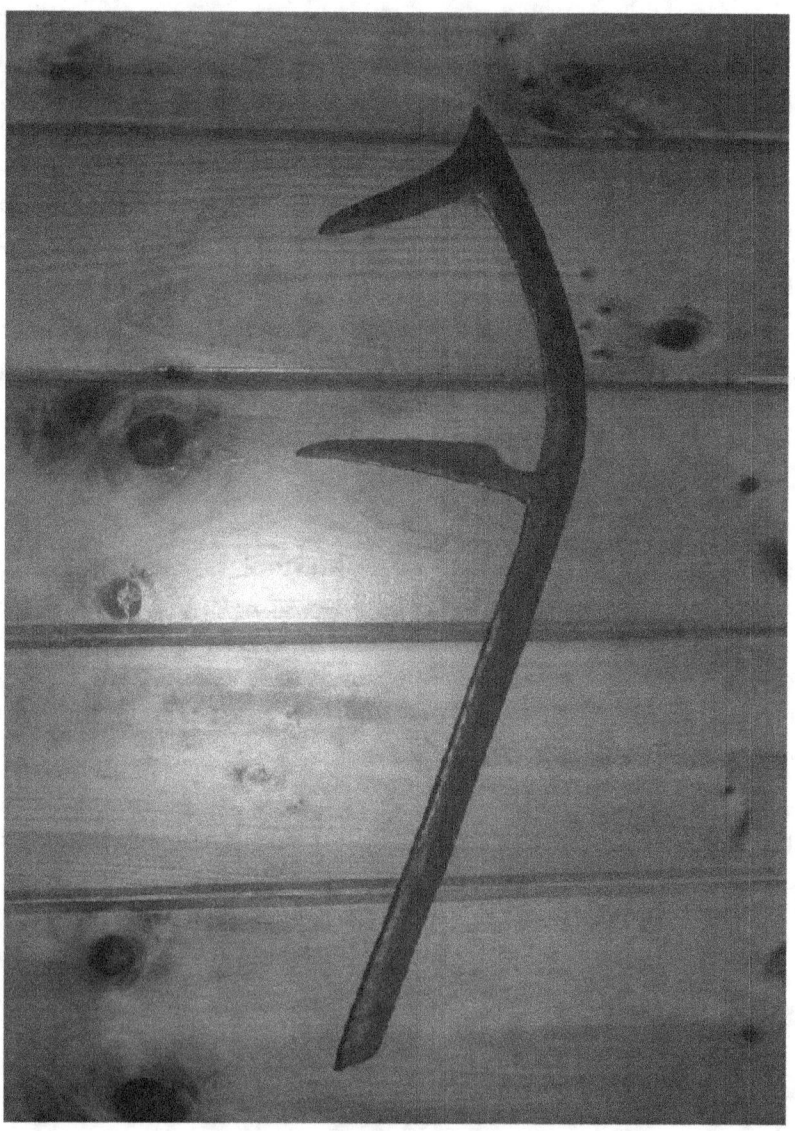

AFRICAN THROWING KNIFE

Tchadian throwing knives *(coute de jete*)*, unlike other African weapon types, were fashioned purely for fighting assailants and protection from attacking wild animals. (Photo by Jim Diamond of his African throwing knife from Bessada, Tchad, Africa)

AFRICAN THROWING KNIFE

I purchased this African throwing knife from the village blacksmith *(forgeron)* of Bessada, Southeastern Tchad, where my late wife, Betty, and I lived for two years as Peace Corps volunteers.

Southern Tchad is believed to be the birthplace of the African throwing knife. In the Sara Madjingaye language, it is known as *angalio*.* These throwing knives, unlike other African weapon types, were fashioned purely for fighting assailants and protection from wild animals.

When people are walking in the bush or very rural areas, they carry their African throwing knife over their shoulders. That is how I personally carried this throwing knife when I was alone in the bush.

When the knife is thrown, it spins, and no matter where it strikes a villain, major damage could be life-threatening or lethal. They can forcibly be thrown by hand at a target with a range up to ninety feet.

Sara Madjingaye blades were unusual in that the sides of their blades were not decorated. The blades were made from heavy metals salvaged from wrecked cars or trucks, for example bumper, spring leaf, or fender. Both sides of the spinning blades were also sharp to cut deep into the flesh wherever it struck its target. The long, narrow shank forming the base for the two knives is also sharply honed, in case it strikes the target first. In other words, this throwing knife was certainly a wicked, dangerous weapon.

I would like to close this narrative with the words of the Tchadian National Anthem that is proudly sung by Tchadians, "People of Tchad, arise and to work! You have conquered the soil and won your rights. Your freedom will be born of your courage. Lift up your eyes, the future is yours."

Even though Tchad is one of the poorest, most corrupt countries in the world Tchadians are a proud people who work hard on land they have conquered. They yearn to one day lift their eyes to look for their future without having to use African throwing knives in combat.

Long live the Tchadian people!

PRELUDE: Shortly after our arrival in Tchad, Africa, we heard tom-toms being played in a far-off distance late at night near Tchad's capital, Njamina. We were mesmerized because it was the first indigenous African village sound we heard. It has been reported that the African tom-tom drum was first created by Mandinka blacksmiths in western Africa sometime around 1300 AD. African tom-tom drums are still used in Africa during ceremonial events, rituals and spiritual healing. I was inspired to write this narrative titled "African Tom-Tom" because while living in Tchad for two years, I heard them played many times for various reasons in several African countries, and I purchased an antique hand-carved wooden African tom-tom in Bessada, Tchad, Africa after the seller played it at a funeral.

AFRICAN TOM-TOM

The village chief of Bessada explained that a tom-tom symbolizes the heartbeat of Mother Nature, regardless of the event where it's played, such as a marriage, birth of a baby, death of a villager, Baya rites* for young girls, or harvesting crops. (Photo by Jim Diamond of an African tom-tom he purchased in Bessada, Tchad, Africa, in 1972)

AFRICAN TOM-TOM

Tom-tom drums are an important component of the various indigenous cultures found in many countries throughout Africa. In the Republic of Tchad (aka Chad) the fifth-largest country in Africa, tom-toms were used to communicate to the people the fundamental intent of an activity or event, such as to celebrate, mourn, inspire, plant, or harvest a crop. They also performed on the tom-toms in times of both peace and war.

The village chief of Bessada explained to me that a tom-tom symbolizes the heartbeat of Mother Nature, regardless of the event where it's played, such as a marriage, birth of a baby, death of a villager, Baya rites* for young girls, holiday celebrations, or harvesting crops. Each event was depicted by certain recognizable drumbeats people have learned to distinguish.

One day, I saw a Tchadian man walking near our house carrying his tom-tom. I greeted him by saying, "*Lapia, ea-toe carie wah.*" (Hello.)

We started to talk in French about his tom-tom. He told me it was possibly more than 100 years old and has been handed down through generations of Tchadians. He said it was hand-carved from a piece of mahogany, with two pieces of dried cowhide attached with rope to the top and bottom. Beeswax was put on top to give the tom-tom more resonance. He also told me he played his tom-tom when the chief declared an event required playing.

After an in-depth discussion, I asked the man if he would sell me his tom-tom. He expressed interest because he knew I would pay him in cash.

"How much would you charge me?" I asked. I knew his price would be high, but I wanted that tom-tom. I agreed to his price, but he told me before he would sell it to me, he had to play it one last time at a funeral.

Two weeks after the funeral, the man brought the tom-tom to me. I paid him, and he was very, very happy to get the money. I was very, very happy to buy the tom-tom and be able to send it to my home in Pennsylvania, and since August 1973, I have displayed that tom-tom in my home.

In the near future, that tom-tom is destined to be permanently displayed in the African-American Museum of Bucks County, Pennsylvania. I had been seeking a permanent home for all my African handicraft and artifacts from Tchad. My in-depth discussions with officials from the African-American Museum of Bucks County focused on preserving African heritage. However after seeing the plethora of items that were being donated to their new museum, they realized they were receiving more than they could envision.

This African proverb summarizes our discussions, "The humble person looks for one thing and sees everything.

PRELUDE: In April 1971, when my late wife, Betty, and I arrived in Tchad, Africa, as Peace Corps volunteers, Terance A. Todman was the United States Ambassador to the Republic of Tchad. Ambassador Todman was an outstanding American diplomat! He served in that post with honor, respect and dignity from 1969 through 1972. Betty and I met with Ambassador Todman on several occasions, and our relationship unfolded into an esteemed friendship. I was inspired to write this narrative titled "Ambassador Terence A. Todman" because of his strong support and genuine interests in Peace Corps volunteer efforts in Tchad. We were saddened to learn that after a stellar diplomatic career, Ambassador Todman passed away on 13 August 2014.

AMBASSADOR TERANCE A. TODMAN

Ambassador Terance A. Todman (13 March 1926-13 August 2014) traveled to Bessada in early February 1972 to observe the opening of a pit silo. He was amazed at the uniqueness of this project. (Photo by Betty Diamond of Ambassador Todman far left, the president's brother far right and Jim Diamond second from right)

AMBASSADOR TERANCE A. TODMAN

Shortly after our arrival in Tchad in February 1971, my late wife, Betty, and I were invited to Ambassador Todman's residence for a short visit to welcome us and get to know each other. He seemed to be very much interested that we keep him apprised of our planned efforts in Bessada, the home village of Tchad's president, Francois Tombalbaye.

Soon after we got settled into our house in the village of Bessada, Betty and I began getting to know the people to learn what kind of skills they possessed, their level of education, their felt needs, who made the decisions in the village and what resources were readily available. When a mutual trust was established between us and the people, we began setting priorities to fulfill our duties to help the Tchadian people help themselves using their skills, knowledge and resources. Betty and I completed thirty-one projects during our tenure in Bessada.

We arrived in Tchad on 28 April 1971, at the height of the annual dry season that begins in the end of September and ends in May or early June. During the annual dry season in Tchad, not one drop of rain fell. There was no hay, silage, grass, or grain to feed oxen.

I wondered how the cattle survived the dry season. The answer was that farmers released their oxen into the bush to fend for themselves. By the end of the dry season, many oxen had died from eating poisonous plants, thirst, or starvation.

When rains arrived, edible grass covered the whole countryside. I once asked a farmer, "Why do farmers not make grass silage as a feed for oxen?"

The farmer responded, *"C'est que cest?"* (What's that?)

I figured out how to make a round silo to store grass in a pit! We solicited village volunteer farmers to try this new idea, and seventeen came forward to try it. They dug a pit, cut grass, carried the grass to the pit and chopped it on a log. When they filled the pit with chopped grass, a thick layer of unchopped grass was placed on top of the chopped grass and two feet of soil on top of the unchopped grass. When they opened the pits five months later, they saw the greenest, best-smelling, best-tasting grass silage one could find anywhere back home in Pennsylvania! Six to seven tons of grass silage would feed two oxen during an annual dry season. We achieved success helping people help themselves by introducing an ingenious modern concept using local skills, knowledge, resources, homemade tools and no cash!

This project became well known throughout Tchad and other countries, and Ambassador Todman learned about this successful effort. In early February 1972, he traveled to Bessada to observe the opening of a pit silo. He was amazed by the uniqueness of this project. Another project Ambassador Todman wanted to see during his visit was a modern chicken house we built using bamboo, grass and indigenous skills. The chicken house was three feet off the ground, featuring slatted bamboo floor, slatted sides, grass thatched roof and four slanted nests enabling the eggs to roll out of the nest into a bamboo trough outside. Ambassador Todman was so impressed with the ingenuity of these two projects using the people's own knowledge, skills and resources that he featured them in his monthly embassy publication.

Peace Corps volunteers must understand that creativity is necessary in developing countries. One should never dismiss an idea that can possibly help people to help themselves.

PRELUDE: In the village of Bessada, Tchad, every Sunday afternoon, Tchadian horsemen loved to race their steeds near the village edge. I learned that when President Tombalbaye visited his home village, the horsemen would ride their horses in front of the president, then race them. There were forty-two horses in the village, and I thought it would be proper if the Tchadian riders would conduct a series of drill movements and patterns with their horses in front of the president, remembering the Pennsylvania State Police Horse Drill Team I used to watch at the annual Pennsylvania Farm Show. I used their impressive riding skills and drill patterns as a model to teach Tchadian horsemen to ride their horses in a series of movements and patterns. I was inspired to write this narrative titled "Bessada Horse Drill Team" to capture the strong enjoyment Tchadian horsemen expressed while riding their steeds and the merriment of village people watching the riders perform and race.

BESSADA HORSE DRILL TEAM

The first thing we taught the riders was to watch their leader's flag and walk their horses in two straight lines. My helper, Nestor, and I walked in front of each line to show the drill format. (Photo by Betty Diamond of Nestor and Jim Diamond walking in front of the horsemen learning how to walk their horses in a straight line in May 1972)

BESSADA HORSE DRILL TEAM

One Sunday, I called a meeting of all the riders and explained how they could put on a noble presentation with their horses during the president's next visit to the village. We named the group "Bessada Horse Drill Team."

The riders expressed a very strong interest in learning how to do the movements and patterns. I agreed to teach them, using the Pennsylvania State Police Horse Drill Team as a model to develop their performances. Like the state police team, they were all volunteers who cared for the horses. It was to be their show from start to finish.

Each Sunday morning, we practiced for two hours in front of the Bessada Elementary School. The only props that we needed were two Tchadian flags and two long bamboo poles. We attached a Tchadian flag to the end of each bamboo pole and each of two team leaders would carry their flags upright.

We divided the forty-two horses into two twenty-one-horse teams. We taught one new drill pattern each Sunday. Each Sunday thereafter, we would practice previous drills, then add a new drill.

The first thing we taught them was to watch the flag held by their leader and walk their horses in two straight lines, keeping a space of about six and one-half feet (two meters) between each horse. My helper, Nestor, and I walked in front of each line to clarify the drill format. The riders were not used to being told where to ride their horses. It was challenging the first couple practice sessions to get them to follow instructions.

After they mastered walking their horses in a straight line, we showed each leader how to go into two circles. This is when the riders began to really cooperate and follow instructions. After they circled twice, we showed them how to get out of the circle and back into a straight line. We practiced these two patterns until they mastered the straight lines and circles. At this point they were really getting excited about their accomplishments. When they mastered the two straight lines and two circles, we then showed them how to go from two circles to four circles. This was a bit complicated at first, but they mastered this pattern rather quickly. From the four circles, we showed them how to get back into a straight line. For their next pattern, the riders would form two straight lines and would criss-cross with their horses in the other line until all the horses in line A were in line B and vice versa.

For the exhibition finale, as each line arrived at the far end of field, horses number one in lines A and B would race across the field. Then horses number two would race. All the horses would race in pairs and that is how we ended practice sessions. After the horsemen knew how to perform their exhibition, they were quite pleased and proud of their new abilities.

The Bessada Horse Drill Team in their traditional garb performed proudly with stateliness for any government dignitary who visited Bessada on Sundays, national holidays, or other special events.

PRELUDE: In the early 1960s, using oxen for animal traction was introduced to rural sedentary farmers in Tchad by the French. Ten years later, rural Tchadian farmers were beginning to authenticate the use of oxen, and more oxen were seen in the villages. They were used mainly to pull ox carts and hand plows to till the soil. The farmers purchased untrained, uncastrated* bull oxen from nomadic Fulani herdsmen. Because the bulls were uncastrated, the farmers had to learn how to safely restrain bulls. I was inspired to write this poem titled "Casting a Bull" because farmers were using very unsafe methods of restraining bulls to castrate them. I taught them an approved method of throwing the bull on its side, which was safe for both farmers and bull.

CASTING A BULL

I explained how to put a halter on the bull, wrap the rope around the heart girth, loop the rope on top and take it over the back and around the hind flanks.

One person would hold the halter, and another person would gently pull the long rope taunt. Then the bull goes down like a big baby.

(Photos by Jim Diamond of Tchadian farmers learning how to cast and castrate a bull in 1972 in Tchad, Africa)

CASTING A BULL

French extension staff introduced oxen to Tchadian sedentary farmers in 1960, but they taught them only how to use the oxen. Purchasing a team of oxen was a major, long-term investment for a farmer. The farmers would purchase untrained, uncastrated bull oxen from nomadic Fulani herdsmen as they passed nearby their village. Because the bulls were not castrated, the farmers had to learn how to restrain bulls.

Uncastrated bulls can be quite powerful and dangerous to farmers working with them. Their temperament can be malicious and dangerous to the handler and to people nearby. When adults handle an oxen, they tend to show fear, and bulls can sense such feelings. That's when a problem can unfold. Ironically, young boys were able to handle the oxen more easily and safely because they did not show any fear. Nevertheless, once the bulls were castrated, they became more docile and easier to handle.

I decided to teach the farmers how to properly castrate their bulls so they would become more docile. I had a Burdizzo* and would use that tool because it was a bloodless way to castrate* a bull.

I asked a farmer if he would throw the bull down on its side and restrain it. Their traditional method of throwing a bull was "any way you could." One person restrained the horns, another person had a rope around the hind legs pulling to the right, a third person had a rope around the front legs pulling to the left, and a fourth person held the tail. Ultimately, the bull would fall onto its side and its legs would be restrained. This method was very difficult and dangerous.

Then I demonstrated how to castrate a bull using a Burdizzo.

I got my rope and halter out of my truck, then I called everyone to gather around the next bull. I explained how to put a halter on the bull, wrap the rope around the heart girth, loop the rope on the bull's top, take the rope along the top of its back, loop it again and place the rope around the hind flanks. (See photo.) Once one person holds the halter and another person gently pulls the long rope taunt, the bull goes down like a big baby. The legs were tied and the bull was castrated with a Burdizzo.

This castration method crushes the testicular chords with no bleeding. This is important because bleeding can cause a fly strike; the flies lay eggs and hatch into maggots, which presents a different problem. After castration, the bull is released.

The farmers could not get over how easy it was to throw a large bull to the ground onto its side using my method. They learned the method quickly.

There were sixteen bulls waiting to get castrated, and the farmers wanted to try their new skill. They went to work throwing a bull. When I looked over to where the bulls were waiting their turn, I saw twelve bulls lying on their sides on the ground. The farmers were very excited and proud they were successful at learning a safer, easier way to throw a bull.

Tchadian farmers must keep their tasks safe and simple and let their newly learned casting technique be the service it provides for the task.

PRELUDE: Creativity is a necessity in developing countries. One should never dismiss an idea that can possibly help people to help themselves. In Southern Tchad, we were able to introduce a modern American concept of feeding oxen quality grass silage by using the people's own knowledge, skills and resources. Grass silage is a nutritious, fermented* feedstuff for ruminants* and would keep oxen strong and healthy during the dry season. French veterinarian Marc Dronne was a very popular veterinarian and a good friend of mine. Tragically, on 13 February 1972, Dr. Dronne was killed in a car accident on his way to show the pit silo project to international guests. I will never forget that very sad day because I was the first American expatriate to find him deceased in the middle of a dirt road along with his colleagues. I was inspired to write this narrative titled "Catastrophic Event" because that was an emotional experience will forever be embedded in my unnerved mental well-being.

CATASTROPHIC EVENT

The damaged station wagon was upside-down with its contents strewn. I saw two bodies lying in the middle of the road. (The above image was not the car I found on the dirt road in Tchad. However, except for the tar road and police car, this scene nearly replicates what I found.)

CATASTROPHIC EVENT

On 28 April 1971, we arrived in Tchad at the height of the annual dry season. During that dry season in Tchad, not one drop of rain fell, yet when rains arrive, edible grass covers the entire countryside.

The French government assigned a very talented veterinarian named Dr. Marc Dronne to work in Tchad. He was a well-respected veterinarian, and the farmers and nomadic herdsmen trusted him because he was not a Tchadian government employee. They knew he was not obligated to report the names of farmers or herders and number of animals to the Tchadian government.

Dr. Dronne had been closely watching the process I used to teach farmers how to make grass silage to feed oxen. He was very pleased that my pit silo and grass silage program was such a success. He invited colleagues from France and Germany to Tchad to see how we made quality silage with indigenous knowledge, skills and resources while introducing a modern concept.

On 6 February 1972, I received a letter from Dr. Dronne informing me he invited a visiting French veterinarian, a German agronomist,* and Tchad's Director of Animal Industry to visit Bessada to observe a pit silo and grass silage being fed to oxen. He asked me to meet him at 8:30 a.m. on 13 February in a village east of Bessada called Bedaya.

Per his itinerary, with the local Tchadian veterinarian, I waited for Dr. Dronne to arrive with his guests. At 10:30 a.m., a native Tchadian boy hurriedly ran toward our car and excitedly informed us there was a car accident ten kilometers east, and the occupants were Europeans.

We immediately departed for the accident scene and were horrified at what we found. The damaged station wagon was upside-down with its contents strewn about the accident scene. Two bodies were lying in middle of the road. I walked over to the bodies and was utterly traumatized to find my good friend and colleague Dr. Marc Dronne lying dead on the road. The other victim was Dr. Godit, a French veterinarian.

A local person who was standing along the road informed me that a Nigerian driver passing by took two seriously injured passengers to a hospital in Koumra: the driver of the car and the German agronomist Dr. Ox.

While waiting for authorities to arrive, I covered the bodies with branches and a sleeping bag. After the authorities and police arrived, I assisted in placing the bodies in the back of a pickup truck, and two Frenchmen transported them to Fort Archambault to be flown back to France.

The following Tuesday, I attended a memorial service at the Koumra Catholic Church.

Tchad and France lost a hard-working, intelligent and skilled veterinarian. I lost a good friend. Dr. David Seymour, Baptist missionary, reported that all of the victims had serious head and neck injuries.

One of the hardest things required of me in Tchad was the day I had to let go as angels carried Dr. Dronne up to heaven. Dr. Dronne is now a cherished memory, but his life and our friendship will be with me during the remainder of my life.

PRELUDE: Featured sounds of Tchadian music include the *coucouma*, a violin-like instrument performed by Bilala shamans* from central Tchad. The *coucouma* sounds portray short, constant repeated rhythmic patterns. Featured *coucouma* sounds are often interwoven with melodies created by a *balafon.* * Another Tchadian instrument often heard being played with *coucoma* melodies is a five- to seven-string instrument called the N'*gambaya* Guitar of Mondou, from Central Tchad in the Logone district (see narrative titled N'*gambaya* Guitar of Mondou). The body of the N'*gambaya* Guitar is wood, covered with a thin animal hide. I was inspired to write this narrative titled *"Coucouma"* because I was able to hear a Tchadian lady play a *coucouma* at a village marriage celebration. I was ultimately able to purchase it from her to fully complement the beautiful-black-and-white painting I previously acquired portraying a lady playing a coucouma.

COUCOUMA

A *coucoma* is a type of violin that is commonly found in Tchad and neighboring countries. Note the lady playing a coucouma in the painting. (Photo by Jim Diamond of his *coucouma* and painting of a lady playing a *coucoma* he acquired in Tchad, Africa, in 1972)

COUCOUMA

A *coucoma* is a type of violin commonly found in Tchad and neighboring countries. The bow is a stick with a ribbon of parallel horsetail hairs attached and stretched between the two ends. The horsehair is coated with rosin* so it can grip the string.

Moving the horsehair across a string causes a stick-slip phenomenon.* An example of the stick-slip phenomenon occurs when musical notes can be made by rubbing a wet finger along the rim of a crystal wine glass.

The *coucouma* has a resonating body with a small bridge implanted in it. Horsehair is stretched from the bridge to the resonating body. In most string instruments, the vibrations are transmitted to the body of the instrument, which often incorporates some sort of hollow or enclosed area. The body of the instrument also vibrates, along with the air inside it. The vibration of the body of the instrument and the enclosed hollow or chamber make the vibration of the string more audible to the performer and audience.

In Tchad, the *coucouma* is usually played by Bilala and Bournauan witch doctors. A medicine man named Amadou Coucouma was the best-known witch doctor in N'djamena (aka Fort Lamy) the capital of Tchad. For a fee, Amadou Coucouma composed eulogies exclusively for people who died. He was also particularly in demand to perform at weddings and other joyous celebrations.

When listening to Tchadian traditional music, one is struck by the similarities of regional sounds. Its magic lies in the subtle differences and the handling of instruments and sounds. String instruments are common in the Saharan and Sahel regions. Music expresses culture, and there is no music in an absolute way. There are different types of music adapted to each tribe and each situation.

The first President of the Republic of Tchad and my dear friend Ngarta Francois Tombalbaye (1960-1975) was a huge fan and promoter of traditional music, which was performed at every official ceremony thereby promoting several artists from the 1960s whose works represented a common heritage. Artists like Toudjibé, the president's favorite musician, have all left their hallmark.

I would like to close this narrative with a Tchadian proverb that goes like this, "If you always walk down the same path, you'll go where you've already been." Even though traditional music in Tchad remains popular and is frequently requested at events or on the radio, the introduction of Western instruments since independence continues to be considered as a sign of emancipation, but this has never impacted traditional music. Today, musicians owning and using modern instruments turn toward traditional music. Tchad residents are witnessing a crossbreeding of ancestral rhythms, mid-way between tradition and modernism.

PRELUDE: On 31 December 1971, my late wife, Betty, and I loaded our luggage into the back of a Peace Corps Land Rover for a grueling 195-mile (325-kilometer) trip to Lake Tchad (aka Chad) north of Fort Lamy. We rode with three Peace Corps volunteers who were assigned to live in a desert village on the edge of Lake Tchad known as Bol. This was a once-in-a-lifetime opportunity, and Betty and I were able to see the lifestyle of people living in remote woebegone desert villages plus observe scant flora and fauna* in the Sahara Desert. What an intriguing experience this promised to be! I was inspired to write this narrative titled "Lake Tchad Expedition" because its water sustained people, animals (which included donkeys and camels), fishing, irrigation and economic activities in Tchad, Cameroon, Nigeria and Niger. Lake Chad was nestled in a low spot within a huge basin in West-Central Africa, but in the past half-century, it has lost most of its water. The once-great lake now spans less than a tenth of the area it covered in the 1960s.

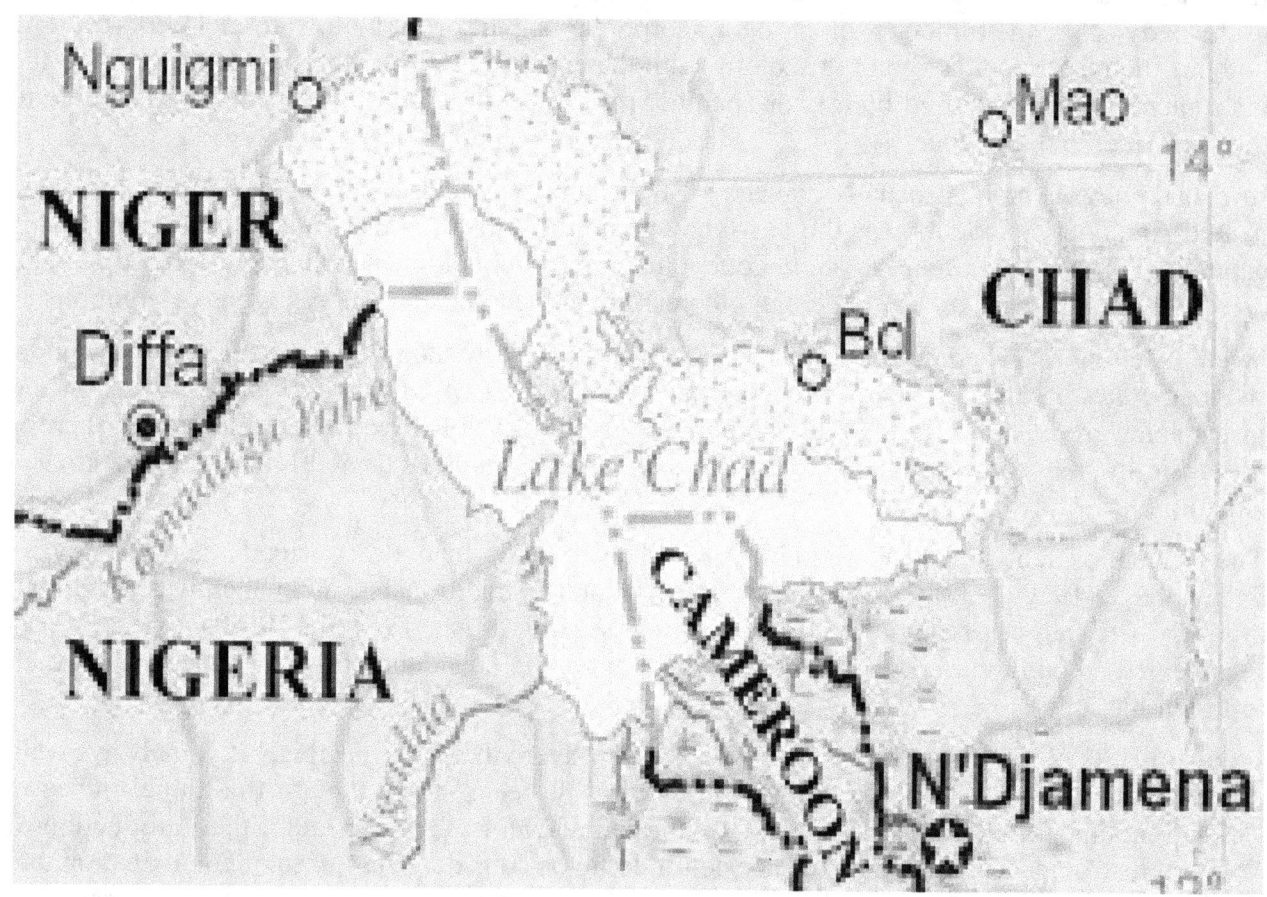

LAKE TCHAD EXPEDITION

During the last three hours of the nine-hour trip, the terrain of the Sahara Desert was nothing but one high sand dune after another. The driver shifted the Land Rover into four-wheel-drive, and he drove as fast as he could down one side of a dune to get enough speed and momentum to climb up the next.

LAKE TCHAD EXPEDITION

The first thirty-five kilometers from Fort Lamy were a rather smooth drive on an asphalt road. When the paved road ended, it quickly turned into a rough, dusty dirt road for several kilometers. The road became narrower and incredibly sandy the farther north-northwest we traveled into the Sahara Desert. The last 145 kilometers followed a track of previous truck tracks in the sand that often vanished. Sand blown by dry desert winds covered the tracks, and they simply evaporated.

Only four-wheel-drive vehicles were able to travel this type of terrain. When the track disappeared, the driver would drive in large concentric circles in the sand until a semblance of a track reappeared. Sometimes the driver knew the general direction he should be driving and drove hopefully in the direction of Bol on the edge of Lake Tchad in barren, harsh, hot, dry, sandy desert environs.

During the last three hours of the nine-hour trip, the terrain of the Sahara Desert was nothing but one high sand dune after another. The driver had shifted the Land Rover into four-wheel-drive, and he drove as fast as he could down one side of a dune to get enough speed and momentum to climb up the next one. When going upward and nearing the top of a dune, the speed and momentum would diminish and all four of his wheels would begin spinning in the sand. The driver would then turn the steering wheel abruptly to the right, then to the left, to the right, then to the left until we got to the top of the dune. The abrupt turning gave the Land Rover just enough traction for us to get to the top. The whole process was repeated over and over as we crossed many kilometers of sand dunes.

One should always travel in the desert in the early morning because the sand is firmer. When the hot afternoon sun heats the sand, air within the sand particles expands and causes it to be more fluid.

Before we reached the dunes, we saw an occasional wild donkey among stressed thorn bushes. The dunes exhibited no flora, at least during that time of the year.

During the entire trip, my late wife, Betty, and our friend Bill Kanapel rode in the cab with the driver. I rode in the back with the other two volunteers. Needless to say, we were exposed to all the elements, such as dust, blowing sand, hot dry air and hot sun.

After nine hours of riding in the back of the Land Rover, we arrived tired and thirsty at the village of Bol. Our first impressions of Bol were of sadness and misery. But it was interesting. We observed that the people who lived there were mostly Arabs, and we found them to be very friendly. The houses of the small village resembled houses that one would have seen during Biblical times. We stayed in a mud brick house, which was complemented by camels and braying donkeys tethered nearby.

I would like to end this narrative by quoting Canadian philosopher and author Matshona Dhilwayo who wrote, " A rose in a desert can only survive on its strength, not its beauty."

PRELUDE: All of North Africa was once an ocean. What's left of that ocean is now known as Lake Tchad, nestled in a huge basin in west-central Africa. Lake Tchad (aka Chad) was once one of Africa's largest freshwater lakes. However, since the 1960s Lake Tchad has dwindled some 90 percent because of declining precipitation. Its water was the central component of the peoples' lifestyles, animals, fishing, irrigation and perpetual economic activity in four bordering countries: Tchad, Cameroon, Nigeria and Niger. Scientists are concerned this striking loss of fresh water will impact more than thirty million people. I was inspired to write this narrative titled "Demise of Tchad's Great Lake" because of my ten-day experience at the edge of Lake Tchad in the village of Bol during the first week of January 1972. At that time, the water level was considered to be normal. Fishing was a prominent source of food and income, a limited amount of fresh water was being used to irrigate vegetable crops, and residents had sufficient fresh water for their daily needs.

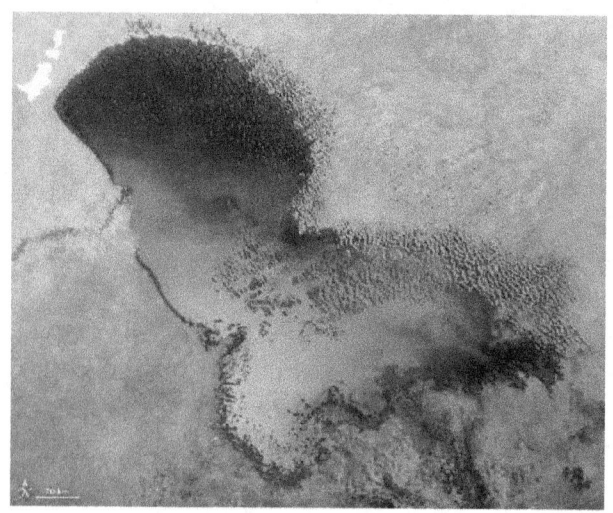

LAKE TCHAD in 1963

NASA Earth Observatory image by Jesse Allen, using Landsat 5 Thematic Mapper data provided by the U.S. Geological Survey. Water level is considered to be normal.

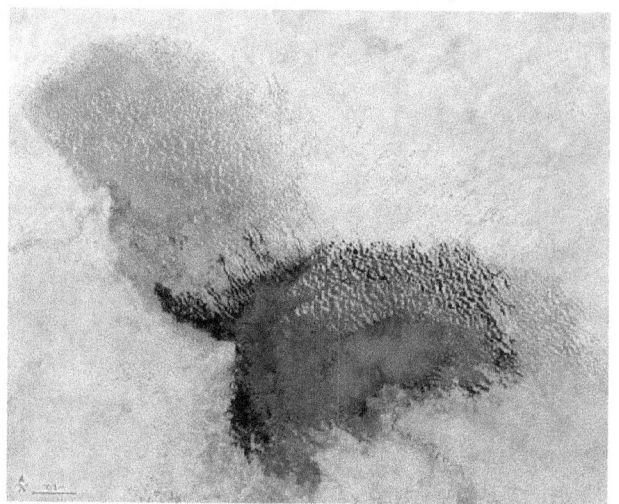

LAKE TCHAD in 1983

NASA Earth Observatory image by Jesse Allen, using Landsat 5 Thematic Mapper data provided by the U.S. Geological Survey. Water level has shrunk to 1/10 of its normal size.

DEMISE OF TCHAD'S GREAT LAKE

All of North Africa was once an ocean. What's left of that ocean is now known as Lake Tchad. Nestled in a low spot within a huge basin in west-central Africa, it has sustained people, animals, fishing, irrigation and economic activity in Tchad, Cameroon, Nigeria and Niger.

DEMISE OF TCHAD'S GREAT LAKE

The source of water for Lake Tchad comes from fresh water flowing northward in the Chari and Logone Rivers and their tributaries. Lake Tchad is a large, shallow natural inland lake of fresh water with numerous inlets jutting into the desert.

When the water receded from the desert inlets during the dry season, the French government provided funds to build earthen dikes to prevent water from re-entering the dried and parched inlets during the rainy seasons. These dried inlets were called "polders." As a result, hundreds of hectares* of deep fertile lake bottom soil had the potential to be a horn of plenty, enabling this poor country to become self-sufficient in food production. In addition to the fresh water in Lake Tchad, groundwater was also readily available. If a hole two to three feet deep were dug into the ground, one would find a water table that had ample water for irrigating food crops.

Bill Kanapel from Washington state, the Peace Corps volunteer assigned to Bol, was a retired farmer with experience irrigating crops on the eastern side of the Olympia Mountains. He taught the Tchadian farmers how to level the land to effectively irrigate crops. He made a broad, camel-drawn, V-shaped drag and properly leveled the land so water could flow and be absorbed uniformly across the field. Using Peace Corps funds, Bill purchased a camel, and with a jerry-rigged* camel-powered water pump he was able to pump irrigation water effectively. It was shaped like a water wheel using a detached rear end of an old Land Rover. Holes were drilled into a large steel plate to align it with the lug bolts on one wheel. Then it was placed upright resting vertically on its rim, firmly supported by the steel plate. On the other wheel rim a long pipe was attached to the camel. When the camel walked in circles around the well, the turning wheel caused the universal joint in the chassis to turn. The universal joint was fastened to a sprocket, which turned a long chain affixed to empty half-gallon juice cans. As the sprocket rotated, the chain with its empty half-gallon cans were simultaneously lowered into the water while lifting full ones. As the full cans reached the top of the sprocket, they automatically emptied water into a wooden trough. As water flowed by gravity into the wooden channel, short hoses were used to siphon water into irrigation ditches between the rows of vegetables growing in rich lake bottom soil. The camel-driven irrigation pump worked very successfully. Water was easily found. Soils were rich. There was a 365-day growing season. People were optimistic this project was going to revolutionize Bol's economy and that particular region of desert in Tchad. However, there was a problem! All of North Africa was once a large ocean of water and what is left is now Lake Tchad. Remnants of the old ocean still existed in the underground water table. Along the wooden channel for irrigation water to flow from the well a white line existed on the two sides, caused by evaporated salt water being lifted from the hand-dug well. The water could be used effectively on the rich soil for year one. During year two, salty water again irrigated into the soil, causing food crops to grow but not as lush and productive as in the previous year. During year three, not even weeds grew. The salt water applied during the first two years caused the soil to become sterile. This irrigation practice resulted in rich, productive lake bottom land to be idle, barren, unproductive sterile fields. Salt water forced this successful water pump project to be deactivated.

PRELUDE: In Tchad's rural bush villages, poultry, namely chickens, was an important food source. Chickens could be purchased directly from the owner, in village markets, or from someone passing by with a bunch of chickens tied by their feet to the back of a bicycle, the top of a truck, or the side of a donkey. There was no electricity for refrigeration in rural villages. People purchased live chickens and at their huts dressed them out (killed, plucked the feathers and removed the entrails) just before preparing them for a meal. Women or teenage girls normally killed and cleaned the chickens. When I visited someone, the Tchadian tradition was to purchase a couple of live chickens and give them to my host upon my arrival. I was inspired to write this narrative titled "First the Chicken, Then the Egg" because there were no poultry management practices in Tchad's rural villages. Chickens ran free and fended for themselves. No local chicken feed was available for purchase. It was survival of the fittest. However, in April each year, healthy indigenous chickens suddenly died from an unknown disease. I did not have a clue what killed chickens in April each year, how to prevent it, how to treat it, or what to do with the dead birds after they died. My mission was to show people how to raise chickens in a modern chicken house built by using their own talents, resources and modern technology.

FIRST THE CHICKEN, THEN THE EGG

Left: Jim Diamond helping Nestor build the modern chicken house frame using bamboo and mahogany poles for the corners. Right: Chickens completely confined on slatted floor with slatted sides and a calabash feeder.

Nestor gathering his eggs that rolled from the nest into a bamboo trough on outside.

(Photos of Jim Diamond teaching how to make a modern chicken house in Bessada, Tchad, in 1972)

FIRST THE CHICKEN, THEN THE EGG

There were no specific breeds of chickens in rural villages. The chickens ran free and fended for themselves; however, everyone knew to whom each chicken belonged.

The indigenous chickens were hardy. They could withstand drought conditions, resist certain parasites and diseases and tolerate heat and dust. Yet I learned 80 percent of all native chickens died in April, which was the middle of the annual dry season—with no noticeable symptoms.

I suspected the disease was caused by a soil-borne organism because most of the village chickens ate what they could glean from scratching the dry soil. I hypothesized that if a modern chicken house was built whereby chickens were totally confined in a chicken house off the ground, the disease would not affect the chickens.

I needed to come up with an idea how to build a modern chicken house using indigenous skills, knowledge and resources. A plan in the *VITA Handbook* helped me to be creative and use resources found in the village. In Bessada, nails, boards, chicken wire, chicken feeders, waterers, cement blocks, cement and roofing materials did not exist. Because bamboo was readily available just outside the village, we used bamboo in place of boards. We used thick layers of dried grass in place of roofing materials, a large gourd cut in half for a chicken feeder and a medium-sized gourd cut in half for a waterer. The locals attached building materials with strips of young tree bark in place of nails. The only tools we needed were a saw, machete and a ruler.

Termites in Tchad were a serious problem with wood products. According to Tchadian villagers, termites would not eat bamboo or mahogany. Based upon their time-honored wisdom, we went into the bush with a machete and cut six mahogany posts three meters long. Four of the posts had to have a forked top. We painted one end of each mahogany post with old used motor oil, dug a hole and set each post into the ground three-fourths meter deep and tamped them tightly. We set three mahogany posts on each corner and one in the middle. Aligning characteristically crooked mahogany posts was difficult. We formed the frame using water-soaked strips of bark to attach long bamboo poles three feet off the ground and on the top. When the bark dried, it shrank and tightened the structure. We cut bamboo poles to fit the width of the bottom frame to form a slatted floor so the manure and water could fall through onto the ground below. Using a machete, we halved bamboo poles, then each half was split into quarters, referred to as slats. Each bamboo slat was attached to the mahogany posts with wet bark having one-inch space between the slats. The slats enclosed the structure to keep the hens confined to a clean, dry space three feet off the ground with air circulation. We used bamboo poles as rafters to form an A-shaped frame for the roof. Thick bundles of dried grass were laid out in rows beginning on the edge of the roof with each preceding layer overlapping the one below it. The thick thatched grass roof protected the chickens from sun, rain and cold. Three short poles were attached horizontally to one side of the structure forming a perch for the hens to fly onto before entering their nests. Short bamboo slats were attached to the bamboo frame to form the sides of four nests. The front of the nest was higher than the back, allowing eggs to roll out of the sloped nest into a bamboo trough.

People in the village stopped daily to observe the chickens; they were amazed that the eggs would automatically roll out of the nests. Using the "modern" chicken house, not one chicken died the following April. Necessity is the mother of invention!

PRELUDE: Ancient Romans used domesticated rabbits for their food and fur. When I was of age, I used to hunt wild rabbits on our farm with my father, carrying a single-barrel Riverside 16-gauge shotgun.* My mother used to make rabbit pot pie and it was delicious. Rabbit meat is called coney,* which is a French word. Coney is white, and it is noted for its low fat, low cholesterol and quality proteins. I was inspired to write this narrative titled "Hare-Raising Story" because I introduced raising rabbits for food to Southern Tchad, Africa, for the first time. The rabbit breed in the photo below was unknown; however, we used the Heifer Project International Project as a model to persuade longevity to our rabbit project. We gave one family a bred female rabbit (doe). After it kindled* and the litter was weaned,* the family was obligated to give one doe from the litter to another family, which was now under the same obligation. After each family satisfied their obligation, they owned the does and remainder of their litter.

HARE-RAISING STORY

When we returned to our village, I began asking people if they would be interested in raising rabbits *(Oryctolagus cuniculus domesticus)* for food. Whoa! The interest level was high. So I wondered, *How am I going to build a hutch?** After some thought, I figured out how this could be achieved. (Photo by Jim Diamond of domestic rabbits in a mud brick hutch with a bamboo floor in Bessada, Tchad, Africa)

HARE-RAISING STORY

I did not see any local Tchadian villagers in Southern Tchad raising domestic rabbits for food. On a very rare occasion, they would catch wild rabbits and harvest them for food. But wild rabbits in Tchad were scant. In two years, I saw only one wild rabbit on the road while traveling in the middle of the night.

Newspaper reporter Ron Harley from the *Los Angeles Times* was writing a story on Peace Corps volunteer efforts to improve the quality of life in rural Tchad, featuring my late wife, Betty, and me. The story was published in several magazines, including *Pennsylvania Farmer*. A lady from Williamsport, Pennsylvania, read the article and was impressed by what we were doing for the Tchadian people. She wanted to help us and mailed me a check to use in an "agricultural project." I had the privilege of determining how to best use that money.

Once a month, Betty and I traveled on a rough road to a town called Sarh to get supplies and go to the bank. Two Peace Corps volunteer friends of ours lived near Sarh, and we had an open invitation to stay at their home. The husband had two riding horses, and on Sunday mornings when we were visiting, we got up before dawn, saddled the horses and rode for a couple hours before breakfast.

One day while riding back to the stable, I saw what looked like rabbit hutches* along the side of a Frenchman's house. Upon closer inspection, I saw several white rabbits in the hutches. I wondered if the people in my village would be interested in raising rabbits for food. That would be a unique way to use the money the lady from Williamsport sent to support an agricultural project. When Betty and I returned to our village, I asked people if they would be interested in raising rabbits for food. Whoa! Theor interest level was high. Next I wondered, *How am I going to build a hutch?*

After some thought I figured out how this could be achieved using indigenous materials and skills. We used traditional mud bricks to build the four-foot-by-seven-foot hutch. We placed the hutch on the West side of a tree so there would be shade during the heat of the day. We laid mud brick four layers high and placed bamboo poles across the brick foundation as the floor and left spaces for the rabbit droppings to fall through to the ground. Then we went up another five brick layers for the sides of the hutch. Across the top, we placed a few bamboo poles for support and laid a thick layer of grass thatch to keep rabbits from escaping and protect them from predators.*

We purchased three does (female rabbits) and one buck (male rabbits) from the Frenchman in Sarh, placed them in the hutch and fed them grass. They adapted to their new hutch quite nicely.

Later, we gave one doe to each of three farmers. I explained to the farmers they were to have their doe bred, and when it kindled* and after they were weaned,* he was to give one rabbit to a friend or relative with the same commitment. The remaining rabbits became the property of the three farmers. Unfortunately, rabbit meat (coney*) was very scarce, and these few rabbits were eaten by the participants. In other words, this rabbit project failed.

I would like to end this narrative by quoting English novelist Richard Adams, who wrote, "Rabbits need dignity and above all the will to accept their fate."

PRELUDE: Teaching American home economics in an African bush village where there is no running water, sink, stove, refrigerator, electricity, kitchen, or dishwasher was challenging, difficult and burdensome. Because there were no supermarkets, grain for making flour was pounded by women in a wooden hand-carved mortar and pestle. Vegetables were grown locally near the village. Fish were caught by fishermen in a nearby river. Bush meat was captured by village hunters. These were the conditions my late wife, Betty, had to contend with during her Peace Corps assignment. She had to identify what skills the women knew, which foods they preferred, how they cooked their food, what kinds of food were locally available, what was the cost of purchasing unprocessed food and how perishable food was stored. I was inspired to write this narrative titled "Home Economics in Tchad" because I was amazed at my late wife's creative home economics abilities teaching Tchadian women American skills that were applicable to village life and conditions, while making do with local resources.

Betty teaching a Tchadian girl how to hang clothes on a clothesline using clothes pins.

Betty teaching a Tchadian girl how to use an oven in a two-burner bottled gas stove.

HOME ECONOMICS IN TCHAD

(Photos by Jim Diamond of Betty Diamond teaching a young girl from Bessada, Tchad, in 1972)

HOME ECONOMICS IN TCHAD

Traditionally, food preparation has been one of humankind's earliest skills. The five domains of American home economics are cooking, child development, home management, budgeting and economics. In Tchad, these domains are bundled into one discipline: survival. Wives are responsible for preparing meals for the men and children and working in the fields in between meals. Men eat separately, and women eat with the children.

The homes have no electricity, running water, stoves, or refrigerators. Women cook their meals on open fires outside their huts. When meat is available, it has to be used the same day it was harvested because there was no refrigeration to keep the meat cool. When hunters brought in a large animal, such as an impala, warthog, or kudu, hunks of meat were distributed to their extended families and friends so the meat could be used within one day. The women cut the heart, lungs, kidneys and liver into small pieces and cooked them in an iron pot over an open fire. When the meat was cooked, they made gravy, which was served over cooked corn or millet meal.

My late wife, Betty, developed a unique program for the village girls ages fourteen to sixteen years of age. The Village Chief would select which girls would enroll in Betty's program. She taught one girl at a time for three five-day weeks. The girls had to be able to speak, read and write French, and they needed to be appropriately dressed.

Each day of the program, Betty would take the girl to the village market to purchase food. They would bring the food back to our house, and in our kitchen Betty would teach the girl how to prepare a different dish each day, using a French recipe from her French cookbook. Betty always gave the girl a sample of the food they prepared for the day to take to their hut to share with their family. Furthermore, she gave each girl 3x4 cards to write the fifteen recipes' ingredients and directions they prepared as a reference to cook on their own.

Other skills Betty taught the girls included how to hook a gas stove to bottled gas, measure ingredients, sweep a floor with a long-handled broom, make a bed, wash dishes, hang clothes with clothespins on a clothesline, put kerosene in a kerosene refrigerator, boil drinking water and set a table.

The girls who successfully completed Betty's home economics program were qualified to be employed as house girls for expatriates. When daughters learned housekeeping skills and became more employable, their fathers would charge a higher dowry* from their suitor.

I would like to end this narrative by quoting renowned chef Thomas Keller, "A recipe has no soul. You as the cook must bring the soul to the recipe."

PRELUDE: A fundamental basic tool for African kitchens is a mortar and pestle, the one instrument that could symbolize the African kitchen. One of the most common images of African life is a woman pounding grain in a wooden mortar and pestle. They are used to grind grain such as maize* (corn), millet, sorghum, teff,* wheat and rice into flour for the day. In rural villages, African women prepare food over open fires outside of their huts. Everywhere in Africa, the thumping sound of mortars and pestles is the sign that cooking has begun. African kitchens do not resemble modern kitchens found in the Western world. I was inspired to write this narrative titled "Mortar and Pestle for Pounding Grain" because I used to watch the women in our village pounding grain near their huts as a precursor to preparing meals.

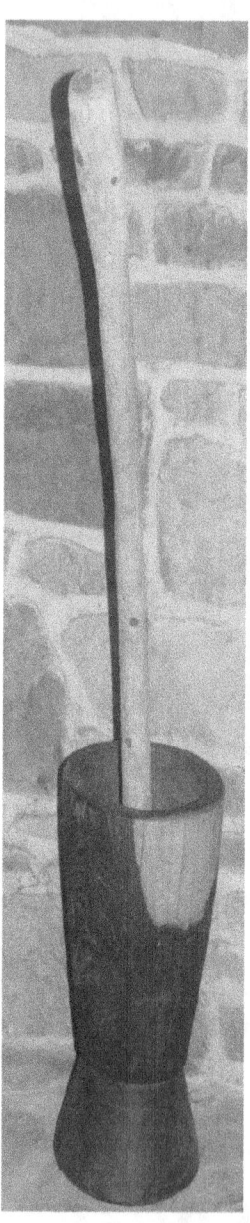

MORTAR AND PESTLE FOR POUNDING GRAIN

I acquired this hand-carved mahogany mortar and pestle at a refugee camp in Swaziland in 1988. It was created by a Mozambican refugee in Swaziland. (Photo by Jim Diamond)

MORTAR AND PESTLE FOR POUNDING GRAIN

The mortar and pestle is the typical kitchen tool for the whole African continent. In many African societies, the mortar and pestle is carved from the wood of a mango or mahogany tree. Unlike the sharp blade of a modern food processor, which bruises the ingredients, the pestle crushes them in a way to help release their fresh flavors and oils. Some purists in rural areas still refuse to take their whole grains to a mill to grind, even though it's faster and easier. They claim it just doesn't taste the same.

Mortars and pestles are made in various sizes, from the smallest used to blend pepper mixtures to the large ones used to prepare flour from grains or beans.

To take the drudgery away from pounding grain in a mortar and pestle, it's often used in cadence with songs, which vary, depending on the occasion: funeral, wedding, birth, or a lullaby to soothe a baby, who is securely on the back of the woman who is pounding.

Sometimes three women generate a rhythm and sing around the mortar while pounding grain into flour. While the first woman pounds the grain, the other two clap their hands, then the pestle is tossed to the second woman, and the first and third clap their hands. This process of singing and clapping goes on and on. The women seemed to really enjoy singing and clapping their hands while pounding grain into flour.

My late wife, Betty, who was a talented singer, once joined the women around the mortar, pounding the grain with the pestle. The Tchadian women enthusiastically enjoyed Betty joining in their circle to use the pestle and participating in their singing and clapping.

Many African societies consider the mortar and pestle sacred. For example, the sound of the mortar should never be heard at night unless there is a funeral, when the mortar is used to crush incense for the ultimate final bath of the deceased.

In some African tribes, the mortar represents the strength of the family. In the Bambara tradition of Mali, a newlywed bride has to sit four times in a row on a mortar. It was believed that the bride subjected to this rite would never divorce. In addition, a bride always brought a mortar and pestle among her belongings when moving in with her new husband.

Among the Soninke people of Southern Senegal, if a stranger enters a house and sees a mortar upside-down with the pestle sitting at its base, it means that there was a death in the family.

I would like to close this narrative with a quote from the World English Bible, "Though you grind a fool in a mortar with a pestle along with grain, yet his foolishness will not be removed from him." In other words, despite the grain being pulverized, its character and traits still exist.

PRELUDE: Founding Dean of the College of Arts and Humanities at McGill University Daniel Levitin argued in his book *The World in Six Songs* that all music can be grouped into six categories: friendship, joy, knowledge, love, ritual and comfort. Music is the art of producing a blend of pleasing, expressive sounds that has melody, rhythm and sometimes harmony that expresses ideas, emotions, thoughts, experiences, opinions, reactions, lessons and memories. Music in Tchad, Africa, was created by handmade wooden xylophones (*balaon´*), indigenous* violins *(coucoma)*, tom-toms, thumb pianos and six-stringed guitars *(N'gambaya)*. I was inspired to write this narrative titled "*N'gambaya* Guitar of Mondou" because on rare occasions in larger cities, we would patronize a restaurant where a man would come by our table and play his *N'gambaya* guitar for a tip. This instrument also was played at national events, weddings, births, funerals, and upon harvesting crops.

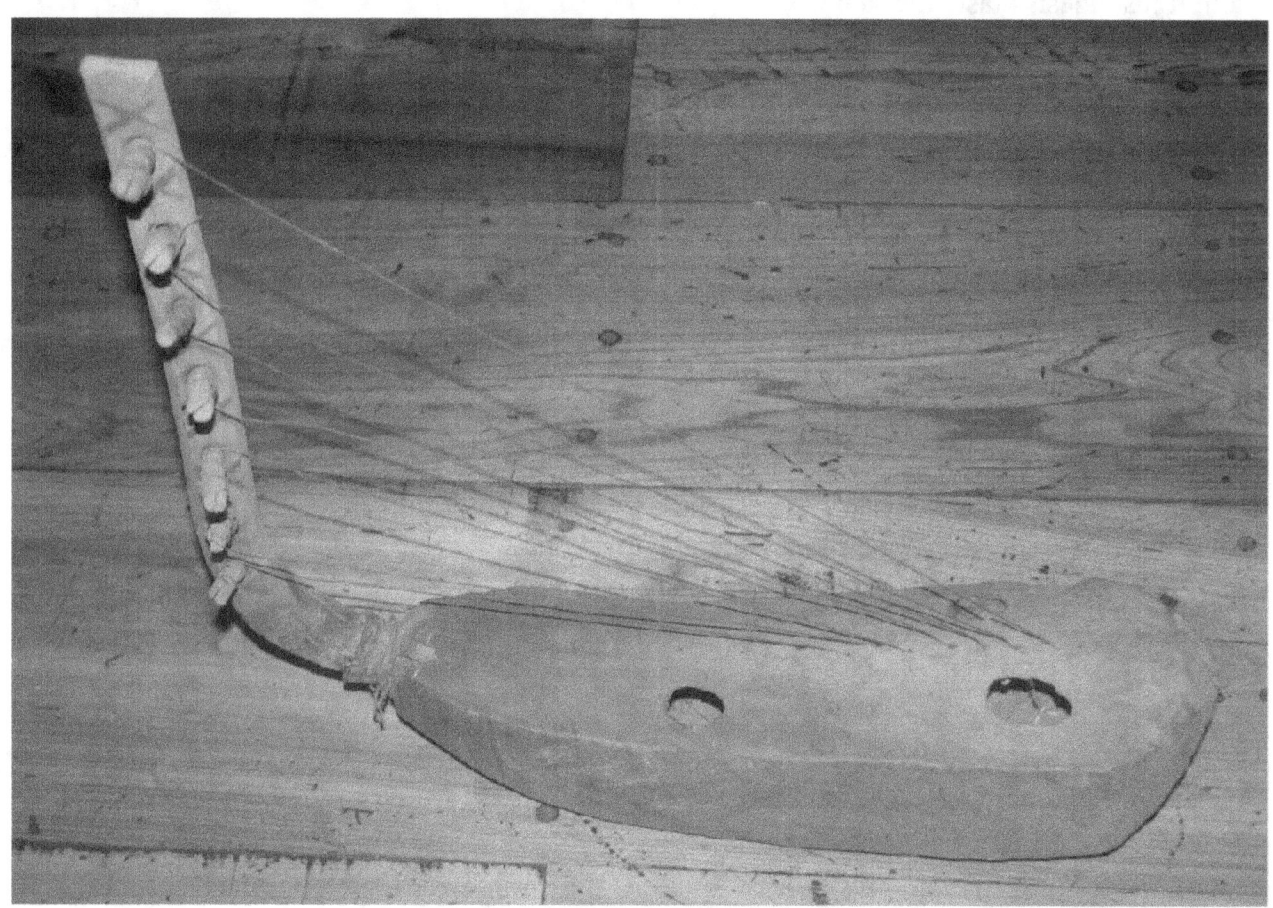

N'GAMBAYA GUITAR OF MONDOU

This guitar bears no resemblance to guitars used in the United States or other countries. Its six strings are spread with a slightly arched bridge over a resonating wood body covered with a thin, dried animal skin. (Photo by Jim Diamond of *N'gambaya* guitar in Tchad, Africa, in 1972)

N'GAMBAYA GUITAR OF MONDOU

Musical sounds are an important attribute to nearly all tribal and expatriate lifestyles featured in all regions throughout the Republic of Tchad. Musical sounds are created using indigenous,* handmade instruments, including six-stringed *N'gambaya* guitars.

Other sounds of music in Tchad are created by indigenous wooden xylophones (balaon^), a type of violin (*coucoma*), tom-toms and thumb pianos. Oftentimes in larger restaurants, a musician would come by the table dressed in traditional clothing and play his *N'gambaya* guitar for a tip. This instrument was played at national events, weddings, funerals, crop harvesting celebrations and births.

Characteristic interwoven sounds performed by Bilala shamans* from Central Tchad included repeated musical melodies created by a *N'gambaya* guitar. The *N'gambaya* guitar originated in the Logone District. This guitar bears no resemblance to guitars used in the United States or other countries. It has six lengths of fishing line attached to a slightly arched bridge over the resonating wooden frame that is encased with a thin, dried animal skin. It is tuned by turning six small pegs embedded into the upper outer edge of the bridge curvature to tighten the fishing line strings on the guitar.

Tchadian musicians present music and dance in all the regions in this landlocked central African nation. Their sounds are interwoven with a vernacular art form that expresses ideas, feelings and emotions in significant forms through rhythm, melody and harmony.

I would like to close this narrative with a quote from an unknown author, "Enthusiasm is everything. It must be taut and vibrating like a guitar string."

From my point of view, music can be a soft or loud sound that arouses emotions relevant to enjoyment, religion, politics, interest and inspiration that sometimes leads to involving speaking in tongues or free-form movements.

PRELUDE: The *Negwenya* Mine is located on the Bomvu Ridge, northwest of Mbabane, eSwatini (Swaziland). This mine is considered to be the world's oldest mine for hematite* ore (anhydrous iron oxide). Hematite ore was used in the Middle Stone Age to extract red ochre, which was mined by the ancestors of the San* people for rock paintings, which are common in eSwatini. *Negwenya* means "crocodile" in the Swazi language. This name comes from the fact that the mountain containing the hematite ore was crocodile-shaped before surface-mining defaced its ancestral shape in the 1960s. The site was known to early man for its deposits of red hematite ore, which was used in cosmetics and tribal rituals. Later, the deposit was mined for iron smelting and iron ore export. I was inspired to write this narrative titled "*Negwenya* Mine" because I have visited this site many times with guests. After each visit to the ancient mine, I always came away with a mystical feeling usually experienced by people with specialized interests in understanding ancient tribal rituals.

NEGWENYA MINE

During archeological digs in the late 1960s and early 1970s, several Stone Age artifacts were found in the *Negwenya* Mine. Radiocarbon dating revealed the age of the oldest mining activities as 41,000 to 43,000 years old. (Photo by Jim Diamond of Betty Diamond exiting the *Negwenya* Mine in 1988)

NEGWENYA MINE

A 2017 publication by R.W.P. Luk titled "A theory of scientific study" defines archeology as the "scientific study of human activity through the recovery and analysis of artifacts, architecture, ecofacts, sites and cultural landscapes." During archaeological digs in the late 1960s and early 1970s, several Stone Age artifacts were found in the *Negwenya* Mine. Radiocarbon dating revealed the age of the oldest mining activities as 41,000 to 43,000 years old. This would make *Negwenya* the world's oldest known mine.

The Swaziland Iron Ore Development Company once was owned by the Anglo-American Corporation and started surface-mining of the hematite* ore deposit in 1964. A Japanese company was the largest consumer of the hematite ore. The open-pit mining took place between 1964 and 1977 when the Goba Railway line was established connecting the mine with the Mozambique Railway System.

Iron can be extracted from two types of iron ores: magnetite and hematite. The primary distinction between magnetite and hematite is that magnetite* is ferromagnetic* (having a high susceptibility to magnetization), and hematite is paramagnetic* (having a lower susceptibility to magnetization, however it's the more important industrial iron ore in terms of the quantity, but has a slightly lower iron content than magnetite.). The hematite iron ore with the iron content of up to 60 percent was explored in the middle of the nineteenth century. An estimated 20,000,000 tons of iron ore were extracted from the mine. However, an estimated 32 million tons of ore yet remain in the soil. Reportedly the Anglo-American Corporation stopped surface-mining the hematite ore because the site was flooded.

In 2008, the Swazi government considered reopening the mine for surface-mining. The Swaziland National Trust Commission submitted the site to the UNESCO's list of World Heritage Sites to protect the ancient *Negwenya* Mine site, but unfortunately the site submission was not accepted by UNESCO.

From 2011 to 2014, an Indian company called Salgaocar formed the Salgaocar Swaziland Limited Company to operate a modern-day surface mine. Before allocating the mine to Salgaocar, King Mswati III dismissed the National Trust Commission's request to protect the area from new mining activities. He replaced the entire board of the commission to permanently stop demands to protect the *Negwenya* Mine site.

The surface-mining operations led to heavy pollution of the water sources that supplied the city of Mbabane, which is the capital of eSwatini. Cases of corruption were reported to get the mining license, including a $28 million donation to King Mswati by Salgaocar. The entire deal established a 25 percent ownership of the mine for the king, 25 percent for the government, and 50 percent to Salgaocar. Reports also claimed that Salgaocar was using Mozambican and South African trucks to avoid paying import taxes. After the Salgaocar-Swazi deals, the 2,500 jobs that were announced were never created. Salgaocar ceased its mining activities in *Negwenya* in 2014.

Funds for construction of a *Negwenya* Mine visitor center were donated by the Peoples Republic of China, and the center opened in 2005. Some ancient tools were displayed in the center. However, sadly, in September 2018, a fire completely destroyed the visitor center. The National Trust Commission declared that all the ancient artifacts in the center were lost in the fire.

PRELUDE: The name Sara identifies numerous tribes of people within the population located in Southern Tchad (aka Chad) sometime during the sixteenth century. The Sara people were principally Christians and Animists with some Muslims, according to Josette Rivallain, author of *"SARA : Echanges et Instruments Monetaires,"* There is little historical evidence written describing the evolution of the Sara people. However, it was learned there were slight differences between lifestyle traits and languages within various Sara tribes. I was inspired to write this narrative titled "Sakania" because I was intrigued about the historical significance of primitive Tchadian money and had many questions that needed answers, such as who made the money, who used the money, what kind of metal was used, where did they get the metal, how did they choose the shape of the coins, and what was the role of the money?

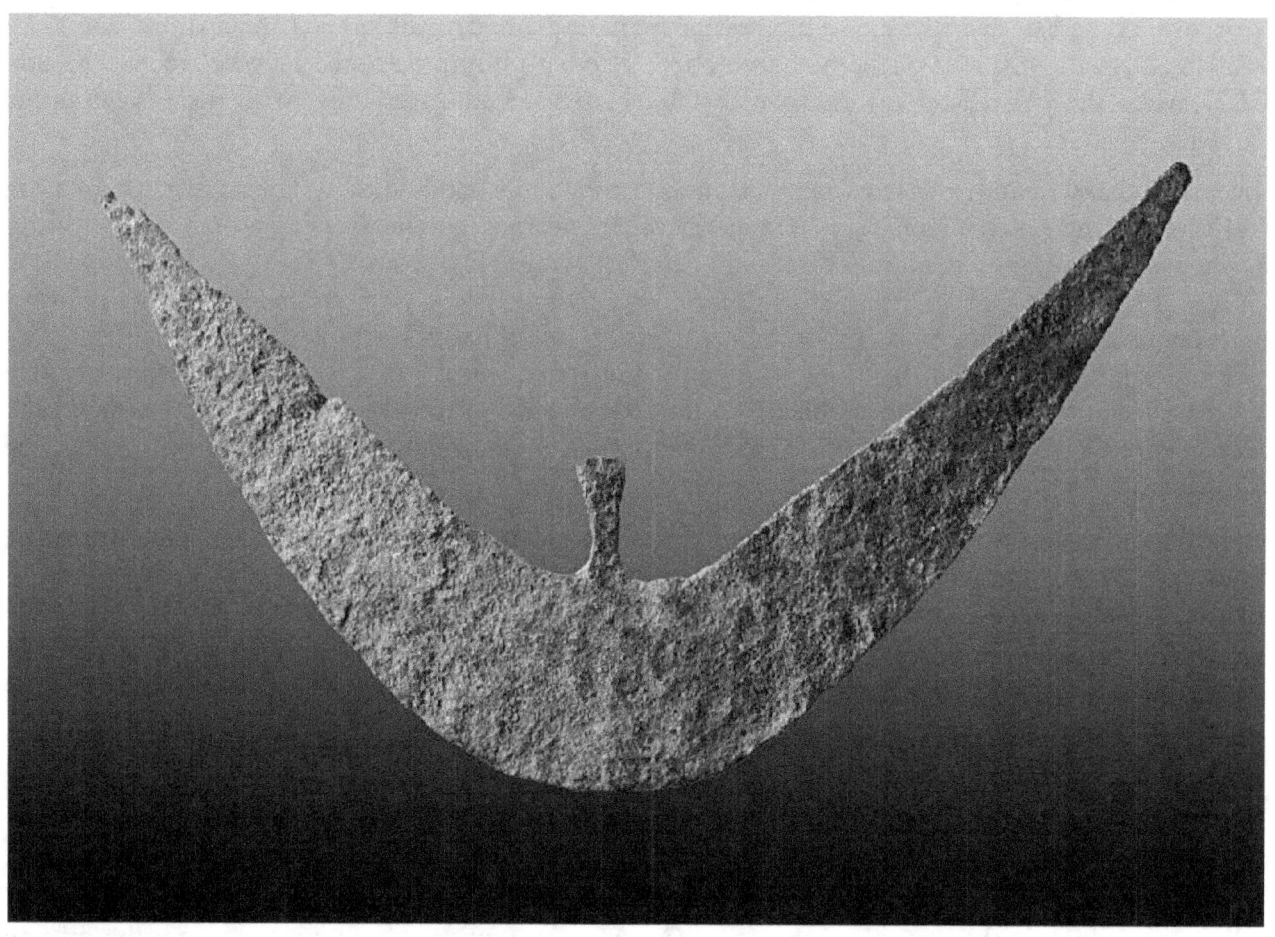

SAKANIA

Voila! Thirty-four years later, I found what I was looking for in an eighteen-page article titled *"SARA: Echanges et Instruments Monetaires"* written in French. Fortunately, I speak French and could understand most of the article. (Photo was from a professional paper titled *SARA: Echanges et Instruments Monetaires* written by Josette Rivallain in 1985.)

SAKANIA

In 1972, during the time my late wife, Betty, and I were Peace Corps volunteers in Bessada, Tchad, Africa, we invited two visiting volunteers to our village residence for a chicken dinner with a cold Gala beer. The volunteers gave us three sakanias (primitive/ancient Tchadian money), which had been found in an archeological dig between the town of Sara (aka Fort Archambault) and east toward the Sudan border.

The two volunteers were part of a Peace Corps well drilling team that was digging wells and installing hand pumps for local people to draw water for daily use. Shortly after archeologists discovered a trove of sakanias (ancient Tchadian coins), our volunteers were talking with the archeologists about their find. The archeologists gave some sakanias to the volunteers, who in turn shared three sakanias with us.

In June 1973, when Betty and I returned to our farm in Bucks County, Pennsylvania, we unpacked all of the Tchad artifacts we collected to display in our home as mementos. All I knew about the sakanias was that they were a form of ancient money.

After Betty and I began reestablishing a routine American lifestyle, I began to search for information about the ancient coins because I had several questions that needed answers. I searched many libraries, books and professional papers, and I watched interviews and found nothing about the sakania. I began to have doubt if they were an authentic form of money and if the coin's name was authentic.

Voila! Thirty-four years later, I found what I was looking for in an eighteen-page article titled *"SARA: Echanges et Instruments Monetaires"* written in French by Josette Rivallain. Fortunately, I speak French and could understand most of the article.

I personally observed that in many areas of southern Tchad and Sudan there were steep mountains containing rich lodes* of iron ore. Because of the masses of iron ore readily available, metal played an important role in lifestyles of Sara villagers. Within the various Sara tribes, there was usually a blacksmith who made hoes, knives and spears and created coins because he had the knowledge and skills to work with iron. In the central and west of the region of Sara tribes (Ngambay, Laka), there were a number of different-shaped coins. However, many Sara people adopted the shape of a hoe (see photograph) for their medium of exchange. Other metal shapes were still used and accepted among the Sara tribes.

I learned the sakania has an ancient history in Sara societies throughout all of southern Tchad. Money started as a solution to problems with bartering between people who had to trade. Money was ultimately created by governments to settle debts. Metal sakanias were used for transactions for merchandise, religious gifts, dowry* for brides, funeral traditions and many other responsibilities as dictated by Sara societal mores. Before coins, taxes were paid with iron knives of various shapes and sizes. Two knives were worth 50 centimes. Once storage facilities were bursting with 10,000 francs' worth of knives, it caused a strong desire to introduce coinage.

I would like to close this narrative with a saying that goes like this, "Just like old librarians, old coins are often more valuable than they appear at face value." I am not yet sure of the value of these three ancient coins, but I truly cherish the thought of placing them in an appropriate museum.

PRELUDE: Slash-and-burn agriculture is a farming method by tribal communities in Tchad, Africa, and other African nations for subsistence farming. Slash-and-burn involves cutting and burning woody plants in a woodland to create a field called a swidden.* Traditionally, the village chief designated an area of dense vegetation by dividing it into cords* (1.23 acres). Every farmer had to plant four cords of cotton and one cord for each wife. Farmers would begin cutting down the trees and woody plants in a designated area. In Tchad, the village chiefs would allow farmers to use fire to remove the immature trees, branches and foliage. The ashes provided nutrients to the soil for planting food crops. Fire was also used to control insects and disease for certain crops. I was inspired to write this narrative because slash-and-burn agriculture was the accepted method of farming in Tchad when I arrived. At first, I was appalled at the use of fire to clear land because it destroys the organic matter that improves soil texture. However, I soon learned from farmers the benefits of slash-and-burn agriculture, and I changed my thinking because some advantages of it outweigh some disadvantages.

SLASH-AND-BURN AGRICULTURE

In Tchad, village chiefs allowed farmers to use fire to remove immature trees, branches and foliage because the ashes sweeten the soil for planting food crops. Note the white ash on the ground and the cleared land that is starting to be visible (Photographer unknown)

SLASH-AND-BURN AGRICULTURE

As an agricultural educator for ten years in Pennsylvania before joining the Peace Corps, my mind was programmed to prevailing crop and livestock production practices in Pennsylvania and other regions in the United States. At the onset of my agricultural endeavors in southern Tchad, the concept of slash-and-burn agriculture contrasted with my learned agricultural knowledge base and approved practices.

When I entered a new village, my *modus operandi* was to keep my thinking and knowledge to myself. I listened, observed, and spoke only to ask questions. I learned a lot about slash-and-burn agriculture that caused me to be less judgmental and study the rationale behind this ancient farming method.

Slash-and-burn agriculture is a process of clearing the vegetation growing on land that was uncultivated for four to six years. When land is unplowed, unharrowed,* and unplanted for a period of time, it enables the soil to naturally re-establish its fertility. This is part of an indigenous* crop rotation strategy to increase production because fertilizer was not available.

The Tchad government required all farmers in southern Tchad to grow cotton because cotton was Tchad's only export. The crop rotation usually followed this schedule: year 1, cotton; year 2, cotton; year 3, sorghum; years 4 and 5, either sorghum or vegetables. After year five, the land was uncultivated to fallow* for the next five to six years. That ancient indigenous crop rotation system differed from what we do in Pennsylvania, but it was functional. They did not need an agronomist* with a PhD to teach them approved management practices.

The Tchad slash-and-burn agriculture system had advantages that addressed necessary survival circumstances for growing food. It enabled people to grow crops on soil with low soil nutrient content and to control pests. The ash from burned wood and grass improved soil nutrition. They also could grow food crops near the village, control some plant diseases, grow crops in places having dense vegetation, and provide communities with a source of food and income from food sales. Furthermore, allowing the land to fallow improved the organic matter in the soil and soil texture.

On the other hand, expatriate critics of slash-and-burn agriculture claim that slash-and-burn agriculture caused deforestation, soil erosion, nutrient loss and biodiversity loss. When this type of agriculture was practiced, it increased carbon dioxide levels. Their points were well taken; however, those issues come about because of irresponsible practices of slash-and-burn agriculture by large numbers of people.

Knowledge of the ecosystem* of the area and people's agricultural competence could provide ways to practice slash-and-burn agriculture in a restorative, sustainable way. That became my job: to teach farmers restorative, sustainable slash-and-burn agriculture.

Archbishop Desmond Tutu best summarized my endeavors in Tchad by saying, "Do your little bit of good where you are; it's those bits of good put together that overwhelm the world."

PRELUDE: In back of our house in Bessada, Tchad, Africa, was an elementary school that was attended by approximately eighty students. The building was unornamented. There were no posters, chalkboards, books, models, magazines, or other items commonly found in an American classroom. The grounds around the school were barren. The playground surrounding the school had no soccer nets, swings, seesaws, climbing bars, or other typical equipment found on playgrounds. One day, Betty and I watched children outside during recess chasing each other playing tag. We decided those kids needed a swing set and seesaws for outdoor activity during recess and before and after school. We began to develop a plan to make that happen. Seeing the children's excitement and happiness on their faces as they took turns using their new swings and seesaws inspired me to write this narrative titled "Swings and Seesaws."

SWINGS

Betty Diamond and two teachers are showing students how to use their new swings. Note the anxiety of all the students awaiting their turn to use the swing

AND

SEESAWS

Betty and I teaching elementary students how to use their new seesaw. Note how these students preferred to sit on the seesaw back-to-back opposed to face-to-face.

(Photos by Ruth Seymour)

SWINGS AND SEESAWS

As a former high school agricultural teacher, I know well that students need an occasional break from their studies, especially elementary school children. Recess breaks are excellent times for students to learn developmental skills that they don't learn in the classroom. For example, an outdoor swing and seesaw can teach motor skills and coordination, provide stress relief, improve social development and sensory skills, increase their attention span, teaching sharing and improve their moods.

After my late wife, Betty, and I estimated the cost for materials, we sent a letter to the Doylestown, Pennsylvania, United Methodist Church where we were members, describing our plan to build a swing set and seesaw at an elementary school in our village in Tchad. We requested $300 from the missions committee to support this project. The church agreed to provide us with the money, and we launched a process to build a set of swings and seesaws. We met with the village chief to explain what we had planned for the Bessada Elementary School, and how we had gotten the money from our church for the project. The chief agreed to let us build it.

The Peace Corps had a well-drilling team, which had a rather large inventory of four-inch steel pipe. We negotiated a price for eleven steel pipes and agreed to purchase them if they would loan me their pipe cutter and threader and deliver the pipe to Bessada in their truck. The Peace Corps volunteers agreed, and that is how we got the materials to the Village of Bessada.

When the pipe arrived, we cut and threaded it so the well-drilling volunteers could return to their village with the pipe cutter and threader. With the assistance of four Tchadian teachers, we assembled the pipe by attaching elbows and forming the shape of both the swings and seesaws. We dug six holes one meter* deep, mixed concrete with water, set the pipe forms into the holes, filled the holes with cement, and allowed the cement to harden. Three days later, we attached the chains to the top cross bar, cutting a board into lengths for two swing seats. With bolts, we attached the chains to the seats, and *voila,* we had a new swing set for the school.

The students did not have a clue how to use a swing, so I asked Betty to sit on the swing seat so I could push her. I said, "Betty, I want you to look like you are really enjoying the swing."

Then we put two students on the swings, and thereinafter, those swings never stopped moving. We did an *encore* with the seesaws, but we noticed the kids preferred not to face each other, but instead they sat on the seesaw back-to-back. Like the swings, those seesaws didn't stop moving after the children learned how to use them.

Thanks to Doylestown United Methodist Church Mission Committee for enabling this mission to be accomplished! Betty and I wished our fellow DUMC members could have seen the horde of happy faces they created by providing a mere $300 to Bessada Elementary School.

PRELUDE: Tchad is a landlocked country in north-central Africa bordered to the south by Central African Republic, to the southwest by Cameroon, to the west by Nigeria and Niger, to the north by Libya, and to the east by Sudan. Tchad has several climatic regions: a desert zone in the north, an arid Saharan belt in the center that includes Lake Tchad, and a more fertile Saharan savanna* zone in the south, which was where my late wife, Betty, and I lived. Throughout Tchad's climatic regions, large gourds called calabashes were common and could be easily acquired and harvested for food. Its hard outer shell was often cut in half to make bowls that are used for various domestic tasks. I was inspired to write this narrative because my late wife purchased several beautifully decorated gourds from Tchad women who lived in our village of Bessada to bring home as gifts for our family and friends.

TCHADIAN CALABASH

The designs on the hard shells of the dried gourds were usually geometric, but they could also include replications of people or animals originating from oral history told by old men. (Photo by Jim Diamond of a Tchadian calabash in Bessada, Tchad, Africa, in 1972)

66

TCHADIAN CALABASH

In the country of Tchad, gourds are left to grow on vines until maturity, then left to dry. Depending upon domestic needs, sizes of gourds, abundance of gourd supply, time and retail market demands, decisions were made how best to use the gourds.

Based upon my observations, domestic and market demands were the greatest influence on how the annual supply of gourds was used. Women made the decisions on the gourds with older women noted for decorating gourds

A type of gourd is a calabash. These gourds are often cut in half, dried, and hollowed out to make bowls. Tchadian calabash bowls were used for many practical purposes, such as serving or storing food or beverages, selling at local markets, holding cosmetics, and storing money by market women.

In addition to being used as containers, calabashes were frequently made into musical instruments, such as the violin for resonance. Small, dried, uncut gourds with their seeds still inside are used as rattles for young children.

Tchadian women amplified the beauty of their calabashes by decorating gourd surfaces with designs. The designs on the hard shells of the dried gourd were usually geometric, but they could also include replications of people or animals originating from oral history or village stories told by old men.

I used to watch women huddled together under a shade tree around a small fire with hot coals. With handmade knives, they would scratch the hard surface of the gourd with the design they desired. Using a small metal tool resembling a screwdriver, they put them into hot coals until they were red hot. The women would take a tool from the coals, then trace their design with the tool burning their blackened image onto the gourds' hard surfaces. When one tool cooled, another hot tool was taken from the hot coals and the burning of the design continued. This process ended when the design was completed. Attractive Tchadian calabash patterns sometimes found in other villages were often used as prototypes.

I would like to close this narrative with a Tchadian proverb, "If the owner of a calabash calls it a worthless calabash, others will join him to use it to pack rubbish." The artist does not appreciate the usefulness of such a beautiful calabash until others see how beneficial it can be to society.

PRELUDE: Embroidery is a talent using a needle to sew thread or yarn to decorate cloth items, such as pillowcases, towels, napkins and tablecloths. Embroidery can also be used to attach pearls, beads, quills and sequins to the design. Learning the skill of embroidery is not difficult. All one needs is a needle, thread or yarn, scissors, needle threader and cloth. Five basic stitches are the cross stitch, whip stitch, running stitch, ladder stitch and back stitch. I was inspired to write this narrative titled "Teaching Women How to Embroider" because my mother and grandmother used to embroider household items as a hobby, and my late wife, Betty, taught many Tchadian women how to embroider. The Tchadian women really enjoyed learning the skill of embroidery.

TEACHING WOMEN HOW TO EMBROIDER

Betty teaching a lady how to hold and use a pencil for the first time to draw a Pennsylvania Dutch design on a piece of white cloth.

Betty teaching women how to embroider a design traced on a piece of white cloth.

(Photos by Jim Diamond in a small village near Bessada in June 1972)

68

TEACHING WOMEN HOW TO EMBROIDER

Teaching embroidery is not difficult, and it does not require a huge investment of money. My late wife, Betty, thought teaching the women the skill of embroidery would be a practical form of recreation for the women who worked so hard caring for their families and working in the fields. A woman only needed a pattern and some supplies. However, there were many obstacles to the women learning how to embroider. Betty found it was impossible to purchase needles in bush village markets. Women who had never heard of embroidery did not know how to hold and use a pencil to draw designs, and they did not have sufficient money to purchase colored thread.

Betty came up with a plan to teach women how to embroider. She presented it to the village chief, who had never heard of embroidery. Because the chief trusted Betty, he reluctantly endorsed her plan.

Betty wrote letters to her mother and mine, asking them to send packets of needles. She was able to purchase the cheapest material (white) and colored thread in village markets.

Then Betty invited the village women to come to our home to learn how to sew. Wow! What a turnout! We expected about ten women, but thirty-two women showed up for a sewing lesson. She intended to teach the women in a room in our house, but all of those women wouldn't fit. So she moved her class outside and taught the women sitting on the ground under a huge mango tree in front of our house.

Betty showed the women one of her embroidered tablecloths. Then she gave each lady one-half meter of white material, one meter of thread and one needle. That is when Betty learned that most of the women did not know how to hold or use a pencil to draw a design on the material. Betty showed them how to hold a pencil to draw a Pennsylvania Dutch design on their white material. (Someday an archeologist is going to find one of those pieces of cloth and wonder, How did Pennsylvania Dutch designs found their way into bush villages in Tchad, Africa?)

She then taught the women how to thread their needles. Her first sewing lesson was how to do a cross stitch. Betty met with the women once a week for two-hour sessions. The women really enjoyed their sewing sessions. They were quite proud of their first completed embroidered designs. The missionaries could not figure out how Betty got them to use white cloth because that was the cloth they used to wrap the deceased before burial. The next batch of material Betty purchased featured solid colors.

Betty's embroidery program became very popular with women in surrounding villages, so she expanded her program to four close-by villages. More than 100 women participated in her embroidery classes. Betty felt her mission was accomplished when the women started to embroider material at their huts.

Former United States President Harry Truman once said, "It is amazing what you can accomplish if you do not care who gets the credit." Betty's credit was the righteous feeling she had as she watched the progress of Tchadian women's embroidery skills unfold under her leadership.

PRELUDE: 2 Corinthians 9:15 states, "Thanks be to God for His inexpressible gift!" Life is a gift from God. Our family, friends, neighbors, and even strangers are all gifts to be savored. Although some days might be full of hardship and sadness, each breath, heartbeat and thought illustrates the beautiful gift of life. A Tchadian farmer who was my friend was certainly a gift from God. Unfortunately, he died as a young man who had been well-loved by his family and friends,. The president's brother Papa John and I arrived in a village called Sebe at 6:50 a.m. and found my friend surrounded by his family as he was dying. I was inspired to write this poem titled "The Gift of Life" because during that sad experience there was nothing I could do to save his precious life. Even in the darkest moments, if we try to see the light, there is promise in this as well.

THE GIFT OF LIFE

An older woman began to wail, and two younger women put their arms around her and slowly walked her next to her dying son where she kneeled down until he died. (Photographer unknown)

THE GIFT OF LIFE

On 15 October 1971, my work was more or less routine because the silage-making program was completed until the end of January 1972. Two young men who worked for me and the president's brother departed our village Bessada for Sebe, a village 11 miles away to check his pit silo. When we arrived in Sebe at 6:50 a.m., we saw around fifty people clustered around a hut.

A young man came running to the road and flagged me down. "A man is sick," he said. My companions and I got out of the car and walked over to the group of people. That's when we saw a 22-year-old dying man lying on the ground. I knew the fellow quite well because he was one of the cooperating farmers who made a pit silo and chopped silage.

I had never felt so helpless. All we could do was stand there and watch him die.

We learned that at 5:30 that morning he drank some homemade beer called *bili-bili*. He didn't know that the day before the bottle had contained an extremely poisonous, concentrated insecticide used to spray on his cotton, and it had not been washed. It didn't take much of the insecticide to be lethal.

Before we had arrived, the young man had gone to his pit silo, felt sick, so he walked a mile back to his village. By the time we arrived he was almost dead. He was soaking wet from sweating, had a lot of fluid in his lungs, and went into convulsions with two men holding his arms.

Two young men pleaded with me to take him to the hospital at Koumra. I was in an awkward situation. I wanted to help, but my better sense told me not to get involved. I knew the young man was almost dead, and I would not have enough time to drive twenty miles to Koumra on the very rough, dirt road. It was no less than a 90-minute ride.

Plus, according to Tchad tribal law, if you take someone from their village to a doctor and the patient dies on the way, the person driving the car is held responsible for his death. Fortunately, the president's brother was with me, and he knew there would not be enough time to make it to the hospital before the young man died, so he replied no to the fellows.

The young man's mother began to wail, and two younger women put their arms around her, locked hands, and slowly walked her next to her dying son, where she kneeled down until he died.

In Tchad, a dead person was wrapped in a white cloth and people sat around the body all day and all night until the next morning, when the body was buried. If the family was Christian, they would sit and sing hymns. If they were non-Christian, they would wail and beat tom-toms. After the burial, friends and family have a three-to-four-day mourning process.

I would like to close this narrative by quoting Casey Golomski, who wrote in his book *Funeral Culture: Cultural Change in an African Kingdom,* "Life is a precious gift to humankind whose value can never be quantified."

PRELUDE: A thumb piano is a popular musical instrument in many African countries. They are properly known as lamellophones. The literature indicates that thumb pianos originated about 3,000 years ago in what is now called Cameroon. The instruments spread into different countries through human migration. Lamellophones are a family of musical instruments consisting of a set of stiff but varying lengths of bamboo, cane, bicycle spokes, narrow strips of metal, or other appropriate material attached at one end of a box or calabash resonator. I was inspired to write this narrative because my late wife, Betty, and I often heard these instruments being played in our village and other Tchadian villages. Because of Betty's interest in playing the piano in church back home in Pennsylvania, she wanted a thumb piano and urged me find someone who would sell their thumb piano to me.

THUMB PIANO

This thumb piano includes a small, enclosed, hollow wooden box with an overhanging sound board under the tines. Its posterior bridge was made from a whittled round piece of wood, and the anterior bridge is a top of an old bicycle rear carrier with two metal sides. (Photo by Jim Diamond of his thumb piano from Bessada, Tchad, in June 1972)

THUMB PIANO

In the village of Bessada, I observed two men who played thumb pianos. The sound of a thumb piano is generated by holding the soundboard in the hands using the thumb or fingers to pluck flexible thin tines of metal or bicycle spokes staggered and attached firmly to a calabash or small wooden box as the resonator.

The thumb piano blends together the musical sounds of several tines set on anterior and posterior bridges, held by a pressure bar attached to a wooden soundboard.* The board is usually held in both hands so that the tines could be depressed with the thumbs. Each tine's thickness and length determine the pitch of the note it produces.

African thumb pianos are used by storytellers to set the pace of their narration, emphasize dramatic moments, and add to the pleasures of listening. They are also used for weddings, funerals, national holidays, and for personal joy.

The thumb piano in the photo includes a small, enclosed, hollow wooden box with an overhanging sound board under the tines. Its posterior bridge is made from a whittled round piece of wood, and the anterior bridge is a top of an old bicycle rear fender carrier with two metal sides. The eleven tines are made from used bicycle spokes, each of a different length with metal shoestring eyelets from an old shoe on each tine. The tines are attached to both the anterior and posterior bridges.

At President Tombalbaye's request, we had a fifteen-acre demonstration cotton field with eleven local villagers working for me hoeing weeds in the cotton. One worker had a thumb piano, and he brought it to the field for several days. While his fellow workers were hoeing under the hot sun, the thumb piano musician would sit under a tree in the shade and play tunes. The other workers became rather annoyed with him as he sat in the shade and played his thumb piano while they endured their assigned chores. I wondered, How am I going to diplomatically get him back to work?

The next day as the man was sitting in the shade playing his thumb piano, I walked over to him and listened to his playing for a few moments. I complimented him on his musical talents, then I asked if he would sell me his musical instrument.

He perked up and asked, "Do you want to buy this thumb piano?"

I responded, "Yes, if we can agree on a price!" After a brief bartering session, we agreed on a price. I purchased his thumb piano and put it in my car. The man was happy, and I got him back to work hoeing cotton.

This event accomplished three things: First, I was happy to get the man back to work with a diplomatic tactic. Second, his fellow workers were happy that he resumed the drudgery of hoeing cotton. Third, Betty now had a thumb piano (displayed in this photograph) to show her friends back home. Now I ask, Is that being a diplomat or not?

PRELUDE: After my late wife, Betty, and I got settled into our house in the village of Bessada, Tchad, as Peace Corps volunteers and got to know the people and identify some of their needs, I noticed several Arabian horses in the village. They were used primarily for riding. From a distance, I noticed the horses were not walking properly. Upon closer inspection, I discovered their feet had never been trimmed and were nearly two feet in length. (That is a fact!) The horses had much difficulty walking and were thin because they could not graze properly. One day at the edge of the village market, I saw a man with a machete hacking off chunks of hoof on his horse. I cringed and thought, *Oh my God! That is not the way to trim a hoof.* I identified this as an important need because the people knew the feet on their steeds needed trimming, but they did not know how to do it. I was inspired to write this narrative titled "Trimming Feet on Horses" because there was an enormous need to teach some people how to trim the feet on thirty-one horses in the village. That was my first project as a Peace Corps volunteer.

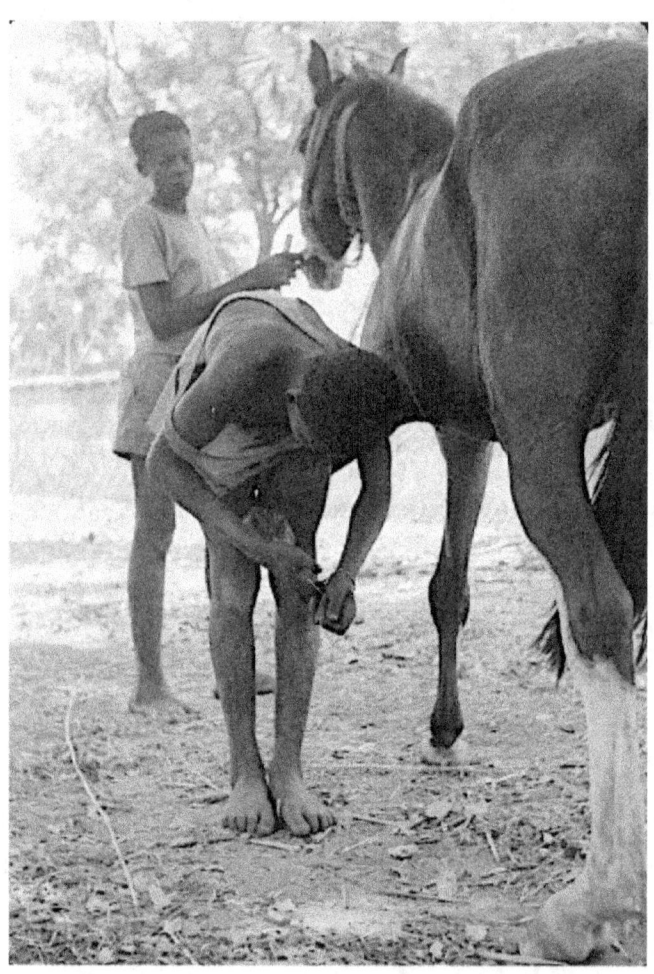

TRIMMING FEET ON HORSES

I met with the village chief to inform him that I was willing to teach two men how to trim feet on horses. I indicated that when the two men become competent in trimming feet on horses, I would give each of them a set of tools so they could develop a small business. (Photo by Jim Diamond of Tchadian man learning how to trim feet on a horse in 1971)

TRIMMING FEET ON HORSES

I was elated when two young men who rode a horse with untrimmed feet came forward and asked me if I could teach them how to trim feet. Whoa, what a coincidence! During the autumn months back in Pennsylvania, before my late wife, Betty, and I joined the Peace Corps, I had completed a course at our local vocational-technical school on horseshoeing taught by a farrier.* I became quite competent at trimming feet on horses.

However, I had no farrier tools to work with in Tchad. Once a month, Betty and I drove sixty miles on a rough dirt road to a city called Sarh to get supplies and gasoline. I went to a store that sold all kinds of stuff, and as I was browsing around, I found a wooden rasp which I could use to file horses' hooves. I continued my search in that store and found a pair of nippers.* I didn't have a clue what they were designed for, but I thought they might work on trimming hooves. I also found a wooden chisel and screwdriver that could be used to clean and trim the bottom of the hooves. I purchased three sets of wooden rasps, screwdrivers and nippers—one set for me and one set for each of the two men I was going to teach.

I met with the village chief to inform him that I was willing to teach two men how to trim feet on horses. I indicated that when the two men become competent in trimming feet on horses, they could charge a reasonable fee for their services. The chief was very pleased that I was willing to teach the men. Now that I had the tools and the chief's blessing, it was time to get a horse and start teaching these two young men how to trim feet on a horse. We asked the village chief to have his village crier announce that anyone who wanted the hooves trimmed on their horse could bring them to the front of my house under the mango tree. Holy mackerel! A whole herd of horses arrived. We had to schedule three horses per day until they all were done.

Seeing the condition of those hooves, I decided that I would do the first trim myself to get the hooves sized and shaped. The hooves were so long that I would trim until I hit blood capillaries, then quit. After that, I asked the horse's owner to regularly walk his horse on a hard surface for a couple weeks to cause the capillaries to recede. Then I asked him to bring the horse back so I could trim some more. It took four to five sessions with each horse to get their hooves shaped and to normal length.

I had asked my two adult students to watch how I trimmed those abnormally long hooves. First, I taught them the parts of the hoof, especially the white ring around the bottom. I showed them how to clean the hoof with a screwdriver, then how to use the wooden chisel and rasp, followed by using the nippers to trim the hooves to the white ring.

When the two men sized and shaped the hooves and some normalcy was achieved, I informed them they were competent in their newly learned farrier skills. At the end of their training, in front of the village chief, I gave them each a set of tools, congratulated them for their excellent accomplishments, and informed them they could now charge a reasonable fee for their services. Success is not an activity, but a process.

PRELUDE: African trypanosomiasis, also known as "sleeping sickness," is caused by microscopic parasites of the species *Trypanosoma brucei,* which infects the blood of oxen. Symptoms include fever, weakness, and sluggishness, which lead to weight loss and anemia. It was transmitted to oxen by the tsetse fly (*Glossina* species), which is found only in sub-Saharan Africa. This pesky tsetse fly is found everywhere in southern Tchad. Sleeping sickness is curable with medication but fatal if left untreated. To prevent oxen from being infected, my French veterinarian friend and colleague Dr. Marc Dronne and I vaccinatated most of the oxen in all the villages in our canton* with a prophylactic vaccine called homidiuim chloride from France. I was inspired to write this narrative titled "Vaccinating Oxen" because most village oxen were prone to be infected with African trypanosomiasis. Because a team of oxen is a major investment for a Tchadian farmer, we were able to prevent many costly, unnecessary oxen fatalities.

VACCINATING OXEN

The length of the oxen chute was about forty feet long. At the end of each row of poles, we planted a log with a fork on it to lie a log across the opening to prevent the oxen from escaping. (Photo by Betty Diamond of Jim Diamond second from right vaccinating oxen in April 1972)

VACCINATING OXEN

Restraining an ox to vaccinate it for African trypanosomiasis was a dangerous task. Most bulls were not castrated, and so they were strong with nasty temperaments. It sometimes took three men to restrain an ox to vaccinate. With the large number of oxen in all the villages to vaccinate, there was a significant risk of someone getting injured.

I knew there had to be an easier way to safely restrain an ox. There were no private, public, or portable cattle restraining chutes in all of southern Tchad like those on beef cattle farms in Pennsylvania. I had to rely upon my creativity to resolve this need.

One morning while my late wife, Betty, and I were eating breakfast, we talked about the dangers of restraining mature bulls to vaccinate. Suddenly, an idea unfolded! After talking it out with Betty, I became convinced it just had to work, and I was willing to try out the idea. I went to the village chief and explained my idea, and he agreed we needed a safer way to restrain bulls. I called a meeting with all the farmers in the village who owned oxen to be vaccinated. I explained the idea concept, what we needed, and about how long it would take to construct. I involved the farmers in making the decision so that my idea became their idea. They all seemed to endorse the idea and were quite cooperative.

After we all agreed to build an oxen chute, the farmers decided to build it at the village edge. Each farmer was asked to go into the bush and bring back two or three medium-size logs at least nine feet (three meters) long. We would plant a straight row by placing the logs upright into the ground three feet deep with the tops gently slanting outward, being approximately six to eight inches apart. A second row was made the same with the chute's bottom being three feet wide and the top four feet wide. The length of the chute was about forty feet long. On the end of each row of poles, we planted a log with a fork in it to lie another log across the opening to prevent the oxen from escaping.

A date was established when the vaccine would arrive, and the farmers would bring their oxen to their improvised oxen chute. Each ox was restrained to a post, and they were tightly packed in the chute. Now all I had to do was reach through the posts and vaccinate each ox on the rump. When all the oxen were vaccinated, they were removed and the next batch entered the chute.

It has been said that necessity is the mother of invention. Our improvised oxen chute functioned beautifully. The ox chute was not fancy to look at, but it worked. It was certainly a much safer way to restrain bulls to be vaccinated, and the farmers were very pleased. Furthermore, the chute became a permanent village fixture for future use. There was no cash outlay. We used indigenous* resources (logs), implemented indigenous skills (digging holes and planting logs), and introduced a modern concept (oxen chute). Thomas Edison once said, "Our greatest weakness is giving up. The most certain way to succeed is to try just one more time."

PRELUDE: Agriculture has always been one of Africa's core industries. For centuries and still today, cotton was Tchad's only exported commodity. The government mandated every farmer to grow two hectares* (4.94 acres) of cotton for themselves and one hectare for each of their wives. Weeding cotton was a dreaded, time-consuming task that included all members of the household. This was a never-ending job because weeds were virtually unmanageable. Farmers weeded their cotton by pulling weeds by hand and using short-handled hoes. One day, I asked my laborers why they did not use long-handled hoes. They told me that short-handled hoes were easier to use. I did not buy that response and decided to do something about it. I was inspired to write this narrative titled "Using a Long-Handled Hoe" because I noticed the workers holding their aching backs when they stood up after using short-handled hoes.

USING A LONG-HANDLED HOE?

At noontime when I returned to the cotton field, the workers were waiting for me. I asked them, "Well, how did you like the long-handled hoe?" One said, "I liked it." Another said, "My back is not as tired." Still another said, "I never thought of using a longer handle on a hoe; this worked well with me." (Photo by Jim Diamond of a Tchadian farmer using a long-handled hoe.)

78

USING A LONG-HANDLED HOE

Whew! What a back-aching job! Weeding cotton was a dreaded, time-consuming task that embraced all members of the household. Men and women would be bent over with short-handled hoes weeding cotton beginning in early morning while it was cool. Because women were responsible for taking care of infants, it was common to see them weeding cotton with babies tied to their backs. Children old enough to weed would also be weeding cotton. I had eleven laborers working in the president's demonstration cotton field, and it was all they could do to keep weeds under control by using short-handled hoes on six hectares* of cotton. I asked them, "Why don't you use long-handled hoes?"

One day while my laborers were working in the field, I purchased eleven new hoes from the village blacksmith. I asked him to bend the hoes just above the top and below where they attach to the handle. He looked at me as if I were out of my mind as he began heating the metal to bend the first hoe. I stood there to make sure he bent the hoe far enough to the way I wanted. He did a very good job and I said, "*Madjingaye* (great) this is the way I want the other ten hoes bent."

By the expression on his face, I could tell he thought this American was lacking good judgment and was quite inexperienced in using hoes. While the village blacksmith was bending my hoes against his better judgment, I went into the bush and cut eleven poles six feet (154 centimeters*) long. When I returned to the village blacksmith, all eleven of the hoes had been bent. After I paid him, I commended him for doing a good job.

I fitted the hoes and poles together to make long-handled hoes. I had to do a little trimming on the poles, but all eleven hoes were comfortable to hold.

The next morning at 5:45 a.m. when the laborers arrived at our house, I greeted them with my usual hearty *bon jour* (good morning) and the traditional handshake, then gave them their work instructions for the day. When I brought out the first three long-handled hoes, those fellows were really surprised. They did not know what to think. They thought the handles had not yet been shortened on those new hoes. While I was inside getting more long-handled hoes, one of the men got a machete and began chopping off the long handle. When I came outside and saw what was happening, I yelled, "*Arrêt! Arrêt!*" (Stop! Stop!) I then explained to the men that I was going to teach them how to use a long-handled hoe. The look on their faces indicated they thought this American must be some kind of idiot!

When we all arrived at the demonstration cotton field, the fellows were not too excited about using those long-handled hoes because it was a major change in their traditional way of weeding cotton. I took a hoe and explained how much easier it was to hoe cotton without having to bend all day using a short-handled hoe. I demonstrated how to hold and use the new hoe. I said to the men, "I want you to try this long-handled hoe until noontime today. If you like it, you can continue using it. If you do not like it, you can shorten it to your liking." They reluctantly agreed with this proposal. I lined them up at the side of the field and assigned each of them a row of cotton to clean with a long-handled hoe. At noon, they were all waiting for me. I asked, "How did you like the long-handled hoe?" One said, "I liked it." Another said, "I never thought of using a longer-handle on a hoe; this new hoe worked well with me."

Not one hoe was shortened during the remainder of the weeding season. AMAZING!

PRELUDE: Lack of access to clean water is one of the most common public health challenges in many communities across the continent of Africa. It's hard to believe that often the clean water desperately needed in rural communities is right underneath them. Water is life! A relatively small investment can get clean water to the people in many areas, and it can make such a dramatic difference in so many lives. Water is a majority of one's body weight. Water is important to nearly every part of your body. It regulates body temperature; helps create saliva; protects body tissues, spinal cord, and joints; helps excrete waste through perspiration, urination, and defecation; maximizes physical performance; prevents constipation; aids in digestion; and improves blood oxygen circulation. In many African societies, people do not drink sufficient clean water to stay healthy. I was inspired to write this narrative titled "Village Water Well" because I have observed many villagers who did not have sufficient clean water to maintain good health.

VILLAGE WATER WELL

Inside of the 110-feet-deep, hand-dug water well in Bessada, Tchad, was our source of water. It had to be brought to a hard rolling boil for twenty minutes and then filtered before it was safe for us to drink. (Photo by Jim Diamond inside of the water well in Bessada, Tchad, in 1972)

VILLAGE WATER WELL

Clean water, reliable toilets, and good hygiene keep people healthy and should be a normal part of daily life everywhere, but they aren't. I noticed several rural African villages where clean drinking water, reliable toilets, and good hygiene did not exist.

In Tchad, the simplest wells have traditionally been hand-dug. They can be fifty feet or more deep. Hand-dug wells are extremely dangerous to build, and many unskilled laborers have been killed in the process. Also, hand-dug wells are often left uncovered, and water is easily contaminated with debris and animal waste. Hand-dug wells aren't always an ideal solution, but when properly built and managed, they can be safe and effective.

One day, a hand-dug well in a village two miles from where my late wife, Betty, and I lived collapsed, leaving the villagers without water. Twice a day, three women would walk two miles to our village of Bessada, each carrying six gallons of water on their heads in traditional, round, hand-made, fired ceramic pots. After the pots were filled, the women would cover the water with mango tree leaves to keep it from splashing out during the walk back to their village. The women took a handful of grass, twisted it, and made a donut-shaped circle to fit the top of a woman's head. Two people lifted the pot and placed it onto the woman's head before beginning the two-mile trek back to their village.

Our well in Bessada was hand-dug to a depth of 110 feet, but it was lined with brick to support the side walls. Mahogany logs were placed over the top of the well to keep people and animals from falling into it. Women would straddle the logs and drop their buckets tied to a rope down to the water. When the bucket was full, it was pulled up and taken to their huts.

It was a common task for women to draw water, not men. At the well, women would socialize. According to tribal morés,* expatriates like Betty and me were not permitted to draw water out of the well. The two boys who worked for us were permitted to draw our water from the well.

Every morning at 5:15, I would start a fire outside of our house, pour water into the pots, bring it to a hard rolling boil, and boil it for twenty minutes to be safe. Afterward, the water was filtered with candle filters before it was safe for drinking.

It was a custom among expatriates that when a visitor visited your home, they were always asked if they would like a glass of water.

The Peace Corps well-drilling team had a very, very successful drilling well project in small Tchadian villages. Small well-drilling rigs were cost-effective and could drill 150 to 200 feet deep in certain regions of Africa. They can be moved with ease and enable drilling a water well quickly. These machines could easily drill through soil and rock, then a casing was installed to keep the hole from collapsing. A concrete base was formed around the casing on top of the well. After the concrete pad was dry and hardened, a pump mechanism was gently lowered into the hole and a hand pump was attached. Fresh clean water flowed from this kind of well because it was sealed from contaminants with a concrete "cap," and it was normally safe to drink without boiling or any other treatment.

I would like to end this narrative with an African proverb, "You don't punish a fish by throwing it into dirty water."

PRELUDE: Josip Broz Tito was a Yugoslav communist revolutionary and statesman, serving in various roles from 1943 until his death in 1980. Tito established diplomatic relations with Tchad in 1966, and in January 1971, he visited President Francois Tombalbaye in N'djamena (aka Fort Lamy), the capital of Tchad. His mission was to sign a friendship treaty with President Tombalbaye to instigate a Communist society in Tchad. President Tito donated to President Tombalbaye an incredible diplomatic gift for the Tchadian people that included a bulldozer with a front blade, a four-bottom plow, a disc harrow,* twenty fifty-five gallon drums of diesel fuel, and a supply of maintenance parts, such as air filters, grease, oil filters and motor oil. This equipment was manufactured by a Yugoslavian company known as 20 October. A Yugoslavian mechanic arrived to teach selected Tchadians how to drive, maintain and repair this equipment. I was inspired to write this narrative titled "Yugoslavian Diplomatic Gift" because I was a Peace Corps volunteer assigned to President Tombalbaye. Unbeknownst to me, President Tombalbaye sent me all that Yugoslavian equipment to be used in his home village of Bessada. Woe is me!

YUGOSLAVIAN DIPLOMATIC GIFT

A replica of the 20 October bulldozer, which was a diplomatic gift from Yugoslavia to Tchad. In addition, there was a front blade for the bulldozer, a four-bottom plow, a disc harrow, 1,100 gallons of diesel fuel and a supply of maintenance parts. (Photographer unknown)

YUGOSLAVIAN DIPLOMATIC GIFT

Late one evening in May 1972 while listening to Voice of America on our shortwave radio, my late wife, Betty, and I suddenly heard a commotion outside on the road. When I went outside to investigate, I found a huge tractor-trailer truck loaded with heavy equipment. On the trailer was a yellow October 20 bulldozer with a front blade, a four-bottom plow, a disc harrow, twenty fifty-five gallon drums of diesel fuel and a supply of maintenance parts, including air filters, belts, grease, oil filters and motor oil. I asked the village chief, "Who was supposed to get this equipment?"

He responded, "You!"

That's when I learned that the president received this diplomatic gift from Yugoslavia, but I was not told this equipment was being shipped to me. The next morning, I asked the French Agricultural Extension team if they were expecting this equipment. Their reply was *"Non!"* (No!) At the Chinese Research Station on the Chari River, I asked if they were expecting this equipment. Their reply was *"不!"* (No!) At the Bedaya Catholic Mission Station, I asked the Italian missionaries if they were expecting this equipment. Their reply was "Nò!" The equipment and supplies were off-loaded and parked along the road in the village, and two days later it was moved to the president's personal premises. The chief was correct: That equipment was assigned to me!

Three weeks later, a Yugoslavian bulldozer expert arrived to teach fifteen Tchadian men and me how to operate the bulldozer. We learned by doing; we cleared land to prepare it for an oil palm tree plantation. One day while plowing with a four-bottom plow, it got it hooked on a root. Instead of the learner backing up, he forged ahead by jerking the plow and sprung it. We had no way of getting parts from Yugoslavia, plus there was no money to pay for parts and shipping. A small building at the president's residence contained the stored spare parts. Under the building was a hive of wild honey bees. The horticultural specialist attempted to get honey by calming the bees with smoke. He built a fire for its smoke but instead caught the building on fire and burned it to the ground, including all the Yugoslavian tractor parts and supplies.

I noticed the supply of diesel fuel was being depleted rather quickly. I learned the president's brother had a fleet of trucks, and the chief was giving diesel to him and selling it to his friends. One day after the Yugoslavian expert departed Tchad, the men were preparing several acres of land to plant oil palm tree seedlings. The tractor had a broken fan belt and all the extras were burned in the fire. That tractor sat there in the field for three years after I departed Tchad. I learned the Tchadian Department of Transportation got the tractor and the equipment for Tchad's dirt road maintenance. At the time, I had no need for such agricultural equipment because farmers in Bessada were just learning how to train and use oxen as animal traction.

This was an example how money is squandered by nations seeking political support with countries not yet ready for modern agricultural equipment for farmers.

I want to close this narrative by quoting Will Rogers, "Too many people spend money they haven't earned, to buy things they don't want, to impress people they don't like."

PRELUDE: Between 1982 and 1991, the agricultural extension system* in eSwatini (aka Swaziland), a country located between the Republic of South Africa and Mozambique, experienced much change. During this period, the Ministry of Agriculture and Cooperatives recognized the benefit of a strong agricultural industry in eSwatini and identified a need for an effective agricultural extension system for Swazi farmers. In 1984, Ministry of Agriculture officials recognized that the old British extension system was not adequately addressing the needs of farmers. A team from the Pennsylvania State University and Tennessee State University helped bring about those changes through the eSwatini Cropping Systems Research and Extension Training Project (CSRET). I was inspired to write this narrative titled "Agricultural Extension in eSwatini" because I was part of the Penn State University team that helped to bring about effective changes through the CSRET.

AGRICULTURAL EXTENSION IN eSWATINI

This four-step agricultural extension planning process was adopted: (1) extension field officers meet with farmers within their respective units to identify and determine the issues that can be addressed through extension education programs; (2) extension officers identify their common subsection needs; (3) senior extension staff identify and prioritize the common subsection needs within their region (these collective needs then evolve into regional agricultural extension plans); and (4) the regional plans collectively become the national agricultural extension plan. (Photo by Jim Diamond of farmers hoeing their maize* with long-handled hoes in 1988)

AGRICULTURAL EXTENSION IN eSWATINI

First organized in 1930, eSwatini's Ministry of Agriculture officials in 1984 recognized that the British system replaced by the new Train and Visit Extension System needed modification to ameliorate eSwatini's agriculture. Under our guidance, they modified the Train and Visit (T&V) Extension System to enable their staff to develop extension plans aimed at the expressed needs of rural people, as opposed to delivering untimely messages. A team from the Pennsylvania State University and Tennessee State University helped bring about those changes through the eSwatini Cropping Systems Research and Extension Training Project (CSRET).

It was apparent that more and more farmers on Swazi Nation Land (land held in trust by the king for the Swazi people) wanted increased contact with extension field officers for agricultural information, nonformal education programs, and advice. Because of many constraints, including transportation, communications, and area of expertise, only a few farmers had access to British-style agricultural extension field officers who focused only on their respective subject expertise. Farmers needed access to the appropriate extension field officer for a specific question or problem.

The T&V Extension System was developed in India and implemented in eESwatini beginning in September 1985. It was designed so local extension officers could quickly disseminate information to farmers through frequent visits to their farms. All extension field officers who were specialists suddenly became generalists. The T&V Extension System implementation increased the number of farmers having contact with field officers. However, implementation was resisted within the rank and file of extension staff during its first year. Upon reviewing the status of eSwatini's T&V Extension System two years after implementation, the extension subject matter specialists, T&V coordinators, extension officers and field officers expressed frustration and confusion with the system. The morale of the staff was very low, and a number of extension officers resigned or requested a transfer. Because the T&V Extension System was not fully accepted by the extension field staff, the system began to flounder. Staff frustrations included: (1) The extension field staff members were unclear about how the system was to function; (2) Many were confused as to what their specific roles and responsibilities were; (3) Field staff and subject matter specialists lacked transportation to attend meetings; (4) Field staff had too many farmers under their jurisdiction; (5) Local chiefs were concerned that field officers were preempting their right to select the contact farmers; (6) Farmers were receiving untimely messages from the extension field officers; (7) And farmers lost confidence in the field officers. The CSRET Project team began the long, tedious process of advising and guiding ministry officials in developing and executing a bottom-up extension program planning process within a traditional top-down governmental administrative system. A four-step agricultural extension planning process was adopted. (1) Extension field officers met with farmers to identify and determine the issues that could be addressed through extension education programs; (2) Extension officers identified their needs; (3) Senior extension staff identified and prioritized the needs within their region; and (4) Regional plans became the national agricultural extension plan. I would like to end this narrative with a Swazi proverb, "The bee that is forced into the hive will not produce honey alone." A national extension plan developed by Swazi Extension Staff and farmers was a sweet success.

PRELUDE: Desmond Tutu, an Anglican Bishop and theologian in the Republic of South Africa, was known for his role as a human rights and anti-apartheid activist. He was the first Black African to become archbishop. He was born on 7 October 1931 and died 26 December 2021. Desmond Tutu was a Nobel Peace Prize winner because of his dynamic role in ending the South African racist regime. He was an influential, respected leader in the efforts to end racial segregation and discrimination enforced by a white minority government. President Cyril Ramaphosa described Tutu as the "spiritual father behind the movement to end racism," a policy of racial segregation and discrimination from 1948 to 1991 that was enforced by a white minority government. I was inspired to write this narrative titled "Archbishop Desmond Milo Tutu" because I was privileged and honored to meet him in person and had a significant, far-reaching, meaningful, relevant discussion with him. He was an easy person to talk to, and he was very selective in choosing words to use that adequately described his thoughts. I was mesmerized as I listened to him talk about how black Africans were treated by white people. Living in nearby eSwatini (Swaziland) I witnessed firsthand the injustice of apartheid he was describing in South Africa.

ARCHBISHOP DESMOND MILO TUTU

Desmond Tutu, as he appeared while sitting in his Air Swazi Airline seat during our discussion, was friendly, interested in my work in eSwatini, and willing to discuss eliminating racism in the Republic of South Africa. (Photo by Jim Diamond of Archbishop Desmond Milo Tutu)

ARCHBISHOP DESMOND MILO TUTU

One day in November 1988, my late wife, Betty, and I were about to begin a long flight from Johannesburg to John F. Kennedy international Airport in New York, then fly to Pittsburgh, then to State College, Pennsylvania. As we walked across the tarmac to Swazi Airlines, we noticed an unusual number of Swazi soldiers with machine guns posted along the way to our airplane. I said to Betty, "I knew we were well known in eSwatini, but it was not necessary to bring out the military to protect us!" After we boarded our airplane and got seated, I looked out the window. That's when I learned the military was not there to protect us. We saw Desmond Tutu walking across the tarmac. After he boarded our plane, he sat directly in front of me.

After a few minutes, while Tutu was getting settled, I stood and introduced myself and Betty. I was amazed how friendly and accepting of us he was and with the kinds of questions he asked! He asked me what I was doing in eSwatini, whether or not we liked living there, where were we going, and how long would it be before we returned.

Tutu told us he had been visiting his son who was a student at Waterford Kamhlaba School located near Mbabane, the capital of eSwatini. Waterford was established in 1963 as a private International Baccalaureate School, and in 1981 it became the fourth of eighteen international schools and colleges in the United World College (UWC) educational movement. Waterford Kamhlaba School was located on a hillside donated by the King of eSwatini near where I lived in Mbabane, eSwatini. I was familiar with the Waterford School, and I knew that Prince Charles of England was on the board of directors. The motto of the Waterford School meshed beautifully with Bishop Tutu's philosophy and thinking, "UWC makes education a force to unite people, nations and cultures for peace and a sustainable future."

That motto led us to some far-reaching topics of discussion. When Tutu learned I was an agricultural teacher and consultant, he informed me he once was a teacher and that after three years he resigned to protest the South African government restrictions on black children's education. After he described his career accomplishments, it was clear he was a very courageous man to resist government officials who favored apartheid principles. He went on to say after he was ordained as an Anglican priest, "I plunged into my inner desire to eliminate racism in my beloved country." He was the first black appointed Anglican Dean of St. Mary's Cathedral in Johannesburg; chaired South Africa's post-apartheid Truth and Reconciliation Commission; was the first black Secretary General of the Interdenominational South African Council of Churches; became the second South African after Chief Albert Lutuli to win the Nobel Peace Prize for efforts to end apartheid; was elected archbishop of Cape Town, becoming the head of the Anglican Church in South Africa, Botswana, Namibia, eSwatini and Lesotho; and was selected by South African President Nelson Mandela to chair the Truth and Reconciliation Commission. Then he retired as the Archbishop of Cape Town and became Archbishop Emeritus.

Whew! What an interesting conversation! I was privileged and honored to have had an opportunity to meet and talk with Desmond Tutu, Archbishop Emeritus.

PRELUDE: Toward the beginning of the end of the civil war in Mozambique, African flights from Swaziland and Maputo were re-established. In 1989, my late wife, Betty, and I were among eleven Americans who flew to Maputo, the capital of Mozambique for a three-day weekend as tourists. Because of sporadic Mozambican military skirmishes, we were not permitted to travel outside of Maputo. We rented a twelve-passenger van and hired a driver who had to stay with the van at all times. We stayed in a hotel where we lodged and purchased our meals, but we went on a dangerous adventure to observe the horrific aftermaths of war. A refugee is someone who flees their home and country out of fear of persecution, war, or violence. During the Mozambican civil war, thousands of Mozambican citizens escaped the perils of war by migrating to two refugee camps located in the neighboring Kingdom of eSwatini (aka Swaziland).

CIVIL WAR REFUGEE CAMP

I visited two refugee camps in Swaziland and was appalled at the squalor refugees had to tolerate. I saw hundreds of people crammed together in tents in a small area. (Photo by Jim Diamond of refugee camp tents in eSwatini [aka Swaziland])

CIVIL WAR REFUGEE CAMP

Mozambique is located on the southeast coast of Africa and is bordered by Swaziland to its south. It had a diverse, rich heritage where Swahili, Bantu and Islam language speakers existed in mutual acceptance. Mozambique was widely known for quality fresh fish and seafood. I now know why Mozambique was known for its seafood. My prawns were absolutely magnificent.

The hotel's souvenir shop featured fantastic Mozambican arts and crafts. Some of our group purchased them.

Mozambique became independent from Portugal on 25 June 1975. A fifteen-year civil war was fought in Mozambique from 1977 to 1992. The dominant political party known as Mozambique Liberation Front became an official Marxist-Leninist political party, and the civil war effort was supported by the former Soviet Union. However, following the collapse of the former Soviet Union, that support ceased.

On our way to the hotel, in Maputo, Mozambique, I saw people sleeping under pieces of plastic along the road against sloping road banks. People were desperate for something to eat, and beggars were everywhere. Destruction from the war was all around us. Buildings, homes and streets were rubble.

For some unfathomable reason, our hotel was spared from destruction. It was within easy walking distance of the beautiful Indian Ocean beach. We walked along the beach but did not swim. After lunch, we took a siesta for a couple hours. During the siesta, I heard a huge "BOOM!" It was a bomb detonated some distance from the hotel. We were confined to the hotel premises and were not permitted to drive around town except where our driver knew it was safe for us to visit, but we had to stay in the van.

Back in eSwatini, I had visited two refugee camps near Caritas and was appalled at the squalor refugees had to tolerate. Caritas, eSwatini was founded in 1977 to empower communities and reduce chronic poverty. During the Mozambican war, Caritas officials and the Ministry of Home Affairs Refugee Section in eSwatini (Swaziland), implemented a mandate of guaranteeing the protection and assistance of poverty-stricken Mozambican asylum-seekers and refugees. Acting together with United Nations High Commissioner for Refugees, they ensured provision of legal protection, education, health, counseling, shelter, food assistance, income-generating opportunities and skills training

I saw hundreds of people crammed together in tents in a small area. Swaziland's Ministry of Agriculture designated an open field for refugees to grow fresh vegetables. Water was made available from a drilled well. Each one of those people had a horrific story to tell about their escape, loss of family members, friends and worldly goods and destruction of their villages. Most of those people would never return to Mozambique! Kudus to the Kingdom of Swaziland for their willingness to help their neighbors.

I would like to close this narrative with a quote from a refugee named Amelia Koulder, "A refugee is someone who survived and who can create a future."

PRELUDE: Dr. Lawrence Ragan, a Macintosh microcomputer expert, was invited to travel to the Kingdom of eSwatini. All employees and officials employed by the Ministry of Agriculture and Cooperatives (MOAC), Mbabane, eSwatini (Swaziland), recently had new Macintosh microcomputers placed in their offices. Each of them was given the opportunity to learn how to use their new microcomputers by enrolling in Dr. Ragan's course, "Learning How to Use Microcomputers." Dr. Ragan was also an expert bird watcher, who was able to call in owls at nighttime. Upon Dr. Ragan's arrival in eSwatini, I informed him, "We work hard during the week and play hard on weekends." I was inspired to write this narrative titled "Owl Calling" because Dr. Ragan presented a stellar nonthreatening microcomputer curriculum to the Swazi audience. Additionally, Dr. Ragan shared his owl-calling expertise to interested American Cropping Systems and Extension Training Team members after hours and on weekends.

OWL CALLING

Dr. Lawrence Ragan, an expert bird watcher, had the capability to call in owls during the nighttime. (Photographer unknown)

OWL CALLING

Antonio Namburete, Mozambique's Attorney General said, "Gun smuggling from Mozambique has contributed to soaring crime in South Africa. The huge demand for illegal firearms in South Africa has led Mozambican gunrunners to seek weapons from members of the armed forces." He told a crime conference in Pretoria, "They have started to lure members of the defense and security forces with easy money to steal arms from their barracks." Namburete went on to say he expected new arrests in connection with the gunrunning and espionage case that involved South African foreign affairs official Robert McBride, who was suspended from his job as director of the Asian desk in the Foreign Ministry.

Malolotja National Park is located on Forbes Reef, eSwatini (Swaziland). It's an upland park for tourists with hiking for all levels, camping, waterfalls and zip-line tours over a forested gorge. Some common species of owls found there include African grass owl, barn owl, African scops owl, Southern white-faced owl, Cape Eagle owl, spotted eagle owl and Verreaut eagle owl.

After I visited Malolotja National Park with Dr. Ragan, he asked if it was possible to call owls after dark. Dr. Ragan was a well-known owl calling expert from State College, Pennsylvania. We went to the park's entrance office and asked permission to enter the park after closing hours. The park ranger was very cooperative and agreed to have a guard open the gate at 9 p.m. to allow us to enter.

After dark, we drove to a mountaintop, got out of the car, and walked a short distance. Larry soon began to call owls. Amazingly, several common species of owls began to swoop around and over us. In some African societies, seeing owls at night is associated with mischief, death, and the supernatural. Their hooting is widely linked to ghosts, evil spirits and misfortune.

While Dr. Ragan was calling owls, I noticed flickers of light far down the mountainside along a river's edge that flowed from Mozambique through eSwatini into South Africa. What I was observing were smugglers who had been carrying arms from Mozambique into South Africa through Malolotja Park, eSwatini. I did not say anything because I did not want to cause alarm amongst the group. When we returned to the car, my late wife, Betty, sitting alone, saw the flickering lights and became very frightened. She got into the backseat and hid on the floor.

The group began to discuss the flickering lights. I explained that I thought they were smugglers' flashlights. Dr. Ragan looked through his binoculars and suddenly said, "Wait! They are communicating with morse code. Let me interpret what they are saying."

Everyone was utterly anxious and very quiet as Dr. Ragan began his morse code interpretation by slowly saying, "B-R-I-N-G the beer!"

Dr. Ragan's humor released all of the anxieties among the group, and everyone laughed at the happy ending. We all departed the national park. We had observed swooping owls, they were unharmed, we observed firearms being smuggled into South Africa, and all of our fears were released with Dr. Ragan's humor. We returned to the motel outdoor bar for the evening and sipped cold beer while chattering about our interesting owl-calling experiences.

PRELUDE: After Britain's Prince Charles's ex-wife Diana's death, he conducted his first foreign tour in Southern Africa to attend a board meeting at Waterford Kamhlaba United World College, Mbabane, eSwatini. He began his eight-day journey with a visit to the tiny Kingdom of eSwatini (aka Swaziland). During his stay in eSwatini, Prince Charles laid a wreath at the grave of King Sobhuza II, who led eSwatini to independence from Britain in 1968. My late wife, Betty, along with a group of other expatriate ladies, had a principled visit with Prince Charles in the guest house at the Waterford Kamhlaba United World College, Mbabane, eSwatini. She reported they acted in accordance with the kingdom's established rules for visiting royalty. It was an exciting time.

PRINCE CHARLES VISITS eSWATINI

Left to right: Person 2, Prince Charles, now His Majesty King Charles; Person 3, His Majesty King Mswati III; Person 4, mother of King Mswati (aka Queen mother) (Photo by Jim Diamond during Independence Day 6 September 1988)

PRINCE CHARLES VISITS eSWATINI

In September 1988, Prince Charles visited the Kingdom of eSwatini, which is one of the few absolute monarchies in the world. On 6 September, 1968, eSwatini became an independent nation. Originally it was a constitutional monarchy, but in 1973, King Sobhuza II assumed full power.

Independence Day in eSwatini, which is also known as Somhlolo Day, is celebrated nationwide. In Prince Charles's first official overseas visit after the death of Princess Diana in a car crash, he was praised for how he handled his personal tragedy. Senate President Lawrence Mncina told Prince Charles during his brief visit to Parliament, "Your immediate response to the news of her death and your immediate departure to Paris touched the hearts of all of us around the world. It undeniably and practically portrayed you as a caring, forgiving and loving man."

Prince Charles, wearing a blue-gray suit, blue shirt and blue-gray tie, was wringing his hands and looked on passively as Mncina spoke. The praise was in marked contrast to widespread criticism in Britain of the royal family as cold and distant following Diana's 31 August death in Paris.

Prince Charles responded by saying, "I am enormously grateful for your kind words with which you greeted me here and for your kind condolences both to my sons and myself."

During his stay in eSwatini, union members disrupted the return of King Mswati III from an international trip. In 1988, eSwatini's government was facing protest campaigns for an end to its absolute monarchy and the establishment of a multi-party democracy. The protest campaign accelerated when police fired tear gas and rubber bullets to disperse a crowd of about 500 demonstrators who tried to block King Mswati's exit from the airport on his return from the Commonwealth summit in Scotland. The protesters, who wanted democratic reforms and higher pay for teachers, threatened to demonstrate when Prince Charles arrived. But the eSwazi police banned the gathering. During the celebration of Independence Day, Prince Charles was escorted with a military honor guard to the dignitary section adjacent to where we were sitting, hence the reason I was able to take this photo.

I would like to close this narrative with a popular expression in the eSwatini language, "*Litsemba alibulali.*" (Hope does not kill.) It means, having hope has never killed anyone, even when it is lost. Be optimistic and never lose hope. Based on personal experiences with my wonderful eSwazi friends, I can safely say the eSwazi people are an optimistic, hopeful people.

PRELUDE: Archeologists claim that stone carvings evolved within cultures throughout eons of time. It has been further claimed that stone carvings reflect the oldest records of civilization. An excellent tradition of renowned soapstone carvings can be found in eSwatini, Africa, at craft markets and small kiosks along the main roads. Carvers use their skilled hands to turn soapstone into everything from palm-sized ashtrays to large animals and human heads. I was inspired to write this narrative because I became acquainted with a well-known, talented soapstone carver named Noah Mdluli. He had a kiosk on Piggs Peak Road, where I often stopped with guests, consultants and of course my late wife, Betty, who purchased his soapstone carvings as extraordinary souvenirs from the Kingdom of eSwatini (aka Swaziland).

SOAPSTONE CARVERS IN ESWATINI

Watching Noah Mdluli perform his incredible craftsmanship was an interesting learning experience. Anyone who appreciates the preservation of tradition and culture would find this an enlightening encounter. (Photo by Jim Diamond of Noah Mdluli carving soapstone at his kiosk along Piggs Peak Road in eSwatini (aka Swaziland) in 1997)

SOAPSTONE CARVERS IN eSWATINI

My friend Noah Mdluli, a soapstone sculptor who had a kiosk on the side of Piggs Peak Road, usually began his carvings by sketching the shapes of his conceptual object on paper or scratching a general outline of the object on the soapstone itself. When ready to carve, Noah began by chipping off large portions of unwanted stone. He told me this is called the "roughing out" stage of the sculpting process.

Watching Noah perform his incredible craftsmanship was an interesting learning experience, and anyone who appreciated the preservation of tradition and culture would find this an enlightening encounter. The only downside I found to soapstone figurines is that they're heavy to transport, so I suggest one consider purchasing a smaller figurines for travel.

Noah's work and vision were evident in the construction of his kiosk as well as in the pieces he produced. He used soapstone as a primary material of choice. Born in Shiselweni, Swaziland, in 1965, Noah began his career in stone carving when he moved at age twenty to Nkhaba. With no formal training, he learned by watching and experimenting with numerous carvers who lived in his area. Through trial and error, Noah quickly learned the skills of the trade, forgoing wood carving for the stronger, more durable soapstone. Noah once told me, "Soapstone is much more work, but more rewarding."

Working at his roadside kiosk, his career began by carving conventional tourist sculptures, such as the big five elephants: cape buffalo, lions, rhinoceros and leopards. During a discussion one day, Noah said, "Carving needs a concept. You must have an image in your mind that you are looking for. This stops many people from starting. I am an artist. I like to create, but I also like to change and grow."

Noah told me that mining and carving soapstone definitely provides such a challenge. The process of locating and mining soapstone is hard work that can take several days, even with help. Although Noah had a license to mine soapstone, the encroachment of urban areas and private property meant that he regularly needed to find new locations to excavate soapstone. Other obstacles included difficult vehicle entry to the mining site and the occasional theft of unattended soapstone. However, Noah continued to regularly produce amazing artwork.

Although soapstone carving seems to be a dying art, Noah was as determined as ever. He once told me, "Soapstone is mine. It's my skill. Everybody can cut grass or hammer a nail, but not everyone can carve out their imagination."

I would like to close this narrative by quoting Noah Mdluli's favorite saying, "Don't limit your challenges; challenge your limits."

PRELUDE: During my late wife, Betty, and my four-and-one-half years working and living in the Kingdom of eSwazi (Swaziland), I felt honored to be invited to many national holiday events and special occasions called by His Majesty King Mswati II. In addition to the Swazi dances and singing, I was astonished to watch Swazi military cadets dressed in their traditional loincloth garb holding their unique Swazi warrior shields and spears. It was so picturesque, yet the cadets wearing their battle garb were more than a flamboyant spectacle. During our tenure in Swaziland, we had an extraordinary series of inspiring experiences. I was inspired to write this narrative titled "Swazi Warrior Shield" because the shields were part of the traditional cadet garb. Also, I was able to acquire a bona fide Swazi warrior shield, spear and knob curry that have been displayed in my Pennsylvania home since 1998.

eSWATINI WARRIOR SHIELD

This photo depicts a cadre of proud Swazi warriors ready to fulfill their duty at the King's Kraal.* Yet Swazis are known for their proverbial compatibility and tranquil lifestyle. They are proud of their independence and self-government. (Photo by Jim Diamond of Swazi warriors during the annual Ncwala Ceremony at the Kraal* of King Mswati II in 1984)

eSWATINI WARRIOR SHIELD

Traditional Swazi parables declare that Swaziland is a nation of peaceful clans. However, the Swazi warrior shield is on their national flag. The Swazi people are peaceful and caring by nature, yet they are also courageous warriors.

In 2014, the Swazi Counselor from the Embassy of Swaziland in Washington, DC, visited my home in Pennsylvania and was impressed to see the Swazi warrior shield, spear and knob curry hanging on a wall in our family room, among other handiworks and articles from eSwatini. She was in awe that we treasured such Swazi memories thirty-one years later.

True Swazi battle shields were made from raw cattle hides of the esteemed breed known as the Sanga-Nguni. That was an important breed of cattle for the Swazi people because owning cattle is a symbol of wealth. War shields were traditionally stockpiled by a chief or king, to whom they belonged, while smaller shields were reserved for their subordinates' personal daily use or as a complement to their dancing ceremonies.

A battle shield was carried in the left hand as the only piece of defensive armor used by the Swazi warriors. Its use was practiced from boyhood by means of stick fighting. Its primary function was to deflect spears or arrows, but they were also carried during lion or leopard hunts. Some warriors bashed their opponents with their shields to knock them off balance or used them to hook the opponent's shield away to enable a stab with a spear.

Shields were used to confuse the enemy; for example Swazi warriors used their enemy's shields to disguise themselves. Warriors were advised to hide behind shields and imitate grazing cattle.

Shields were also used as protection against the weather or as shelters when camping. When a king was sitting in the open, his subordinates would hold shields over him to shade him from the hot sun.

Shields were also used at weddings or as screens at a bridal procession. Also, it has been said that a small shield placed over a house means that the house owner is married.

The use of shields declined when firearms were introduced to conflicts. When lions and leopards were nearly exterminated by firearms, shields also lost their usefulness in hunting.

Even though there are a plethora of other Swazi warrior shield customs, traditions, rituals and morés,* I would like to close this narrative by lifting a stanza from my narrative titled "A Kingdom of Peace," "Swaziland is a nation of peaceful clans as parables declare. Calm by nature, firm to endure, proud warriors struggle yet not too rapt to care."

PRELUDE: When my late wife, Betty, and I arrived in eSwatini in August 1986, we toured Mbabane, the capital of eSwatini, and surrounding communities. eSwatini's King Mswati had an official residence nearby where many official functions took place, which enticed tourists to the area. Near the roads and streets and in hotel lobbies were many exhibits featuring woven Swazi tapestries. Entrepreneurs exhibited beautiful weavings made by Swazi women that portrayed Swazi scenes. These weavings are sometimes called tapestries, but the tapestry technique was a European tradition developed for weaving pictures that is different from most weaving in eSwatini. Swazi weavers focused on geometric patterns. A popular tapestry shop where many high-quality tapestries were made was called *Phumalanga* (rising sun). I was inspired to write this narrative titled "eSwatini Tapestry" because a tapestry hanging in our home reminds me of the weaving process and the Swazi women's skills in making such beautiful wall hangings from mohair* and homemade dyes.

eSWATINI TAPASTRY

Before photographing it for the weaver, Jim Diamond examines ancient Bushman paintings on a rock overhang found at the trails end in Pine Valley near Mbabane.

Our dyed mohair* tapestry portrayed an ancient Bushman painting photographed by Jim Diamond in Pine Valley. Mohair yarn shown is being woven into the warp.*

eSWATINI TAPASTRY

As my late wife, Betty, and I began exploring eSwatini during our first week in the country, we noticed many shops in hotels and kiosks along the roads selling Swazi artworks, soapstone, carvings, and Swazi tapestries. They were beautiful! I sensed Betty wanted a tapestry, but we decided to wait until a later date to purchase one for our home back in Pennsylvania.

After living and working in eSwatini for three years, we decided to start looking for a tapestry that we liked. I told Betty, "It would be more meaningful if a little bit of Jim and Betty was in the tapestry." One of our favorite hikes near Mbabane was into Pine Valley on a narrow footpath that meandered among single-story, crudely constructed Swazi homes and fertile farmlands. It was a three-mile hike into the valley and at the end of the trail was a huge rock overhang, upon which were ancient Bushman paintings.

Because of its mountainous terrain, the area where the tapestry workshop was located is known as the "Switzerland of Africa." Tapestries were woven by Swazi women in a workshop called *Phumalanga* (rising sun). I photographed the Bushman paintings at the end of the trail in Pine Valley. I took a beautiful photo to the Phualanga Weaving Workshop and asked the weaver, "Can you make me a tapestry from this photograph?"

She said, "No problem!"

I had learned that when she got a photograph, they would make twenty tapestries of that image. I asked her to make our tapestry exclusive. She agreed, and our tapestry has the number one woven into it.

I photographed different stages of our tapestry's development. The mohair* was imported from the nearby Kingdom of Lesotho. The women carded* the mohair, spun it into yarn and dyed it in soft pastel colors using homemade dyes. A Swazi artist made a painting of the image I gave him on an easel the size of our tapestry, three feet by four feet. It was placed behind the warp* to give the weavers guidelines of which color of yarn to weave into the warp. It took thirty days for the weavers to complete our magnificent tapestry.

The San* rock painting on our tapestry is an animal called Eland de Derby. Researchers have reported a special relationship existed between the San and the Eland de Derby. San men were hunters, and San women were gatherers. The Eland was highly prized by the San because it was central to San *rites de passages,* for example a boy's first kill and a girl's first menstruation. To the San people, all cultural traits and rituals are one.

I cherish that tapestry. When a person enters our home, it is the first African artifact they see, so that tapestry has given rise to many discussions with guests shortly after their arrival.

PRELUDE: The Nile perch (aka Capitan in Tchadian) are a freshwater fish that can grow up to six feet long and weigh more than 400 pounds. Nile perch are native to African lakes and rivers in Tchad, Niger, Congo and Senegal. Nile perch are abundant and a bountiful source of food. Sometime around 1962, the Nile perch were intentionally inaugurated into Lake Victoria for commercial fishing purposes. There they copiously reproduced and spread throughout several aquatic environments in Africa. When using industrial fishing techniques, large Nile perch were easy to catch in shallow water. Their white meat is absolutely delicious, especially when baked slowly, garnished with onions, ketchup, hot paprika, garlic powder and black pepper. The bone-free flesh is rich with protein and nutrients, including omega three fatty acids, which are vital for human nutrition and well-being. I was inspired to write this narrative titled "Nile Perch" because they were readily available in the Chari River near where I lived and worked in Tchad. While working in Tanzania as a consultant for the United Nations, my late wife, Betty, and I boarded a ship to cross Lake Victoria. We observed hundreds of gigantic Nile perch on the dock that were processed and smoked for domestic and international markets.

NILE PERCH

A Tchadian fisherman went fishing with his nets early each morning and placed his Nile perch (*Lates niloticus*) on the back wheel of his bicycle to transport it to local markets to sell. (Photo by Jim Diamond of a Nile perch on a bicycle being transported to the market near Njamina, Tchad, Africa, in 1972)

NILE PERCH

According to an agrotechnical school professor in Tanzania, Nile perch were originally indigenous* to the Ethiopian region of Africa. However, Nile perch (*Lates niloticus*) were introduced into Lake Victoria about 1962 for commercial fishing. The Nile perch ultimately became the dominant predator* fish in Lake Victoria. Mature Nile perch have silver skin with a vague blue sheen and blazing black eyes ringed by luminous yellow.

The huge volume of Nile perch my late wife, Betty, and I observed on the Mwanza docks at Lake Victoria supported the claim that Nile perch was a thriving fish export industry for the three countries that adjoin Lake Victoria, Kenya; Uganda; and Tanzania.

According to the captain of the ship *Lake Victoria*, the number and size of Nile perch have diminished in recent years due to commercial fishing. A Tanzanian government decree encouraged fishermen to harvest thousands of Nile perch from the lake because of their ferocious predatory nature. Many indigenous small fish of Lake Victoria were endangered, nearly extinct, or extinct.

However, over the years Tanzaniansts were not concerned about the small fish. Catching and selling Nile perch was a major source of income to support their wives and many children. Not only did the Nile Perch enable fisheries to unfold, but this one fish species impacted fishery employment opportunities. Laborers loaded twenty to twenty-five huge fish onto two-wheeled carts and wheeled them to a large nearby smokehouse. After the fish were smoked, they were delivered to local markets or exported to surrounding countries.

In Tchad, a fisherman from the village of Bessada would go fishing with nets early each morning, placing his fish into a wooden box attached over the back wheel of his bicycle. He covered the wooden box with a wet burlap bag to keep the fish moist until he got to the village market to sell. He would push his bicycle with his fish past my cotton field. I would stop him, look at his daily catch, negotiate a fair price for his fish, and purchase eleven fish, one for each of my workers.

At 10:00 a.m., the men would take a break from the cotton field, and I would give them each a fish to eat as a morning snack. They built a fire and roasted the fish whole—not cleaned or de-scaled. They ate everything, even the eyes. That was probably their most nutritious meal for the day.

I would like to close this narrative by quoting a Chinese proverb, "Give a man a fish, and you feed him for a day. Teach a man to fish, and you feed him for a lifetime."

PRELUDE: An authentic Oriental rug is an heirloom that can be handed down for generations, and they are great investments that actually accrue in value over long periods of time. This stunning wool Oriental rug is a durable hand-woven work of art by a Uyghur (pronounced wee-gar) family who lives in Kashgar, China. Oriental rugs are typically produced by highly skilled artisans in and around Kashgar, and each Oriental rug exhibits a great investment of time and overall labor. I was informed that it took a large Uyghur family one month to make this rug. I was inspired to write this narrative titled "Oriental Rug" because it was given to me in 1996 by the Uyghur family who made it. It was a truly sincere token of their appreciation for visiting their village representing the Food and Agricultural Organization of the United Nations with a mission to improve and support their agro-technical school by introducing new teaching methods.

ORIENTAL RUG

Oriental rugs are primarily distinguished by their impeccable craftsmanship and beautiful materials. Even an experienced Uyghur rug maker will spend up to six months to create a single six-by-nine-foot Oriental rug. (Photo by Jim Diamond of his Oriental rug from Kashgar, China)

ORIENTAL RUG

The Uyghurs are native to the Xinjiang Uyghur Autonomous Region in northwest China. They are one of China's fifty-five officially recognized ethnic minorities. I found the Uyghur people to be very friendly, good-looking, cooperative, helpful and good-natured. I made a lot of friends in Kashgar, especially in their agrotechnical school.

While in Kashgar, China, I observed many stunning Oriental rugs! They were durable, heavy, hand-woven works of art. Because my rug has a wide range of color schemes that includes many shapes and styles, it can easily be coordinated with an existing color scheme. This rug fit beautifully almost anywhere in our rural log home.

Oriental rugs are primarily distinguished by their impeccable craftsmanship and beautiful materials. Even an experienced Uyghur rug maker will spend up to six months to create a single six-by-nine-foot Oriental rug. Oriental rug creators painstakingly stretch individual strands of wool, cotton, or silk across looms, weaving them together into beautiful, storytelling designs that have an incredible amount of cultural meaning within every square inch.

Vertical looms on which Oriental rugs are made look different when viewed from the top instead of the bottom. There are many types of Oriental rugs, including all-over geometric Moroccan rugs, tribal geometric Moroccan rugs, Shag Oriental area rugs, Oushak Indian rugs, Moroccan trellis rugs, Oushak Agra rugs, Agra area rugs, Indian rugs, Oushak Turkish area rugs and Chinese area rugs.

My late wife, Betty, really loved this rug, especially for the reason it was given to us. She wanted to make sure the airlines would ship it to the United States, so she tightly rolled it and fit it into her suitcase. With the rug and her clothes compressed into her suitcase, it was very heavy, and I feared it would cost a lot of money to ship. Luckily, Betty checked in at the Kashgar Airport with no additional luggage weight charges.

I would like to close this narrative with a Uyghar proverb, "A multitude of friends is wisdom and strength." Personally I am not sure about the wisdom, but I am undeniably blessed with a multitude of lasting Uyghar friends in Kashgar, the Republic of China.

PRELUDE: Upon my arrival at the Huangyuan Animal Husbandry and Veterinary School in Huangyuan County, China, I was warmly welcomed by the director and many faculty members. An Israeli official from the Food and Agriculture Organization of the United Nations, Rome, Italy was traveling with me. After we got settled in our rooms, we met with the director to plan an itinerary for our weeklong visit. Among many grueling visitations, duties, responsibilities, and talks, our Chinese colleagues felt we needed a mid-week break. We were informed that we would be attending a formal concert at the auditorium on Thursday evening. My Israeli colleague and I were delighted that we would see Chinese student musicians, actors and dancers perform. After attending the theater on Thursday evening, it was the peoples' way of paying homage to my Israeli colleague and me. I was moved by the people and the performers to write this narrative titled "Square Dancing in China."

SQUARE DANCING IN CHINA

This photo shows the Chinese version of square dancing after teaching them the American square dance: Allemande left and allemande right, circling back to your partner to swing her twice around. (Photographer unknown)

SQUARE DANCING IN CHINA

At 6:00 p.m., a driver dressed in an appropriate taxi driver hat, scarf around his neck, in a suit and tie drove to our dormitory to fetch my Israeli colleague and me to the main auditorium in town.

Wow! When we arrived at the colossal auditorium, we saw at least 200 people milling around on the beautiful steps leading up to the entrance. The driver opened our doors and helped us out of the car. When all of those people saw that we had arrived, they quickly lined up, forming a corridor for us to go up the steps as they applauded our arrival.

Inside the immense auditorium, we saw no less than 1,000 people present to express their gratification that two representatives of the United Nations were in their midst.

We were escorted to the front of the auditorium and seated in the first row, next to the town mayor and the director of the school. The emcee was my interpreter. She was a beautiful young Chinese lady with long black hair and long fire-engine-red dress, who spoke impeccable English. She came from behind an enormous maroon curtain and welcomed everyone and introduced us as her guests. Her program featured an awesome itinerary of talented, masterfully adroit dancers, singers, and musicians. I heard musicians playing an *erhu*, a bowed, two-stringed instrument that represents China and vocalists singing traditional Chinese folk songs. We observed Chinese dancers perform long-established, time-honored dance routines and much more.

Half-way through the two-hour program, the emcee came down off the stage, walked toward us, and asked my Israeli colleague if he would teach the Chinese audience an Israeli folk song. He said there was no way he would go on stage to participate. She then turned to me and asked if I would teach the audience an American folk song. I agreed, but as I climbed the steps to the stage, I wondered, *What am I going to do?* As I walked behind the curtain, I saw many young people waiting their turn to perform behind stage props. I thought, *Voila! There is my answer!* I decided I was going to teach and demonstrate to the audience a traditional American square dance.

I requested my interpreter to ask four girl and four boy volunteers to come onto the stage. I went to the microphone with my interpreter and gave a brief, historical overview of square dancing in America. Then I turned to the eight young people and squared them into four boy-girl couples. I explained and demonstrated each step of the dance, beginning with do-se-do your corner, bow to your partner, promenade her round the circle back to home, allemande left and allemande right, circling back to your partner to swing her twice around.

I walked each couple through each step until they were able to do the dance called "Dive for the Clams and Duck for the Oysters." I went back to the microphone with my interpreter and told the audience, "I need some euphonic sounds for the dancers to perform." I demonstrated how I wanted them to clap in unison. Whoa! I had more than 1,000 people clapping in cadence. Turning to the dancers, I started them by calling the square dance moves, which they well remembered.

Those young people danced wonderfully! The audience really enjoyed observing a traditional American folk dance, and they gave my volunteers a standing ovation.

I would like to close this narrative with a Chinese proverb, "Hear your song and dance your soul."

PRELUDE: The word "bell" itself is traced to the old Saxon word "bellon" and the Latin word "belare," meaning to bellow or bleat like an animal. Animal bells are icons throughout the world that symbolize pastoral lifestyles. They are worn by domesticated cows, horses, sheep, goats, cats, dogs, turkeys, water buffalos, camels, oxen, yaks, donkeys, mules, bulls, llamas, reindeer and elephants. Presently, I have collected and displayed eighty-one domestic animal bells from thirty-two countries at my home near Ottsville, Pennsylvania. My friend Rose Sandler from Poway, California, recently gifted me a new reindeer bell that she obtained in Mongolia. I was inspired to write this narrative titled "Chu Chu" because of Rose's kindness.

"CHU, CHU!"

On a snow-covered tundra* during an early sunlit morning, Mongolian nomadic herder Erdenebat Chuluu from the village of *Tsagaannuur* shouted, "Chu, Chu," words of encouragement to the reindeer he was riding. (Photo by Jim Diamond of a reindeer bell at his home near Ottsville, Pennsylvania)

"CHU, CHU!"

On snow-covered tundra* during an early sunlit morning, Mongolian nomadic herder Erdenebat Chuluu from the village of *Tsagaannuur* shouted "Chu, Chu," words of encouragement to the reindeer he was riding. Chuluu lived all his life in the centuries-old tradition of his Dukha ancestors, who are renowned for their reindeer herding and hunter-gathering skills in forests of the rugged Sayan Mountains straddling the border.

Kelly Rick indicated in our discussion during lunch that a former student of hers from California traveled to Mongolia and brought home some reindeer bells. I immediately asked, "Would her name happen be Rose Sandler?"

Stunned, Kelly excitedly and with exhilaration looked at me and responded, "How do you know her?"

I said, "I received one of her reindeer bells from her mother for my domestic animal bell collection from around the world last Wednesday!" What a small world we live in!

My new friend Kelly Rick and I were ecstatic how a reindeer bell from Mongolia warmly linked Rose Sandler of Poway, California; with Kelly Rick of Gainesville, Florida; with Lisa Sandler of Pipersville, Pennsylvania; with Jim Diamond of Ottsville, Pennsylvania.

Whew! What a wonderful twist of fortuity.

Mongolian herders find their reindeer by listening for jingling bells hanging on straps around their necks. Depending upon the weather and a bell's size, it can be heard up to one mile away.

Often Mongolian reindeer herders use bells with different resonating peals on reindeer singled out for a specific purpose. In addition to identifying an animal's location, the herders quickly learn by various tones of the bells if the reindeer are grazing, lying down chewing their cud, walking, running, or being chased by a predator.*

Animal bells are an alarm system that alerts the herder if a thief is stealing an animal under the cover of darkness. Recently, modern technology has reached Mongolia, where reindeer herders now use satnav GPS collars on reindeer to locate them in the event traditional bells cannot be heard.

I would like to close this narrative with a Chinese proverb, "Look deep into nature and then you will understand everything better."

Looking into the friendly nature of the Chuluu people has made me feel less alone in the world.

PRELUDE: Albania, a very poor country by European standards, is located in southeastern Europe, nestled between the shores of the Adriatic and Ionian Seas and the borders of Greece, Macedonia, Serbia and Montenegro. It obtained its independence from the Ottoman Empire on 28 November 1912, and its capital is Tirana. Since 1990, the Albanian people have experienced substantial political and social upheavals following the demise of communism and the shift to a market economy. In 1998, the government of Albania confirmed that its agricultural sector was forever important in its national economy. Both the Ministry of Education, Agriculture and Agricultural University of Tirana had the responsibility to coordinate training of agricultural extension officers* and agricultural teachers. Hence the reason I was summoned to Albania via Volunteers for Overseas Cooperative Assistance, which was awarded the project contract by the United States Agency for International Development. I was inspired to write this narrative titled "Albanian Goat Bell" because of my excitement upon finding this goat bell in an antique shop on the way to Kurja, Albania, in May 1998. I have an extensive collection of domestic animal bells from around the world, but until then, none from Albania.

ALBANIAN GOAT BELL

This goat bell was estimated to have been made around 1950 by a local Albanian blacksmith. It is rusted from being exposed to outdoor elements. This bell was made from a flat piece of scrap metal by cutting, heating and bending it into a rectangular shape and riveting each of the two sides with three handmade rivets. (Photo by Jim Diamond of the Albanian goat bell in his home.)

ALBANIAN GOAT BELL

Because of political uneasiness in Albania and a concern for our personal safety, our travels were confined to the city of Tirana. Just weeks before my arrival, homes had become armed camps in which reports of deaths became increasingly common. At least twelve people were killed and fifty wounded a week earlier. And at least one tank rumbled down the main boulevard in Tirana at night in an area populated by government buildings. We wanted to travel up a mountain outside Tirana to Kurja, but three weeks earlier five people from England were ambushed and killed near Kurja.

Only one Saturday did we have clearance from the embassy of the United States of America to leave Tirana and travel to Kurja to visit a refurbished ancient castle. On our way up the mountain in a van, we drove past a lone antique shop, but we did not stop. We decided to stop on our way back down the mountain toward Tirana.

When we reached the top of the mountain, a military blockade stopped us from going any further. The soldier seemed to be friendly and congenial when they sensed we were Americans and would obey their commands. Nearby stood an elderly lady outside her old stone house. She invited us into her home for a cup of tea. We asked the soldiers if that was okay, and they agreed.

We had a delightful experience supping tea and nibbling homemade scones with that lady. She intended her hospitality to be complimentary, but we of course paid her a handsome sum for her friendliness and warm reception to complete strangers. Before departing her home, we profusely thanked her and bid her a very warm goodbye with a hug before getting back into our van.

As we journeyed south toward Tirana, we stopped at the antique store near Kurja. As we would do in the United States, we got out of the van, walked around and browsed. We found a lot of interesting items, but nothing I wanted to carry home—until I spotted an animal bell with a wooden collar on a table in the back of the shop. WOW! What a find!

In 1996-1997, Albanian farmers sold most of their livestock and invested their money into governmental pyramid schemes purported to make them a lot of money quickly. Unfortunately, the pyramid schemes shortly collapsed, and the farmers lost most of their money. Some farmers made a little extra money by selling their used bells to antique dealers, who in turn sold them to tourists. I purchased this distinctive bell because its collar was made from carved wood and would have a personality of its own in my collection. I was informed that the wooden collar had to be soaked in water to soften it so it could be opened to put it on or take it off the goat.

This goat bell was made around 1950 by a local Albanian blacksmith. It is rusted from being exposed to outdoor elements. This bell was made from a flat piece of scrap metal by cutting, heating, bending it into a rectangular shape and riveting each of the two sides with three handmade rivets. In 1997, a new clapper* was made and installed by an Albanian blacksmith to replace the old broken clapper. When the clapper strikes the inside of this bell, it makes a loud clanging sound.

I would like to close this narrative with a quote from an unknown Albanian farmer who had bells on his goats and said, "How awesome is that! Such a sweet sound, to do a serious job as a herd protector, it's like music on the farm." He captured my feeling when I heard bells ringing on my sheep . What a magnificent way to close each day with a soothing evening lullaby.

PRELUDE: Albania is a small, mountainous country on the Balkan Peninsula bordered on the east by Republic of Macedonia, on the northeast by Kosovo, on the northwest by Montenegro and on the south by Greece with coastlines that span the Adriatic and Ionian seas. Crossing the middle of Albania are the Albanian Alps. The location of its capital, Tirana, can be likened to a bottom of a soup bowl, having mountains surrounding it. Tirana is the site of their National History Museum and Et'hem Bey Mosque. The Ottoman Empire and Stalinist Communism formally ruled Albania. In 1992 elections, communist rule under Enver Hoxha ended forty-seven years after World War II. Enver Hoxha was a staunch isolationist who did not align his country with other countries, whether communist or non-communist. Many of the 3.2 million people departed Albania to seek employment and a life elsewhere. Under the current leadership, efforts are being made to revive Albania's frail economy so it can become a member of the European Union. In 1998, while I was on a project in Albania, there was political unrest plus widespread corruption and crime. Extension officials endeavored to have an effective, efficient non-formal educational system to help farmers help themselves throughout all of Albania. The purpose of writing this narrative titled "God Bless Albania!" was to describe efforts to initiate sustainable progress among Albanian extension officials who wanted to improve their economy and quality of life in a land they loved.

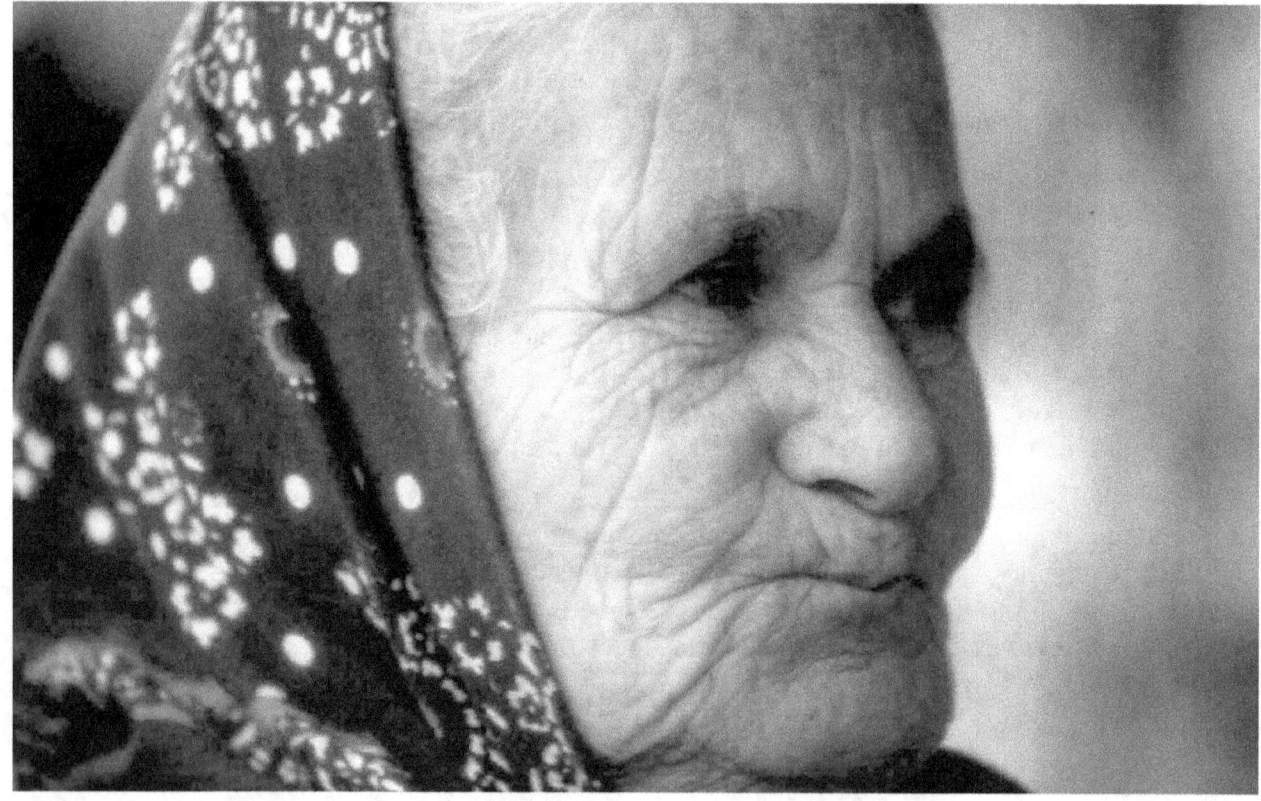

GOD BLESS ALBANIA!

Poverty-stricken farmers' constraints consisted of low levels of income; reluctance to take the risks of implementing new practices, technologies, or skills; small, scattered plots of land; and little interest in extension programs because they lacked confidence in extension officers. (Photo by Jim Diamond of an Albanian woman on her farm near Tirana, Albania)

GOD BLESS ALBANIA!

Before any nation can become strong, it must develop its agriculture. Albania's future was in the hands of agricultural extension officers and teachers. To assist Albanian extension officers, a ten-day teaching session was planned and implemented that included "Concepts of Rural Agricultural Extension," "Role of Extension in Rural Development," "Extension Planning Process," "Role of Non-Formal Farmer Training Programs," "Developing Action Plans," and "Program Evaluation."

"Learning by Doing" was the leading principle for teaching adult extension officers. As an integral part of the curriculum, extension participants had many opportunities to use their newly learned information with local farmers. However, agricultural development was constrained by factors that could not be addressed without changes that were specific to agricultural policies.

I admired the extension officers' sincerity in wanting to learn. However, my feelings and emotions were wounded after becoming conscious of their bleak destiny. Their numerous external constraints included a worsening macro-economic framework after the collapse of pyramid schemes in 1997. Internal constraints hinged on uncertainty of titled and untitled land ownership, lack of credit, and inefficient systems of production and transportation.

Agricultural extension constraints were abundant! They had little access to research results, lacked experience, had no transportation to travel long distances between remote villages and farmers, no operating budget, and too many farmers per extension worker. Poverty-stricken farmer constraints consisted of low levels of income, reluctance to take a risk of implementing new practices, lack of understanding technologies, inadequate skills and small scattered plots of land. Farmers also had little interest in extension programs because they lacked confidence in extension officers.

In spite of these constraints, the government of Albania placed high priority on the agriculture sector and was committed to developing an extension system that would offer assistance to farmers by providing timely management information. In 1990, when the country began to reshape their government and political system, state farm systems disintegrated and all state holdings were privatized. As a result, a need evolved for development of an agricultural extension system* to serve thousands of private farmers. To have strong agricultural non-formal education programs for farmers and agricultural education in schools, well-qualified extension officers and teachers were essential. The need for teaching inexperienced extension officers to become competent in teaching farmers agricultural production skills was imperative.

After participants evaluated their teaching session, it was reported that the extension officers became familiar with non-formal agricultural extension programs and understood the agricultural extension officer's* influence on rural development. Achieving goals of a teaching session made us feel good, but we were not yet convinced that extension officers would be able to cope with existing constraints that faced them in Albania. Education is the most powerful weapon that can be used to change any nation.

God bless Albania!

PRELUDE: Tirana is the capital of the Republic of Albania, which is located in southern Europe on the strait of Otranto. In 1997, a significant number of Albanians sold their homes and livestock to invest their money in a government-sponsored pyramid scheme. It was estimated that $1.5 billion was invested. The failure of the pyramid scheme triggered a rebellion that escalated into a civil war that toppled the government after 2,000 people were killed. Albania is considered Europe's poorest country, and Sali Berisha was a deeply unpopular president and authoritarian ruler who refused calls for his resignation. Citizens barricaded themselves inside their homes in terror as gunfire rattled across the capital while people bid up the prices of the last food supplies in the face of uncertainty and chaos. The people were desperate because they lost their money and sold any items they had left to antique dealers to generate income to exist. I was inspired to write this narrative titled "Reinvigorating Albanian Agriculture" because after their beautiful agricultural university was destroyed during the rebellion, I was the first person to offer a course in a refurbished classroom.

REINVIGORATING ALBANIAN AGRICULTURE

The social unrest of early spring 1997 did not spare the Agricultural University of Tirana, which was looted, ruined and burned. The furniture and equipment were destroyed. My mission was to develop and implement an extension training program to reinvigorate Albanian agriculture and support the development of an effective agricultural extension system* for Albania. (Photo by Jim Diamond of social unrest destruction of Agricultural University of Tirana in April 1998)

REINVIGORATING ALBANIAN AGRICULTURE

The Republic of Albania is an extremely poor country by European standards. In 1997, it was reported that much of Albania's economy was derived from agriculture. During the opening ceremony of the Extension Training Program on 31 April 1998 for Albanian Extension Leaders, I stated, "Before any nation can become strong, it must develop its agriculture."

To have strong agricultural extension programs, there must be a sufficient number of well-qualified extension officers to teach. Because agriculture is an important economic sector for the Albanian economy, the government intended to strengthen and expand its nationwide public agricultural extension system* to disseminate technical, management and economic information to farmers. I was in Albania to develop and implement an extension training program to reinvigorate Albanian agriculture and support the development of an effective, efficient agricultural extension system for Albania.

The extension training program had six objectives: (1) Defining the concepts of agricultural extension; (2) Explaining the role of extension in rural development; (3) Clarifying the roles of agricultural extension officers; (4) Defining agricultural knowledge information systems; (5) Naming methods for planning and implementing extension programs; and (6) Determining farmers' needs and preparing an action plan.

Learning by doing was the leading learning principle for teaching, and participants had many opportunities to visit local farmers to use their newly learned information.

Albania's agricultural development had constraints that prohibited rural and agricultural development from reaching its fullest potential. External constraints included a worsening macro-economic framework after the collapse of pyramid schemes in 1997. Internal constraints included uncertainty of land ownership, very small family farms, and lack of market channels and credit. The agricultural extension officers had little access to Ministry of Agriculture research results and no operating budget. For various reasons, farmers did not carry out the extension officers' recommendations. Farmers were reluctant to take the risk of implementing new practices, technologies, or skills. They lacked confidence in extension officers, and they had little experience in management and decision making.

Albania was the last communist country in Eastern Europe to reshape its political structure, and it was dubbed the "last domino." Even though the Albanian people were still struggling with the throes of a changed process, the resilience of the Albanian people was Albania's hope for a dignified emergence into the European economy.

The fate of Albanian farmers who crave to invigorate Albanian agriculture was transferred to the hands of competent agricultural extension officers.

Mother Teresa once said, "Be faithful in small things because it is in them that your strength lies."

PRELUDE: The Republic of Bulgaria is a Balkan nation dating back to the fifth century with the ancient city of Sofia being its capital. Since 1989, the citizens of Bulgaria struggled with the restitution* process because of the uncertainty of making a transition from a centralized state-controlled economy to a free Bulgarian market economy. There were strong-willed Bulgarian farmers with vastly diverse land ownership. The restitution* process pointed them toward a free-market economy, which they yearned for during so many years of socialism. The ancient Greek philosopher Plato once said, "Need is the mother of invention." New farmers needed guidance! A group of farmers learned that producing cheese with water buffalo milk was a profitable enterprise and started a farm near Lozenets, Straldzha municipality, Yambol District. My mission was to recommend options to prevent buffalo manure from being washed into a small river where it contaminated the Straldzha water supply. I was inspired to write this narrative titled "Murrah Buffalo in Bulgaria" because the farm owners' pessimistic attitudes needed adjustment to enable their livestock venture to be cost-effective in buffalo milk and cheese production without jeopardizing the local villagers' water supply. Ultimately, we succeeded

MURRAH BUFFALO IN BULGARIA

A group of farmers organized a Murrah buffalo farm near the village of Lozenets, Straldzha municipality, Yambol district, Bulgaria. They owned Murrah buffaloes and produced and sold buffalo milk and cheese. (Photo by Jim Diamond of Murrah buffalo near Lozenets, Straldzha municipality, Yambol District, Bulgaria)

MURRAH BUFFALO IN BULGARIA

Since 1989, strong-willed Bulgarian people with lands so vastly diverse, the restitution* process pointed new farmers toward a free-market economy and new enterprises. A group of farmers organized a buffalo farm named Murrah 2002 Ltd. near the village of Lozenets, Straldzha municipality, Yambol district. They owned more than 600 Murrah buffaloes and produced their own animal feed. Because the farmers owned so many buffaloes, they needed to build a new barn, and they needed to expand and renovate an existing barn that had the capacity for 240 Murrah buffaloes.

The current barn was on top of a moderately high mountain with a narrow river flowing toward several villages, including Lozenets. That river was a water supply for those villages' residents and businesses. The buffalo were confined in a barnyard, which was positioned within an important watershed. During rains, gushing water moved a copious amount of buffalo excrement into the narrow river. The contaminated water seriously jeopardized the residents' healthful living downstream. My mission was to meet with the farm owners and an agricultural extension officer* to present and discuss various options to rectify this situation.

Upon our arrival, an armed guard opened a gate and greeted us coldly. The guard informed my late wife, Betty, that she was not permitted to get out of the car.

As I walked toward the gate with the guard, Betty spotted an unusual bird on a post. She got out of the car with her binoculars to study the bird. The armed guard stopped and gruffly ordered Betty to get back into the car.

When I entered the meeting room in the barn, six men stared at me as I walked to my chair. Quite frankly, I began to feel uncomfortable. I was introduced as an American expert who had come to tell them how to run their farm. I was asked several questions that were aimed at establishing my qualifications to advise them.

One man said, "You are just another highly-paid American who was sent here to tell us how to manage our business."

I finally got an opportunity to present some options for them to discuss and reach their own decisions, including enabling the farm to become cost-effective and competitive in buffalo milk and cheese production. It is important the farm complied with European Union standards on work safety, ensuring compliance with the EU Nitrates Directive on the protection of waters against pollution. Pollution is caused by nitrates from agricultural sources and lowers the cost of veterinary interventions due to improved hygiene conditions for the buffaloes.

After our departure, the agricultural extension officer informed me that those men were strongly linked with the Bulgarian mafia. Hence, their gruff attitudes.

I would like to close this prose narrative with a Bulgarian proverb, "When too many people give advice, things do not work."

PRELUDE: Memories and friends are two of life's most precious treasures. The older we grow, the more precious they become. On 11 July 2011, my late wife, Betty, our two dear friends Dave and Connie Kantner, and I boarded the *m/s Prinsendam* for a Celtic cruise around Great Britain to create a plethora of memories to cherish and reinforce our friendship. We departed London Cruise Terminal from Tilbury, England, and fourteen days later, we returned to the same terminal. Our objective was to indulge our bird-watching passion and record the sea and land birds we sighted. The following narrative was a pleasurable effort to describe the delight of seeing by chance a rare bird that was nearly extinct just a few years ago.

WHITE-TAILED SEA EAGLE

With a fish in its talons, the white-tailed sea eagle *(Chaliaeetus albicilla)* set in motion hearty wing beats to lift it upward far above sea level to its nest to feed young eaglets. Wow! What an exhilarating encounter! Seeing that rare eagle in the wild was truly a twitcher.* (Photo by Jim Diamond of a white-tailed sea eagle near Portree on Isle of Skye, Scotland)

WHITE-TAILED SEA EAGLE

The cloudy overcast morning of 16 July 2011, our cruise ship *m/s Prinsendam* made a scheduled day stop at a scenic fishing village called Portree on the Isle of Skye, Scotland. Many passengers went on a three-hour chartered bus tour to see the famous Dunvegan Castle. Because my late wife, Betty, and I had seen enough castles during our world travels, we were not interested in seeing another.

So we did what we liked to do best! We got off the ship and slowly strolled around a picturesque fishing village to enjoy the ambience of small village life, window-shopped at small boutiques, and looked for a pub to sup an ale. When we found one, we went in, sat at a small table for two, and ordered two ales.

As we relaxed and enjoyed our ales, we struck up a very interesting conversation with local residents. For the price of two ales, we got a heartwarming life experience. Then we decided it was time to say goodbye to our new friends and trek back to the ship.

As we walked down a long ramp to board the dinghy to take us back to the ship, we saw a man and woman at a small table with a sign stating, "See a White-Tailed Sea Eagle by Boat." Having a strong interest in birdwatching, we stopped to ask about the white-tailed sea eagle. The man told us the white-tailed sea eagle was quite rare and in recent years it was nearly extinct.

I asked the gentleman, "Am I going to see a sea eagle?" He replied, "It's nature!"

I rebounded and said, "That's not what I asked." He said, "We see them most of the time."

I then asked, "What does that mean?" He finally said, "We see it 85 to 90 percent of the time." That was what I wanted to hear, so I purchased two tickets.

Choppy waves made the moored boat go up and down next to the dock. Because of Betty's disability, she was somewhat leery about getting into the boat, but I assured her that we would safely get her on board, which we did. The boat crossed choppy waters parallel to a high cliff separating the bay and the Atlantic Ocean. Our guide showed us a blown-up photograph of that high cliff and pointed to a tree on top of the northeast side of the cliff where a white-tailed sea eagle built a nest. I looked through my binoculars, and sure enough far away and very high I saw the tree and a speck of a nest just like he told us. Also in the nest, I saw a tiny figure of a sea eagle.

Bobbing up and down in the boat, our guide reached into a cooler and removed a small fish. He threw the fish in the air, and as it hit the water, a herring-gull grabbed and swallowed it. The guide threw two more fish into the water for a herring seagull encore. After some twenty minutes sitting quietly in a bobbing boat, our guide took another fish from the cooler, tossed it into the air and yelled, "Get your cameras ready!" A white-tailed sea-eagle was approaching with its head down, wings spread, and talons ready to grab a fish. As the sea eagle swiftly glided down on the starboard side of our boat, it grabbed a fish in its talons, then its hearty wingbeats lifted it up toward its nest.

Several wise leaders in the Republic of Finland set measures into action to protect the nearly extinct bird. Numbers of white-tailed sea eagles increased in Finland and nearby Scotland. What an exhilarating encounter! Seeing a wild rare white-tailed sea eagle was a "twitcher,*" which is a British term that is used when one gets so excited seeing a rare bird that they start to twitch.

PRELUDE: In Southern Poland near Krakow is a town called Wieliczka. This UNESCO World Heritage Site is where Wieliczka Salt Mine is located. It was opened in the thirteenth century to produce table salt and is considered one of the world's oldest salt mines. In 1996, salt mining was suspended because of flooding in the mine and low salt prices. It continued on a much smaller scale in continuous operation until 2007. After visiting Wieliczka Salt Mine in 2010, I was inspired to write this narrative titled "Salty Legend" to document the unique beauty of the mine's many statues and chapels carved into walls of rock salt by miners.

SALTY LEGEND

Generations of self-taught salt miners created an unusual subterranean art gallery on saline walls. (Photo by Jim Diamond of Joseph and Mary engraved on a salt wall in Wieliczka Salt Mine in Wieliczka, Poland, in 2010)

SALTY LEGEND

Visiting the Wieliczka Salt Mine in Wieliczka, Poland, was an awesome event. On our walking tour, we learned the mine is about 900 feet deep and roughly 178 miles long.

Rock salt looks much like unpolished granite with its many shades of grey. The Zupy Krakowskie Salt Mines company opened in the thirteenth century. Commercial mining was discontinued in 1996 due to low salt prices and mine flooding. It is considered to be one of the world's oldest salt mines. After rock salt was discovered, many shafts were dug over hundreds of years to enable miners to remove salt from the mine. The mine produced table salt continuously until 2007.

The mine attractions include dozens of statues and four chapels carved out of rock salt by the miners. The older sculptures were supplemented with new carvings made by contemporary artists. Each generation of miners working in the mine left its mark on the saline sidewalls.

It was incredibly fascinating that generations of self-taught salt miner artists created an unusual subterranean art gallery on the saline walls. The mine has always provided an inspiration to artists, who would go there in throngs to fulfill their inspiration for their artistic works. Their stay in the Wieliczka salt mine yielded views of sculptures, paintings and even literary works that conformed to the high standards of art.

The salt miner artists exhibited their skills, portraying their discriminated judgment and personal sensitivities. The Wieliczka Salt Mine is often referred to as the "Underground Salt Cathedral of Poland."

During the Nazi occupation, several thousand Jewish people were transported from forced labor camps to the Wieliczka Salt Mine to work in an underground armament factory set up by the Germans. However, manufacturing never began because the Soviet offensive was nearing. Some of the machines and equipment were disassembled, and the Jewish people were transported to factories in the Czech Republic and Austria.

I would like to close this narrative by declaring that the ancient Wieliczka Salt Mine, which was begun in the thirteenth century, is now a UNESCO World Heritage site. Seeing the carved religious scenes, sculptures and chapels by self-taught miner artists in that underground saline art gallery was an extraordinary life experience that I will cherish forever.

PRELUDE: Oscypek* (pronounced os-TSEH-peck) is a smoked cheese made from salted sheep's milk in the Tatra Mountains in the southern region of the Republic of Poland. Oscypek cheese is made by a supervising shepherd who is also a cheesemaker known as *baca* (pronounced bah-tsa). Oscypek is a popular traditional holiday cheese in several European countries. While traveling in southern Poland, my late wife, Betty, and I had departed Zakopane and headed north-northeast to cross the Tatra Mountains when I sighted a small roadside tent where a lady was selling what looked like brown bricks neatly stacked onto a table. Curious, we stopped to learn what she was selling. She gave us a phenomenal description of the cheese-making process, which inspired me to write this narrative titled "Smoked Oscypek Cheese."

SMOKED OSCYPEK CHEESE

We saw smoked Oscypek* cheese being sold along the road under a small tent north of Zakopane, Poland. I purchased only one spindle* of cheese to try. Whoa! What a tantalizing taste! I was dismayed that I had not purchased several pieces of smoked Oscypek cheese to ship back to Pennsylvania. (Photographer unknown)

SMOKED OSCYPEK CHEESE

On 2 May 2010, my late wife, Betty, and I visited the University of Podlasie, Shedlce, Poland, to attend the university's fiftieth anniversary celebration. During that event, my colleague Helen Nelson and I each were presented an award to acknowledge our well-merited friendship with the university.

After the festivities, Betty and I decided we were going to rent a car to visit sites throughout Poland we had not yet seen.

When Rector Antonio Jowke learned of our plans, he called me to his office and said, "I heard you are going to rent a car and tour Poland. I will give you a car and driver and have a professor guide you throughout Poland at no charge." Whoa! What a wonderful friendship gesture.

During our fabulous weeklong tour, Betty and I visited Zakopane in the Tatra Mountains, which is where the Polish Olympic Committee bid to host the 2006 Winter Olympics. Although Zakopane was one of six candidates, it failed to be short-listed. However, the town was a Polish centerpiece. In a horse-drawn carriage, Betty and I rode past gorgeously decorated mountain-style homes before approaching an outstanding ski slope. Polish mountains are ideal for skiing, especially alpine skiing, cross-country skiing and ski jumping.

One of the highlights of the trip was discovering smoked Oscypek* cheese. As Betty and I departed Zakopane, we observed a number of roadside kiosks featuring the cheese sold by shepherds. I found it appealing that the cheesemaker shepherds still wore the traditional clothing of the region: black felt hat, leather vest, shirt made of homespun flax and leather moccasins.

The shepherds explained to us their centuries-old traditional method of making smoked Oscypek cheese. They need a particular breed of sheep called Polish mountain sheep, a shepherd, apprentice shepherds, a small mountain hut with a hearth and pastureland where the sheep graze on fresh mountain grass.

During the sheep milking season of May to September, the apprentice shepherds rarely leave the mountains. They milk the ewes (female sheep) three times a day. After each milking, the unpasteurized* milk is poured through a linen cloth into a wooden bucket where dried rennet* is added. Next, the curdled, unpasteurized, salted sheep's milk is turned into cottage cheese, repeatedly rinsed with boiling water, and then the curds are squeezed to separate the whey.

Next, the shepherds formed a seven-to-nine-inch spindle*-shaped cheese by placing it on a wooden mold. Then it was dipped into a brine-filled barrel for a night or two before being placed under the hut's roof where it was smoked with a cold smoke from a small fire in the hut's hearth. After seven to fifteen days, the cheese was fully cured with its distinctive flavor and golden color.

Oh God, that smoked Oscypek cheese had its own scrumptious personality and tasted so delicious.

PRELUDE: Iceland's Blue Lagoon is a geothermal spa in southwestern Iceland that was founded in 1992 as a bathing facility. It is now known as one of the twenty-five wonders of the world. The spa is located in a lava field near Grindavík in front of Mount Þorbjörn on Reykjanes Peninsula in a location favorable for geothermal power.* Power is supplied by water used in nearby Svartsengi geothermal power station. Its bioactive seawater has attracted people from around the world because it is enriched with elements and minerals that are believed to have healing, nourishing effects on the skin. The water's milky blue shade is caused by a high content of silica. The silica forms soft white mud on the bottom of a lagoon that bathers rub on themselves. I was inspired to write this narrative titled "Iceland's Blue Lagoon" to document my observations during a visit to this facility in a land sculpted by forces of nature.

ICELAND'S BLUE LAGOON

The Blue Lagoon is a geothermal spa in southwestern Iceland. The spa is located in a lava field near Grindavík in front of Mount Þorbjörn on Reykjanes Peninsula, in a location favorable for geothermal power. It is supplied by water used in the nearby Svartsengi geothermal power station. The water's milky blue shade is caused by a high content of silica and blue-green algae in the water. (Photo by Jim Diamond of Iceland's Blue Lagoon on 20 September 2021)

ICELAND'S BLUE LAGOON

Iceland has a long history of using geothermal energy.* It has been used for heating buildings and for cooking, such as baking bread by burying it in the ground. Some Icelanders heat their homes by taking boiling hot water directly from the ground and pumping it into the radiators of their houses. The Svartsengi plant drills bore holes for boiling water around 392° Fahrenheit.

Because the Blue Lagoon water is full of dissolved minerals mixed with seawater, it is not suitable for direct use to warm up houses. The minerals would damage the pipes. Instead, the water is released into a nearby porous lava field, and then it is pumped to nearby urban areas.

Contrary to popular belief, the Blue Lagoon is not a natural hot spring. It is a pool created by a manmade structure over a volcanic hotspot. It is waste water from a power plant that is drilling for steam and hot water.

It has been reported that the water is completely clean and that it does not contain harmful chemicals, only natural minerals that have been proven to be very good for people's skin. From the power station, a new batch of superheated water renewed with minerals such as sulfur and silica flows into the lagoon every two days at 99 to 102° Fahrenheit, making sure it stays clean.

Wow! You can really smell the sulfur in the water. It's a strong odor that you have to get used to.

It's not known exactly why the water is so good for the skin. Some people believe it is due to the dissolved minerals in the water. Others think it's the blue-green algae that thrives in the water and a type of bacteria that is only found in the Blue Lagoon.

The algae purportedly is the reason for the water's milky blue color, but the lagoon has a more greenish tinge when the algae blooms on sunny days.

I would like to close this narrative with an Icelandic proverb: "It is better to see things one time than to hear about them 100 times." That was why I visited Iceland: I wanted to see it once because I was tired of hearing about it hundreds of times.

PRELUDE: The Icelandic horse is a small breed of horse developed in Iceland measuring twelve to fourteen hands* (fifty-two to fifty-six inches) tall. Even though the Icelandic horses are small, most horse registries for the Icelandic refer to them as horses instead of ponies, which are shorter than twelve hands tall at the withers.* Icelandic horses are long-lived and hardy. They suffer from few diseases, which is why Icelandic law prevents other horses from being imported into the country and exported animals are not allowed to return. According to the literature, selective breeding over the centuries developed the Icelandic horse into its current form. Natural breeding also played a role because the harsh Icelandic climate eliminates many horses through cold and starvation. As the only breed of horse in Iceland, Icelandic horses are popular internationally, and sizable populations of them exist in Europe and North America. The breed is used for traditional shepherding in Iceland as well as for leisure, racing and showing. I was inspired to write this narrative titled "Icelandic Horses" because of my animal science interests and the uniqueness of this breed.

ICELANDIC HORSES

It has been reported that the Icelandic horse (*Equus ferus caballus)* was developed from ponies taken to Iceland by Norse settlers in the ninth and tenth centuries. The Icelandic horse was the first breed of domestic animals created in Iceland. (Photo was provided compliments of the International Federation of Icelandic Horse Associations in 2021)

124

ICELANDIC HORSES

It has been reported that the Icelandic horse was the first breed of domestic animals created in Iceland. Today, the breed is represented by organizations in nineteen different nations, organized under a parent association, the International Federation of Icelandic Horse Associations.

Icelandic horses are long-lived and hardy. In Iceland, they have few diseases. They are the only horse breed found—in fact the only breed allowed—in Iceland.

In the winter, the Icelandic horse grows extensive hair. In the summer, they shed their winter coat, and they look completely different. The Icelandic horse is known for its ability to cross rough terrain, and they are also excellent swimmers.

The Agricultural Society of Iceland, along with the National Association of Riding Clubs, organizes regular shows with a wide variety of classes. Some horses are bred for slaughter with much of the *chevaline* (horse meat) being exported to Japan.

Most horses move in different ways, which are called "gaits." They naturally walk, trot,* gallop and canter (which is actually a variation of gallop), depending on how fast they need to move. The Icelandic horse moves in two additional gaits called "tolt" and "pace.*" Here are descriptions of these gaits.

Walk: It is a good rule to begin and end all horse riding with walking.

Trot: This is the most common gait around the world. When a person rides a horse in a trot, they will go up and down with each step. A good way to ride trot is to step strongly into the stirrup and move with the horse.

Canter/gallop: There is a small difference between the canter and the gallop, but most people consider them to be the same. This gait is common amongst other horses in the world, and it can be ridden both fast and slow.

Tölt: This is an additional gait that the Icelandic horse possesses. They are naturally able to Tölt from birth. It is a smoother, more comfortable gait than other gaits.

Pace: Also called "flying pace," this is the other gait unique to the Icelandic horse. It is a particularly popular gait in racing because the horses can reach an incredible speed. This gait can only be performed by five-gaited horses.

I would like to close this narrative with a popular quote among horse lovers in Iceland. It goes like this: "Let a horse whisper in your ear and breathe on your heart. You will never regret it."

Long live horses that love people, and long live people who love horses.

PRELUDE: The Republic of Iceland is a geological hotspot. It is one of the most active volcanic regions on planet Earth! In particular, the Reykjanes Peninsula is comprised of lava fields, geothermal waters, hot springs and lava caves. On Friday 19 March 2021, a volcanic eruption began in a valley called Geldingadalur, behind the Fagradalsfjall Mountain. That volcano has been dubbed the "tourist eruption" due to its location. It has a hiking approach on a rugged walking path that is manageable to the volcano. During my visit there, I elected not to hike it because of a physical issue and my age. However, I chartered a helicopter flight over the Fagradalsfyall Vocano to fulfill a lifelong yearning. In the helicopter, I got so close to the eruption site that I felt the heat of the magma. I marveled at the power within the Earth. I was inspired to write this narrative titled "Iceland's First Mantle Eruption" because I have seen several inactive volcanos and climbed a volcano in California, but that was the first time I saw an active volcano.

ICELAND'S FIRST MANTLE ERUPTION

On 19 September 2021 I boarded an Atlantsflug helicopter for an ultimate volcano tour. Whew! Flying in a helicopter over the Fagradalsfjall Volcano in Iceland was an exciting life experience. We saw the simmering, steaming crater, black flowing lava stream and a copious black lava field.(Photo by Jim Diamond of Fagradalsfjall volcano in Iceland on 19 September 2021

ICELAND'S FIRST MANTLE ERUPTION

Eruptions of the Fagradalsfjall Volcano on the Reykjanes Peninsula in Iceland were ongoing during my visit to the site. Lava pulses erupting from the vent alternated with quiet phases every twelve to sixteen hours. According to measurements reported by the Iceland University Department of Earth Sciences on the recent flow and chemical composition of the magma in the eruption in Fagradalsfjall, the lava flow had increased to forty-two feet per second.

The Fagradalsfjall Volcano eruption marks a turning point in geological history. It was the first mantle eruption of historical times. (The mantle is the main layer of the Earth that is always covered by the Earth's crust.) According to geoscientist Haraldur Sigurdsson, "The eruption was of great importance for geoscientists to view and study."

Fagradalsfjall Mountain is a tuya* that erupted during the last glaciation under the ice shield. A tuya is a flat-topped, steep-sided volcano that is formed when lava erupts through a thick glacier or ice sheet. Tuya are rare throughout the world, but recently this tuya occurred in Iceland's volcanic system. A tuya comprises an area of eruptive fissures, cones and lava fields found in the southern part of Iceland's Reykjanes Peninsula. A strong seismic crisis began in the area near Fagradalsfjall in late February 2021. It was elucidated as an intrusion of magma at a shallow depth, which led to Iceland's first historic mantle volcano eruption on 19 March 2021.

This volcano was unusual. Magma usually comes from the Earth's crust, but in this volcano, the magma came from ten to twelve miles below the crust with a lot of carbon dioxide, sulfur, high temperatures and low viscosity.

On 19 September 2021, I boarded an Atlantsflug helicopter at Reykjavik Domestic Airport for the ultimate volcano tour. Whew! What an exciting life experience. The tour lasted about 45 minutes. We saw the simmering, steaming crater, black flowing lava stream and copious black lava field.

The volcano eruption site is always changing due to increased gas pollution and the growing height of the crater, which makes it almost impossible to see into the crater from a safe spot on the ground. The best and safest way to see the volcano is from a helicopter flight over the eruption.

As we flew, the helicopter pilot pointed out parts of the volcano that we couldn't have seen from the ground, hiking to the site. He hovered over the top of the crater as it heavily expelled smoke and steam. The blackened lava covered a colossal area as it filled a wide valley with hot lava. The pilot explained that when the blackened lava crystalizes, the hot lava under it continues to flow.

During the helicopter flight, the power of nature was certainly evident. Many Icelanders fear that more eruptions will occur in the future. However, what we witnessed could have been the beginning of a quieting phase, and the volcano could possibly lay dormant for the next hundreds or even thousands of years. Or it could erupt every twelve hours!

I would like to close this narrative with a quote from an unknown author that goes like this: "Stay active. Keep your inner fire burning. It's okay to let off steam, go with the flow, be uplifting. It's all a matter of time. HAVE A BLAST."

PRELUDE: Iceland's mud pots, which are also called "mud pools" or "mud volcanoes," are a kind of hot spring or fumarole* with limited water causing bubbling pools with the consistency of mud or clay. Mud pots can be found in many places around the world, such as Yellowstone National Park in Wyoming, Lassen Volcanic National Park in California, and Rincón de la Vieja Volcano National Park in Costa Rica. I was inspired to write this narrative titled "Iceland's Mud Pots" because I was amazed that this bubbling phenomenon was a natural occurrence in certain parts of the world, and Iceland was one of those volcanic sites, exhibiting slurry mud pots for me to observe.

ICELAND'S MUD POTS

Viewing and sensing the bizarre mud pots made me feel that I was on an inharmonious planet. When I closed my eyes, I heard bubbling and smelled sulfur. (Photo by Jim Diamond of a mud pot in Iceland on 19 September 2021)

ICELAND'S MUD POTS

I found it interesting that Iceland's largest mud pot is known as Big Boiler. It has high-velocity steam and a temperature as high as 322 degrees Fahrenheit, making it the hottest hydrothermal mud pot on planet Earth.

A mud pot is a natural double boiler! Surface water collects in a shallow, impermeable depression where the soil is rich in volcanic ash, clay and other fine particulates and has no direct connection to an underground water flow. Thermal water beneath the depression causes steam to rise through the ground, heating the collected surface water.

A fumarole,* or steam vent, exists when a hydrothermal feature has so little water in its system that the water boils away before reaching the surface. Steam and other gases emerge from the feature's vent, sometimes hissing. Steam vents are often superheated with temperatures as high as 322° Fahrenheit. The thickness of the mud usually varies with seasonal changes in the water table. The mud in a mud pot becomes a viscous, bubbling slurry.

Viewing and sensing the bizarre mud pots made me feel I was on an incongruous planet. When I closed my eyes, I heard bubbling and smelled sulfur.

When I opened my eyes, steam from beneath the Earth's crust pushed mud slurry upward to the surface. I smelled even more sulfur. The assorted formations of the mud pots were common.

The mud pots' bizarre landscape contrasted with the conventional beautiful sights on planet Earth, creating in me a strange, creepy feeling. Yet it was exciting to sense the geothermal actions of Mother Nature.

I would like to close this narrative by expressing feelings I had while observing natural traits within Iceland's mud pots: I am an amateur author of narratives driven by passion, captured by obsession, fascinated by ability, enthralled with interpretation, filled with compassion, consumed with elegance, and astounded by inspiration. Thank you, dear reader, for acknowledging my thoughts, impressions, empathy and reasoning.

PRELUDE: While delving into Iceland's mysterious natural features, my sister Jane Ross and I came across Iceland's North American and Eurasian exposed tectonic plates. Iceland lies on the Mid-Atlantic Ridge, and it is split by the movements of the shifting tectonic plates. The plates are moving apart, one to the east, the other to the west, and both the North American and the Eurasian systems are slowly moving northwesterly across Iceland. Hence, Iceland is splitting along its spreading center between the North American and Eurasian plates. I was inspired to write this narrative titled "Iceland's North American and Eurasian Tectonic Plates" because of this awesome yet intimidating off-the-beaten-path sight for visitors to witness.

ICELAND'S NORTH AMERICAN AND EURASIAN TECTONIC PLATES

The tectonic plates whose turbulent interactions formed Iceland are the Eurasian Tectonic Plate on the left and the North American Tectonic Plate on the right. (Photo by Jim Diamond of Iceland's North American and Eurasian tectonic plates on 20 September 2021)

ICELAND'S NORTH AMERICAN AND EURASIAN PLATES

The tectonic plates whose turbulent interactions formed Iceland are the North American and Eurasian tectonic plates. Spanning the Mid-Atlantic Ridge, Iceland emerged as a result of a distinct spreading boundary between these two plates.

The North American and Eurasian plates are moving away from each other along the line of the Mid-Atlantic Ridge. The Mid-Atlantic Ridge, like other ocean ridge systems, was developed as a reaction of the opposite motion between the Eurasian and North American, and African and South American Plates.

Most tectonic plate boundaries are underwater, but at one place in Iceland, we can actually see above ground the two different tectonic plates from the Mid-Atlantic Ridge. Plate tectonics have shuffled the Earth's landmasses around and continue to carry forward. When two continental slabs collide, they buckle and form mountain ranges like the Alps.

A research team used a technique known as "nano-indentation"* to more accurately match the strength of the lab rocks to those found in the natural world. The nano-indentation experiments showed how the rocks that make up tectonic plates are weak enough to break and form new plate boundaries. The variability among previous calculations of rock strength depends on the volume of material being tested.

To determine this, nano-indentation experiments were used with a microscopic diamond stylus pressed into the surface of an olivine* crystal. These experiments reveal the strength of the crystal, which depends on the size of the indentation.

I would like to close this narrative with Iceland's motto: *Petta Reddast.* Translated, it means, "It will all work out okay."

We can have hope that it all will work out okay because researchers can make better predictions of the evolution of stresses on earthquake-generating faults, which likely depends on the size of the individual crystals that make up the rocks involved.

PRELUDE: Icelandic sheep have remained unchanged during thousands of years on the island country. The Icelandic breed of domestic sheep is a Northern European short-tailed sheep. It is larger than most breeds. It is thought that Icelandic sheep were introduced to Iceland by Vikings in the late ninth century or the early tenth century. In September, it is common to see farmers herding their sheep from the plateaus of Iceland after they grazed freely in the wilderness during the summer months. I was inspired to write this narrative because of my interest in sheep science and my experiences raising sheep, shearing sheep, selling tanned sheepskins, and marketing sheep blood for research by pharmaceutical companies. Raising sheep was an important component of the early years of my wonderful career, and I was interested in learning about Icelandic sheep management practices.

ROAMING ICELANDIC SHEEP

In early October shepherds begin the process of herding Icelandic sheep *(Ovis aries)* from the wild. Shepherds herd the sheep on country roads, riding trails, well-used paths, and sometimes even main roads to fenced corrals. In the corrals, the marked sheep are sorted to ensure rightful reclamation by the farmers.

(Photos provided by the Government of Iceland's Minister of Fisheries and Agriculture in 2021)

ROAMING ICELANDIC SHEEP

In Iceland, sheep numbers exceed 500,000. They are a quarter of the total Icelanic agricultural output. Icelandic sheep are not a fragment breed,* but rather they are a commercial production breed that can be raised and fattened on grass.

Icelandic sheep are "triple-purpose" sheep, which can be raised for meat, fiber and milk. In Iceland, the primary focus of sheep raising is for meat production, and Icelandic sheep produce gourmet-quality meat. They also yield a fleece known for popular yarn, the best fleece for felting and luxurious pelts that lead the worldwide market in price.

Icelandic sheep are hardy, medium-sized, with open faces, legs and udders. They are foragers on rangeland pastures during the summer and fed silage or hay during the long, cold Icelandic winters.

Rams are docile, but they can be aggressive and protective of their flock. Adult rams will breed sixty ewes,* and ram lambs will breed thirty ewes. Icelandic rams are extremely fertile and easily settle* their ewes.

After the lambing season, Icelandic ewes and lambs are housed for two weeks before they are released to fenced farmland for a couple weeks to adjust to the climate and diet. Then farmers open the gates to release the flock to freely spend the summer in the wild, grazing on Iceland's plateaus. Lambs are finished on pasture, not on grain. Yearling lambs will breed, and ewes (female sheep) can produce lambs until they are age thirteen or even older. Most ewes will produce twins in their second year of age and thereinafter.

Icelandic ewes are known for their milking ability. Their high milk production causes nursing lambs on good pasture to gain up to one pound per day. Either sex can be polled* or horned. Horned rams (male sheep) develop a full double curl horn, and horned ewes develop a backward sweeping half circle horn.

The ewes tend to guide their lambs to succulent grazing grounds to feed on seaweed, heather,* forbs* and other young sprouts. The sheep will forage over large wild areas to munch on natural feeds. This causes the lambs to gain a remarkable amount of weight. However, weather conditions can negatively impact vegetation and jeopardize the lambs' weight gains.

In early October, shepherds begin to herd the sheep back from the wild. Shepherds herd the sheep on country roads, riding trails, well-used paths, and even sometimes main roads back to a fenced corral. In the corral, the marked sheep are sorted to ensure rightful reclamation by the farmers.

Farmers mark their ewes and rams with three markings: a mark on the horn to refer to its province, a plastic ear tag to identify its district, and an earmark to identify the owning farmer. The annual sheep roundup is a festive social occasion. Flasks of spirits are passed around, and good friends gather to dance and sing as they rejoice in the year's production.

Icelandic sheep are free of pneumonia, foot rot and scappie*! Because it is forbidden to import sheep into Iceland, the Icelandic sheep is of one the purest breeds of sheep in the world.

I would like to close this narrative with an experience at the Food Cellar Restaurant in Reykjavik. I had for the main course the most flavorful, tender, juicy, sumptuous leg of lamb I ever tasted. Lamb is the "lobster tail of red meats." Mmmm good!

PRELUDE: Near the town of Laugarvatn, Iceland, my companions and I had the unique opportunity to watch bread being baked geothermally at the Laugarvatn spa—and then taste it. The bread is a favorite of the spa members. Our host invited us to accompany him on a short walk on the warm, black volcanic sand to the edge of a small lake where steam was rising from the water because heat from underground lava caused the water and sand mixture literally to boil. He then explained and demonstrated how to bake bread buried in the hot sand. I was inspired to write this narrative titled "Icelandic Rye Bread" because baking bread without a stove or kitchen was so extraordinarily different than how we bake bread in ovens in our kitchens in Pennsylvania.

ICELANDIC RYE BREAD

Bread still covered with tinfoil and plastic wrap.

Fresh rye bread being sliced after baking for twenty-four hours in boiling water heated by underground lava. It was Mmmm good!

(Photos by Jim Diamond of freshly baked Icelandic rye bread near Laugarvain, Iceland, on 17 September 2021)

ICELANDIC RYE BREAD

Baking a delicious loaf of bread in Iceland doesn't require a kitchen or even an oven. Iceland is a nation of volcanoes, underground lava and hot springs. The only necessities to transform raw dough into rye bread are a cooking vessel, a long-handled shovel and a hole in the sand exhibiting boiling water.

After a short walk with our host on wet black volcanic sand to the beach of a small steaming lake, I noticed a small cone-shaped mound of sand with a small rock on top. Our host told us to close our eyes and listen. Then he asked, "What do you hear?" Nearly all of us responded we heard boiling water.

At the steaming site where bread was being baked, our host removed the rock from the mound. He used a long-handled shovel to remove the black sand to the depth where the bread was located. We heard a clinking sound.

"There it is," our host said as he uncovered a large, stainless steel pot. He delicately lifted the pot out of the hole with his shovel, being careful not to touch the steaming hot metal with his bare hands. He put on a pair of gloves and opened the pot to show us the steaming rye bread. The loaf of rye bread weighed seven pounds. It was a gorgeous dark brown color and smelled so good.

The natural hot water "oven" had a temperature of 212 degrees Fahrenheit, which was warm enough to bake a loaf of bread in twenty-four hours. Our host informed us his recipe included four cups of rye flour, two cups of wheat flour, two cups of sugar, four teaspoons of baking powder, one quart of milk and a pinch of salt.

When our host carefully sliced the bread for us to sample, the final product appeared to have a cake-like texture. It was served with a healthy portion of butter and was surprisingly sweeter than I expected for rye bread. It was delightfully gratifying.

"You could make that delicious rye bread again," I told our host.

Our host said, "My mother, grandmother and distant kinfolk used this method of baking bread. A lot of the local Icelandic people do it here as well."

I would like to close this narrative with an Icelandic proverb that goes like this: "The generous and bold have the best lives." I found the Icelandic people to be both generous and bold as they shared their traditions and customs, such as baking bread in a black sand pit with geothermal heat, which resulted in contented, gleeful people. The Icelandic people seemed to be thrilled to share the thought-provoking, enthralling, interesting customs and traditions that are still practiced in their island country.

PRELUDE: Strokkur Geyser is a fountain geyser located in a geothermal area in southwest Iceland. It generally erupts every six to ten minutes to a height of fifty to sixty-five feet, sometimes up to 130 feet. A geyser is a spring characterized by an intermittent discharge of water ejected turbulently upward and accompanied by steam. Strokkur Geyser is one of a very few natural geysers that erupts frequently and reliably. Geysers are formed by peculiar groundwater hydrology conditions that exist in only a few places on Earth. All geysers are located near active volcanic areas. I was inspired to write this narrative titled "Iceland's Strokkur Geyser" because of its uniqueness and my close proximity to the geyser's vent. Hearing the sudden, brief eruption of pressurized water and steam when it was turbulently discharged through the vent sounded like an eerie hydrothermal explosion.

ICELAND'S STROKKUR GEYSER

All geysers are located near active volcanic areas, and geysers evolve because of their close proximity to super-hot magma. Strokkur Geyser is one of very few natural geysers that erupt frequently and reliably. (Photographer unknown)

ICELAND'S STROKKUR GEYSER

Strokkur Geyser was first mentioned in 1789, after an earthquake helped to unblock the conduit for the geyser. It continued to erupt until the turn of the twentieth century, when another earthquake blocked the conduit again. Our tour director Peter Maast informed us that in 1963 local people cleaned the blocked conduit and the geyser has been erupting regularly ever since.

All geysers are located near active volcanic areas, and a geyser evolves because of the close proximity of super-hot magma. Generally, surface water works its way down to an average depth of about 6,600 feet where it contacts hot rocks. Boiling pressurized water results in a geyser spraying hot water and steam out of the geyser's surface vent. Water from a geyser can be a blistering 200 degrees Fahrenheit, and the steam can be hotter than 350 degrees Fahrenheit.

Strokkur Geyser is located in Iceland's Haukadalur Valley. It was first discovered in 1294, making the "Geysir" the oldest known geyser on the planet. Hundreds of years later, the original spelling of the word geysir was changed to geyser.

Our guide Peter Maast explained that many of Iceland's geysers no longer erupt. Hot springs in Iceland are full of very hot geothermal waters that spout from vents in the Earth's surface. He said geysers in Iceland are a nature lover's overwhelming and astonishing thrill, but they can also be dangerous. Getting sprayed with very hot geothermal steam and water can produce one of the worst burns a person can experience.

I personally remained a safe distance from the geyser, yet still the experience of hearing and seeing the geyser erupt was indeed overwhelming and astonishing. I watched it erupt three times.

I would like to close this narrative with an Icelandic proverb titled "One Step at a Time." It goes like this: "Don't overwhelm yourself by taking on everything all at once. Just take one step at a time. This is one of the surest ways to make progress and get where you want to be in life."

Hearing the natural sound of a geyser's eruption, seeing the steam and water explode high into the air, and looking at its beauty was one of the many personal experiences that I had yearned to witness throughout my eighty-three-year-old life.

PRELUDE: In May 1973 after crossing the North Sea with our new Volvo car on a ferry to the Republic of the Netherlands, my late wife, Betty, and her parents, Bill and Mary Rohrman and I arrived in Amsterdam. We were ready for a break from our travels. We registered into two hotel rooms on the second floor. Climbing the long set of steps carrying our luggage seemed like we were ascending heaven. We found our rooms to be small but comfortable. After resting for a while, we decided to go for a walk to explore Amsterdam. WHOA! What a riveting, captivating, alluring walk that was both amusing and entertaining. I saw sights that this country farm boy had never before experienced. I was inspired to write this narrative titled "Red Light District in Amsterdam" because that was our first experience seeing such sights in an urban neighborhood.

RED LIGHT DISTRICT IN AMSTERDAM

To be frank, everything I had previously heard about the Red Light District was true. From brothels to sex shops to sex museums, the Amsterdam Red Light District had it all. Seeing it was *avant-garde,* (innovative, unconventional) and a phenomenal life experience for all four of us. (Photographer unknown)

RED LIGHT DISTRICT IN AMSTERDAM

Contrary to what people might think, the Amsterdam Red Light District had a very friendly atmosphere, and it wasn't as dangerous as I had heard it used to be. Amsterdam prides itself on liberal attitudes by welcoming people who might be involved in prostitution and pornography. Instead of criminalizing them, they respect the righteousness of it all. The name "Red Light District" comes from the red neon lights that highlighted the 300 windows where women were working. At the time of our visit, prostitution was legal in the Netherlands but not on the streets. Prostitutes in Amsterdam market their bodies by standing or sitting behind a window showcasing their private room. Since October 2000, window prostitutes have been allowed to legally offer their services. When a window curtain is closed, it indicates the girl has a customer.

Today, prostitutes in the Netherlands are also taxpayers. Because it is a legal profession, the government can ensure that all prostitutes are able to access medical care and work in better conditions by regulating and monitoring working practices and standards.

During our slow stroll about the streets of Amsterdam, honestly unbeknown to us, we lumbered into De Wallen, Amsterdam's main red light district that offered legal prostitution and a number of coffee shops. The concierge at our hotel had informed us that if we were interested, the best time to see excitement was after 11:00 p.m. Usually between 11:00 p.m. and 2:00 a.m., the district is swarming with people, and neon lights illuminate shadowy canals and streets.

We also learned that the Amsterdam Red Light District is not only about prostitution. One can find a variety of sex shops, peep shows, strip clubs, sex theaters, museum of prostitution and eroticism, and Dutch brown cafes.

We were advised not to take photos of occupied windows, to watch out for pick-pockets, to visit the district in a group, and not to buy from dealers. Remember that sex activities are not the only interesting attribute of Amsterdam.

Betty and her parents were lifelong Methodists, and I am a Presbyterian. As we walked in the Red Light District, our religious backgrounds kicked in and created ignominious feelings. Betty's mother started to giggle when she saw the girls sitting in the windows. Betty, her dad and I looked at the scenario around us as a form of amusement and a diversion from our Christian lifestyles.

Nevertheless, it was a once in a-life-time experience. I thank God what we experienced was not our way of enjoying life.

I would like to close this narrative with a quote from American author John Green that goes like this: "Some tourists think Amsterdam is a city of sin, but in truth, it is a city of freedom. And in freedom, most people find sin."

Amsterdam is truly a city of freedoms.

PRELUDE: The Kingdom of the Netherlands is a country located in northwestern Europe bordered by Germany, Belgium, and the North Sea. Holland is a region and former province on the western coast of the Netherlands. However, the name "Holland" is often used informally to refer to the entire country. Tulips (*Tulipa*) are the pride of the Netherlands, and flower lovers travel from many parts of the world to see Holland's hundreds of acres of tulips and to express their admiration for the radiance of tulip seasonal blooms. However, tulips originated in central Asia, and the tulip's name comes from the Persian word for turban because in full bloom tulips have a turban-like shape. I was inspired to write this narrative titled "Holland Tulips" because we were fortunate to see the astounding tulip blooms at their peak in early May 1973 near the town called Lisse. While at Lisse, we learned the famous Keukenhof Gardens were nearby. Oh my! What beauty!

HOLLAND TULIPS

Holland is known worldwide for its tulips. Whew! We got lucky and arrived near Lisse by chance where a plethora of tulip fields painted with vibrantly hued tulips was located in an outdoor wonderland. Oh my! What beauty! (Photo by Jim Diamond of a field of tulips near Lisse, Holland)

HOLLAND TULIPS

On our way home from Tchad, Africa, my late wife, Betty, and I flew to Sweden where we purchased a new Volvo sedan at the factory and met her parents who accompanied us during three weeks of European travels.

In early May, when we arrived in the Netherlands, by chance we drove into the town of Lisse and learned the famous Keukenhof Gardens were nearby. Netherlands produces around 90 percent of the world's tulips. Whew! We got lucky and arrived near Lisse where a plethora of tulip fields painted with vibrantly hued tulips were found in an outdoor wonderland. Oh my! What beauty!

Originally, growing tulips was a hobby of the wealthy. However, people of the middle class also began growing tulips to reflect their prosperity as well.

Tulips are in the same family as lilies and onions. Tulip bulbs should be planted in the fall, and they bloom in the early spring into summer. We learned from a signpost that the blossoming tulips were about ready to have their beautiful petals harvested. Removing the petals causes the bulbs to enlarge. Then the enlarged bulbs are harvested and sold to markets worldwide.

We also learned that the harvested petals were fed to dairy cattle. As we drove around the tulip fields, we noticed that some of the blossoms had already been harvested. We saw huge mounds of colorful tulip petals waiting to be fed to cattle.

Tulips often symbolize perfect and deep love because tulips are one of the first flowers to bloom in the spring. Tulips can also represent rebirth. We also learned that red tulips are the traditional symbol for eleven-year wedding anniversaries because they are represent devotion and love.

Other tulip colors exemplify other meanings. For instance, pink tulips symbolize happiness and confidence. Purple tulips symbolize royalty. Yellow tulips symbolize cheerful thoughts. White tulips symbolize forgiveness.

Holland is known worldwide for its tulips. Traditionally, the annual tulip season opens with a celebration of National Tulip Day in January in Amsterdam. On that day, tulip growers build an enormous tulip garden from the 3,000 different tulip varieties on Dam Square where people can pick a free bouquet of flowers.

I would like to end this narrative by quoting American author and spiritual leader Marianne Williamson, who once wrote: "A tulip doesn't strive to impress anyone. It does not struggle to be different from a rose. It does not have to. It is different! And there's room in the garden for every flower color." She was implying that it matters not people's skin color, language, religion, politics, or level of education. There is room for everyone.

PRELUDE: In December 1984, I was summoned to Rome, Italy, by the Food and Agricultural Organization of the United Nations (FAO) to meet with two officials to review a new concept for developing instructional materials for agricultural teachers, extension workers and farmers throughout the world. Our dear friends Bill and Judy Lindley hosted us at their Rome apartment. Judy was the perfect hostess and took my late wife, Betty, and me to sites in Rome that most tourists do not see, including the ruins of the Colosseum. What an experience! Imagining the Colosseum's rich history, I thought of the plethora of events that transpired in this facility, such as gladiator contests, animal hunts, group battles and executions. Being there witnessing the site and imagining all the excitement that once took place within that structure inspired me to write this narrative titled "Colosseum" to document my encounter with ancient history.

COLOSSEUM

To increase their popularity, emperors used the Colosseum to entertain the public with free gladiatorial contests that lasted from one to several days. These contests took on many forms, from animal hunts to group battles to one-on-one competitions. Additionally, the arena was the site of public executions. (Photo compliments of Dreamstime. Colosseum Rome stock photos are available royalty-free)

COLOSSEUM

Whew! When I was in Rome as a consultant for the FAO,* I walked past the Colosseum from my hotel to the international FAO office, carrying my briefcase. After dark, the Colosseum is lit with a beautiful, soft light.

To many visitors, the Colosseum is just the remains of an ancient structure. Although two-thirds of the Colosseum has been destroyed by vandalism, earthquakes and fires, when one visits the Colosseum, they step back into ancient times to study its loathsome, despicable history.

The Colosseum is an iconic landmark of Rome because it was used for entertainment for nearly 400 years. It has been estimated that some 400,000 people died within the walls of Rome's amphitheater. If those ancient bricks could talk, they could tell hundreds of blood-soaked facts and stories.

Nowadays, I spend my weekends watching baseball, soccer and football games on television in the comfort of my home. In ancient times, Romans spent their time watching gladiators—who were often slaves, criminals, ex-soldiers, prisoners of war and sometimes volunteers—fight to their bloody end. The stakes were extremely high in a gladiator battle. It was literally life or death.

Often the Colosseum was filled to its capacity of around 50,000 spectators. Seats were separated into sections, depending on one's social status—rich or poor. The better seats were given to wealthier spectators. There were no admission fees, and oftentimes free food was distributed during long events.

Gladiators were told the correct way to die—gracefully, with honor, showing no fear, and being brave to the very end. That was important to both the gladiators and spectators.

Not only gladiators were killed in the Colosseum arena. During the nearly 400 years, around one million animals died in a sport called *venatio* (hunting). Animals used for the hunts were exotic critters from other continents that spectators would never see otherwise, such as leopards, bears, tigers, hippopotamuses, wild boars, lions, crocodiles and elephants. Usually during the hunt, the animals were killed. But sometimes hunters were killed who did not have the strength of their animal opponent and were no match for such a wild animal,

Another way of using wild exotic animals was to execute convicted lower-class Roman citizens. This was called *estias* (prisoner alone in the arena with one or more vicious wild animals).

Even though the underground rooms were exposed, I wanted to experience where the gladiators and animals were kept and to sense what they must have felt while waiting for their fate.

I would like to close this narrative by citing Saint Florus, who once said, "Those who read about Rome get to know not only the history of one city but also about all of mankind."

PRELUDE: On 30 December 2007, we departed Christchurch, New Zealand, on Quantas Airlines for Sydney, Australia. On 31 December 2007, my late wife, Betty, and I dined with dearest friends Dave and Connie Kantner and George and Barbara Perry at the Restaurants of the Rocks next to a window overlooking Sydney's Darling Harbor Bridge to celebrate the arrival of the New Year. Wow! My longtime dream to spend time in Australia finally became a reality. To reserve this table for six, we had to book it eleven months in advance. The restaurant was an old warehouse that had been converted into an elegant restaurant. Pyrotechnic displays were electrifying events on New Year's Eve at midnight. The fireworks exploded off the arches, catwalk and roadway of the Harbor Bridge, including the Opera House, moored yachts, nearby city buildings, and up to eight barges evenly divided on both sides of the bridge. Seeing these fireworks was awesome, thrilling, and exciting! I was inspired to write this narrative titled "A Dream That Became a Reality" because I was so enthralled with this experience that I felt the need to document such an unforgettable event with my late wife and four magnificent friends.

A DREAM THAT BECAME A REALITY

The fondest life memories are made when gathered around a table with cherished and esteemed friends with kindred spirits. Sitting around the table in the Restaurant of the Rocks in Sydney, Australia, on New Year's Eve was an awesome memory. From left to right: Barbara Perry, Connie Kantner, Dave Kantner, Betty Diamond, Jim Diamond and George Perry

A DREAM THAT BECAME A REALITY

Because of my keen interest in sheep shearing and raising sheep, I hoped to one day travel to and study the Australian sheep industry. For many years, that was my fondest dream.

After waiting nearly a lifetime, my late wife, Betty, and our dear friends Dave and Connie Kantner and George and Barbara Perry and I finally arrived in Australia. After planning our trip for nearly a year, we finally arrived at Salville 2 Bond Street Hotel in Sydney, Australia, and together we began making memories.

Sitting around the table in the Restaurant of the Rocks on New Year's Eve 2007 with cherished friends with kindred spirits was an awesome memory. The cuisine was a delectable four-course gourmet menu. The sparkling wine was sensational. The dessert was luscious. The waiter was gentlemanly. The discussion was amicable, and most important, our friends were charming, dignified and gracious. We consumed a pleasing, tasteful meal with lifelong, loving friends.

Following our tasteful dining experiences, our fellow patrons kick-started the excitement for the approaching New Year's Eve celebration. Sydney's New Year Eve's celebration is always focused on an annual theme. The celebration is viewed by more than one million people surrounding the harbor, especially the midnight fireworks. The theme for the 2007/2008 fireworks that we observed in Sydney was "A Time of Our Lives."

Shortly before our arrival in Sydney in 2007, the bridge acted as a seventh barge for the first time, shooting fireworks throughout the display instead of just the beginning and finale. Sydney firework displays are enhanced by rope lighting displays on Harbor Bridge called the "bridge effect." Prior to our visit to Sydney, the bridge effect was designed by Brian Thomson to complement the fireworks. The rope lights were attached to a panel and truss system that showcased a variety of symbols related to the annual theme.

After the fireworks, as we walked amongst thousands of people back to Salville 2 Bond Street Hotel, the mood was festive and congenial.

The event's theme was certainly befitting for those six astonished Pennsylvania first-time travelers to Sydney, Australia. "A Time of Our lives" was without doubt a time of our lives.

PRELUDE: While traveling through Australia in 2008 with dear friends Dave and Connie Kantner and George and Barbara Perry, my late wife, Betty, and I were escorted into the state of New South Wales where we visited a roadside fruit stand. We learned New South Wales was one of the largest producers of sour (also called tart) cherries in Australia. Because George and Barbara Perry once owned a pick-your-own sour cherry orchard, they had a keen interest in Australian cherries. The cherries we observed looked mouth-watering and were nicely displayed. That type of cherries are commonly used in desserts, especially cherry pie and jam and of course wine. Cherries are packed with essential elements needed by the body, including antioxidants, vitamins, carbohydrates and minerals such as potassium, zinc, calcium, manganese, phosphorous and iron. I was inspired to write this narrative titled "Australian Sour Cherries" because I make sour cherry wine back home in Pennsylvania as a hobby. My sour cherry wine usually scores high at wine-tasting parties. I would have loved to have had twenty pounds of those Australian cherries shipped to the United States to make into my sour cherry wine.

AUSTRALIAN SOUR CHERRIES

Australian sour cherries *(Prunus cerasus)* are loved for their delicious flavor and ruby red color. They can be enjoyed in many ways every day. (Photo by Jim Diamond of Australian cherries yet to be picked to be sold at a roadside stand in 2008)

AUSTRALIAN SOUR CHERRIES

I learned that Australian sour cherries are grown in six states, with New South Wales, Victoria, and Tasmania being the three largest sour cherry growing states and South Australia ranking fourth. These four states export most of their cherries.

Both Western Australia and Queensland are small cherry growers. They focus their cherry sales on the East Coast domestic markets. However, a large percentage of their cherries are marketed to the local tourist trade through roadside stands like the one we visited. We were informed that cherries contain many antioxidants, but no fat or cholesterol. Furthermore, it was claimed that phytonutrients contained in cherries might offer protection against heart disease, reduce inflammation, and ease arthritis and gout pain.

Cherries are loved for their appealing flavor and ruby red color. They are enjoyed in many ways every day. They are perfect for a summer picnic, lunchbox treat, or snack while watching television or at family gatherings.

I like to serve guests glasses of chilled, homemade dry cherry wine prior to and during dinner. A sweetened sour cherry wine is especially enjoyable after dinner as a treat to satiate the appetite. Oh, how I yearned to have those beautiful Australian cherries to crush, ferment,* bottle, age and serve back at my home in Pennsylvania.

I would like to close this narrative by briefly describing the significance of cherry blossoms in Washington, DC. Many tourists travel to Washington, DC, to see the annual National Cherry Blossom Festival. Depending upon the weather, this event takes place between 20 March and 17 April.

The festival celebrates the 1912 gift of 3,000 cherry trees to Washington, DC, by the mayor of Tokyo. In Japanese culture, the significance of the cherry tree goes back hundreds of years. In Japan, the cherry blossom represents the fragility and beauty of life. It's a reminder that life is almost overwhelmingly beautiful, but it is also tragically short.

Much like the Japanese culture, a glass of aged, homemade sour cherry wine is overwhelmingly tasteful and beautiful, but it is tragically short because the bottle is quickly emptied.

PRELUDE: The Sydney Opera House is a multipurpose performing arts center in Sydney, Australia. Located on the banks of Sydney Harbor, it is widely regarded as one of the world's most distinctive buildings and a masterpiece of twentieth-century architecture. According to an expert evaluation report of UNESCO, "It stands by itself as one of the indisputable masterpieces of human creativity, not only in the twentieth century, but in the history of humankind." The building's design was entirely unlike anything that had been seen before. Pressures piled up on its architect, Jørn Utzon, who left Australia midway through construction and never returned to see the building completed. Nevertheless, Utzon's masterpiece redefined the image of Australia. It was an extraordinary work of art built for the performance of art and to bring together people who believe in the power of imagination. Seeing the opera house was an awesome and overwhelming experience, sensing the feeling of this aristocratic, creative structure. Because opera is my favorite music, I yearned to attend an opera performance in the Sydney Opera House. Unfortunately, there were no performances scheduled during our stay.

SYDNEY OPERA HOUSE

Since its official opening in 1973, the Sydney Opera House has been home to many of the world's finest artists, its most refined performances, and a proper meeting place for matters of local and international significance. (Photo by Jim Diamond of the Sydney Opera House while cruising in Sydney Harbor in 2008)

SYDNEY OPERA HOUSE

The Sydney Opera House sits on Bennelong Point, a former island in Sydney Harbor. In 1956, 233 designs were submitted for the opera house, and the design submitted by Jørn Utzon from Denmark was selected.

Construction began in 1959 and took fourteen years. Paul Robeson climbed the scaffolding and sang "Ol Man River" to the construction workers while they ate lunch. The final cost of the opera house was $102 million, which was paid for by a state lottery.

The opera house was opened by Queen Elizabeth II on 20 October 1973. In 2007, the Sydney Opera House was placed on UNESCO's World Heritage list.

When the Sydney Symphony Orchestra is performing on stage, the indoor temperature must be 72.5 degrees Fahrenheit to safeguard the tune of the instruments. The heating and air-conditioning in the opera house control the building's temperature by circulating seawater that is pumped directly from the harbor through twenty-two miles of pipes.

According to an expert evaluation report to the UNESCO World Heritage Committee in 2007, the Sydney Opera House stood alone as one of the indisputable masterpieces of human creativity in the twentieth century. The architecture of the opera house combines both ancient and modern structural influences. The site of the opera house was sacred to local Gadigal people for thousands of years.

Today, the opera house is one the most recognizable buildings in the world. The creativity of the architecture by Jørn Utzon yielded a building that was technologically far ahead of its time, which changed the image of an entire commonwealth.

Since its official opening in 1973, the Sydney Opera House has been home to many of the world's best artists, most refined performances, and a proper meeting place for matters of local and international significance. It is now Australia's number-one tourist destination, welcoming more than eight million visitors during recent years. It also has evolved into one of the world's busiest performing arts centers, presenting more than 2,000 shows 363 days a year. The breadth of those experiences reflects the Visionary 1961 Act, which obligates the opera house with the promotion of philosophy of art across all art forms and also "scientific research and encouragement of new forms of entertainment and methods of presentation." Furthermore, the flagship arts company is home to First Nations' arts culture, talks, ideas, theater, dance and the superstars of classical and contemporary music.

I would like to close this narrative by quoting the famous Greek singer Nana Mouskouri, who said, "One of the most wonderful memories in my life was when I sang at the opera house in Sydney. I will never forget; it is one of the most beautiful houses I have sung in."

I too will never forget having the opportunity to see such a beautiful opera house.

PRELUDE: New Zealand's most famous fjord* is called Milford Sound, which is located in the southwestern corner of the South Island. With dear friends Dave and Connie Kantner and George and Barbara Perry, my late wife, Betty, and I took a day cruise to the South Island's Fjordland. Most of New Zealand's Fjordland is dominated by the steep sides of the snow-capped Southern Alps, deep lakes, and its steep, glacier-carved and now ocean-flooded western valleys. I was inspired to write this narrative titled "New Zealand Fjords" because I was awestruck by their overwhelming natural beauty.

NEW ZEALAND FJORDS

New Zealand's fourteen fjords* are in the southwest of South Island. They were carved out of the mountains about 20,000 years ago by glaciers. When the ice melted, the Tasman Sea came in and filled the fjords. (Photo by Jim Diamond of Milford Fjord on Thursday 27 December 2007)

NEW ZEALAND FJORDS

According to *National Geographic* magazine, a fjord* is a deep, narrow, elongated sea with steep land on three sides. The opening toward the sea is called the mouth of the fjord, and it is often shallow. The fjord's inner part is called the sea bottom. If a geological formation is wider than it is long, it is not considered a fjord.

New Zealand's fourteen fjords are in the southwest South Island, where they were carved out of the mountains about 20,000 years ago by glaciers. When the ice melted, the Tasman Sea came in and filled the fjords. Because mounds of rock block some of the entrances, there is little flow of water between the sea and the fjords. However, many cruise ships navigate through the fjord to reach the Tasman Sea.

Even though it was raining nearly all day, our Milford Fjord voyage was thrilling, inspirational and sensational. Waterfalls enhanced the beauty of the fjords. (See photo.)

Our voyage on a boat named *Red Boat's Discover More* included a buffet lunch. The friendly staff gave us raincoats and encouraged us to go outside on the front deck in the rain to enjoy the sights.

The captain sailed the boat quite close to a waterfall, and the feeling of torrents of extremely cold water splashing down on me was quite memorable.

There are two permanent waterfalls in Milford Sound: Lady Bowen Falls (531 feet high) and Stirling Falls (508 feet high). The water in Milford Sound is a combination of salt water and fresh water. The top thirty-three feet of water is considered fresh water. The fresh water comes from the annual twenty-three to thirty feet of rain that empties into the sound via its many rivers and waterfalls. Under the fresh water at 869 feet deep, the sound's water is salty.

Milford Sound is so magical that famed British writer Rudyard Kipling called it the Unofficial Eighth Wonder of the World. In fact, of the many unofficial wonders of the world, seven of them are in New Zealand.

The seven unofficial wonders of New Zealand are Milford Sound, White Island, Fox and Franz Josef Glaciers, Poor Knights Island, Rotorua, Tongariro National Park, and All Blacks. These seven wonders have withstood the test of time, and they continue to leave many amazed with their magnificence.

New Zealand is covered by the Southern Alps running down the center of the island. Milford Sound has mountains too, but they jut straight from the Earth and tower 1,000 meters above the water. It's truly a staggering sight.

I would like to close this narrative by quoting English author Douglas Adams, who said, "Fjordland, a vast tract of mountainous terrain, is one of the most astounding pieces of land anywhere on God's Earth. One's first impulse while standing on a cliff top surveying it all is simply to burst into a spontaneous applause."

I personally felt the urge to applaud the beauty that was truly in the beholder's eye.

PRELUDE: The Republic of Honduras is located in Latin America bordered on the northwest by Guatemala, the southwest by El Salvador, and the south by Nicaragua. Coastlines include the Gulf of Fonseca between Nicaragua and El Salvador, and to the northeast by the Gulf of Honduras, a large inlet of the Caribbean Sea. Honduras is the home to many cultures. Probably the most well known are the Mayans, who dominated the land before the Spanish invasion in the sixteenth century. Spanish settlers introduced to the Mayans their Spanish customs, language and religion of Roman Catholicism. Honduras is a mountainous land with rainforests on the interior and on Caribbean and Pacific coastal plains where farmers grow coffee, tropical fruit and sugar cane. The capital is Tegucigalpa. During January 2009 and 2013, I had the privilege and joy of being part of two volunteer teams with Discovery Services Projects. We traveled to Honduras to carry on a series of projects at the Residential Home for Children located at San Buenaventura. That unique experience inspired me to write this narrative titled "Building a Greenhouse in Honduras" as a manifestation of my insight of this exclusive encounter with missionaries and the Honduran people.

BUILDING A GREENHOUSE IN HONDURAS

Within a short period of time, my Honduran colleagues and I decided to build a practical greenhouse, using indigenous* materials. But then the cost factor unfolded. We had little to no money to construct a greenhouse. No problem! (Photo by Jim Diamond of greenhouse construction at the Residential Home for Children located at San Buenaventura, Honduras, in January 2009)

BUILDING A GREENHOUSE IN HONDURAS

What a joy it was to be among eager volunteers who devoted strenuous labor to make life more enjoyable for sixty orphaned children. My mission was to recommend a process to introduce a horticultural unit into the curriculum for elementary schoolchildren up to grade six. Within a short period of time brainstorming with Honduran colleagues and missionaries, we decided to build a greenhouse using indigenous* materials so the children could learn practical horticultural skills.

Once the decision was made, the cost factor unfolded. We had little to no money budgeted to construct a greenhouse.

No problem! Nearby, we found an abandoned, aged concrete foundation that had been constructed for another purpose. For some unknown reason, eleven perpendicular pipes were buried on each side of the foundation, at least two feet deep.

Next, lying in tall grass, we found a pile of rusty rebar* left over from when the school had been built. Serendipitously, the diameter of the embedded pipe was the exact size for us to insert the rusty rebar to make the greenhouse hoops.

Putting the first end of each piece of rebar into the embedded pipes was easy. However, bending the rebar to fit into the embedded pipe on the opposite side was a difficult, laborious task. Four people together tugged on a rope to bend the eleven pieces of rebar to form the eleven hoops. On the positive side, those hoops will last forever!

Next, we purchased one-by-two-inch slats. We attached them lengthwise to stabilize each side of the hoops.

On top of the foundation, we attached second-hand aluminum roofing to the hoops to keep critters like goats, sheep and chickens out of the greenhouse. We closed the two ends of the greenhouse with wood boards with a door frame. We made Dutch doors* so only the top half could be opened for air circulation while the bottom half could be kept closed to keep critters from entering.

We covered the hoops with a plastic roof. Then we covered the floor with gravel.

By gravity, recycled water was piped from the cafeteria to the greenhouse. We filled raised beds, pots and old tires with soil in which to plant seeds.

The schoolteachers taught their students appropriate gardening skills to plant, grow and harvest the vegetables in the greenhouse. They also taught the children how to process and cook the vegetables for the orphanage cafeteria. The results were phenomenal!

No one could put a value on the outpouring of love, dedication and Christian endeavors that contributed toward improving the quality of life for those children at the Residential Home for Children at San Buenaventura, Honduras.

PRELUDE: On 11 October 2023, a beautiful autumn day, I took a walk. October is my favorite month of the year on our farm in Nockamixon Township, Bucks County, Pennsylvania. The sun's rays sprinkled onto towering trees of multicolored leaves as they lazily trickled downward to the understory covering the forest floor. Our fields and woodlands are truly "at the place of soft soil," as the Lenni Lenape Tribe would say. According to my friend the late Maurice Goddard, former Secretary of the Pennsylvania Department of Forest and Waters, settlers built cabins in the palisade forests on the river side of Bucks County. There was no organized township north of Tinicum at the time as settlers built cabins here and there in the woods as high up as the tributaries* (forks) of the Delaware River. I was inspired to write this narrative titled "At the Place of Soft Soil" because this farm has been an important part of my adult life for sixty-three years. I cherish its aesthetic assortment of gorgeous wildflowers, wildlife and towering trees and the relaxing sounds of the flowing Rapp Creek.

AT THE PLACE OF SOFT SOIL

"At the place of soft soil" at 120 Tabor Road, Ottsville, Pennsylvania. "I found it, I found it" near Ottsville, someplace far away in Upper Bucks County. We continue to be gratified that Ottsville is the address for our small farm in Pennsylvania.

AT THE PLACE OF SOFT SOIL

Country music artist Hal Ketchum wrote and recorded the song titled "Someplace Far Away." For me that song portrayed the "someplace" far away in Upper Bucks County that got me excited.

During the summer of 1961, when I found a home near Ottsville, Pennsylvania, I got to shout, "I found it!" My late wife, Betty, and I were gratified that Ottsville, in Nockamixon Township, would become our address at the small farm we did find seemingly someplace far away. At the time, Nockamixon Township seemed so far from Doylestown, Pennsylvania, where we had lived. Betty and I named our land Cedar Brook Farm because the acreage was masked with Eastern Red Cedar Trees, which is a common tree indigenous* to the area.

In 1738, when Tinicum was organized, a huge tract of land immediately north of it was left without local government. In 1727, the Durham ironworks was established even though there was no organized township north of Tinicum. In 1742, Nockamixon was organized by English-speaking settlers, and subsequently, German settlers overran the township. On the back of the petition to the court asking to have the township organized, a couple of English settlers wrote, "As rocks in Nockamixon meet the skies, so let this town Nockamixon rise."

Since 1727, although there was no organized township north of Tinicum, settlers had claimed land and built cabins in the woods as high up as the forks of the Delaware River. Settlers were generally found on the river side of Bucks County. The opening of Durham Road invited settlers to penetrate such a wilderness to settle in the woods near or along Rapp Creek in Nockamixon. Records indicate that some of the early English-speaking settlers included Richard Thatcher, Joseph Warford, William Morris, John Harwick, John Henry Hite, David Buckherd, Jacob Richards and Thomas Blair.

As the township became more established, villages expanded where larger numbers of people settled. Villages were named Harrow (located at the end of the river road, which was a regular stopping place for the Philadelphia and Easton stage coaches), Bucksville (one of the earliest villages founded in the township), Revere (Jacob Buck, Nockamixon tax collector, established the Sorrel Horse Inn in what would become Revere around 1800), and Kintnersville (the largest community in the township named for George Gintner (Kintner) who settled in Nockamixon in 1749 after serving in the Revolutionary War and entered the pottery business), and Narrowsville (a small hamlet at the lower end of the narrows on the Delaware River).

In 1784, the population of Nockamixon was 629, living in 116 dwellings. Sixty-three years ago, in 1960, my late wife, Betty, and I lived above the County Theater in Doylestown, Pennsylvania. It was our temporary living space until we decided which direction destiny would guide us. Being a farm boy, living in town was like living in a cage.

In January 1961, when I accepted a full-time teaching position at Delaware Valley University, we looked for a more permanent, rural living space. In July 1961, we experienced excitement, ecstasy and jubilation at discovering for sale a small farm secluded in a beautiful dell (wooded valley) near Ottsville, Pennsylvania. At the time, we were the only residents on Tabor Road, and that farm became our home and an agricultural production unit. I have often wondered if the early settlers in Nockamixon Township felt the same excitement and ecstasy as we did when we first saw it.

155

PRELUDE: While I served as the Dean of Agricultural and Environmental Sciences at Delaware Valley University (DVU), I traveled with Pennsylvania Secretary of Agriculture Dennis Wolff to Mexico to deliver and implant frozen Holstein embryos into several dairy cattle for two dairy farmers who lived south of Mexico City. Secretary Wolff was the owner of Pen-Col Farms and a fifth-generation Pennsylvania dairy farmer. In the 1980s, Secretary Wolff took Pen-Col Farms international and entered the world market for fresh and frozen bovine* embryos. The farm has since shipped embryos to more than thirty countries. The Pen-Col herd has received international accolades for their impact on the global Holstein breed. The DVU delegation accompanying me was composed of one Animal Science Professor and three undergraduate dairy science students. We observed a Mexican veterinarian implant five thawed embryos into four "primed" heifers and one cow on a dairy farm owned by our hosts Amando and Juan Schievenini. I was inspired to write this narrative titled "Frozen Embryos for Dairy Cattle" reflecting on Secretary Wolff's frozen embryo expertise and the knowledge I acquired about managing a Mexican dairy farm.

FROZEN EMBRYOS FOR DAIRY CATTLE

Embryo transfer for dairy cattle is the process of removing one or more embryos from the reproductive tract of a high-producing dairy cow sired by a superior bull. Embryo transfers are used to increase the number of offspring from genetically outstanding dairy cows and bulls to improve the offspring of surrogate cows, particularly heifer calves for replacement stock. (Photo compliments of Australian Broadcasting Corporation)

FROZEN EMBRYOS FOR DAIRY CATTLE

Embryo transfer for dairy cattle is the process of removing one or more embryos from the reproductive tract of a high-producing dairy cow sired by a superior bull. Embryo transfers are used to improve the genetic potential of offspring from genetically outstanding dairy cows and bulls, particularly heifer calves for replacement stock. Embryos are transferred to one or more genetically inferior surrogate cows.

It can offer a genetic advantage for Mexican dairy farmers to focus on their best genetics with sexed semen for breeding their domestic superior-end cows; or importing frozen sexed semen from the United States to produce desirable replacement heifers. In Mexico, there was a need for much improvement of the genetic capability of dairy cattle to increase milk quality and quantity.

The dairy farm we visited was perhaps one of the most advanced in Mexico. Our DVU delegation observed a Mexican veterinarian perform the implantation process of the thawed embryos into five heifers and one cow. We toured the dairy with co-owner Juan Schievenini, and he thoroughly described his Mexican dairy cow management practices. We learned that Schievenini's practices were somewhat different from those in the United States, especially the outdoor milking system.

After touring the farm's milk production facilities, we drove fifteen miles to a milk-processing unit. The Mexican milk tank trucks loaded milk from the farm milk tanks the same as we do at DVU here in Pennsylvania. Cool raw milk was trucked from the farm to a state-of-the-art processing plant where the milk was pasteurized* and homogenized.* Some of the milk was flavored. The milk was then bottled in glass bottles or paper cartons, and then transported to markets in the surrounding communities.

During our flight back to the United States, my companions and I landed at the San Antonio International Airport where we had to deplane, show our travel documents in customs, have our luggage inspected, and undergo an interview process.

Beforehand, I warned our delegation they were going to ask, "Were you on a farm in Mexico?"

I instructed them to say "yes!"

When an official began to interview us, I interrupted him and said, "Sir, we are all affiliated with an agricultural university in Pennsylvania. We were on a Mexican dairy farm delivering frozen cow embryos. I would appreciate it if you would please explain to these dairy science students why you are asking such questions to make this activity a learning opportunity."

I was very impressed with the airport official! He seemed to really appreciate being asked to describe the nature of his duty to the dairy science students. He carefully named all of the diseases he was attempting to prevent from entering the United States. When he asked everyone's permission to disinfect the bottoms of their shoes, he even explained why.

It was very informative. The airport official's geniality was superb. This quality discussion time at the airport was an educational highlight of our overall trip.

PRELUDE: As their name implies, the Guernsey breed of dairy cattle originated from the British Channel Island of Guernsey. Our dear friends Dave and Connie Kantner accompanied my late wife, Betty, and me to Guernsey island, which is the second-largest island in the English Channel some thirty miles west of Normandy, France. The island came to the attention of Robert the Magnificent, Duke of Normandy. He sent a group of militant monks to educate the natives on how to cultivate the soil and defend the land. The monks brought with them the best bloodlines of French Guernsey cattle. Around September 1840, Guernseys were introduced to America when Captain Belair of the *Schooner Pilot* brought three cows to the port of New York. Later, Captain Prince imported two Guernsey heifers and one bull from Guernsey Island. Those six original animals evolved into the popular Guernsey breed that is nationally known in the United States today. I was inspired to write this narrative titled "Guernsey Cow" because of my experiences with this dairy breed. I found them to be hardy in our climate and docile to handle. They are able to produce milk with high butterfat, protein and carotene, which gives their milk its golden color. Furthermore, the milk is rich in flavor.

GUERNSEY COW

According to the United Nations Food and Agriculture Organization, the Guernsey cow *(Bos taurus taurus)* originated from the British Channel Island of Guernsey. (Photo of a Guernsey cow compliments of the Livestock Conservancy, whose mission is to protect endangered livestock and poultry breeds from extinction)

GUERNSEY COW

The Guernsey breed is a medium-sized bovine.* It is orange/red and white in color. Many farmers that I know have said that the Guernsey is one of the easiest breeds to work with because of its amiable disposition. This dairy cow breed is also known for its rich-tasting milk!

Guernsey cows weigh an average of 1,200 pounds. They are known to live long lives, which enables them to produce milk for a longer period of time. When compared to other dairy breeds, Guernsey milk contains 12 percent more protein, 30 percent more cream, 33 percent more vitamin D, 25 percent more vitamin A and 15 percent more calcium.

In the 1930s, two private dairies on Guernsey Island processed milk from the 500 dairy farms on the island: Grove Dairy and the Farmers' Cooperative Dairy. In the late 1930s, both dairies were purchased by the Guernsey Island government, which merged them to form one central dairy.

While I was traipsing around Guernsey Island, I wondered what happened to the Guernsey cows when German forces occupied Guernsey Island during World War II. Before the Germans took control of Guernsey Island on 30 June 1940, nearly half of Guernsey Island's men, women and children were evacuated to England. Because the island then had a much smaller population requiring milk, the remaining farmers began trading individually. The Germans seized control of the milk supply on Guernsey Island, and they ordered the dairy farmers to stop trading cows. Instead, all milk produced on the island was to be sent to one central facility for processing. Even after Guernsey Island was liberated in 1945, milk continued to be processed by that central dairy.

During our delightful meandering around the mesmerizing Guernsey Island, I noticed a beautiful golden domestic goat in a lush green pasture. Being inquisitive about livestock because of my animal science background, I learned that the breed of goat was named the Guernsey goat for the Guernsey Island. The Guernsey goat is a rare dairy goat breed that originated on the Channel Islands off the coast of Britain. It has been reported feral goats flourished on Guernsey Island for about 200 hundred years, and as those feral goats mated to local Anglo-Nubian and Swiss breeds, that inaugurated the golden breed plus the other breed traits Guernsey goats exhibit today.

I would like to close this narrative by sharing a joke by my favorite television host and comedian the late Johnny Carson, who once said, "There was this billy goat at a movie studio who found and ate a can of film. When a nanny asked him how he liked it, he said, "It was all right, but I liked the book better." There was more fact to his joke than just humorous comedy. Goats eat almost anything. For example, two of their favorite foods are poison ivy and newspapers. Yum, yum!

PRELUDE: The Western honeybee, which is also known as the European honeybee *(Apis mellifera)* is the most common of the seven to twelve species of honeybee worldwide. The genus name *Apis* is Latin for "bee," and *mellifera* is Latin for "honey-bearing." *Apis mellifera* is known for their construction of beehives* from wax, the large size of their colonies, their surplus of honey production, and their storage of honey. Their hives are a prized foraging target of many wild animals, including honey badgers, bears, skunks, raccoons and possums, as well as people. I was inspired to write this narrative titled "Honeybees" because I have always been awestruck by their stewardship of the environment and the importance of their capability to pollinate food crops. It is well known that the scarcity of pollinators could endanger our ecosystem.*

HONEYBEES

Learn all you can about honeybees *(Apis mellifera)* before starting a hive. All beginning beekeepers should be able to say yes to these four questions: Are you ready to learn about beekeeping? Are you interested in raising bees? Do you want to raise bees? Does the idea of keeping bees intrigue you? (Photo by Jim Diamond of a beehive on his farm near Ottsville, Pennsylvania, in July 2014)

HONEYBEES

Each morning on our farm nestled in a valley near Ottsville, Pennsylvania, draws out the beauty of permanent pastures, a red barn and an old farmhouse that stirs the soul. This was no conventional farm with its hilly and rocky land, lots of wildflowers and shaggy paths that wiggle through the woodlot management syllabus. We even have the rippling Rapp Creek flowing with water collected from an Exceptional Value Watershed (waters of high quality). These attributes were powerful enough to motivate me to raise honeybees.

Are you considering beekeeping? Learn all you can about honeybees before starting a hive. All beginning beekeepers should be able to say yes to these four questions: Are you ready to learn about beekeeping? Interested in raising bees? Do you want to raise bees? Does the idea of keeping bees intrigue you? If the answers are yes to these four inquiries, select a competent instructor, buy an excellent bee book, and subscribe to periodicals that together will teach you the best management practices for beekeeping.

Make sure you learn and understand these topics: What beekeeping is all about, the benefits of keeping bees in a top bar hive and frame hives, how to make your own top bar hive, where to set up your apiary, how to manage bees in your hive, how to get your hive occupied with bees, how to extract beeswax, and how to make simple candles and beeswax polish. Furthermore you should have an interest in learning different ways to keep bees, in low-cost beekeeping, in producing high-quality bee products for sale or home consumption, in bees and the natural environment, in protecting honeybees, and in improving the quality biodiversity and the natural environment.

Honeybees are a vital link in growing fruit trees, ornamentals and other plants that need pollination.* Approximately one-third of all the food we eat is dependent upon pollination. Bees need a variety of flowering plants throughout the spring, summer and fall, and they mostly like to visit plants with small flower heads. Think Queen Ann's Lace, not tulips. Be sure nearby pesticides injurious to honeybees are not used when those flowers are in bloom.

In most seasons, honeybees produce up to 100 pounds of honey per hive. Honey can be sold at roadside stands, natural food stores, commercial grocery stores, and through mail order. Honey can be harvested fresh from the hive and consumed immediately.

Periodic hive inspections are necessary to ensure the colony's health, abundant food and a prolific queen. Furthermore, inspections are necessary to check for mites, disease, colony collapse disorder and other pesky disorders.

I would like to close this narrative by quoting Saint Francis de Sales, a Bishop of Geneva who is revered as a saint in the Catholic Church, who once stated, "The bee collects honey from flowers in such a way as to do the least damage or destruction to them and leaves them whole, undamaged and fresh, just as it found them. It would be wonderful if humankind could benefit from their environment without destruction and leave it behind just as they found it, undamaged for future generations."

PRELUDE: Agronomists* and horticulturalists* believe that pumpkins originated in North America around 9,000 years ago. The oldest pumpkin seeds have been found in Mexico. They date back to between 7000 and 5550 B.C.* Pumpkins and other kinds of squash have been an important food among Native American, African, Asian, Hispanic and European societies. One cup of one-inch cubes of pumpkin contains 30 calories and a good amount of the daily value of the following nutrients, 11 percent potassium, 2 percent carbohydrates, 3 percent magnesium, 5 percent vitamin B6, 4 percent iron, 2 percent calcium, 2 percent protein and 17 percent vitamin C. I was inspired to write this narrative titled "Pumpkins" because of my experiences while hosting a group of guests from the Republic of Mali, Africa, and two weeks later a group from the Republic of Tchad—both at a time when the pumpkin harvest was at its peak. When my guests visited farmers markets to see how pumpkins were sold, they were appalled that Americans spend money on purchasing nutritious, delicious food for Halloween decorations, then throw them away. They thought of the hundreds of thousands of people back in their home countries starving and their need for nutritious food.

PUMPKINS

Contrary to popular belief, pumpkins *(Cucurbita moschata)* are a fruit. The word "pumpkin" comes from the Greek word *pepon*, which means "large melon." (Photo by Jim Diamond of pumpkins and Halloween decorations on Tower Road near Ottsville, Pennsylvania, on 12 October 2022)

PUMPKINS

Native Americans grew and ate pumpkins and their seeds long before the pilgrims reached North America. Pumpkin was most likely served at the first Thanksgiving feast celebrated by pilgrims and Native Americans in 1621.

Pumpkins have been prepared in many ways, from soups to stews to desserts, since the immigration of the first European settlers. The earliest pumpkin pie made in America was quite different from the kind we enjoy today. Pilgrims and early settlers made pumpkin pie by hollowing out a pumpkin, filling the shell with milk, honey and spices, then baking it. The early settlers also dried pumpkins shells, cut them into strips, and wove the strips into mats.

Morton, Illinois, is the pumpkin capital of the world because 85 percent of the world's canned pumpkin is packed in the Nestles/Libby's plant located in the center of Morton. According to the Research Service of the U.S. Department of Agriculture, in 2020, Illinois increased its pumpkin acreage and leading position by 15,900 acres. However, Half Moon Bay, California, which is south of San Francisco, also claims to be the pumpkin capital of the world because farmers along the Half Moon Bay coastline produce more than 3,000 tons of pumpkins every year.

The Guiness World Record for the heaviest pumpkin belongs to Stefano Cutrupi of Peccioli, Italy, who grew a 2,702-pound-and-13.9-ounce pumpkin. Cutrupi's pumpin received confirmation from the Guinness World Records on 26 September 2021.

Annually, October 17 is recognized around the globe as the International Day of Poverty Eradication. Poverty does not discriminate; it affects people around the world. I wrote this narrative to expose how some societies waste food while hundreds of thousands of people suffer from hunger. Poverty entails more than the lack of income and productive resources to ensure sustainable livelihoods. It also includes hunger, malnutrition, limited access to education, social discrimination and lack of participation in decision-making.

In October 2019, I hosted a delegation of guests from the Republic of Mali, Africa, and two weeks later a delegation of guests from the Republic of Tchad to study American food production practices. My guests were astonished at how much food was produced on just one farm. When my guests visited local farmers' markets to see how pumpkins were sold, they were appalled that Americans would purchase nutritious, delicious pumpkins for Halloween decorations, then throw them away. Those pumpkins would be food in their home villages. When they thought of the hundreds of thousands of people back in their home countries starving and in dire need of food, they became angry that Americans were so wasteful.

I would like to close the narrative by saying poverty is overwhelming among 700 million people in global populations, which means they are surviving on less than $1.90 a day per person. The UN Ending Poverty One goal has been focused on ending poverty by 2030. To end poverty, we need policies and laws to allow everyone fair access to basic sanitation and food resources. Furthermore, Americans need to seriously curtail their food wastefulness, including decorative pumpkins. When my wife, Sue, bought a pumpkin, we would set it on the porch until Halloween, then bring it into our kitchen to cook into puree for soups and pies.

PRELUDE: Suffolk sheep originated in England within four counties: Suffolk, Essex, Norfolk and Kent. The breed evolved from crossing Old Norfolk ewes (female sheep) with improved Southdown rams (male sheep). Around 1859, the name Suffolk was adopted when the breed was first exhibited at a show held by the Suffolk Agricultural Society. In 1886, the breed was officially recognized by the Royal Agricultural Society of England. The Suffolk breed is unique because of its wool-less black head and legs. Suffolk sheep are small, hornless ruminants* with wool. I was inspired to write this narrative titled "Suffolk Sheep" because they were docile and hardy, they lambed easily and had good mothering instincts, and they were easier to shear than other breeds. Also, my late wife, Betty, and I liked their appearance.

SUFFOLK SHEEP

Suffolk sheep *(Ovis aries)* are raised for meat, fleece* and milk. Meat from younger sheep is called lamb, and meat from older sheep is called mutton. Occasionally, sheep are raised for their pelts, as dairy animals, and as science research animals. (Photo by Jim Diamond of one of his four-year-old Suffolk ewes nursing its lamb who was sired by R.L. Roe ram from St. Ansgar, Iowa)

SUFFOLK SHEEP

Sheep (*Ovis aries*) were one of the earliest animals to be domesticated for agrarian* purposes. Consequently, sheep are deeply entrenched in human culture, and they are represented within both modern language and symbology.*

A group of domestic sheep is called a flock. Domestic wool is harvested by shearing, and it is a widely used animal fiber. Beginning each shearing season from April to mid-June in eastern Pennsylvania, I sheared 2,000 sheep. That was how I paid my way through college. Over the years, working for various farms, I observed a plethora of management systems and learned much about the traits of various sheep breeds.

After my late wife, Betty, and I purchased our small farm, we decided to raise Suffolk sheep to supplement my income as an agricultural science teacher. We purchased a small farm flock of fifty to sixty purebred registered Suffolk ewes and one ram. We exposed our ewes to the ram in mid-September so our lambing season would be in mid-February to early March. (An ewe's gestation period lasts five months.)

Lambing season was always exciting and fun. Our goal each year was to have a 150 percent lamb crop, which means two lambs born to each ewe. We often surpassed that goal. Our small farm flock produced four commodities: Lambs for breeding and market, wool, tanned sheepskins, and blood, which we sold to pharmaceutical companies for research.

When we harvested our market lambs, we always got the hides back, salted the meat side, and transported them to a local tannery. Each year, we sold between fifty and sixty-five absolutely beautiful, tanned sheepskins. We developed a technique for bleeding one liter of blood from each of our forty-five to fifty mature ewes every eight weeks. With partners, we established a company named Lampire to market our blood to pharmaceutical companies for research. The combined income from breeding lambs and marketing lambs, wool, tanned sheepskins and blood, plus custom shearing I did made our sheep enterprise profitable. Betty was very instrumental in the success of our management system, especially during the busy lambing season.

Through experience, we learned that sheep have good hearing, and they are sensitive to noise, especially when being handled. Sheep have horizontal slit-shaped pupils. Because sheep have excellent peripheral vision, they can actually see behind themselves without turning their heads. However, sheep have poor depth perception, and shadows and slopes on the ground can cause sheep to shy away. Sheep tend to move from dark areas into well-lit areas. They also prefer to run uphill when being chased. One objection we had with the Suffolk breed was the scant fleece* weight, which averaged between six and seven pounds. Occasionally, a few black fibers were sprinkled throughout the fleece. Wool colors of domestic sheep range from pure white to dark brown, and they can be spotted. Because white fleeces are easily dyed, that is the preferred dominant trait, especially for large commercial markets. There is a niche market for colored fleeces for handspinning.

I would like to close this narrative by quoting Roman scholar and philosopher Marcus Tullius Cicero, who once said, "Every man can tell how many sheep he possesses, but not how many friends." Sheep are expendable, but friends are not. That's why it is important to know how many trustworthy, loyal, devoted friends one has come by during one's life.

PRELUDE: In 1961, the Northeast Chapter of the American Littoral* Society was founded by Dr. Lional A. Walford of the Sandy Hook Marine Lab to be a bridge between science and the public. Its mission is to serve members in New York state and New England to empower people to care for the Atlantic Ocean coast through programs focused on advocacy, education and conservation. The organization is headquartered in Broad Channel, Queens, adjacent to the Jamaica Bay Wildlife Refuge. It focuses on the protection, preservation and restoration of New York's urban wilderness along the Atlantic Ocean coast, including Cape May, Montauk, Sandy Hook, Assateague and others as needed.

AMERICAN LITTORAL SOCIETY

The American Littoral* Society Emblem reflects the public caring for and protecting the Atlantic Ocean coast. (Photo provided by American Littoral Society)

AMERICAN LITTORAL SOCIETY

Since 1961 the American Littoral* Society has empowered people to care for the Atlantic Ocean coast through advocacy, conservation and education. Members provide a voice for the coast, and they also give concerned citizens the knowledge and tools they need to raise their voices. When the society restores a habitat, such as restoring a dune or rebuilding an oyster reef, it also motivates people to take responsibility for a piece of the coast and become committed stewards.

The American Littoral Society promotes the study and conservation of marine life and habitat, protects the coast from harm, and empowers other people to do the same. The term "littoral" denotes the zone of a seashore between high and low tides or the zone near a lake shore with rooted vegetation.

Cornerstones of the American Littoral Society's efforts are managing and promoting New York State's participation in the annual International Coastal Cleanup and the Jamaica Bay Guardian program, which protects, preserves, and enhances the Jamaica Bay Estuary, which is one of the largest remaining areas of open space in New York City. It's an important urban oasis.

The society provides a plethora of activities for people and groups that are aimed at education, political, economic, and social institutions. Examples of the society's activities include:

- Discovering the diverse wildlife inhabiting the Atlantic Ocean coast
- Establishing buffers along a stream that contain wetland trees, shrubs, and native plants
- Defending a valuable diving spot off Fire Island from salvage for scrap iron (A wreck remains a popular dive site today.)
- Publishing *Fish and Man: Conflict in Atlantic Estuaries* to alert the public to the threat of water pollution to development
- Founding the volunteer fish-tagging program to enable fishermen to work with scientists
- Managing and protecting the largest all-volunteer fish-tagging program in the United States
- Restoring beaches
- Winging It, their summer bird walk
- Operation oyster
- Whale watch
- Salt marsh restoration of living shorelines

These activities are examples of how American Littoral Society volunteers promote the study and conservation of marine life and habitats, protect the Atlantic Ocean coast from harm, and empower other people to do the same.

I would like to close this narrative by quoting the title of a film *How to Let Go of the World (And Love All the Things Climate Can't Change)* by Josh Fox. With American Littoral Society volunteers, there are circumstances that climate warming just cannot alter.

167

PRELUDE: The Bucks County Conservation District Board of Directors work to educate and assist citizens and communities to look after the natural resources in their community, including soil, water, wildlife, trees and other plants. The Bucks County Conservation District was designated by the Pennsylvania Department of Environmental Protection to administer Chapter 102 (Erosion and Sediment Control) of PA Title 25 (Environmental Protection). This Pennsylvania law requires that anyone planning to do an activity that will result in 5,000 square feet or more of earth disturbance must present a written Erosion and Sedimentation Control Plan. I was inspired to write this narrative because I was once a member of the Conservation District Board of Directors.

BUCKS COUNTY CONSERVATION DISTRICT

Engineered plans must show erosion controls, which prevent soil particles from leaving the disturbed areas. (Photo provided compliments of Bucks County Conservation District)

168

BUCKS COUNTY CONSERVATION DISTRICT

Before and during 1961, it was determined soil resources and soil erosion were problems of public concern throughout all of Bucks County, Pennsylvania. To address the need for soil conservation, the Bucks County Conservation District (BCCD) was created in a resolution by the Bucks Commissioners on 24 April 1961. BCCD agricultural services were prioritized to prevent soil loss from agriculture practices over other needs.

During the past fifty or more years, a distinct non-agricultural metamorphosis in land use in Bucks County has occurred, yet erosion and soil loss are still the priority for BCCD. Commercial development in parts of the county causes serious negative soil erosion effects on society and the welfare of communities.

An Erosion and Sedimentation Plan review is required to approve a permit site compliance. This task has become a priority for BCCD. Still there remains a strong feeling of the board for agricultural cooperation and now development for both resource management and public education. Many Bucks County municipalities require developers to submit written plans to the BCCD for review for approval prior to issuance of any building permits.

Some municipal zoning ordinances require that a plan be submitted when an area of more than 1,000 square feet of earth disturbance is proposed. These engineered plans must include erosion controls, which prevent soil particles from leaving the disturbed areas. The district monitors environmental regulation by reviewing submitted plans and ensuring their adequacy.

Once a project is underway, it is the district's responsibility to inspect the construction site, provide written inspection reports if a site is found to be out of compliance with state law, and impose monetary penalties for violations. Even though BCCD does not enforce PA Code Title 25 Chapter 102, all Bucks County inquiries regarding stream obstructions and encroachments must be directed to the Pennsylvania Department of Environmental Protection Southeast Regional Office.

The services offered by BCCD include application for services, the dirt and gravel and low-volume road program, watershed management, watershed assessment reports, watershed improvement and riparian buffer programs, Paddle with a Purpose, remove water chestnut, spotted lanternfly, educational resources, agricultural conservation, and manure and nutrient management.

In addition to these BCCD responsibilities, many other programs have become part of the BCCD mission as allowed by Conservation District Law. The BCCD was formed as an agricultural assistance provider, but in recent years, it has expanded its role to include watershed management and protection as well as environmental education.

During the past sixty years, I have taken good care of my land by having soil conservation plan. I am a member of a forest stewardship program. I have an approved wildlife habitat. I preserved my land, and an exceptional value watershed flows through my farm. My father always said, "Buy land and take care of it because they are not making any more of it."

I would like to close this narrative by quoting Franklin D. Roosevelt who said, "The nation that destroys its soil destroys itself."

PRELUDE: Sometime around 1817, the first use of coke* in an iron furnace occurred at Isaac Meason's Plumsock Puddling Furnace in Fayette County, Pennsylvania, which is located within the county's Klondike Region. After that, Fayette County became a rich source of bituminous coal* for making coke. Coke was used as a fuel in smelting iron ore in blast furnaces. In the early 1880s, steel production became important in the United States, and coal mining and coke production formed the economic focal point for Fayette County. Coal was king! My father was a coal miner who had worked in various mines in both Fayette and Greene counties for forty-four years. He once told me, "I never want you to work in a coal mine." To this day, seventy years later, I have never even been in a coal mine. Coal mining was a very dangerous occupation, and the working conditions in coal mines were dreadfully unsafe. John L. Lewis, President of the United Mine Workers of America led union efforts that forced coal companies to implement improvements to working conditions that protected coal miners. Being a son of a coal miner and living in Fayette County where coal mining, strip mining,* and coke ovens were an integral component of the ecology that influenced my early life, I was inspired to write this narrative titled "Coke Ovens: Industrial Scars" to reflect memories of that godforsaken ecosystem.

COKE OVENS: INDUSTRIAL SCARS

In communities near where I grew up, scars of the coke* industry were everywhere. Crumbling remnants of coke ovens lie hidden under wild plants and tree overgrowth in close proximity to small coal mining patches* and towns. (Photo by Gary B. Fuess of coke ovens near Village of Shoaf, Fayette County, Pennsylvania, in 2013)

COKE OVENS: INDUSTRIAL SCARS

Millions of tons of bituminous coal* were burned in coke* ovens, which were also called beehive ovens, to make coke for the steel mills in Pittsburgh, Pennsylvania and other American communities. Bituminous coal was shoveled into brick coke ovens and burned at high temperatures with restricted oxygen, which converted it into a material called coke. Coke is grey, hard, porous and high in carbon.

Coke ovens were found throughout all of southwestern Pennsylvania near coal mining patches* such as Grey's Landing, Leckrone, High House, Continental #3, and Shoaf; at outskirts of towns like Brownsville, Uniontown, Smithfield, Masontown, Connellsville, and along the Monongahela River. Smoke containing a sulfurous pollutant was a horrible, filthy byproduct from burning bituminous coal in coke ovens.

That toxic smoke drifted over the homes in coal-mining villages, farms and urban areas. Entire populations were affected by the bituminous coal smoke from coke ovens. At night on the horizon, various shades of orange colors reflected burning coke ovens. For years, residents breathed hazardous coal smoke, resulting in severe black lung,* silicosis,* chronic obstruction pulmonary disease and other related health issues. In addition to the smoke, wastewater from making coke was highly toxic and carcinogenic.

After the coal was burned into coke, the coke was loaded from the ovens directly into railroad cars and shipped to mills where it was used to make steel to help build America.

In recent years, steel manufacturing in Pittsburgh dwindled, causing the coal and coke industries to dissipate. The coal industry in Fayette County wavered. Demand for coal was strong by coal-powered electric generation plants along the Monongahela River until recent years as U.S. government agencies mandated coal-powered electric generation plant closures and encouraged them to convert to natural gas.

In communities near where I grew up, scars of the coke industry are everywhere. Crumbling remnants of coke ovens lie hidden under wild plants and tree overgrowth. Many of the ovens were ruined by residents scavenging for brick to build walkways, driveways and buildings.

Despite coke oven scars, the historical coke-making legacy will live on to enlighten future generations of how pollutants affect societies and why Fayette County influenced the economic and industrial development of America. But because of the coke industry's demise in the Klondike region, coal is no longer king, leaving Fayette County wounded and scarred!

PRELUDE: An ice cave near Coudersport, Pennsylvania, is an underground cavity that paradoxically has summer ice deposits that melt in the winter. The cave is approximately forty feet deep, eight feet wide, and ten feet long. For several decades, the ice cave was open to the public, but it was closed in 1987. In 2013, new owners purchased the property, and they restored and reopened the facility. On 29 July 2021, I visited the ice cave. Even though the outside temperature was 81 degrees Fahrenheit, I could feel coolness from the ice that had formed inside the rocks. The ice I observed was clear, sparkled from lights and appeared in various shapes and forms. Inside the ice shaft, I saw huge icicles from one to three feet thick and from fifteen to twenty-five feet long. I was inspired to write this narrative because of the cave's eccentric, mysterious ability to form ice in the hot summer months that melts during the bitter cold winter months.

COUDERSPORT ICE CAVE

The Coudersport ice cave was discovered by prospectors searching for silver with divining rods. When the rods pointed to a likely silver node, the prospectors began digging. Although they didn't find any silver, they did discover this unusual subterrestrial seam of ice. (Photo by Jim Diamond of the Coudersport Ice Cave on 29 July 2021)

COUDERSPORT ICE CAVE

It might sound absurd to travel 241 miles from Ottsville, Pennsylvania, to Coudersport, Pennsylvania, to the Coudersport Ice Cave, but my personal desire had to be satisfied. Concurrently, my dear friends Roland and Valerie Duperron, who lived near the ice cave, accompanied me to view, study and gather data there.

The late John Dodd, lifetime Potter County farmer and landowner, had heard a plethora of stories about Native Americans carrying silver ore out of a mountainside cave in Sweden Valley east of Coudersport. Dodd went searching for silver ore with his farmhand Billy O'Neil, who knew how to use a divining rod. In 1894, prospectors speculated that rich deposits of silver were in the earth of the mountainous hills around Coudersport. Those silver prospectors had dreams of becoming wealthy.

When Dodd and O'Neil searched for silver ore with a divining rod, it pointed to a spot, indicating this might be the location of the wealth. The pair began digging vigorously. After much digging for silver, they came up empty-handed. However, they unintentionally discovered a subterrestrial seam of ice—the Coudersport Ice Cave.

In 1987, the owner closed the cave to the public, and sadly, the cave was dormant and neglected for more than twenty-five years. In 2014, Diana and Gary Buchsen purchased the ice cave, and they beautifully restored the viewing house, gift shop and grounds. The Buchsens promoted the uniqueness of the ice cave on television, websites, and the radio. Each year, the cave opens on Memorial Day and closes on Labor Day. Access to the cave is 10:00 a.m. to 6:00 p.m. Wednesdays through Sundays.

The Coudersport Ice Cave is believed to be the largest ice cave east of the Mississippi River and the coolest place in Pennsylvania in the summer. The shaft of ice is approximately forty feet deep, ten feet long, and eight feet wide.

The ice cave is a puzzling geological phenomenon. While standing on a viewing platform at the top of the ice cave peering into an atypical icy shaft, our escort informed us that the dynamics that drive this counterintuitive process are not yet fully understood. However, geologists and physicists are studying the cave to learn more about the natural phenomena at work.

The hypothesis for the origin of this cave states that from May to September cold air trapped in the rocks during the preceding winter comes in contact with warm percolating summer rains, forming ice during the hot months of the year. From October to late winter, the trapped warm air in the rocks from the preceding summer escapes and completely melts the ice. Our escort went on to say, "During frigid winter months, the annual cyclic icing process begins an encore."

I would like to close this narrative by quoting American writer Richard Bach who wrote, "The best way to pay for a lovely moment is to enjoy it." I truly enjoyed a lovely memorable moment at the Coudersport Ice Cave with two longtime friends.

PRELUDE: On my farm near Ottsville, Pennsylvania, I usually see daddy longlegs *(Opiliones)* during the summer. According to the literature, they are also known as harvestmen or harvesters. Their name daddy longlegs reflects their exceptionally long legs in comparison to their tiny body size. They are normally found in or near dark, moist places, and they eat decomposing vegetable and animal wastes. I was inspired to write this narrative because one day I observed a daddy longlegs walking on the railing on my deck. A little later, I observed another one crossing the sidewalk leading up to my deck. I was amazed how these long-legged creatures could navigate so elegantly, appearing stylish and dignified. I took its picture and decided to write this narrative because I was flabbergasted by the uniqueness of this harmless long-legged creature prancing around on my deck.

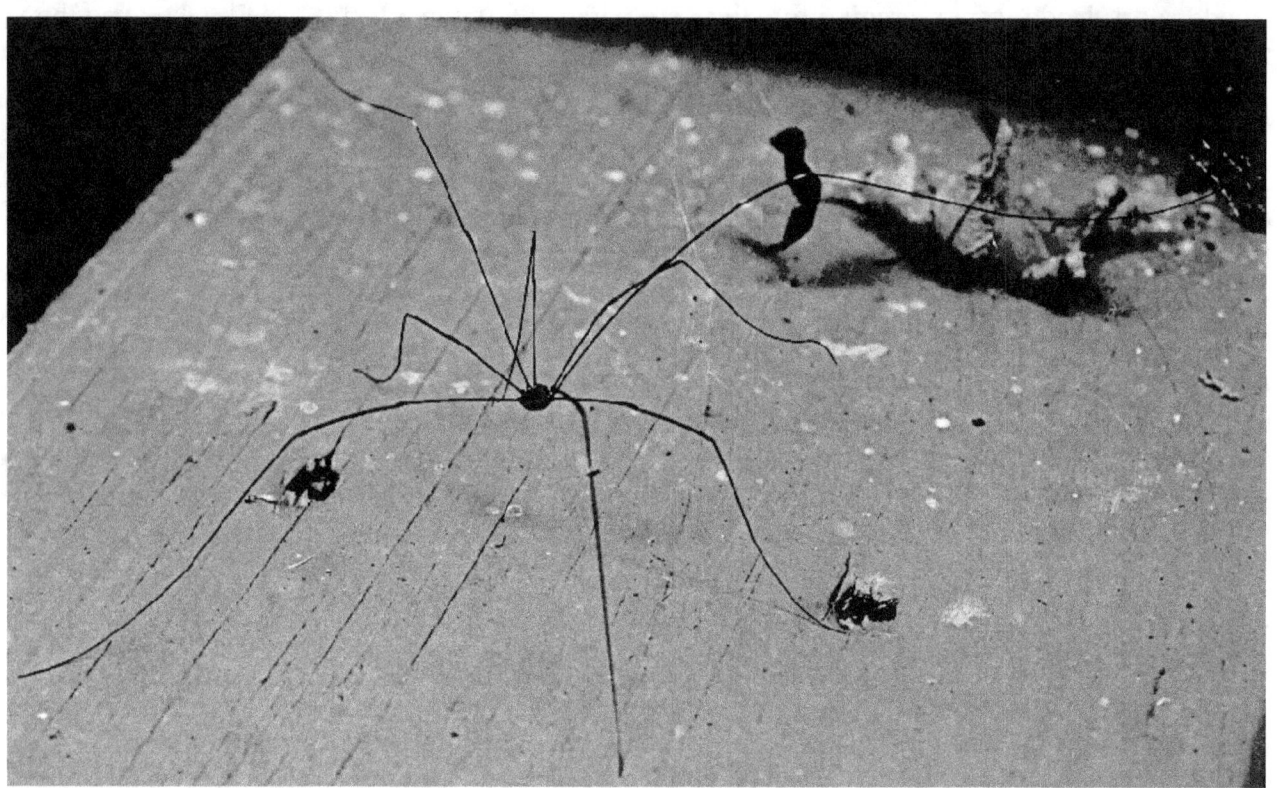

DADDY LONGLEGS

Daddy longlegs *(Opiliones)* are generally beneficial because they have a broad diet that includes spiders, earthworms, insects, insect eggs and plant pests such as aphids. (Photo by Jim Diamond of a daddy longlegs on a deck attached to the outside of his home near Ottsville, Pennsylvania, in July 2021)

DADDY LONGLEGS

Contrary to old wives' tales, leave these guys alone! These are the good guys. Unlike common household spiders, you should leave these guys alone if you spot them in your house. They are not poisonous to humans because their mouths are too small to penetrate human skin.

Daddy longlegs look like spiders, but technically they are not. Daddy longlegs are generally beneficial because they have a broad diet that includes spiders, earthworms, insects, insect eggs and plant pests like aphids. Furthermore, daddy longlegs scavenge for dead insects and decaying plant material, and they will eat bird droppings. They live in piled moist soil and dark places. Daddy longlegs are rarely found inside finished living spaces of homes. Chemical control is rarely needed to get rid of them.

Daddy longlegs have one pill-shaped body section, two eyes on a little bump, a segmented abdomen, eight long legs, and a different respiratory system.

Even though daddy longlegs are somewhat like true spiders, they do not produce silk, spin webs or capture prey. They also do not have venom glands, fangs or injectable toxins.

Daddy longlegs are ground-dwelling, outdoor creatures. Hundreds of daddy longlegs can be found in daunting clusters, and when they are disturbed, they scatter about confusing raiders.

A daddy longlegs' legs are designed to fall off so that they can escape predators*. A detached leg can twitch continually for up to an hour, distracting the predator while the daddy longlegs hobbles away on its remaining seven legs.

Although daddy longlegs are harmless annoyances, they lurk around homes and gardens in the spring and summer, especially in dark, damp places near water sources. That's why they are commonly found in basements, garages, and crawl spaces. Female daddy longlegs lay their eggs in moist soil, under stones, or in cracks in wood during the fall. The eggs hatch during the spring.

I would like to close this narrative by quoting American singer, songwriter and musician Bruce Springsteen, who sang, "Walk tall, or baby, don't walk at all."

PRELUDE: According to the United Stated Department of Agriculture (USDA), an adult deer tick *(Ixodes scapularis)*, which is sometimes called a black-legged tick, has eight dark brownish-black legs, brownish-black head and a spot behind its head called a dorsal shield. Ticks are external parasites that feed on the blood of mammals, birds and sometimes reptiles and amphibians. Most tick bites are painless and cause only minor signs and symptoms, such as a change in skin color, swelling, or a sore. I was inspired to write this narrative titled "Deer Tick" because in the wooded area of my farm, whitetail deer and deer ticks are quite common.

DEER TICK

Depending on their age, gender, species and fullness, adult deer ticks *(Ixodes scapularis)* are between three and five millimeters long. (Photograph of an adult deer tick provided by United States Department of Agriculture)

176

DEER TICK

There are several types of ticks in the United States. However, the ticks found more commonly in the Central and Eastern United States are deer ticks, dog ticks and Rocky Mountain wood ticks.

Some ticks require multiple molts* before reaching maturity over three years to reach full adulthood. Once a tick has reached maturity, its sole purpose is to reproduce. A male tick will die soon after mating.

Deer ticks are very small! Adult deer ticks are about the size of an apple seed, nymphs are about the size of a poppy seed, and larva are the size of a grain of sand—not much bigger than the period at the end of this sentence. Tick larva have three legs and translucent abdomens.

Deer ticks feed during three points in their lifespan: as larvae before they molt into nymphs, as nymphs before they molt into adults, and as adults before they lay eggs. Adult female deer ticks feed preferably on white-tail deer—and also on humans—in the spring and summer before they lay their eggs. While a tick is feeding, the color and size of its abdomen changes, becoming shades of yellow to dark bluish-grey. Also when ticks feed, they swell with blood, which can make them easier to spot.

Most tick bites are painless and cause only minor signs and symptoms, such as a change in skin color, swelling, or a sore. But some ticks transmit bacteria that cause Lyme disease and Rocky Mountain spotted fever in people.

Pennsylvania has one of the highest incidences of Lyme disease in the United States, likely because its climate and abundance of green space are hospitable to ticks and their white-tail deer hosts. To avoid Lyme disease, medical personnel recommend applying insect repellent while outdoors to protect from deer ticks. Also, people should check themselves and their children and pets for ticks after spending time outdoors.

Without treatment, Lyme disease can cause neurological conditions such as nerve pain, facial palsy and meningitis symptoms that include fever, stiff neck and severe headache.

Deer—or humans—provide a food source for adult ticks that meet their mates while feeding on blood. Female ticks produce up to 3,000 eggs. Entomologists claim that because of their small size, deer ticks are rarely found or eaten by predators* such as birds.

One day, my friend Lisa Sandler was explaining to me how to have a tick identified and tested for bacteria. Suddenly, I felt something itching. I looked at my right forearm, and WHOA, I saw a dog tick crawling amongst the hair. What a surprising coincidence! Lisa then demonstrated how to put the tick on scotch tape and send it off to a lab for testing.

I would like to end this narrative by quoting Dr. Kathleen Jones, Professor of Education specializing in Mathematics and Science at Juanita University. When I asked her what she thought of deer ticks, she said, "They are nasty little buggers!"

PRELUDE: At this writing, autumn in the Northern Hemisphere began on Wednesday, 22 September 2021 and ended on Tuesday 21 December 2021. Autumn is the season when duration of daylight becomes conspicuously shorter and temperatures considerably cooler. During early autumn, depending upon the species of trees, their leaves begin to change into shades of red, yellow, orange and brown. Leaves contain xanthophyll, which makes the leaves look yellow, and carotene, which makes the leaves look orange in late September and especially October when the leaves begin falling to the ground to form detritus.* I was inspired to write this narrative titled "Leaf Colors" because autumn is my favorite season. It is a time to rejoice in nature's artistic skills to paint exquisitely on the rolling countrysides.

LEAF COLORS

Nature's strokes of color beautify the countryside. Neither talented artists nor expensive cameras can replicate Mother Nature's elegance. Various parts of the Northeastern United States display vibrant displays of fall foliage colors. (Photo by Jim Diamond of fall foliage on trees in his woodlot management program in 2021)

LEAF COLORS

Nature's strokes of color beautify the countryside. Various parts of the Nnortheastern United States display vibrant fall foliage colors. Sadly, nature will take down her quilted beauty by dropping those gorgeous leaves onto the detritus* (forest floor). It seems odd that people get such delight from the annual death of those gorgeous leaves from deciduous* trees.

Unlike animals who can hibernate, migrate, or otherwise escape a harsh winter, plants cannot. Dormant naked trees must stay where they are rooted and adapt to natural conditions around them.

With all their dead leaves on the forest floor, trees will pose naked during the winter months. However, Mother Nature will cover the trees' nakedness periodically with blankets of white snow.

Snow also helps soil conserve moisture over the winter, and snow is a very good insulator against chilling temperatures that injure trees. Snow on the ground prevents injury to roots, which can't withstand extreme cold. Without snow, milder temperatures and the sun warm the soil, leading to damage by soil heaving, which can break roots and dry out plant parts.

Have you ever wondered why leaves change colors in the autumn and why some years they are more brilliant and last longer than others? Scientific environmental cues cause leaves to change out of their summer green color. Let's talk a bit about the science of leaf colors.

Chlorophyll is the pigment responsible for the green color in leaves. Sunlight energizes the process of photosynthesis; carbon dioxide enters the stomata*; and carbon combines the water to form carbohydrates (sugars and starches), water and oxygen is given off as gas for plant growth.

Carotenoids are leaf pigments responsible for orange and yellow colors in leaves in the autumn. They are actually present throughout the growing season but are camouflaged* with green chlorophyll. That is why plants that are stressed during the summer turn yellow. One type of these carotenoids is "xanthophyll" for yellow. Carotenoids are responsible for absorbing wavelengths of mainly blue-green and green light that chlorophyll doesn't. Trees with leaves that are mainly yellow, or yellow and orange, in the fall include sugar maple trees, hickory trees, beech trees, birch trees and tulip poplar trees.

Ideal conditions for fall color are an early moist growing season and a dry late summer and early fall, with sunny warm days and cool nights. Early in the summer, rain is beneficial for creating fall leaf color; however too much rain means more clouds and less sun, which spoils fall leaf color brilliancy. Cooler temperatures in late summer accompanied with plenty of sunshine often cause brighter leaf colors. Cool is good, but too cold (freezing) can kill leaves early.

I get nostalgic when I see the gorgeous beauty the trees on my farm display in the autumn. Watching sunshine flow onto the trees makes me think about life and hope for a future when our lifestyle is more peaceful and serene.

I would like to close this narrative with a quote from Scottish-born American naturalist John Muir, who once stated, "Nature's peace will flow into you as sunshine flows into trees."

PRELUDE: Air pollution is the presence of toxic chemicals or compounds, including those of biological origin, in the air we breathe. Compounds at levels not normally present naturally pose health risks to humans and animals. Furthermore, lower-quality air causes damage to the ozone layer and global warming. The Pennsylvania Constitution states that people have the right to clean air in Article 1 Section 27:

> The people have a right to clean air, pure water, and to the preservation of the natural, scenic, historic, and esthetic values of the environment. Pennsylvania's public natural resources are the common property of all the people, including generations yet to come. As trustee of these resources, the Commonwealth shall conserve and maintain them for the benefit of all the people. (May 18, 1971, P.L.769, J.R.3)

It has been reported that nearly 40 percent of Americans live in areas with unhealthy levels of smog, which is formed when industrial emissions from power plants, factories, cars and other sources react with heat and sunlight in the atmosphere. Smog is a hazy brown soup of pollution hanging over the skyline, especially in the warmer months. It is known more specifically as ground-level ozone. I was inspired to write this narrative titled "Protect the Air We All Share" because my first asthma* attack was caused by a succession of air pollutants in the Peoples Republic of China.

PROTECT THE AIR WE ALL SHARE

This aerial image is of the coal-fired Hatfield Ferry Power Station, located near Masontown just across the Monongahela River in Greene County, Pennsylvania. The Hatfield Ferry Power Station was one of thirteen plants that Duke Energy's Fayette Energy Facility sold after announcing that earnings in the power generation market had been weak. (Photographer unknown)

PROTECT THE AIR WE ALL SHARE

Residents of Masontown, Pennsylvania, and surrounding communities (including my father) complained about the yellow smoke pouring from the chimneys of the nearby coal-fired Hatfield's Ferry Power Station, which left a yellowish film on their cars, homes and crops.

The Hatfield Ferry plant violated the Clean Water Act 33 times since 2006. For those violations, the company paid less than $26,000. During that same period, the plant's parent company earned $1.1 billion. Five states sued the plant's owner, Allegheny Energy, claiming air pollution was causing respiratory diseases and acid rain.* Allegheny Energy installed scrubbers to clean the plant's air emissions. The scrubbers sprayed water and chemicals through the plant's chimneys, trapping pollutants before they escaped into the air.

After the scrubbers were installed, each day Allegheny Energy dumped thousands of gallons of wastewater into the Monongahela River containing chemicals from the scrubbing process. The Monongahela River provided tens of thousands of people with drinking water and flowed into Pittsburgh. Now instead of breathing the poisonous pollutants, the residents had to drink them.

The situation in Pennsylvania was far from unique. According to a *New York Times* analysis of the Environmental Protection Agency (EPA), as an increased number of coal-burning power plants across the nation reduced their air emissions, many of them created their water pollution, going into lakes, rivers and landfills. Power plants are the nation's boundless producer of toxic wastes.

As the number of scrubbers across the United States increased, environmentalists became increasingly worried. The EPA projected that roughly 50 percent of coal-generated electricity in the United States will come from plants that use scrubbers or similar technologies, creating vast sources of polluted wastewater.

For instance, according to EPA records, only one in forty-three power plants across the nation limits how much barium they dump into nearby waterways. Barium has been linked to heart problems and diseases in other organs. State officials placed no limits on water discharges of arsenic, aluminum, boron, chromium, manganese, nickel, or other chemicals that have been linked to health risks, all of which have been detected in plant wastewater samples.

While I was working in China, I observed a fine dust on the horizon coming from the Gobi Desert. Outside, the smog was incredibly thick. I sat all day in meetings where other people smoked cigarettes, so I breathed in secondhand smoke. One evening on a train, I was suddenly unable to breathe, and I didn't know why. The toxic brew of secondhand cigarette smoke, fine dust from the desert, and smog from industrialized cities had triggered my first asthma* attack.

I would like to close this narrative quoting former President Barack Obama, who visited a plant making solar panels and said, "Here at this site, Solyndra expects to make enough solar panels each year to generate 500 megawatts of electricity. And over the lifetime of this expanded facility, that could be like replacing as many as eight coal-fired power plants." Former President Obama's vision aligned with my concept that our future electric power will be a combination of solar, wind, tidal, and to some extent atomic energy.

PRELUDE: Wood is a renewable source of energy from the sun that is stored in trees as they grow. When we burn firewood, the stored energy is being released. When we release such energy in a blazing fire in a wood stove or hearth during a cold winter day, the warmth resembles a bit of calm summer sun in the house. I was inspired to write this narrative titled "Releasing the Sun's Energy" because I truly enjoy the warmth and coziness of a blazing fire in my wood stove on cold, uncomfortable days while reading a good book or playing cards with dear friends.

RELEASING THE SUN'S ENERGY

Burning wood releases carbon dioxide (CO_2), which trees absorb as they grow. This is the cause of global warming. (Photo by Jim Diamond of cut, split and stacked ash firewood in an enclosed woodshed, in March 2022 for the 2023 winter months)

RELEASING THE SUN'S ENERGY

Firewood contains energy from the sun, which was stored by the tree as it grows. When burning wood, the stored energy is released as heat. When firewood burns, it releases carbon dioxide (CO2) like the fossil fuels oil, natural gas and coal. However, as young trees grow, they absorb and recycle carbon dioxide. So it can be said that burning wood warms inhabitants, not the globe.

I am a member of a forest stewardship program. One day, a forester who was marking mature trees for a timber sale informed me that if I could replace the BTUs* released from burning a cord* of firewood with the same number of BTUs released from burning a fossil fuel such as fuel oil, I would save $500.

Each year, I burn four to five cords of wood. When a storm interrupts the electrical source to homes, barns and businesses, the conventional systems that rely on electricity are useless. The heat pump falls silent, the oil furnace won't work, the milking machines won't milk, water cannot be pumped from the well, and lights won't turn on; however, the wood stove will enable one to cook and keep residents warm, cozy and safe.

In the winter, one of life's small pleasures is coming indoors from a freezing snowstorm, standing near a fiercely burning wood fire, and rubbing your hands together. That warmth quickly warms the innermost self. Similarly, in an evening after an exciting afternoon of cross-country skiing, a soft glowing wood fire is a cherished backdrop for a friendly conversation with gathered friends and family relaxing, talking, and laughing in comfort. Gazing into the fire, your imagination is free to flee from the harsh cold world outside to the depths of the innermost self. It is very possible you will find solace in the flames.

One type of firewood is kiln-dried firewood, which is the most efficient wood you can buy and is great for heating a home. However it is more expensive than other types of wood. It is made by placing green wood in a kiln at a temperature of 160 to 200 degrees Fahrenheit, until the moisture content of the logs is below 25 percent. Kiln-dried wood is exceptionally light. It contains no bugs, mold, or fungus. It creates no creosote buildup, and it leaves little ash.

Naturally seasoned firewood is wood that's been split and then stored properly for twelve months to allow the pieces to dry. It typically has a moisture content of less than 40 percent. Seasoned wood loses its color and bark. It has no mold or fungus. It has cracks on the ends, and it makes a crackling noise when two pieces are struck together.

Hardwoods such as maple, oak, ash, birch and most fruit trees are the best burning woods that give a hotter, longer burn time. These woods have the least pitch and sap, and so they are generally cleaner to handle.

Nevertheless, in many areas, dry firewood is the cheapest heating fuel one can use to warm the innermost self. Because I burn wood in my wood stove, when I walk through the woods and see a dead tree, I see valuable firewood. A forester once told me, "A dead tree in the forest is just as important as a live one."

PRELUDE: A solar panel is an assembly of photovoltaic (PV) cells mounted in a framework for installation. Solar panels use sunlight to generate direct current electricity.* A collection of PV modules is called a PV panel, and a system of PV panels is called an array. Arrays of a PV system supply solar electricity to electrical equipment and appliances. According to the US Department of Energy Solar Energy's Technologies Office and the National Renewable Energy Laboratory, by 2035, solar energy could account for as much as 40 percent of the nation's electricity supply. I was inspired to write this narrative titled "Solar Energy" because I believe this alternative carbon-free electrical energy source will supply homes and businesses across the United States.

SOLAR ENERGY

It has been projected that by 2050, ground-based solar technologies will require a maximum land area equivalent to 0.05 percent of the contiguous United States surface area. (Photographer unknown)

SOLAR ENERGY

The members of the United Nations have indicated that global climate change refers to long-term shifts in temperatures and weather patterns. In some cases, these shifts might be natural; however, since the 1800s, human activities have been the main cause of climate change, hastening it through the burning of fossil fuels such as coal, oil and natural gas, which produce heat-trapping carbon dioxide (CO2).

It has been claimed that 95 percent decarbonization of the electric grid can be achieved by the year 2035. Furthermore, studies indicate that decarbonization of the electric grid can become a reality without increasing electricity prices because decarbonization and electrification costs are fully offset by savings from technological improvements and flexibility of demand.

Electrification of fuel-based homes, businesses, motorized vehicles, and industrial processes will reduce emissions. It has been projected that by 2050, ground-based solar technologies will require a maximum land area equivalent to 0.05 percent of the contiguous United States surface area.

This requirement could be met by using disturbed or contaminated lands unsuitable for agriculture. For example, when I was a boy growing up in Fayette County in southwestern Pennsylvania, thousands of acres of land were disturbed to extract bituminous coal* and natural gas. On my father's farm, 300 acres were disturbed by strip-mining coal. Furthermore, sulphur water from the mining and stripping coal sites was not potable and unsafe for livestock to drink. It caused major fish kills and was unsuitable for agriculture production. I never knew what a freshwater stream with fish was like until I settled in eastern Pennsylvania. Such disturbed land could be used for ground-based solar panels.

In a recent issue of *Lancaster Farming* weekly news, farmers expressed concerns that electric companies should not place ground-based solar panels on high-producing class 1 or class 2 farmland. Using such prime farmland would be detrimental to Pennsylvania's number one industry. Many land areas in Pennsylvania that were disturbed and/or contaminated can be used for ground-based panels,

With continued technological advances, electricity prices should not increase through 2035. Achieving decarbonization will require significant acceleration of clean energy deployment, which will employ more than 500,000 people in solar jobs by 2035. Challenges must be addressed so that solar costs and benefits are distributed equitably. Land availability should not constrain solar deployment use if Class 1 and class 2 lands is kept to a minimum.

I would like to close this narrative by quoting American technologist Ramez Naam, who said, "Solar power is going to be absolutely essential to meeting growing energy demands while staving off climate change." Personally, I am of the opinion that the time has arrived where we must heed Naam's thinking by relying upon solar, wind and tide energy to assist humankind in curbing global climate change.

PRELUDE: It seems to me that humans, plants, animals, fish, sun, day, moon, night, air, wind, water, time, and the four cardinal directions all have a symbiotic relationship that supports life forms to exist on the planet Earth. All living organisms have their respective characteristics and functions as they relate to order, sensitivity (response to stimuli), adaption, growth, reproduction, regulation and energy. Each of these traits are holistic components in a definition of life. I was inspired to write this narrative because these traits are a given; there are no access charges or fees. Everyone was born with access to systematic symbiotic relationships to survive an existence within the environment provided.

SYMBIOTIC RELATIONSHIPS

The sun is the center of the solar system and the source of all life and energy here on Earth. Since the beginning of history, human have understood the sun's importance to our world, its seasons, the diurnal cycle,* and the life cycle of plants. (Photo by Jim Diamond of a sunrise in Alaska in 1998)

SYMBIOTIC RELATIONSHIPS

Symbiosis can be defined as the intimate living together of two or more dissimilar organisms in a mutually beneficial relationship. In other words, organisms that depend upon each other to survive.

When I look out my window, I see a plethora of tall trees on a steep hillside. On many trees, green lichens* grow, usually on the north side of each tree. Lichens on trees are a good example of a symbiotic relationship. Lichens are slow-growing plants that typically grow on trees, rocks and stone walls. These plants growing on trees consist of a fungus, which contains photosynthetic algae cells. They get both their water and nutrients from the air and energy from the sun, and so the symbiotic components are tree, fungus, algae, air, water and sun.

According to a Buddhist saying, "You cannot hide the sun, moon or truth." The sun is the center of the solar system and the source of all life and energy here on Earth. Since the beginning of history, humans have understood the sun's importance to our world, its seasons, the diurnal cycle,* and the life cycle of plants and animals.

The moon is the brightest and largest object in our night sky; it moderates the Earth's wobble that leads to a relatively stable climate, causes tides, and creates a rhythm that has guided humans for thousands of years. An essential truth is not a thought, an idea, a reaction, or an action; its most important characteristic is that it is an ontological presence. Like the sun and moon, it has a substantive existence.

The four cardinal directions are north, south, east and west. North always points to the North Pole, and south points to the South Pole. Directions can represent the four stages of life (birth, youth, adult, death); the four seasons of each year (spring, summer, winter, fall), the four aspects of life (spiritual, emotional, intellectual, physical).

Air is a mixture of gases in the Earth's atmosphere, consisting of oxygen, nitrogen, carbon dioxide and small amounts of other gases. This gaseous mixture is a component of the symbiotic relationships for both fauna and flora* on Earth. A day is the time it takes the sun to move around the Earth, and night occurs when the moon or clouds cover the sun. Humankind is always under the same sky, looking at the same moon and same sun.

According to Webster's New Collegiate Dictionary, four is defined as "something having four units" as it relates to quantitative measurements, which reflect systematic relationships. Now I need to ask, "Why are there four stages of life, four seasons, four cardinal directions and four gaseous components in air?"

I would like to end this narrative by quoting American artist and author Gloria Vanderbilt, who once said, "I love to think that animals and humans and plants and fishes and trees and stars and the moon are all connected."

What do you think?

PRELUDE: People worldwide need a climate that ensures their communities are tolerable for personal health and well-being. Forests throughout Nockamixon Township, Bucks County, Pennsylvania and countries around the world absorb and store carbon monoxide from the atmosphere. They cleanse our water supplies, provide shade, produce edible fruits, create beautiful countrysides, and provide lumber, wildlife habitats and many other useful benefits to humankind. Protecting our forests by replanting trees implements approved woodland management practices that symbolize humankind's commitment to protecting the significant benefits which trees provide for rural countrysides and urban communities. I was inspired to write this narrative titled "Trees: The Necessities of Life" because I have managed my forty-acre woodlot to prevent erosion and provide shade for livestock, which is considered the best use of classes three and four land. A forester selectively marked mature trees for harvesting. Furthermore, we provide wildlife habitat while simultaneously cleansing the water and air in my community.

TREES: THE NECESSITIES OF LIFE

A good stewardship of land includes sustainable, active management by minimizing soil disturbance, maintaining an open overstory canopy with a dense understory, leaving many desirable big tree species, maintaining existing water resources and protecting wetlands and riparian zones. (Photo by Jim Diamond of his woodlot before a selective harvest of timber to open the canopy in 2009)

TREES: THE NECESSITIES OF LIFE

With many global challenges within splintered and in some cases fractured societies around the world, I believe there is nothing impassioned, sincere, caring people can entirely agree on that significantly impacts our broken world except planting trees.

I am compelled to be a good steward of my land by sustainably, actively managing it. My management goals include minimizing soil disturbance, maintaining an open overstory canopy with a dense understory, leaving many desirable mature seed tree species, generating periodic income from timber production, maintaining existing water resources, protecting wetlands and riparian zones, and promoting vegetation that displays attractive wildflowers.

Most of the soil on our forty acres is woodland—except for an eight-acre hayfield. The hayfield is incorporated with Klinesville Croton very channery silt loam,* the wooded acreage is extremely stony Lansdale silt loam, and the southwestern corner of the farm is Croton silt loam.

A field of corn has to be harvested after five to six months of growth. A woodlot has to be harvested after 50 to 100 years of growth, hence, our woodlot is considered to be a productive part of our farm (timber, wildlife, clean water, clean air and soil stabilization). The species of trees which are favored include sugar maple, red maple, red oak, white oak, hickory, chestnut oak, walnut and wild cherry. In 2009, harvesting my trees enhanced the overall health of our woodlot. Harvesting trees is the best way to prevent an invasion of internal or external insects and diseases.

A plethora of tree species live around the world with individual traits, such as bark design and color, hardness of wood, leaf shape and color plus appearance, flowers and fruits. Like trees, people live all around the world, each with individual traits, such as skin color, language, religion, government, interests and skills.

Regardless of humankind differences, planting a tree is a cordial, nonviolent, unwarlike task nearly all societies do in peaceful unison. Regardless of individual traits, trees should be protected by community citizens adopting acceptable policies and regulations that will protect environmental, scenic and economic benefits of trees.

I would like to close this narrative by saying that trees are humankind's inheritance from previous generations, and hopefully they will be our legacy to future generations. Long live the trees for future eras. They are necessities for peaceful, secure, happy lives of humans around the world.

PRELUDE: A child has two adoring grandmothers. Traditionally, grandmothers are warmhearted people with a unique mixture of love, wisdom, laughter, kindness, praise, respect, friendship, and happiness who cherishes each grandchild. Barbara Cage, known for her quotes on love, marriage, mothers, and daughters said, "A grandma is warm hugs and sweet memories. She remembers all of your accomplishments and forgets all of your mistakes." This photograph reflects an extraordinarily happy grandmother making life-long memories sitting on a chair outdoors with a contented smile on her face holding her happily sleeping first granddaughter. I was inspired to write this narrative titled "A Happy Grandmother" because it was such a pleasant experience to observe a grandmother's genuine happiness and contentment.

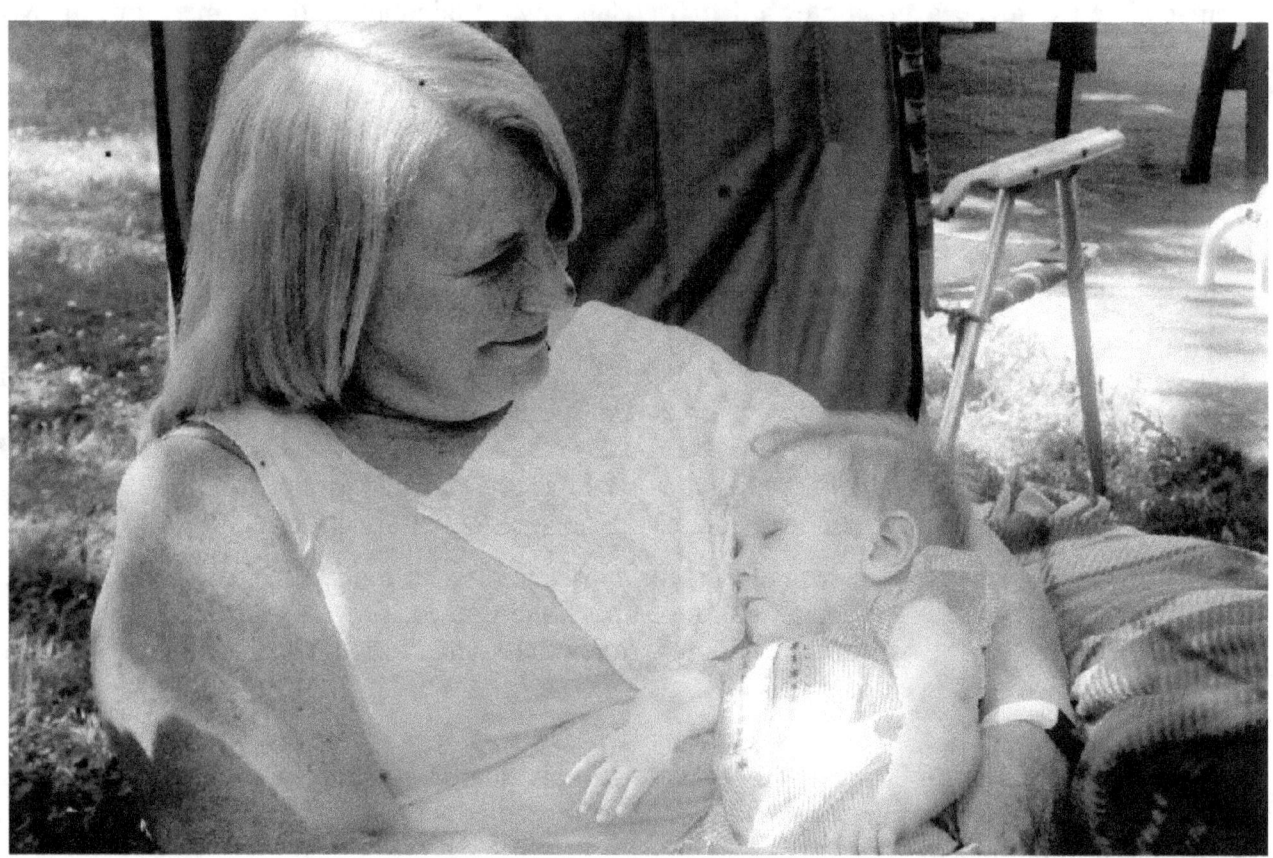

A HAPPY GRANDMOTHER

A grandmother is a remarkable woman. Grandma SaraJane Hamilton dispenses a superfluity of hugs, love, laughter and respect. (Photo by Jim Diamond of a happy grandmother at Plumsteadville Grange Farm Market, Plumsteadville, Pennsylvania, on 13 July 2019)

A HAPPY GRANDMOTHER

SaraJane Hamilton is a remarkable grandmother who dispenses a superfluity of hugs, kisses, love, laughter and respect. SaraJane recalled that when her daughter Kaitlyn informed her she was pregnant, "All I could do was cry with happiness. It is so special seeing your daughter have a baby. She is still your baby, no matter how old she is."

SaraJane's first granddaughter, Lorelei Gilbert, was born a triplet. Her sisters, Evelyn and Layla, lived for two days before being called home to be with God. Grandmother Hamilton said, "God was felicitous by allowing me to hold Evelyn and Layla before they left us."

When Lorelai was born prematurely in October 2018, instead of her expected birth month of January 2019, she weighed only one pound, two ounces. One of my greatest joys was watching her grow to eleven pounds while in the hospital. Since Lorelei was released from the hospital, she has grown normally. Today, Lorelei is a happy, healthy child, and when she smiles, all of the people around her melt with happiness.

SaraJane said, "There are no rules for grandmas: My job is to spoil her. There is nothing better than holding my first grandchild."

A lot of family and friends watch Lorelei grow who yearn to spend time with this bundle of love. Family and friends have said that Lorelei fills an empty space in their hearts where they did not realize such emptiness existed.

Grandchildren quickly learn that a grandmother is a devoted friend who provides them with wisdom and security. SaraJane is a grandmother who has ears that listen, arms that hug, and a heart that gives an unending supply of love. SaraJane's body and facial expressions in the photo reflect how Lorelei is an awesome blessing to her grandmother's life.

As Lorelei has grown from infancy (birth to age one), toddler years (two to three years), and childhood (four to eight years) and will grow into puberty (nine to thirteen), older adolescence (fourteen to eighteen years), and adulthood (beginning at age nineteen), Grandma SaraJane will hold her tender hand. Regardless which life stage Lorelei is in, Grandma's love for Lorelei will forever be deeply embedded in her heart.

PRELUDE: A centenarian is a person 100 years old and older. According to Iscovich Reports on 2 June 2021, out of the 7.8 billion people in the world, there are only about 316,600 centenarians living. That's 0.004 percent of the population. It is estimated that this age group will grow to almost 3.7 million by 2050. In 2022, the life expectancy of women was 75.6 years and of men was 70.8 years. I was inspired to write this narrative titled "Centenarians" because I was invited to attend the 100th birthday party for my long-time friend H. Calvin Weikel. What a joyful experience. Calvin immediately recognized me and called me by my name. He was great! With Calvin's enthusiastic personality and sharp memory, a stranger would not have believed he was 100 years old. I have been blessed to know Calvin, his dear wife and their wonderful children for more than fifty years.

CENTENARIANS

This photo of my longtime cherished friends H. Calvin Weikel and his wonderful wife, Doris, was taken at Calvin's 100th birthday party at the Plumsteadville Grange on 16 October 2022. They were surrounded by a plethora of friends and relatives who came to wish him a happy, healthy birthday. (Photo provided by David Weikel)

CENTENARIANS

People who reach the age of 100 are called "centenarians." Those who reach 110 years of age are known as super-centenarians. Most centenarians lived heathier longer than their peers. Often they didn't experience any serious disease or disability until they reached 90 years of age. According to a 2015 study by Ash et al, 25 percent of centenarians reached the age of 100 with no serious chronic illnesses, such as depression, osteoporosis, heart disease, respiratory illness and dementia. Centenarians are more likely to experience a rapid terminal decline very late in life, meaning that for most of their adulthood and even older adult years, they were relatively healthy when compared with other older adults.

According to Guinness World Records in 2016, Jeanne Louise Calment was the longest living person at 122 years and 164 days old. She was born in 21 February 1875 and died 4 August 1997 in Aries, France.

Longer life spans tend to run in families, which suggests that genetics, lifestyle, or both play an important role in longevity. Brothers and sisters of centenarians typically also lived long lives, and they are more likely to remain healthy longer than their peers. At age seventy, people with centenarian parents are less likely to have the age-related diseases that are common among older adults.

Scientists who study centenarians have found that centenarians have healthy lifestyles, do not smoke, maintain a healthy weight and cope well with stress. Because of their healthy habits, these older adults are less likely to develop age-related chronic diseases such as high blood pressure, heart disease, cancer and diabetes, than their same-age peers.

On 16 October 2022, a plethora of friends and family came to wish Calvin Weikel a happy 100th birthday at the Plumsteadville Grange in Plumsteadville, Pennsylvania. The mood of the huge crowd in the grange hall was festive, with lots of laughter and heartfelt emotions. As I admired the crowd, I remembered well when several of them were high school sophomores, juniors and seniors in high school. Today, many of them today are grandparents, and hopefully they too will live to be centenarians.

Calvin's 100 years of life have been defined by his religion. the support of his lovely wife, raising their children, making a super-abundance of friends, helping people in need, and working long, hard hours on his dairy farm. May Calvin Weikel's good deeds and moral standards have the power to guide and influence his family and friends far into the next century.

Time goes fast when you're having fun!

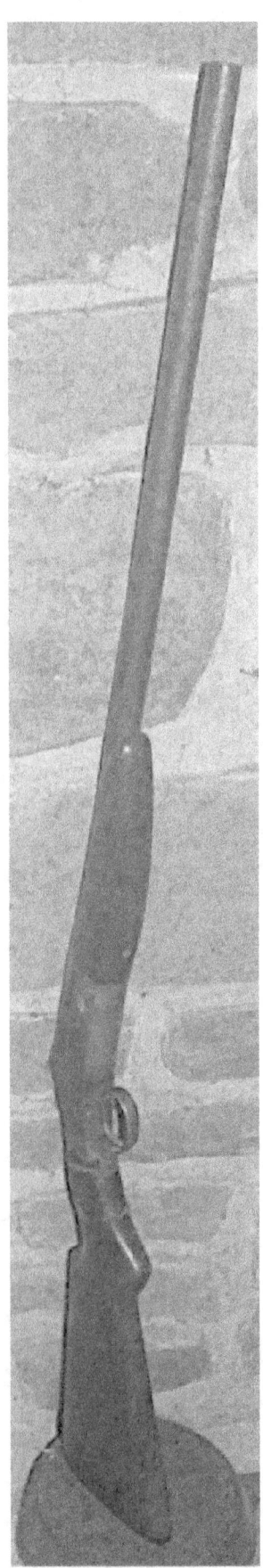

PRELUDE: Riverside Arms Company was in business in the late nineteenth and early twentieth centuries. In July 1916, Riverside Arms Company was purchased by J. Stevens Arms and Tool Company, which began using Riverside Arms Company as a brand name for their line of economy gun products. This single-shot, single-barrel, break-open 16-gauge shotgun* was reported to be a variant of the Riverside Model 315, which was made between 1915 and 1929. The gun's National Rifle Association rating is "fair." Unfortunately, no records exist to give an exact date when this gun was made. I was inspired to write this narrative titled "Damn! I Forgot My Shotgun" because my father gave me this gun, which is the only gun I ever used for hunting small game and shooting on New Year's Eve to celebrate the arrival of a new year.

DAMN! I FORGOT MY SHOTGUN

One day while we were playing pinochle, my friend George said, "It is 11:50 p.m. We need to get our shotguns ready." Instantly, I remembered that I had left my shotgun at home on the couch. I slammed my hand abruptly on the table and loudly said, "Damn! I forgot my shotgun!" (Photo by Jim Diamond)

DAMN! I FORGOT MY SHOTGUN

New Year's Eve 2020 was a special time when people awaited the arrival of 2021. People across America and around the world were under much duress from the Covid-19 pandemic. Hundreds of thousands of people had died, and many more had been hospitalized.

The year 2020 was marked by masking, avoiding crowds, staying six feet apart, washing hands multiple times each day, and canceling meetings, reunions, conventions and travel plans. Public and private elementary, middle, and high schools were closed, and classes were offered to children via computer at home.

The Covid-19 virus rapidly spread around the world. It had no cure and many unknowns to scientists. Finally in mid-December 2020, a vaccine became available to inoculate people against the virus.

Getting back to New Year's Eve 2020, traditionally, I celebrate the closing of the old year and the welcoming of the new year with my close friends the Kantners and the Perrys. When we assembled in the afternoon, we got into a good discussion solving the world's problems, nibbled on hors d'oeuvres, swapped some 2020 stories (and lied a wee bit), updated each other on immediate family members, watched a football game and played pinochle.

While we were playing pinocle, George suddenly said, "It is 11:50 p.m. We need to get our shotguns* ready."

Instantly, I remembered that I had left my shotgun at home on the couch. I slammed my hand abruptly on the table and loudly said, "Damn, I forgot my shotgun!"

Whoa! Dave and George picked up on my negligence and will never, and I mean never, allow me to forget that.

However, it has been said, "Never judge people for their mistakes. Judge people on how they fix them."

I can reassure George and Dave that under no circumstances will I ever again forget my shotgun on New Year's Eve. Woe betide me if I ever do.

PRELUDE: The Great Salt Lake is the largest saltwater lake in the Western Hemisphere and the eighth largest terminal lake* in the world. It is located in northern Utah and has a substantial impact on the local climate, especially through lake-effect snow. The Great Salt Lake has been called "America's Dead Sea," and it is a habitat for millions of indigenous* shorebirds, waterfowl, and brine shrimp. In July 2002, with our dear friends Gary and Alma Fuess, my late wife, Betty, and I visited the Great Salt Lake. I was inspired to write this narrative titled "Great Salt Lake" because we were somewhat disappointed to find vast areas around the lake void of water. As the photo reflects, Gary and I walked on the salty lake bottom with blue salt water a long way from where we were standing.

GREAT SALT LAKE

The Great Salt Lake is a remnant of Lake Bonneville, which was a prehistoric body of water that covered much of western Utah. In July 2021, the Great Salt Lake reached a historic low of ten feet below its average level, exposing vast swaths of dry lake bottom. (Photo by Betty Diamond of Jim Diamond and Gary Fuess walking on a dried Great Salt Lake bottom in July 2002)

GREAT SALT LAKE

In prehistoric times, Lake Bonneville covered much of what is today western Utah. The Great Salt Lake is a remnant of Lake Bonneville and today is the largest saltwater lake in the Western Hemisphere and the eighth largest terminal lake* in the world.

Three major tributary* rivers flow into the Great Salt Lake: Webber River, Bear River and Jordan River. This trio of rivers deposits water and minerals into the lake. Because the lake has no outlet, water evaporation increases the lake water's salinity and density so much that that is actually greater than seawater. The high salinity helps swimmers to float effortlessly. The Great Salt Lake is so salty that the only living things in the lake are algae, bacteria, brine flies and brine shrimp.

In the 1980s, the lake reached a historic area of 3,300 square miles. At the time, evaporation was the only way to reduce the lake's water level. However, the state of Utah constructed the West Desert Pumping Project to reduce the high water level of the lake to mitigate the damage it caused. The flood-control project pumped water from the lake into the nearby desert and expanded the normal evaporation process.

Sadly, today the Great Salt Lake is drying up. At the end of July 2021, after years of drought and increased water diversion upstream of the lake, it fell to its lowest recorded area—just 950 square miles, exposing vast swaths of dry lake bottom. This made boating unnavigable and jeopardized the many industries that rely on the lake for transportation and other uses.

The Great Salt Lake's surface elevation reached lows not seen since 1963. Late summer heat and lack of rain further reduced the lake to its current level at ten feet below the historical average. According to University of Utah professor Dr. Kevin Perry, a dry, dusty lake bed exposed by receding water is susceptible to dust storms and full of tiny dust particles that make it difficult to breathe, especially for people with asthma* or other breathing issues.

The wetlands surrounding the Great Salt Lake are one of the most important migratory bird habitats in North America. Annually, around 250 species of birds feed and nest at the lake. Some of the most common birds migrating are the barn owl, American avocet, snowy plover, bald eagle and golden eagle. The most significant source of animal life in the lake is brine shrimp.

In July 2002, with our dear friends Gary and Alma Fuess, my late wife, Betty, and I visited the Great Salt Lake. While Gary and I walked on the salt, we found it to be crunchy, similar to the crunching of dried leaves in Pennsylvania under our feet in November. Gary and I courageously tasted the saltwater! However, I wouldn't recommend more than a lick because it smelled indescribably bad.

We learned that a few bacterial sulfates make hydrogen sulfide, low depth and low oxygen in the water as the bacteria quickly decompose. Also, industrial waste dumped into the lake adds to the smell. Adding to the bad odor are the large amounts of algae and brine shrimp that wash onto the shore each day. These smells combine into the unique odor on the widespread desert-like shore. The Great Salt Lake is an interesting place to relax and appreciate the sights and sounds of the lake—but not the smells.

I would like to close this narrative by citing Dale L. Morgan, an American historian, who said, "Great Salt Lake is an ironical joke of nature—water that is itself more desert than a desert."

PRELUDE: When the former chaplain of Plumsteadville Grange Rowland Carlson retired from the pastoral ministry, he and his wife, Barbara, had an idea to form an alliance with Rolling Hills United Methodist Church to establish Discovery Service Projects (DSP). Barbara's beloved husband has since passed, but she continued to honor his memory and DSP's mission by traveling with clergy and volunteers from many faiths to build much-needed churches, clinics, civic buildings, schools and residences in developing Central American countries and challenged areas in Mexico and the United States. I was inspired to write this narrative titled "Our Friend Barbara Carlson" because I was fortunate enough to travel to Honduras with Barbara twice to participate in projects and work with other Christian volunteers. Barbara Carlson was a real blessing in Honduras!

OUR FRIEND BARBARA CARLSON

Plumsteadville Grange member Barbara Carlson co-founded Discovery Services Projects (DSP), which provides construction, scholarship and mission works to improve the lives of individuals and cultures. The Plumsteadville Grange, Rolling Hills United Methodist Church and Bucks County Pomona Grange supported DSP financially, plus several of DSP members have traveled to Central American countries to participate in various projects. (Photo by Jim Diamond of Barbara Carlson in Tegucigalpa, Honduras)

OUR FRIEND BARBARA CARLSON

Our friend Barbara Carlson gave more than seventy years of her life to help thousands of people. She taught, influenced and guided people, taking them far beyond their wildest expectations. Her legacy is a lasting expression of her humility to foster and mentor people.

Barbara was a master at managing people. I observed her people management skills with Discovery Services Project, and I hold Barbara's *modus operandi* of mentoring and managing people in high esteem.

Memories are one of life's most precious treasures, and the older we grow, the more precious they become. I met Barbara and her late husband, Rowland, when they came to Doylestown United Methodist Church in Doylestown, Pennsylvania. We became dear friends.

My late wife, Betty, praised Barbara and admired her ability to play the organ. Barbara supported Betty and encouraged her to sing solos at Rolling Hills United Methodist Church. In my mind's eye, I can still see Betty standing at the end of this organ singing the Lord's Prayer with Barbara accompanying her on the organ. I have a trove of memories of Barbara that will be forever remembered, and our church congregation misses her devoted organ playing on Sunday mornings.

Barbara never made anyone feel she was more important or better than them. She never pretended to be someone she wasn't. Whether Barbara was talking with a governor, president of a large corporation, distinguished author, professor, staff, janitors, or a homeless person, she was always the same Barbara Carlson. That trait made her very effective in communicating with people, especially the young.

As a public school educator and mentor, Barbara taught her students principles of respect, character, integrity and leadership. Her consistency in teaching those virtues, led her students to become honorable citizens in their communities, churches, states, nations and to some extent the world.

To end this narrative, I would like to say, "The best teachers teach from the heart, not from the book." Barbara taught from the heart! A teacher effects eternity, and a teacher like Barbara can never tell where her influence stops. Nelson Mandela said, "Education is. the most powerful weapon which you can use to change the world."

Barbara, thank you for your contributions and service to changing the world.

PRELUDE: In Philippians 1:3-5, it is written, "Every time I think of you, I give thanks to my God. I always pray for you, and I make my requests with a heart full of joy because you have been my partner in spreading the Good News." Pastor Steve McComas brought much joy to our congregation at Rolling Hills United Methodist Church in Pipersville, Pennsylvania, and he is a true friend. In 1996, a famous Chinese poet wrote a poem for me that expresses his appreciation for my works in China. I share part of the poem here because it applies to Pastor Steve when he was transferred from Rolling Hills United Methodist Church to Hatboro: "If you are a real friend, even though you are far away, we are near." Even when Pastor Steve was far from me, I felt him near. Throughout life, we meet close confidants, colleagues, coworkers, classmates, relatives, peers, and mere acquaintances. People have latent needs* for friendship with other people in their society. A Swazi farmer once said to me, "If you make an enemy your friend, you no longer have an enemy." Sydney Smith said, "Life is fortified by multitudes of friends. To love a friend and to be loved by a friend is the greatest happiness of existence." Helen Keller stated, "If you have friends, you can endure anything." I was inspired to write this narrative titled "Our Friend Pastor Steve McComas" to share my feelings that guided me in strengthening our church and friendships over the years.

OUR FRIEND PASTOR STEVE McCOMAS

I thank Pastor Steve for being a friend to the multitudes. Because centers for the spheres of friendship are everywhere, friendships enfold societal acceptance and dissipate loneliness. (Photo of Pastor Steve McComas provided by RHUMC)

OUR FRIEND PASTOR STEVE McCOMAS

Among life's most precious blessing are friends. Friendship comes to people who are first a friend. Multitudes of friends unfold during life endeavors and societal interactions. The potential for number of friends is countless, and when perceived as a sphere, the sphere's center is everywhere and its circumference is nowhere.

Spheres of friendship emanate mutual acceptance and dissipate loneliness. Dissipating loneliness begets well-being and happiness. Pastor Steve taught that our well-being and happiness enhance the numbers of our friends. Mustering spheres of friends is a life endeavor that fulfills an indigenous* desire because God envisioned the indigenous craving for friendship as compellingly human.

Human craving for friendship cleanses the soul of malice, betrayal, deceit and greed. Making a friend provides a glorious feeling of fulfillment. It's an inner feeling that no other quest can satisfy.

I thank Pastor Steve McComas for being a friend to the multitudes. People who are friends talk to each other and spend time together. They trust one another and also help each other when they are in trouble or hurt. Friends can be looked up to and trusted.

Pastor Steve McComas is a person who can be looked up to and trusted. I am grateful to him for pleasing our desire for friendship and cleansing our souls. May God bless him forever!

PRELUDE: In Proverbs 12:4, it is written, "A wife of noble character is her husband's crown." Behind every successful leader is a supportive, loving spouse. Many leaders credit their spouses with enabling them to excel in their chosen fields. CEO of Pacific Brands Sue Morpet said, "Having a supportive partner is critical to our success." Every Grange Master in Pennsylvania yearns to have spouses the caliber of Edith M. (aka Meg) and James (aka Jim) Lomax. We are very proud and pleased that Meg and Jim emigrated from England and became American citizens in 2010. I was inspired to write this narrative titled "Two Peas in a Pod" because it is such a blessing to have Meg and Jim Lomax as active members of Plumseadville Grange. The Lomaxes have learned to speak "American" quite well, but occasionally a British word unintentionally slips out, and they say an English term, such as swindle, cheeky, bloody, loo, dodgy, knackered, smash it, telly, or chap.

TWO PEAS IN A POD

Meg and Jim Lomax consistently portray an extraordinary reflection of British customs, cultural traits, morés* and their love for their homeland. It is a joy and delight to work with Meg and Jim as they address their Grange office responsibilities and volunteer their creativity to make Plumsteadville Grange activities successful. (Photos by Jim Diamond of Meg and Jim Lomax, members of Plumsteadville Grange, Plumsteadville, Pennsylvania)

202

TWO PEAS IN A POD

Meg and Jim Lomax are two esteemed members of Plumsteadville Grange in Plumsteadville, Pennsylvania. They are talented in so many ways. Meg as Lecturer then Secretary and Jim as Treasurer gave profound cognizance to their duties and responsibilities. Plumsteadville Grange members looked forward to Jim and Meg's unique programs. Their ability to plan such interesting programs attracted several new members to the Grange.

Meg and Jim consistently portray an extraordinary reflection of British customs, cultural traits, morés* and their love for their homeland. The evening after their citizenship swearing-in ceremony in Philadelphia, they presented an enlightening program to Grange members describing their experiences and feelings at the ceremony. Their presentation provoked interesting, educational, illuminating, didactic knowledge about our beloved country, the United States of America.

Meg and Jim are excellent people managers. They know how to effectively get people involved and accept responsibility. An example of this talent was reflected in their role as managers of the Plumsteadville Grange Farm Market, where they increased the number of purveyors to twenty-five and got them to implement new Department of Health regulations. Meg successfully established a tea room for community members at the market, and she worked with a local farmer to make artisan cheese while encouraging him to sell his cheese at the market.

Meg is a humble person who expresses recognition and gratitude to all of the people who do well under her watch. She is particularly talented in writing, producing, and directing skits and plays, especially for Christmas holidays. In fact, Christmas would not be the same without seeing Grange and 4-H Club* members perform Meg's Christmas play following our holiday covered-dish dinner.

Jim is remarkably trustworthy in keeping the Grange financial records, investing funds, paying monthly bills, and having the financial books audited. Meg and Jim are Grange members who stay in the background out of the limelight and encourage, coach, promote, influence, and support the effectiveness of others. They pat others on the shoulder and say, "Well done!" or "Good job!" or "Congratulations."

Meg and Jim are very dependable, trustworthy, responsible, sincere and straightforward. They also possess charismatic personalities, and their magnetic enthusiasm causes others to be cooperative and supportive.

Like two peas in a pod, Meg and Jim are always together. They do things together, perform together, travel together and live a spirited lifestyle together.

Let me close this narrative with a British proverb, "Our friends are our mirrors and show us ourselves." We are proud that Jim and Meg Lomax are our friends; they show us who we are!

PRELUDE: A wool spinning wheel* converts carded* wool fibers into yarn. Yarn is long, continuous, interlocked wool fibers used for knitting, crocheting, sewing, weaving, embroidering and making rope. Spinning grease wool* into yarn is an ancient textile art. For thousands of years, wool fibers were spun by hand, using a simple tool called a spindle. A spindle is a straight, round piece of wood weighted near the bottom with a round ceramic ball called a whorl.* One woman spun the spindle with a small whorl near the end as another woman fed the wool onto the spinning spindle. Around 1030, the spinning wheel was invented in the Islamic world. By the eighteenth century, mass production of woolen yarn dramatically increased with the Industrial Revolution. I was inspired to write this narrative titled "Wool Spinning Wheel" because of my excitement when I once purchased a spinning wheel for my late wife, Betty, on our second wedding anniversary. In January 1973, I observed the ancient practice of wool spinning with a weighted spindle by Dogon women who lived at the base of the Bandiagara Cliff in Northern Republic of Mali.

WOOL SPINNING WHEEL

According to Spinning & Yarn Barn of Kansas, the spinning wheel* in the photo is an Ashford Elizabeth 2. It is called Ashford's "fairy tale" wheel because it has a traditional fairy tale look. Its twenty-four-inch wheel diameter means less treadling and less effort becuase the wheel just keeps turning. (Photo by Jim Diamond of a spinning wheel in his home)

WOOL SPINNING WHEEL

Because I am a shepherd and professional sheep shearer and my late wife, Betty, was a competent shepherdess, we had great interest in the wool produced from our flock. Betty yearned to have a spinning wheel* because she wanted to learn how to use it to make yarn.

To surprise Betty, I spent a chunk of money from our meager budget to purchase a spinning wheel for her to celebrate our second wedding anniversary. It was a rather large wool spinning wheel, and Betty truly liked it and looked forward to learning how to spin.

Because of its size, we put the spinning wheel in our living room. Guests used to comment on our beautiful spinning wheel's uniqueness. Three years after I bought the wheel for Betty, a former student of mine and his new wife visited us. They adored our spinning wheel.

My former student asked, "Would you be willing to sell that spinning wheel?"

I said, "Yes, if we can agree on a price."

I more than doubled my purchase price and sold them the spinning wheel. I promised Betty I would get her another, smaller spinning wheel that would fit better in our home. As our destiny together unfolded, forty years passed, and I had not yet fulfilled my promise to buy Betty a smaller spinning wheel. (Woe is me.)

Betty and I had two extraordinary friends, Dave and Connie Kantner, who over the years became steadfast, affectionate members of our surrogate family. Dave also had an interest in sheep, and he too could shear them. Sometimes he and I would work together shearing a flock of sheep.

One day, Dave visited a shop in Ocean City, New Jersey, that was going out of business, and he spotted a spinning wheel for sale. He purchased it as a piece of moveable furniture for their home. The spinning wheel remained as a fixture in the Kantner house for many years to depict their interest in raising sheep. Plus it was a great topic for conversation with visiting friends and family.

The Kantners reached an age when they began to downsize to ultimately sell their home and move into an assisted-living facility. During the downsizing process, they remembered I never fulfilled my promise to give Betty another spinning wheel, so they decided to give Betty their spinning wheel—with one stipulation. I had to promise that I would never sell Betty's wool spinning wheel.

Giving Betty that wool spinning wheel was a reflection of Dave and Connie Kantner's uniqueness as thoughtful and kind human beings. Since then, that wool spinning wheel has been displayed in our living room. It's observed by visiting guests and generates interesting discussions.

I would like to close this narrative with a quote by Margaret Mead, who was raised in Doylestown, Pennsylvania, and attended Buckingham Friends School, "Always remember that you are absolutely unique. Just like everyone else."

PRELUDE: Likely, backgammon is the most predominant of table games. It is more than 5,000 years old, and it was enjoyed by ancient Greeks, Romans and Egyptians. It involves a combination of strategy and luck from rolling dice. Backgammon is a two-player game where each player has fifteen pieces, known traditionally as "men," short for "table-men." Players move their pieces along twenty-four points according to the roll of two dice. The objective of the game is to move your pieces around the board to remove them and be the first player to remove all your pieces from your table. This is called "bearing off." Even though backgammon is quite popular in many countries, some people do not know much about this prepossessing game. I was inspired to write this narrative titled "Backgammon" because of my many challenging, fun experiences playing over the years with my late wife, Betty, and longtime friend Dr. Kathleen Jones. We all found the game to be more than the luck of rolling of the dice, and we expressed our feelings with customary felicity.

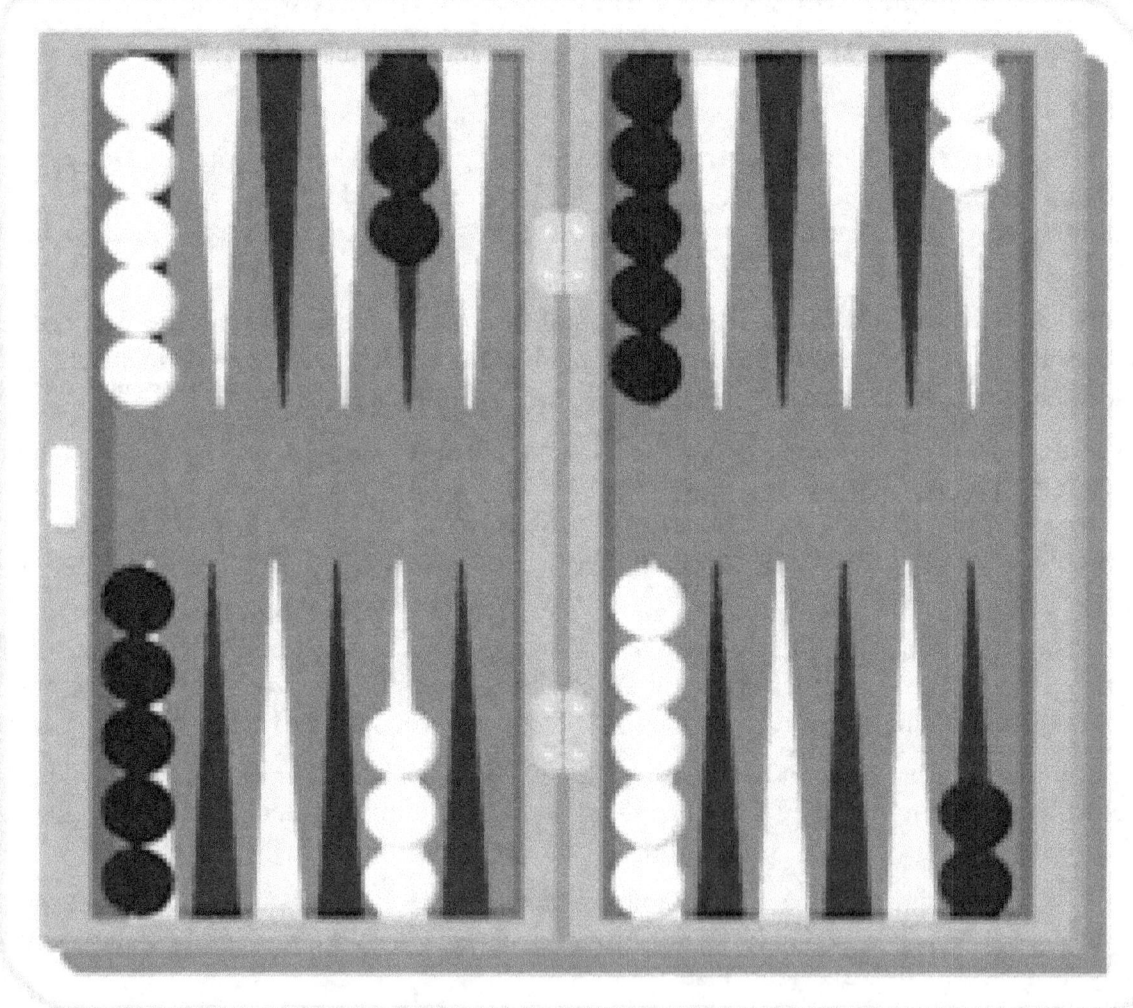

BACKGAMMON

Having been played for more than 5,000 years, backgammon is one of the world's oldest board games. It is still played around the world by both young and old generations. (Photographer unknown)

BACKGAMMON

Having been played for more than 5,000 years, backgammon is one of the oldest board games still in existence. It is still played around the world by both young and old generations. The oldest known evidence of this game comes from Iran. It is believed the word "backgammon" most likely derived from "back" and the Middle English *gamen*, which means "game" or "play." The earliest use of the word "backgammon" was documented by the Oxford English Dictionary in 1652.

Backgammon requires two players compete using strategy, tactics, counting and probability. The objective of the game is to move fifteen pieces around the board to remove them and to be first to remove all your pieces from the board.

During the sixteenth century, the Catholic Church didn't approve of backgammon. They ordered the boards to be burned, proclaiming them to be unholy.

Even people who play it often do not know much more about it than the rules. The first international backgammon tournament was held in 1964. It was organized by the Imperial Prince Alexis Obolensky, who was a stupendous fan of backgammon and very good at playing it.

After international backgammon tournaments became more frequent, players had more chances to compete against other skilled players in official events. Sadly, they do not get a lot of media coverage.

Backgammon boards can be made from different materials, including plastic, wood, metal and Bakelite.* Bakelite is definitely the best material for backgammon boards because it is extremely durable and the pieces slide well on it. Old Bakelite backgammon sets are very valuable and highly collectible.

Today, more and more people play backgammon online. However, in my opinion, playing on the computer can't replicate the feeling of sitting at a table with a friend or foe and rolling the dice.

I would like to close this narrative by quoting Georges Mabardi who wrote the book *Backgammon to Win,* "Two expert players will never disagree. Knowledge of backgammon, after all, is finite."

My longtime friend and frequent backgammon opponent Dr. Kathleen Jones and I never disagreed. I could be chagrined at her astonishing ability to roll doubles, which made her wins so predictable. Playing against Kathleen was always entertaining, enjoyable, relaxing and fun.

PRELUDE: When I was a graduate student at Penn State University, downhill skiing was a common topic of conversation among faculty and graduate students during the winter. Most everyone knew how to ski and spent their free weekends at the well-known Tussey Ski Area Slope near State College, Pennsylvania. I had never skied and was oblivious to the adroitness and terminology of the sport. One day, my classmate and dear friend David L. Kantner asked me to go skiing with him and his son. He promised he would get me safely down the beginner's slope if I did everything he instructed. I accepted his invitation and learned to downhill ski in one day on the beginner's slope at Blue Mountain All-Seasons Resort. However, cross-country skiing was more to my liking. I was inspired to write this narrative titled "Cross-Country Skiing" to chronicle my skiing experiences on the slope.

CROSS-COUNTRY SKIING

The classic style of cross-country skiing is used on prepared trails with two parallel tracks cut into the snow. However, you can also cross-country ski on snow without tracks. In cross-country skiing, one ski is pushed forward from the other stationary ski in a striding, gliding motion. (Photo by Jim Diamond of his dear friend Jim Lomax cross-country skiing on his farm near Pipersville, Pennsylvania, in February 2021)

CROSS-COUNTRY SKIING

Cross-country skiing is the oldest winter sport in Scandinavian countries. Finland, Norway and Sweden each claim to be the fatherland of the sport.

I enjoyed downhill skiing, but only when there were not too many other skiers on the slope. However, the only time I could go skiing was when everyone else could go skiing as well, so the slopes were always crowded. I zig-zagged down the slope to control my speed, and other skiers zinged past me like I was standing still.

Because I am totally blind in my left eye, I feared that I was going to turn toward a rapid skier on my left and cause an accident on the slope. I worried that someone was going to get hurt—probably me.

I decided to consider another option of skiing, cross-country skiing. Cross-country skiing is a form of skiing whereby skiers traverse snow-covered terrain without the use of ski lifts or other assistance. It requires perseverance, persistence, tenacity, dedication, commitment. It's a lot more tiring than downhill skiing. Cross-country skiing builds strength, and it is considered to be an excellent cardiovascular exercise!

My friend Dave taught me how to cross-country ski, which was more my pace. That experience led me to develop a love for cross-country skiing and enabled me to join ski discussions with my colleagues.

The classic style of cross-country skiing was my favorite. It is used on prepared trails that have two parallel tracks cut into the snow. However, one can also cross-country ski on ground without prepared tracks. To cross-country ski, one ski is pushed forward from the other stationary ski in a striding, gliding motion.

In short order, I learned how to safely fall down, get up, sidestep up a steep slope, slow down and stop. And also importantly, I know when to rest.

My favorite time to cross-country ski was at night with a full moon. A small group of graduate students and faculty and I would cross-country ski several miles in a line on an old railroad bed. After a couple hours of skiing, we would go back to my home where my late wife, Betty, would have prepared hot chocolate and her famous homemade cinnamon flop.* We all laughed as we shared humorous classroom stories, funny occurrences with colleagues, and much more.

Those evenings were a lot of fun and took our minds off studying, writing professional papers, preparing lectures, correcting papers, advising students, and our many other duties and responsibilities. Cross-skiing with university graduate and undergraduate students was full of surprises, amazement, wonderment and jubilation.

To end this narrative, I would like to quote the late Warren Miller, ski bum turned filmmaker, who said, "If you don't do it this year, you will be a year older when you do."

Well, I'm more than a year older now, and I don't ski any more.

PRELUDE: Bells originated in Asia in the 800s BC. The word "bell" is traced to the old Saxon word *bellon* and the Latin word *belare*, which means to bellow or bleat like an animal. Traditionally, bells have been used before religious services to summon worshipers to their place of worship. Animal bells symbolize pastoral lifestyles. Domestic animal bells are worn by cows, horses, sheep, goats, cats, dogs, turkeys, water buffalos, camels, oxen, yaks, donkeys, mules, bulls, llamas, reindeer and elephants. I have collected eighty-one domestic animal bells from thirty-two countries on five continents, and they are on display in my home. I was inspired to write this narrative titled "Domestic Animal Bells from Around the World" because each animal bell has a fascinating story about the material from which it was made, its size, where and how it was used, and how I acquired it. Each of my bells has its own personality.

DOMESTIC ANIMAL BELLS FROM AROUND THE WORLD

Domestic animal bells are hollow metal or wooden vessels that have a loosely attached clapper* inside the vessel that when jostled strikes against the side of the vessel, causing a distinct sound. (Photo by Jim Diamond of his domestic animal bell collection from around the world at his home in 2022)

DOMESTIC ANIMAL BELLS

Domestic animal bells are hollow metal or wooden vessels that have a loosely attached clapper* inside the vessel that when jostled strikes against the side of the vessel, causing a distinct sound. The clappers can be made from metal, bone, horn, or wood. Most animal bells are made by local craftsmen using indigenous* materials.

Animal bells are attached to the animal's neck with a leather strap, piece of wire, length of rope, or lightweight chain. Animal bells save a shepherd or herder a great deal of walking and searching because the bells' sounds indicate the wherebouts of their animals. Herders quickly learn how to tell by the bells' if an animal is grazing, lying down, walking, running, or being chased.

Bells can also shatter the boredom and drudgery of using domestic animals for transportation of cargo or people. For example, camel herders crossing a desert appreciate the clunking sound of a bell around a camel's neck because it breaks the monotony and quietness of trudging across miles of sand and dunes.

Bells are also practical. Clanging bells on horses communicate to walking pedestrians that a horse is approaching. In many states, farmers put bells on their domestic farm animals during large game-hunting seasons to prevent hunters from mistakenly shooting them. Animal bells are also an alarm system that alerts the owner if a thief is stealing an animal under the cover of darkness.

Here are some of my favorite animal bell stories.

- While traveling in Tibet, I bought a yak bell that has a clapper made from a yak horn.

- I got a water buffalo bell made from wood with two clappers while I was working with agricultural schools on Hainan Island in the South China Sea.

- In Ethiopia, a man in a cart made from an old Land Rover chassis was pulled by a horse wearing a unique homemade bell. We stopped the car, and I got out. The man was very uneasy, even after I explained that I wanted to buy the bell that was on the horse. He gave me an inflated price, which I paid, and now the bell is displayed in my collection.

- Most of the bells in my collection are metal. One non-metal water buffalo bell was brought to America from Indonesia in 1946. In Indonesia, not much metal is available, so all of the livestock bells are hand-carved out of wood and have wooden clappers.

- While I was a professor at Penn State University, one of my graduate students, Wail al Tikriti, was in Saudi Arabia. He saw a camel caravan crossing the desert and thought its bell would be a nice addition to my collection. Tikriti approached the caravan, and the camel owner was open to selling the bell. They negotiated a price, Tikriti removed the bell from the camel, and brought it back to State College for my collection. This bell is extra special because Tikriti was the nephew of the former president of Iraq, Saddam Hussein. Tikriti came to America in 1978 because he wanted to get away from his family. He enrolled at Penn State, but never finished because he had a massive heart attack and died.

I would like to close this narrative by quoting influential lyricist and librettist of the American theater, Oscar Hammerstein II, who wrote, "A bell's not a bell til you ring it. A song's not a song til you sing it. Love in your heart wasn't put there to stay. Love isn't love til you give it away!"

PRELUDE: Each November, hunting season normally opens for small game, namely rabbits, squirrels, pheasants and grouse. Going small-game hunting was always a joyous and exciting time for me to get away from daily routines, enjoy the marvels of nature, and socialize with fellow hunters while anticipating a well-trained hunting dog to point and flush a pheasant. While on a two-day hunting expedition with longtime friends George Perry, Jim McCoy and Harry Carey at Perry Acres in Berks County, Pennsylvania, it mattered not whether we harvested enough small game for a hearty dinner featuring baked rabbit or fried pheasant. Our annual event emphasized being together and enjoying the excitement of hunting rabbits and ring-necked pheasants. I was inspired to write this narrative titled "Don't You Ever Come Back Here Again!" to capture Jim McCoy's ability to protect his reputation and to accurately shoot his expensive shotgun* during our pleasurable small-game hunt.

DON'T YOU EVER COME BACK HERE AGAIN!

Four of us hunted ring-necked pheasants and rabbits as we slowly, safely walked in a straight line across an alfalfa field. Three hunters carried expensive Remington shotguns* that could hold three 12-gauge shells, while I carried my single-barrel 16-gauge Riverside shotgun with only one shell. (Photo by Barbara Perry of four hunters: Left to right: George Perry, Harry Carey, Jim McCoy and Jim Diamond, with black Labrador retriever Barney in front, November 2002)

DON'T YOU EVER COME BACK HERE AGAIN!

Four friends hunted ring-necked pheasants and rabbits as we slowly, safely walked in a straight line across an alfalfa field. Three hunters carried expensive Remington shotguns* that could hold three 12-gauge shells, while I carried my single-barrel 16-gauge Riverside shotgun with only one shell that had a cracked stock* wrapped with black tape.

If one hunter missed his shot, the others eagerly waited to "jerk his chain." Suddenly Harry yelled, "There goes a rabbit!" As the rabbit quickly ran toward Jim, it was his shot, so he quickly lifted and aimed his expensive 12-gauge shotgun at the rabbit and pulled the trigger. His first shot missed the rabbit, and a puff of dust flew up behind the rabbit as it hopped uphill. Jim's second shot also missed, and another puff of dust flew up behind the rabbit. Jim's third shot missed, and a third puff of dust flew up behind the rabbit as it safely hopped over the hill and out of sight.

After missing that rabbit three times, Jim looked down at the three of us, knowing we were going to tease him for the entire afternoon. To forestall such a destiny, as we all gawked at him smiling, Jim quickly turned to look where the rabbit hopped over the hill, raised his arm, shook his index finger, and loudly hollered, "Don't you ever come back here again!"

We all broke into a long-lasting, hearty laugh. What could we say? We continued our joyous hunt with smiles on our faces and laughter in our hearts.

PRELUDE: Once a year with our longtime friends George and Barbara Perry and Dave and Connie Kantner, my late wife, Betty, and I would travel to a racetrack for a delicious gourmet dinner and after-dinner entertainment of ten horseraces. We each selected a horse in each race, bet the minimum $2, then watched the horses race to the finish line. I have no intention of making this narrative titled "Harness Horseracing" appear to talk about a trustworthy, steadfast gambling business that originated in a horse stable. My intention was to document delightful times with lovely friends that evolved into harness horseracing memories. Even though none of us became wealthy from our winnings, we sure had some exciting moments when our horses were making last-ditch efforts to be first crossing the finish line. Sharing enjoyment, excitement, thrills, entertainment and good food strengthened our longtime bond and inspired me to document those beautiful times in this narrative.

HARNESS HORSERACING

Since ancient times, people have raced horses to see which horse can run faster. (Photo by waitress at Penn National Race Course near Grantville, Pennsylvania, in September 2013. From left to right: George Perry, Betty Diamond, Barbara Perry, Dave Kantner, Jim Diamond and Connie Kantner)

HARNESS HORSERACING

Racing horses is an ancient equestrian sport where jockeys* ride their steeds around an established racetrack counterclockwise. The reason why they race counterclockwise has been lost to history. The purpose of competitive horse racing has been unchanged since ancient times: to determine which horse can run faster.

Although there are several types of horseracing, my friends and I enjoy watching harness horseracing the most. In a harness horserace, steeds either trot* or pace* while pulling a sulky* and its driver.

Even though horses are raced for sport, a major portion of horse racing revolves around gambling. Spectators enjoy choosing a horse to win,* place,* or show,* then they bet at least $2 on their selected horse. Racetracks offer other bets to place on races, but they are more risky and complicated.

Some people select a horse to place after intensely studying statistics in their printed program, which includes previous race dates, times, jockey names, condition of track, track length, previous position at finish line and other pertinent data. Other people select a horse to place based on the horse's name or color or even the color of the jockey's silks (shirt).

Normally, a horseracing event includes ten races. With the minimum bet of $2, if a person bets on each race and loses every one, their total cost of betting during their enjoyable, memorable evening of entertainment with dear friends was only $20.

I would like to end this narrative by quoting Thomas Jefferson, who said, "Difference of opinion leads to inquiry, and inquiry to the truth."

Horseracing has led me to differences of opinion, and to this day I still inquire, "Why do jockeys race their steeds counterclockwise?"

PRELUDE: On 29 October 2022, my dear friend Susan S. Yeske, who later became my wife, and I boarded a Reading Blue Mountain and Northern Railroad vintage railroad car at Port Clinton, Pennsylvania, to journey through central Pennsylvania and look at the beautiful autumn foliage colors. We departed Port Clinton promptly at 9:30 a.m., and we arrived in historic Jim Thorpe, Pennsylvania, at 11:20 a.m. The sights from our windows included scenic mountains, charming towns, spectacular bridges, rolling hills, farmlands, forests, and rivers. They were marvelous! I was inspired to write this narrative titled "Reading Blue Mountain and Northern Railroad" because we had the opportunity to experience the recently refurbished Iron Horse Ramble-Steam Engine 2102. It was beautiful and looked like a brand new steam engine. It burned anthracite coal to make the steam and puffed out a lot of black smoke.

READING BLUE MOUNTAIN AND NORTHERN RAILROAD

This photo shows engine 2102 entering the railroad station at Port Clinton, Pennsylvania, stopping for passengers to board who were destined for Jim Thorpe station. (Photo by Jim Diamond of Engine 2102 on 29 October 2022)

READING BLUE MOUNTAIN AND NORTHERN RAILROAD

At the end of World War II, the Reading Company was looking for heavier and more powerful steam locomotives. But in 1956, the Reading Company discontinued steam operations, so engine 2102 was retired from revenue service and sold to the Allegheny Railroad.

Engine 2102 was reverted to its Reading appearance, but it was re-lettered as "Allegheny." In 1985, it was sold to operate on the Reading Blue Mountain and Northern Railroad. The locomotive was restored to operating condition, and it returned to service in April 2022.

My wife, Susan, and I were looking for a unique way to enjoy the beautiful autumn colors of central Pennsylvania's landscapes so we reserved two seats on the Reading Blue Mountain and Northern Railroad that departed from Port Clinton, Pennsylvania, station with the destination of Jim Thorpe, Pennsylvania.

Because of the strong demand for seats in October to see the beautiful autumn colors, we were advised to reserve our seats in September. There were only three seats available for the weekend we requested. The cost was $39 per person for travel from the Port Clinton station to Jim Thorpe station and back.

Interestingly, at that time common carrier railroad tickets were not subject to Pennsylvania sales tax, and unused tickets were good forever.

During our train ride, Susan and I saw rolling farmlands, beautifully colored mountains and glistening lakes as we passed through several small towns along the main railroad line. Furthermore, we traveled over bridges and through tunnels.

When we arrived in Jim Thorpe, we had three-and-a-half hours to explore restaurants and shops and see local attractions before boarding the train for our return trip to Port Clinton station.

Because every autumnal color in God's palette can be seen during fall in Pennsylvania woodlands and other eastern states, I would like to end this narrative by quoting Vincent William van Gogh, a Dutch Post-Impressionist painter who posthumously became one of the most famous, influential figures in Western art history, who wrote, "As long as autumn lasts, I shall not have hands, canvas and colors enough to paint the beautiful things I see."

PRELUDE: Sailing is a popular pastime that requires wind to propel a sailboat on the surface of open waters. Learning to sail a boat can be a lifelong skill that can be accomplished on water with a sailboat, on ice with an iceboat, and on land with a land yacht. Sailing a boat might not look challenging, but it actually requires a substantial amount of skill to master. When one can envision the vessel in the mind while sailing, the fundamentals of sailing become clearer. Being able to visualize the physics of wind on a sailboat is an influential constituent in sailing. I was inspired to write this narrative titled "Sailing" because I once sailed a boat in the San Francisco Bay and truly enjoyed the experience. However, I was with a dear friend and fellow former Peace Corps volunteer with me in Tchad, Africa, He expertly taught me how to handle the sails.

SAILING

Sailing a boat might not look difficult, but it actually requires a time to master. One fundamental of basic sailing rules is positioning the sail in the direction of the wind so the boat can move forward. (Photo by Jim Diamond of a sailboat on Lake Nockamixon near Ottsville, Pennsylvania)

SAILING

Sailing might look reasonably effortless, but beginners must master several sailing fundamentals. Mastering the basic skills enables beginners like me to build on their sailing knowledge and practice until these basics become intuitive.

One basic sailing fundamental is positioning the sail in the direction of the wind so the boat can move forward. If the wind is not centered in the sail, the sailboat will slide. Learning how to stabilize a sailing vessel is very important. One needs to recognize the points of a sail and the angle to harness the full power of the wind and navigate the vessel to where you want to go.

Understanding the following basic sailing terms can enable the learner to better understand sailing concepts.

- Aft: Back of the ship

- Bow: Front of the ship

- Starboard: Right-hand side of the boat as one faces the front of the ship

- Port: Left-hand side of the boat as one faces the front of the ship

- Windward: The main direction that the wind is blowing

- Leeward: The direct opposite of the main direction that the wind is blowing

- Rudder: A paddle under the boat that controls the boat's direction by displacing water

- Mast: The main point where the sail is raised

- Boom: A horizontal pole that extends out from the main point where the sail is raised for adjusting the sail's direction

- Tacking: Turning the boat's bow into the wind, changing it from one side of the boat to the other

- Jibing: When the stern of the boat goes through a changing wind that exerts its force from one side of the sail to the other (When jibe occurs, the boom has to quickly shift across the cockpit to catch the wind on the new side.)

Some important safety precautions when sailing are: Know how to use a life jacket, how to properly anchor the vessel, what to do if there is a fire, how to follow emergency procedures, and the location of the radio and how to use it.

One can learn how to sail with an experienced friend. Additionally, one can learn to sail at a sailing school, by reading books, volunteering with a crew, or a combination of all these learning sources.

I would like to close this narrative by quoting John Rousmanier, an American author of thirty technical and instructional books on sailing who said, "The goal is not to sail the boat, but rather to help the boat sail itself."

PRELUDE: Snorkeling is the practice of swimming on the surface of a body of water equipped with a diving mask, a breathing tube called a snorkel, and swimming flippers. The mask gives the swimmer clear vision underwater. The breathing tube enables the swimmer to breathe with their face underwater for long periods of time. And the swimming flippers (which are also called fins) enable the swimmer to move with less effort. With this equipment, a swimmer can enjoy the beautiful underwater vista and excitement of swimming with fish and other underwater life. I was inspired to write this narrative titled "Snorkeling in the Caribbean Sea" because I immensely enjoyed my first and unfortunately only snorkeling experience.

SNORKELING IN THE CARIBBEAN SEA

After putting on the snorkeling equipment, I went into some shallow water to try out this new experience. WOW! I didn't realize before how much beauty there is underwater. (Photographer unknown)

SNORKELING IN THE CARIBBEAN SEA

From January to March 1971, my late wife, Betty, and I were in a Peace Corps French language program in St. Thomas, Virgin Islands. On Saturday afternoons and Sundays, we were free to explore the island.

One Saturday in February, we hiked to a beach along the Caribbean Sea at Coki Point to swim. Upon arrival, we discovered that snorkeling was popular there. We saw a nearby shop where we could rent the necessary equipment for the afternoon.

I had no snorkeling experience, but another Peace Corps volunteer explained how simple it was and how reasonable the cost was to rent the equipment. Furthermore, he said snorkeling required no special training or strong physical effort.

"I'm going to rent the mask, snorkel, and flippers and see if I can snorkel," I told Betty, who decided to sit in the sun on the beach instead.

After I put on the equipment, I went into some shallow water to try out the new experience. WOW! I hadn't realized before how much beauty there is underwater. I was so enthralled that I snorkeled nonstop all afternoon. In a short period of time, I was staring at fish in more-than-fifty-foot-deep water. In the crystal clear water, I saw octopus, great barracuda, four-eye butterfly fish, and many more species I could not identify. I also saw plant life and rock formations on the bottom of the sea, which enhanced the Caribbean underwater exquisiteness.

Because I was so captivated by what I was seeing, I gave no thought to the fact that I had been exposed to the tropical sun for such a long period of time. As a result, I developed a horrible, painful sunburn on my head, back and backs of my legs.

Oh did I suffer! I was a scarlet red, blistered, gruesome sight for ten days until I finally began to heal. I could not sit, walk, nor sleep comfortably.

I want to close this narrative with a French proverb, "Learning is the eye of the mind."

That day, I learned an important painful lesson that I will never forget. However, I also will never forget the beauty I observed underwater in the Caribbean Sea.

PRELUDE: The Franklin Horse Company is one of Bucks County's last remaining links to the nineteenth century. This organization was originally formed in 1810 in Dedham, Massachusetts, to track down horse thieves and recover stolen horses. Recovered horses were returned to their owners and thieves were turned over to the local sheriff. If a horse was not found, the organization purchased a new horse with member dues. Back then, the organization was known as the Society for Apprehending Horse Thieves, and the society warned local farmers, "It is evident that villains through the northern states would probably continue and frequently escape from the hand of justice." In 2022, the Franklin Horse Company held their annual membership meeting, featuring speaker Jim Bongiovanni, who described his studies on the tyranny of the Doan Gang of Plumsteadville Township. I was inspired to write this narrative titled "The Franklin Horse Company" because I am a dues-paying member, and the organization continues to meet annually in Bucks County at the Plumsteadville Grange, Plumsteadville, Pennsylvania. There its members enjoy a bit of bluegrass music and a home-cooked roast beef dinner while they report any local animal thefts and tell tales from the good old days.

THE FRANKLIN HORSE COMPANY

In 1810 in Dedham, Massachusetts, the Society for Apprehending Horse Thieves was formed. On 24 February 2020 Retired news editor Carl La Vo wrote, "There was no messing around when it came to law and order in Bucks County's early history," in his article titled "Villains Were Brought to Justice in Bucks County." Burglaries required every member of the company to baffle and suppress robbers. Tracking down robbers sometimes failed even though property was recovered. The Franklin Company once employed five bounty hunters and posted $100 rewards for the arrest and conviction of horse thieves.

THE FRANKLIN HORSE COMPANY

The Franklin Horse Company was like an insurance company, said the late Glenn C. Dutterer, past-president of the Franklin Horse Company of Holicong. "If someone stole your chickens or horses, the members rode out in a posse in search of animals and perpetrators. If they couldn't find your horses, they would pay you a claim."

Dutterer went on to say the police chief of Buckingham lost a revolver through a theft the past year. As a member of the Franklin Horse Company of Pineville, the chief filed a claim for his gun and received $75. The late Robert Beck, a Chalfont resident, served as secretary of the group and kept minutes of annual meetings. He claimed that at one time the company employed five full-time bounty hunters. Company members observed strict rules while attending the meetings. A page from an 1800s minutes book reveals that a member who attended the meeting intoxicated would be fined five cents. Uttering a profanity during the meeting could cost a nickel. Beck wrote that the Franklin Company officially went out of the insurance and posse business after company members determined that horse thieves were no longer a problem in Bucks County.

Retired news editor Carl La Vo wrote, "There was no messing around when it came to law and order in Bucks County's early history." LaVo indicated in 1786, John Hough stood before Judge Henry Wynkoop to be sentenced for horse thievery. Justice was swift, and Hough was fined forty English pounds, which is equivalent to $6,720 today. He also had to stand for one hour in public disgrace in stocks in downtown Newtown, Pennsylvania, where he received thirty-nine whip lashes, then went to prison for six months. Even worse, he had his ears cut off! Horse thievery wasn't the only crime citizens in Colonial Bucks County had to deal with. Theft of farm equipment, holdups and vandalism were among villainous behaviors at a time when law enforcement was stretched thinly across the county. "Horse companies" were insurance enterprises dedicated to thwarting thieves. Stolen horses that were valuable were ridden out of the county for easy sales elsewhere. If someone reported a horse was stolen, the Telegraph Committee issued a call to ride. At the company's annual meeting, usually in January, members would pay their dues and were assigned areas to cover in cooperation with neighboring companies (especially those close by in New Jersey). The Franklin Company took responsibility for areas from telegraph headquarters in Lambertville to Doylestown. Ephraim Slack and Robert Heston covered Lahaska to Mount Holly. Samuel Doughty and Henry Carver covered Buckingham to Philadelphia. James Shaw and lawyer N.B. Heacock"examined stables and farms on roadways leading to New Brunswick, New Jersey.

Burglary required the utmost efforts of every company member to thwart and suppress robbers. Tracking down robbers sometimes failed, even if property was recovered. The Franklin Company once employed five bounty hunters and posted $100 rewards for the arrest and conviction of horse thieves. In covering one loss, Franklin Company valued Alfred Ely's missing horse at $80 and paid him $60. When bandits robbed John Umstat of Carversville, he submitted a claim for stolen wheat, corn, lard, twelve cans of fruit, and two grain bags. He received $11.90.

Over time, horse companies started to taper off. By the 1940s and 1950s, they dwindled as cars replaced horses. Today, they are social organizations dedicated to preserving history. I would like to close this narrative by quoting Napoleon Bonaparte, who said, "There is one kind of robbery that law does not strike at: stealing time." Time is precious.

PRELUDE: This 30-40 Krag-Jorgensen bolt-action rifle was manufactured by the Springfield Armory. Its bolt-action was a Norwegian design that was adopted in 1892 as the standard United States Army military long-arm. It was the first American military rifle cartridge designed to use smokeless powder. Because this new cartridge used a 30-caliber bullet propelled by 40 grains of smokeless powder, the cartridge earned the name 30-40. The new 30-40 Krag was well liked among military leaders who were keen on its performance. Between 1892 and 1903, the 30-40 Krag famously served as the long-arm during the Spanish American War. Even though the 30-40 Krag has been around for a long time, it is still a very capable gun for hunting many species of big game. Considering its age, the cartridge is also a surprisingly popular choice for many hunters, including me. Unfortunately, currently there are only two factory ammo choices for the 30-40 Krag: one from Remington and one from Hornady. I was inspired to write this narrative titled "30-40 Krag Rifle" because in 1952 when I was fourteen years old, my father took me deer hunting for the first time in the snow-covered Allegheny Mountains near Fairchance, Pennsylvania. He gave me his 30-40 Krag rifle and twelve shells with instructions on safe use of the rifle. For the following sixty-five years, that is the only rifle I used to hunt deer. I still use it as I write this narrative, although now I mostly hunt with a camera. There is an old saying that the 30-40 Krag has shot at every large animal that walks in North America.

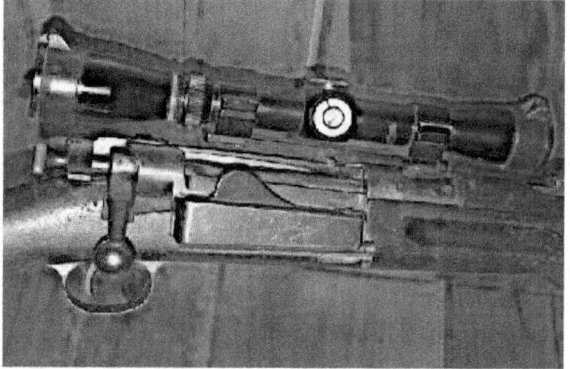

30-40 KRAG RIFLE SHELL MAGAZINE

The hinged magazine is the Krag's distinguishing feature. It takes a lot of time to load five cartridges into the magazine and one in the chamber.

30-40 KRAG RIFLE

Notice the 2- to 7-power Leopold telescope and walnut wood stock.* (Photos by Jim Diamond of his 30-40 Krag in December 2020)

30-40 KRAG RIFLE

Hunting with a 30-40 Krag is like dragging a cannon up a mountain and through the woods. However, make no mistake, a well-placed 30-40 Krag bullet is deadly on all North American big game, such as whitetail deer, mule deer, moose, pronghorn, feral hogs and black bear. If a 30-40 Krag is used for elk or moose hunting, it is best suited for close-range shots.

A 30-40 Krag doesn't offer the same level of performance as a Springfield 30-06, but make no mistake, the cartridge is absolutely deadly on North American big game. Even though 30-40 Krags were popular for hunting big game, the side-loading magazine mechanism is slow and cumbersome to reload. All versions of the Springfield model 1892–99 Krag-Jorgensen rifles were Norwegian-designed bolt-action rifles, and they all were manufactured by the Springfield Armory between 1892 and 1903. Accordingly, the model 1898 in this photo with a serial number 284808 engraved on this 30-40 Krag was the last of the Krag series built by the Springfield Armory.

Today 30-40 Krag factory-loaded cartridges contain 180 grams of smokeless gunpowder. Those loads are perfect for big game, including deer and elk at a moderate range. I have harvested several whitetail deer over the years using the 30-40 Krag rifle in this photo. It accompanied me in snow, rain, ice, cold weather, warm weather and high winds.

One must be well dressed while standing motionless next to a large tree from before dawn to after dusk in cold weather conditions. Waiting for a deer to appear within shooting range requires three virtues: patience, persistence and perseverance. Sometimes I asked myself, *Why in hell am I standing here?* while shivering with ice-cold hands and feet.

Once while I was hunting with George Perry in his dad's apple orchard in Blair County, I aimed at a small buck. When I pulled the trigger, my gun went "click." I had cleaned my gun with gun oil, and the cold oil caused the firing pin to go slow and click. That deer got away.

Experience has taught me that deer hunting in cold weather can be challenging, but with greater odds of success because the cold makes the deer more likely to step out. Standing in the rain can be worthwhile because the sound of the rain dampens the sound of crunching leaves, and deer take less meticulous movements in the rain. Hunting in the dull daylight of dawn and reddish or dull light of dusk is often a hunter's best time for success. According to studies, most bucks are harvested in the wild between 9:00 a.m. and 10:00 a.m.

In December 2003, I harvested a huge ten-point buck with one shot at 9:30 in the morning running more than 100 yards from my stand. It scored 138 on the Boone Crockett scoring scale measured by Frank Meno. My dad taught me to pay attention to the wind to ensure your scent does not blow your cover, and stay as quiet as possible near your favorite hunting spot.

When hunting with my 30-40 Krag, regardless of the weather, I am often in the woods before sunrise and after sunset. Even when I don't see game animals, watching the first rays of sunlight peep through a dissipating morning fog and hearing birds singing while flitting from one naked branch to another is worth every moment in the woods, maximizing my experience and rejuvenating my soul.

I will end this narrative with a quote by President Joseph Biden, "A bad day deer hunting still beats a good day working at the office."

PRELUDE: Since the early nineteenth century, square dancing has been derived from jigs and reels from Scotland and Ireland. Traditional square dancing that I am familiar with is considered a North American folk dance preferably with a caller* accompanied by live music. The old-time music was played on acoustic instruments, such as fiddle, banjo, double bass, guitar, piano, or accordion. I was inspired to write this narrative titled "Traditional Square Dancing in America" because during my formative years, I had much merriment at square dances, and they were my only form of acceptable social recreation. On Saturday nights, there was always a square dance at one of six grange halls in Fayette County. I truly enjoyed square dancing. There was a short period of time when I could even call a square dance.

TRADITIONAL SQUARE DANCING IN AMERICA

"All join hands and circle eight around to the right. Now do-se-do your corner; bow to your partner and promenade her round the circle back to home. Allemande left and allemande right, circling back to your partner to swing her twice around. (Photo of four couples circling eight around to the right.)

TRADITIONAL SQUARE DANCING IN AMERICA

Alll join hands and circle eight around to the right. Now do-si-do your corner; bow to your partner and promenade her round the circle back to home. Allemande left and allemande right circling back to your partner to swing her twice around."

This is one way a caller* would begin calling a square dance in cadence with a fiddle, banjo and piano playing lively, old-time music. Square dancing is an American country folk dance with four couples dancing to movements sung out by a caller in tempo with music. Both adults and youth consider square dancing good for the body and mind, easy to learn, and a way to make new friends.

When beginning a square dance, the couple whose back is to the music and the couple facing the music are considered the "head couples." The other two couples are called "side couples." The caller often gives instructions by naming these couples. Square dance figures are generally danced four times featuring each couple once.

Experienced square dancers know the basic figures of a particular dance, such as Dive for the Oysters and Duck for the Clams. They find it easy to follow the callers' instructions. Callers are very patient with new dancers who are unfamiliar with the figures, and they often walk the dancers through the figure before calling the dance.

In most American forms of square dance, the dancers are prompted through a sequence of steps and figures by a caller who sings calls to the beat of a recognizable melody. The primary purpose of singing calls is to help dancers relax and dance well together as a group while simultaneously enjoying the caller's song and accompanying musicians.

Square dancing can be a family activity. My mother and father enjoyed square dancing with adults their age while young people danced with people their age. Refreshments were always available, and often after much energetic and exuberant dancing, some dancers would sit out a dance to repose. Sometimes there was a break for everyone to rest and munch on refreshments, the musicians would play lively polka music and spirited beaus with their dates, and some adults would dance a polka for a short time.

In rural areas where square dancing was popular, a saying went, "You don't stop dancing because you grow old. You grow old because you stopped dancing."

PRELUDE: Christmas 2020, my niece Lisa Sova and her husband, Shawn, sent me a unique, practical gift that I will cherish each time I use it while trekking.* It is a ravishing, handmade trekking pole made by my then-ten-year-old great-nephew, Marty Diamond. Whether you are trekking a short or long distance or heading out for a weekend outing, trekking poles can add a lot of stability, safety and comfort to your trek. Trekking poles should be considered essential. I was inspired to write this narrative titled "Trekking Pole" because I like to trek, and this pole is very special to me personally because of who made it and who gave it to me.

TREKKING POLE

When senior citizens like me go trekking,* using two trekking poles takes much strain off various joints, such as hips, knees, shoulders and lower back. I find that using two trekking poles gives me more symmetrical support than one. (Photo by Jim Diamond of a trekking Pole made by my great-nephew, Marty Diamond, January 2021)

TREKKING POLE

TRekking* poles are often used in pairs because they provide more benefit, especially for senior citizens. Uses of trekking poles include, pushing aside thick bushes across the trail, clearing away cobwebs, pushing aside thick grass, supporting the trekker when going uphill, keeping your balance when crossing streams, reducing your speed when walking down a steep hill, and giving you stability on rough ground.

When senior citizens like me go trekking, using two trekking poles takes a lot of strain off joints, such as hips, knees, shoulders and lower back. I find that using two trekking poles gives me more confidence and symmetrical support than one pole alone. Furthermore, I often find my trekking speed to be a bit faster when using two poles. However, some trekkers prefer using just one. Some people claim that trekking poles enable them to trek more miles and have fewer backaches and rubbery knees.

Select a pole that is six to eight inches taller than the height of your elbow from the ground when standing straight. If you plan to trek up steep slopes, the trekking pole should be a little longer. Be careful when trekking on rocky and hilly terrain. If you place your pole between two rocks or if it slips between two rocks, you might fall or snap the pole if you do not pull it straight back out.

Trekkers should be physically fit before trekking a long distance. Do not overwhelm your body if it is not in physical condition. When trekking, stay hydrated, determine your pacing rhythm, dress appropriately, wear comfortable shoes, and have some snacks in a pocket or backpack.

Think of your trekking poles as an extra pair of legs that give you additional stability, allowing you to trek longer distances, safer and faster. At the end of your trek, do your body a favor with some stretching.

I would like to close this narrative by quoting American essayist and poet Henry David Thoreau, "I took a walk in the woods and came out taller than trees."

Each time I went for a walk in my woods, my late wife, Betty, always knew I had something on my mind. I invariably would come out of the woods feeling taller than the tallest oak tree, particularly when I had dissipated some form of stress.

PRELUDE: A-Day* is held each year on the last full weekend (Friday, Saturday and Sunday) in April at Delaware Valley University (DVU) located at 700 East Butler Avenue, Doylestown, Pennsylvania. A-Day is a phenomenal student-planned and implemented event that brings together DVU students with surrounding members of local communities and people from across Pennsylvania, New Jersey, New York, Maryland, Connecticut, Massachusetts, and other states. A-Day features educational exhibits, demonstrations, competitions, entertainment and loads of fun. Among the yummy features of the event are homemade milkshakes by students who use whole milk and real ice cream. I was inspired to write this narrative titled "A-Day at Delaware Valley University" because as a student at DVU, I was co-chair of the 1961 A-Day committee, and as Dean of Agricultural and Environmental Sciences, I was one of the A-Day advisors for six years. What a magnificent experience it was working with such dedicated, enthusiastic, faithful undergraduate DVU students.

A-DAY AT DELAWARE VALLEY UNIVERSITY

A-Day* is filled with educational exhibits, demonstrations, competitions, entertainment and loads of fun. Students make homemade milkshakes with whole milk and real ice cream. (Photo provided compliments of Delaware Valley University marketing and communications staff)

230

A-DAY AT DELAWARE VALLEY UNIVERSITY

A-Day,* stands for "activities day." This three-day family-friendly event is organized, planned, and administered by a huge cadre of Delaware Valley University (DVU) undergraduate students with minimal guidance from the university's staff, faculty and administration. The student A-Day planning committee meet and begin working on next year's A-Day within a week after the conclusion of the current year's.

The first A-Day was held on 21 May 1949 on the campus of the National Agricultural College (now Delaware Valley University). At that time, A-Day was a single-day event when students showcased agricultural displays and exhibits.

In July 2003, Jason Smith, 2004 A-Day Chairman, came into my office and asked, "Dr. Diamond, what can we do different for next year's A-Day?"

I said, "Jason you may want to consider making A-Day an official Pennsylvania Fair because you do everything required except there is no fair catalog and participants do not receive any premiums for their winnings. If all the necessary fair fund requirements are fulfilled, A-Day will qualify to receive state fair funds for paying premiums, judges, equipment, loudspeakers, and anything needed for A-Day to be successful. Let's go share your idea with Dr. Tom Leamer [DVU President]."

We met with Dr. Leamer, who thought it was a great idea and suggested we talk with Samuel Hayes, Pennsylvania Secretary of Agriculture. We returned to my office and made a conference call to him. Jason explained A-Day to Secretary Hayes, who was very supportive. He referred us to the PA State Association of County Fairs Board of Directors. Three of their board members visited the 2004 A-Day Executive Committee Meeting and explained to the students that to qualify for fair funds they had to pay premiums, publish a catalogue, and expand A-Day to a three-day program open to the public.

The students fulfilled the board's requirements, and each year various members of the PA State Association of County Fairs Board of Directors visited A-Day and were astonished and impressed that a fair of that magnitude was planned and implemented by undergraduate students. A-Day became part of the Pennsylvania State Association of County Fairs. In 2007, the A-Day executive committee received their first check for $10,000 to defray the costs of conducting the 2007 A-Day. Every year thereafter, A-Day committee received reimbursement for their A-Day expenditures.

Bucks County residents, university employees, students, 4-H Club* members, Scouts, FFA* members and the public are invited to enter their food, artwork, hay, grain, vegetables, fruits, canned goods, handicrafts and more in the fair for judging. The first year as an official fair, all the exhibits fit on one table. Now a whole room is filled with exhibits to be judged. Each year 30,000 to 40,000 people attend A-Day at Delaware Valley University.

I would like to close this narrative by quoting our former President of the United States John F. Kennedy who said, "Every accomplishment starts with a decision to try."

PRELUDE: An annual university homecoming can be defined as a time when groups of former students and friends return to their university to reminisce about the good and bad times; visit classmates, athletic teammates and professors (if they are still alive); attend an athletic event(s), visit new facilities; acknowledge the changes on campus; and often end the day with a banquet. I was inspired to write this narrative titled "Homecoming: Delaware Valley University" because being an Aggie means so much more to me than the mere definition of "alumni." Aggies who do unfeigned good for humankind in the world are the real measure of wealth. Since 1896 when Joseph Krauskopf founded the National Farm School, which is now known as Delaware Valley University, the alumni have created 128 years of a profound, significant, historic heritage that enhances the institution's image. At our annual homecoming, graduates bring their profound career achievements that further grow the heritage of the institution. Every student who enrolls at Delaware Valley University inherits 128 years of our Aggie historic heritage.

HOMECOMING: DELAWARE VALLEY UNIVERSITY

Being a part of a family of classmates is one of life's most precious treasures. And the older we grow, the more precious those classmates become. (Photo compliments of Delaware Valley University marketing and communications staff)

HOMECOMING: DELAWARE VALLEY UNIVERSITY

Homecoming at Delaware Valley University (DVU) is a special time for alumni and alumnae to link together common career and personal similarities that strengthen friendships, which ultimately evolve into a powerful family of former classmates. Being a part of a family of classmates is one of life's most precious treasures, and the older we grow the more precious those classmates become.

Making a friend creates a glorious feeling of fulfillment. It is difficult to find words to adequately describe the emotions that are felt when two classmates see each other once again after many years apart building their careers and lives. The stronger a family of classmates becomes, the stronger their allegiance will be toward their alma mater.

At university homecomings, good friends refresh their respective memories. They bring forward the good times, bad times, fun times, jovial times, festive times and hilarious times.

In particular, homecoming football games are always exciting. It's fun to cheer on the home team. There's nothing better on a Saturday afternoon than surrounding myself with fellow Aggie fans.

During a recent DVU homecoming, I enjoyed seeing old friends from Maryland, Virginia, New Jersey, New York, North Carolina, Texas, Connecticut and of course, from all over Pennsylvania. It was thrilling to visiting the new Life Sciences Building for alumni who had not yet toured its state-of-the-art modern classrooms and laboratory facilities. Also it was mind-boggling to check out the new state-of-the-art Swine Science Center for alumni who remembered the old facilities.

Prior to each DVU homecoming, a distinguished Alumni Awards Committee recommends to the DVU President highly qualified alumni who have achieved extraordinary career accomplishments for commendation. These recipients receive a beautiful prestigious plaque. During the awards ceremony, current and former professors glow with pride as they observe career achievements of their former students being acknowledged by their alma mater.

It is difficult to find words that can adequately describe my emotional feelings and pride felt during DVU homecoming events. This is what homecoming is all about!

PRELUDE: The Ida M. Block Chapel at Delaware Valley University (DVU) is a welcoming symbol of diversity and inclusion for students, faculty and staff. The chapel was donated by Ida M. Block's husband and family in 1899. The chapel was one of the first buildings erected at the National Agricultural College (now DVU). The university's founder, Dr. Joseph Krauskopf, conducted nonsectarian services regularly in the chapel until his death in 1923. I was inspired to write this narrative titled "Ida M. Block Memorial Chapel" because when I was a student at the National Agricultural College, I spent some time in the chapel thinking, pondering my destiny, studying and practicing my trumpet.

IDA M. BLOCK

Ida M. Block said, "Do all the good you can for people while they are living. Don't wait until they are dead." She also said, "Flowers are for the living. Strew them where they will brighten someone's life."

Chapel Farmschool Fall 1926

IDA M. BLOCK MEMORIAL CHAPEL

(Photos of Ida M. Block and the Ida M. Block Memorial Chapel were provided by Dr. Joseph Krauskopf Memorial Library of Delaware Valley University, Doylestown, Pennsylvania)

IDA M. BLOCK MEMORIAL CHAPEL

Ida M. Block was a well-known leader in Bucks County Jewish community organizations, charities and the local community. The non-denominational chapel named in her honor provides students and faculty a place to pray, ponder, study, think, and hold memorial services and marriage ceremonies. It is open to and accepting of all faiths because Ida M. Block insisted on non-sectarianism in her philanthropy.

To the best of my knowledge, the door to the chapel has never been locked. It has been available to students, faculty and staff twenty-four hours each day for more than 120 years.

The Ida M. Block Memorial Chapel was donated in memory of Mrs. Block by her husband and family in 1899. It is one of the oldest buildings on Delaware Valley University's (DVU) campus in Doylestown, Pennsylvania. During Dr. Joseph Krauskopf's time as president of the university, he provided regular non-denominational services for students of all faiths at the chapel.

As I write this narrative, some structural segments of the chapel need to be refurbished. As an integral component of DVU's exultant celebrations of its 125th anniversary, efforts were made to raise funds to restore the chapel. This effort to carry on the legacies of founder Dr. Joseph Krauskopf and Ida M. Block assures a non-denominational space for DVU undergraduate and graduate students and staff.

When I was a student at DVU, which was then called the National Agricultural College (NAC), I used the chapel for quiet time to think about my courses, ponder my destiny and study. One day inside the chapel on the back left side, I found a trap door in the floor. When I opened the trap door, I found a ladder to climb down to a lower level with a dirt floor. On the rafters, I found a single electric lightbulb with a pull string to turn it on. I played the trumpet and sometimes French horn in the college's marching band and had been looking for an isolated place where I could practice. I FOUND IT! After that, at least twice a week, I would go into the chapel basement and practice playing my trumpet. No one could hear me there, and so I didn't disturb my classmates who were studying in their dormitory rooms.

In the 1950s and early 1960s, the NAC marching band was composed of a small number of students who played three trumpets, two clarinets, two trombones, a bass drum and a French horn. We also had two banner carriers. We practiced each Thursday evening to perform at all home and away football games. All members of the band were male, except at home games we borrowed a majorette from Central Bucks High School to lead the band onto the football field at halftime. We played three numbers, then marched off the field. Even though we were not the best musicians, we sure had a lot of fun. Sadly, the marching band dissolved when our band director passed away.

I would like to close this narrative by quoting George Parks, Director of the University of Massachusetts Minuteman Marching Band at University of Massachusetts-Amherst, who said, "A band is not proud because it performs well; it performs well because it is proud." Our NAC Marching Band did not always perform well; we performed because we were proud Aggies at National Agricultural College.

PRELUDE: In 2003, when I was the Dean for Agricultural and Environmental Sciences at Delaware Valley University (DVU), we established a formal linkage with the University of Guanajuato in Guanajuato, Mexico, to provide opportunities for student and faculty exchanges, special projects, information sharing, and many other appropriate activities. On two different occasions, Adriana Celis and Dr. Manuel Collado from the University of Guanajuato visited DVU. In March 2004, I traveled to Guanajuato on behalf of DVU with my late wife, Betty, DVC Professor of Animal Science Dr. Pamela Reed, and three DVU students majoring in Dairy Science. I was inspired to write this narrative titled "University of Guanajuato Exchange Program" because the University of Guanajuato facilities were similar to those at DVU. I also wrote this narrative with a fond memory of the warm welcome we received from Dr. Collado and his faculty at the University of Guanajuato.

UNIVERSITY OF GUANAJUATO EXCHANGE PROGRAM

In March 2003, Delaware Valley University in Doylestown, Pennsylvania, established a formal linkage with the University of Guanajuato, Guanajuato, Mexico. (Photo by Jim Diamond of the University of Guanajuato in 2003)

UNIVERSITY OF GUANAJUATO EXCHANGE PROGRAM

Baha'u'llah, the founder of the Bah'i Faith, once said, "The world is but one nation and humankind its citizens."

We now live in a world that has a global economy, agriculture, travel, science, education, art and trade. I firmly believe that educators have the professional responsibility to offer and support programs that enable young people to have international experiences, which should be an integral component of their undergraduate and graduate programs.

St. Augustine said, "The world is a book, and those who do not travel read only a page."

In March 2003, Delaware Valley University (DVU) established a formal linkage with the University of Guanajuato in Guanajuato, Mexico, to provide opportunities for Mexican and American student and faculty exchanges, special projects, information sharing and many other appropriate activities.

When I visited the University of Guanajuato in March 2004, I found that the Mexican university's facilities were similar to our facilities at DVU. However, through our deliberations, we learned that literature on agricultural education in Mexico was not part of the information mainstream in national and international databases. Furthermore, we learned that there was little scholarly Mexican literature on academic agricultural education programs. I realized that by exchanging DVU and University of Guanajuato faculties, together we address the issue of mainstreaming agricultural education information into Mexican databases.

On two different occasions, Adriana Celis and Dr. Manuel Collado from the University of Guanajuato came to Bucks County, Pennsylvania, to visit DVU and to formalize the linkage agreement. On both occasions, my wife, Betty, and I hosted them as houseguests at our home for the duration of their visits to Delaware Valley University.

Back then and still today, on a wall of our great room, I display of my collection of domestic animal bells from around the world. During each visit, Dr. Collado carefully studied the display of bells, looking for an animal bell from Mexico. He learned I had no bells from Mexico.

During my visit to University of Guanajuato in March 2004, one day before lunch we all congregated in a small auditorium for an official ceremony welcoming us to Mexico and the University of Guanajuato. During the welcoming program, Dr. Collado asked me to come forward.

When I arrived at to the podium, Dr. Collado handed me a wrapped package and said, "This is not much of a gift, but it will fit nicely into your collection of domestic animal bells from around the world."

When I opened the package, I found a cowbell and sheep bell that had been made in Mexico. Dr. Collado could not have given me a finer gift. It was an awesome gesture to reflect the warmth and kindness of our officially approved joint exchange accord.

"Necessity is a great teacher," and I look back with fondness on our exchange program that addressed the necessities of agricultural education in Mexico. I would like to close this narrative with a Mexican Proverb: "They tried to bury us. They didn't know we were seeds."

PRELUDE: We live in a world with a global economy, agriculture, travel, art, medicine, politics and trade. Today, university graduates will likely begin their careers having some form of international roots. I would like to begin this narrative with a quote often attributed to St. Augustine who once said, "The world is a book, and those who do not travel read only one page." I firmly believe that educators have the professional responsibility to offer programs that enable young people to have an international experience as an integral component of their academic programs. We established the Piszek/Diamond Exchange Program to provide Delaware Valley University (DVU) students opportunities to travel to the University of Podlasie in the Commonwealth of Poland to study Polish agricultural practices and culture. Helen Nelson, a member of the DVU Board of Trustees, indicated that the Copernicus Society of America would provide funds to support the expenses for this unique exchange program. The Copernicus Society of America was founded by her late father, Edward Piszek, who was the founder and Chief Executive Officer of Mrs. Paul's Foods. I was inspired to write this narrative titled "University of Podlasie Exchange Program" because of its success and impact on students' appreciation for people who speak a different language and have different customs and lifestyles.

UNIVERSITY OF PODLASIE EXCHANGE PROGRAM

Left: On behalf of the University of Podlasie faculty and students, Professor Antonio Jowko (pronounced yuf-ko), Deputy Rector for International Relations and Research, bestows a medal of honor on Dr. James E. Diamond, Dean of Agricultural and Environmental Sciences at Delaware Valley University, to express his appreciation for Dr. Diamond's cooperation in establishing the exchange program.

Right: Dr. James E. Diamond, Dean of Agricultural and Environmental Sciences at DVU, delivers a talk to the University of Podlasie faculty and students, encouraging them to travel to other countries to study, do research, explore and scrutinize other cultures and customs as an integral component of the university education programs.

(Photos by Betty Diamond of Jim Diamond receiving a medal of honor and speaking at the University of Podlasie in May 2007)

UNIVERSITY OF PODLASIE EXCHANGE PROGRAM

The idea for the Piszek/Diamond Exchange Program came when Helen Nelson, a member of the Delaware Valley University (DVU) Board of Trustees, asked to meet with me to discuss an idea she had.

The essence of our discussion was brainstorming how to develop an exchange program between DVU students and Polish students. We decided to search for an agricultural university in Poland that resembled Delaware Valley University for the partner exchange school.

After our meeting, Helen met with Jerzey Bystrowski, who was very knowledgeable about institutions of higher learning in Poland. Jerzey traveled to the University of Podlasie in Poland to meet with Professor Jowko (pronounced yuf-ko), Deputy Rector for International Relations and Research and other officials to discuss the possibility of establishing an exchange program with Delaware Valley University.

The Polish professors were very interested, so through email we drafted a Memorandum of Understanding.

On 20 May 2007, a five-member delegation from DVU traveled to Poland where we were hosted by University of Podlasie officials. There we signed the Memorandum of Understanding with the University of Podlasie Rector, creating the well-planned, ten-day exchange program featuring Polish agricultural and culture.

Helen indicated that the Copernicus Society of America would provide funding for this unique exchange program. The Copernicus Society of America was founded by Helen's late father, Edward Piszek, to support programs that internationalize the education of Polish and American young people.

Douglas A. Bocchino, a senior majoring in Ornamental Horticulture at DVU, participated in the second exchange in Poland. Upon his return to DVU, Douglas reported that the highlights of his trip were living in a Polish home, learning about their culture and traditions, eating Polish food, learning about advanced Polish agricultural practices and interacting with Polish students. Douglas's comments helped us to feel that we were meeting the mission of the DVU and University of Podlasie international exchange program.

We are truly indebted to the DVU and University of Podlasie families, who graciously opened their homes to host our exchange students. Three DVU students—Beth, Liz and Kyle—told me that living with a Polish host family was a major highlight of the program. The student delegates from both DVU and the University of Podlasie represented their universities and countries with distinction and dignity.

I would like to close this narrative with a Polish proverb that goes like this, "Keep learning because knowledge is the key to power."

PRELUDE: A Christmas wreath is an assortment of flowers, pine or cedar branches, dried fruits, leaves, pine cones and ribbons that decorate a stiff wire ring. Typically, in English, French, German, Italian and Spanish-speaking countries, wreaths are placed on doors, over fireplaces and outdoors on decks or porches as Christmas decorations. When driving through Doylestown, Philadelphia, Easton, Plumsteadville, Newtown and most other American towns during the Christmas holiday season, one will see Christmas wreaths on many front doors. The art of hanging Christmas wreaths originated with the Romans, who hung wreaths on their doors as signs of victory and of their status in society. In ancient Greece, sports winners were awarded laurel wreaths. Most people don't think about the rich history attached to these beautiful Christmas decorations. I was inspired to write this narrative titled "Christmas Wreath-Making" because Plumsteadville Grange hosts an annual Christmas Wreath-Making Workshop at the Grange Farm Market for grange members and people from the surrounding communities.

CHRISTMAS WREATH-MAKING

Plumsteadville Grange members and friends show off their holiday cheer with their beautifully handmade Christmas wreaths, which are magnificent decorations for homes, offices, or public buildings. (Photo by Amanda Penacale of the 2021 Christmas Wreath-Making Grange Event at Plumsteadville Grange on 11 December 2021)

CHRISTMAS WREATH-MAKING

Christmas wreaths are easily made by twisting evergreen branches into a large circle and decorating the circle with pinecones, dried fruit and other tree ornaments and topping it off with a bow.

One particular type of holiday wreath is an Advent wreath, which is a wreath with four candles in it. In many traditional Christian homes, on each of the four Sundays preceding Christmas Day (the season known as Advent), an Advent candle is lit while a prayer is said. Advent is celebrated in the Christian faith to prepare for the birth of Jesus Christ. Lighting the Advent candles symbolizes newness, eternal life and the birth of Christ. The candlelight can also symbolize the light that Jesus brought into the world.

According to Ace Collins, author of *Stories Behind the Great Traditions of Christmas,* hanging a wreath on a door is almost as essential to Christmas as decorating a Christmas tree. He claimed that the two traditions come from the same place: The trees gave birth to the wreaths.

The Christmas tree tradition of bringing an evergreen tree into the home in the winter began in the sixteenth century. Germans are usually credited with starting the Christmas tree tradition. However, Eastern and Northern Europeans followed the custom as well. Back then, pruning an evergreen tree was part of the preparation process. Branches were cut to make a tree more uniform in shape and better able to fit into a room. Instead of throwing away those cut evergreen branches, the Europeans braided them into wreaths. Then those wreaths were often hung on the family's front door.

Near my home in Pennsylvania, the Plumsteadville Grange hosts an annual Christmas Wreath-Making Workshop at the Grange Farm Market for grange members and people from nearby communities. Each year, it was interesting to observe the wreath-making talents of the members of the grange and local artists, who had jingled their way to the Grange Holiday Market for the workshop.

The enthusiasm, dedication and festive mood of the participants were notable. The participants exchanged wreath-making ideas and shared their wreath-making supplies with each other.

In addition to making Christmas wreaths, the workshops also featured local vendors selling their homemade Christmas items, such as apple butter, bread, honey, sourdough pretzels, goat's milk soap, greeting cards, beeswax candles and food wraps, alpaca dryer balls and knitting yarn, framed photographs, hand-painted Christmas tree ornaments, water and oil paintings and much, much more.

I would like to close this narrative with the following American proverb, titled "Wreaths," "Hung to fill our homes with holiday cheer, they are made in circles with no beginning nor end to symbolize the endless connection we have with God, family and dear friends."

To me, this proverb reflects the joy expressed during the grange's annual Christmas wreath-making event where Christmas was love in action; hence the real reason for the season.

PRELUDE: On 11 May 2021, Pennsylvania State Grange officials made history on behalf of 8,208 subordinate and lifetime grange members. Per the recommendation of the Pennsylvania State Grange President and Executive Committee, we purchased the new Pennsylvania State Grange home at 26 CJEMS Lane, Mifflintown, Pennsylvania. (CJEMS is an acronym for Central Juniata Emergency Medical Services.) I was inspired to write this narrative titled "New Chapter for a 150-Year-Old Grange" because I am a third-generation grange member, and I have been a grange member for more than 70 years. I was utterly delighted to be part of the team effort to acquire the property for the head office for all of Pennsylvania's 173 subordinate granges.

NEW PENNSYLVANIA STATE GRANGE HOME

Above right: The Pennsylvania State Grange President signs documents at the settlement on the new Pennsylvania State Grange headquarters. (Photo by Lizzie Bailey of Wayne Campbell, PSG President and Buyer, Betsy Fairman and Paula Frymoyer, sellers signing closure documents with Jim Diamond at right representing the PSG Executive Committee witnessing this historical event on 11 May 2021)

Center: On 26 May 2021, this new sign was installed by Debbie Campbell and Wayne Campbell at the new Pennsylvania State Grand headquarters. (Photo by Debbie Campbell just minutes after the sign was installed)

NEW PENNSYLVANIA STATE GRANGE HOME

In 1871, the Pennsylvania State Grange (PSG) was established. Over the years, the grange's rich heritage has contributed a plethora of services to rural communities, local residents and people in need both domestically and internationally.

Nelson Mandela said, "If you want the cooperation of humans around you, you must make them feel they are important, and you do that by being genuine and humble."

The genuine, humble leadership of Pennsylvania's subordinate granges encourages its members to contribute copious endowments, which ameliorate the well-being of needy citizens, regardless of their educational level, nationality, language, or religion. Grange members work hard, have fun, make history and help many people.

Grange members from across the Commonwealth of Pennsylvania yearned to acquire a permanent state grange headquarters located somewhere near the center of the state. A Realtor contacted state grange President Wayne Campbell, indicating he had a building for sale that fulfilled criteria established by the state grange president and executive committee.

When the grange executive committee visited the site, they determined that the building needed very little remodeling and that it was adequately acceptable to be the new state grange headquarters. In April 2021, the PSG executive committee voted to approve the purchase of the building for the new state grange headquarters. The Pennsylvania State Grange members were excited and happy to have found a new home.

The new state grange headquarters fulfills many needs of the state grange, including space to conduct its daily business, conferences, executive committee meetings and conclaves. It will even be the site of a museum to exhibit grange objects of historical significance that have been stored away in boxes for many years.

Furthermore, the new headquarters building has access to municipal sewage and water, magnificent road frontage for a large state grange sign and ample parking adjacent to the building. The location is also easy to find.

Tuesday, 11 May 2021, grange members closed on the new property. The meeting was attended by Wayne Campbell, buyer and State Grange President; Betsy Fairman and Paula Frymoyer, sellers; Marianne Stiely, paralegal representative; and James Diamond and Ruth Vonda, representatives of the Pennsylvania State Grange executive committee. Lizzie Bailey, Pennsylvania State Grange public relations and membership consultant, and her husband, Cliff Bailey, recorded the event.

Today, all subordinate grange groups and members are welcome to call the Pennsylvania State Grange office to schedule a tour of their new headquarters.

The building has some unique history. The wide plank boards and German siding on the walls had been removed from the previous building on the land before it was torn down. The former owner hand-stamped each individual brick design on the cement floor of the conference room. Conceivably, the Pennsylvania State Grange will enjoy this beautiful, historic site for another 150 years of life. Long live the benevolent endeavors for humankind by the Pennsylvania State Grange!

PRELUDE: The Plumsteadville Grange Farm Market was established when a group of enthusiastic grange members convinced the membership that there was a need for a farm market in the community. On the first Saturday of June 2002, the first farm market was open. The farm market is sponsored by members of Plumsteadville Grange. It is a community service activity for local residents to market their homegrown food and hand-crafted products. The market is located adjacent to the Grange Hall in Plumsteadville, Pennsylvania. The only rule about selling products at the market is: The vendor has to produce or make the products being sold. I was inspired to write this narrative "Plumsteadville Grange Farm Market" because I was president of the grange when it was founded, and oh what a joy it was to work with such a dedicated, faithful, steadfast, enthusiastic group of local grange members. This effort is part of Plumsteadville Grange history, and I felt the details described herein needed to be documented.

PLUMSTEADVILLE GRANGE FARM MARKET

Pat Worthington is shown selling her fresh vegetables at her Plumsteadville Grange Farm Market table. (Photo by Jim Diamond of a local farmer selling vegetables produced in her garden in June 2006)

PLUMSTEADVILLE GRANGE FARM MARKET

Plumsteadville Grange Farm Market is a spectacular success story. The market is supported by enthusiastic vendors who are dedicated to both the grange and to their local consumers,

This success story began in 2001, when a group of dedicated, faithful, steadfast, enthusiastic local grange members met with the grange president (me) to discuss their idea to start a farm market. I appreciated the group's enthusiasm, so I encouraged them to move forward with their ideas. Then, as per my usual modus operandi, I got out of their way and let it happen!

The excited group convinced the grange membership that a farm market would be a great use of the barn on the newly purchased property next door. That unique group of people included Karen and Don Moss, Annette and Dan Crooke, Helen and Royal Doner, Toni and Pete Keller and Edith Ott.

Many tasks were needed to transform the barn into a farm market. They included repairing the barn's sides and roof, painting the sides, concreting a slab on side of the barn, and establishing a safe flow of traffic into and out of the farm market. We also needed to advertise the opening of the farm market to attract local clientele.

Each June, July, August, September and October, the farm market is open on Saturday mornings from 8:30 to 12:30. The goods for sale depend upon the season and can feature vegetable plants, cut and potted flowers, a variety of vegetables and fruit (including beets, tomatoes, lettuce, radishes, sweet corn, broccoli, cabbage, cauliflower, eggplant, and strawberries), honey, baked goods (cookies, bread, muffins), quilts, books, wood carvings, fence posts, pottery and more. In addition to homegrown foods and hand-crafted items for sale, the farm market also offers entertainment, including local musicians, demonstrations, exhibits and shows.

Young 4-H Club* members and FFA students are encouraged to sell their homegrown food and hand-crafted products. An example of a dedicated local entrepreneurial vendor family is the eight young members of the Macri family—Connie, Barbara, Irene, Stephen, Maria, Logan, Jenna and Christine. Connie, the eldest, started baking and selling cakes, cookies, biscotti and Italian bread. Her products were very popular with customers. She documented all her recipes with ingredients and nutritional value. She studied catering at college and obtained a degree in food science at Delaware Valley University and now works in the food science industry.

Over the past twenty-three years, the farm market has yielded thousands of local dollars transacted by the local vendors and their supportive community customers.

An enjoyable socializing custom has unfolded at the farm market. The highlight of many senior citizens' week is a visit to Plumsteadville Grange Farm Market to purchase a cookie made by the Macri family or 4-H members and sup a free cup of coffee while "swapping some lies" with longtime friends and neighbors.

PRELUDE: On 4 December 1867, the National Grange of the Order of Patrons of Husbandry was founded, usually simply called the National Grange. This social organization encourages families to band together to promote the economic, social and political well-being of their community and agricultural endeavors. My local grange, the Plumsteadville Grange, is noted for its commitment to the community through its local leadership, financial and organizational strength, and ability to make a difference in the lives of people of all ages. As described previously, one of the many successes of Plumsteadville Grange is its Saturday morning farm market. I was inspired to write this narrative titled "Roundtable Chats" because I look forward to attending the Plumsteadville Grange Farm Market each Saturday morning to chat with members, friends, neighbors and even strangers over free cups of black coffee, a bowl of Scott Guiser's homemade vegetable soup and cookies. We discuss and debate a plethora of interesting topics.

ROUNDTABLE CHATS

Roundtable chats are informal discussions on current topics that are important or interesting to the participants and provide a venue to share with and learn from other people. (Photo by Jim Diamond of a roundtable chat at the Plumsteadville Grange Farm Market on 15 October 2022)

ROUNDTABLE CHATS

Most granges across America help people through community service endeavors and volunteer work that bring diverse people together. For example, my local grange, the Plumsteadville Grange, has active members who are carpenters, electricians, plumbers, chemists, secretaries, teachers, computer technologists, feed salesmen, extension educators, housewives, farmers, meat cutters and much more.

Our frequent, informal roundtable chats at Plumsteadville Grange are friendly discussions or debates that bring in different points of view from the attendees. The attendees always seem to enjoy the roundtable chats, whether they are actively participating or just listening.

A roundtable chat can be about practically anything—a myriad of local, county, state, national and international topics. Some roundtable chats have a purpose, such as acquiring or sharing information, promoting an idea, or explaining an issue to help attendees work toward a common goal. It's helpful to ask specific questions or make major points to avoid misunderstandings or vague answers.

Roundtable chats provide opportunities for people, especially rural community residents, to express thoughts, ideas, opinions, experiences, feelings, reactions, lessons and memories without restraints.

I find it a joy to talk with and listen to longtime friends and meet new ones. Together, we solve the "world's problems" at our roundtable chats. Some of our previous discussions have included the Philadelphia Phillies, Philadelphia Eagles, hunting, fishing, book writing, effects of the hot weather, drought, health issues, travel, life experiences, social concerns, future of agriculture in Bucks County, educational issues in public schools, religious concerns and much, much more. Often the roundtable chats address sales, contact information and recruiting new grange members.

One topic that is not discussed at grange roundtable chats is politics because the grange organization is non-partisan. The grange supports only policies, never political candidates or parties. Avoiding political issues helps the mood of the discussions or debates remain congenial and meaningful.

Remember: Words make you think a thought, a thought makes you feel the words, and good discussion makes you feel thoughtful words.

I would like to close this narrative by quoting American writer and aviator Anne Morrow Lindbergh, who wrote, "Good conversation is as stimulating as black coffee and just as hard to sleep after."

Personally, I would rather think about stimulating discussions than sleep, hence the reason my kitchen and our grange always have an endless supply of free coffee on hand.

PRELUDE: The expression "We have always done it this way" is one of the most fatalistic sentences in the English language. They obstruct growth and change within the framework of any organization, such as granges. A plethora of granges in rural and suburban communities across Pennsylvania and America have provided enormous benefits to local residents. However, societal changes dictate the need for mission adjustments of local granges. I was inspired to write this narrative titled "We Have Always Done It This Way" because I have observed many local well-meaning, successful granges dissipate from their communities because their memberships resisted change, preferring to say, "We have always done it this way."

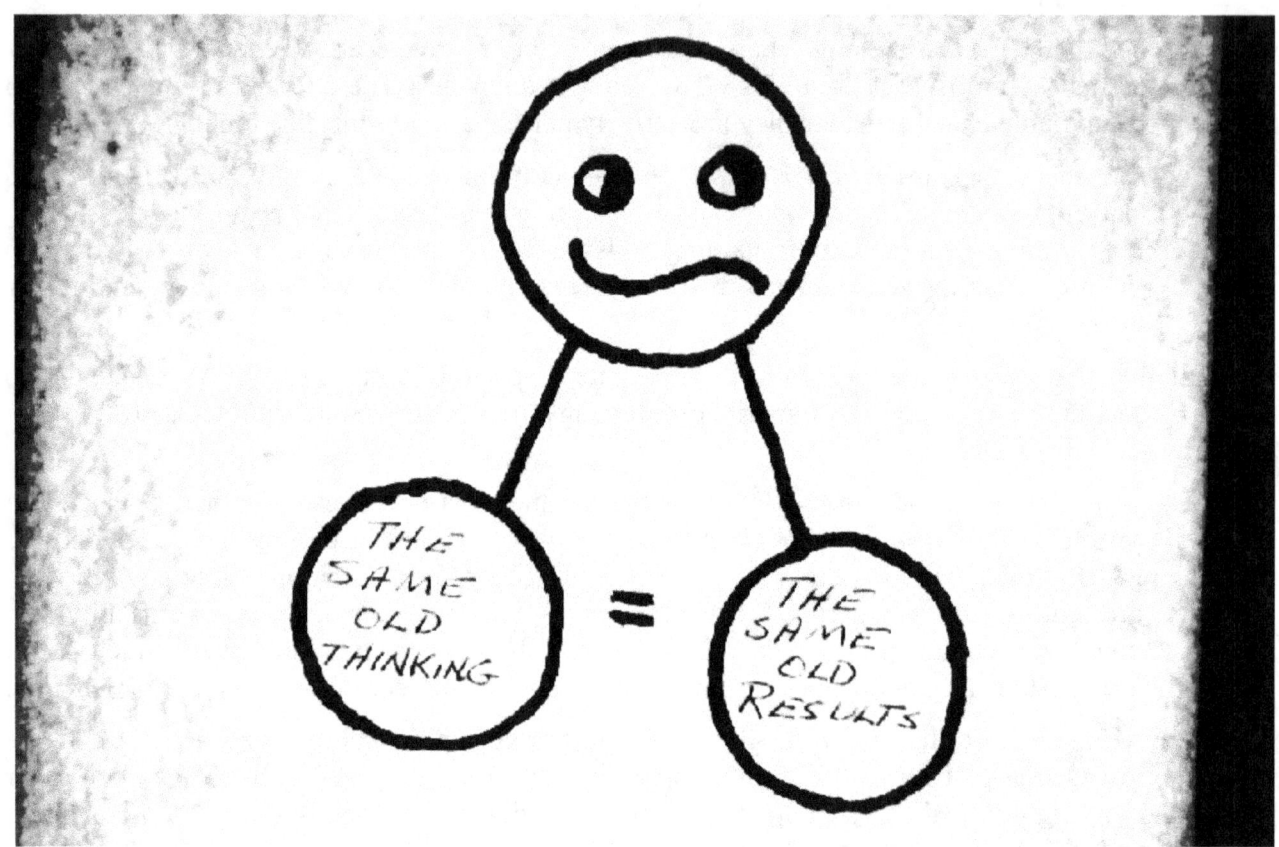

WE HAVE ALWAYS DONE IT THIS WAY

Many granges with innumerable years of existence have provided valuable, useful, profitable, beneficial, rewarding benefits to their communities. However, resting on one's past laurels is often a last-ditch effort to remain relevant. (Illustration by Jim Diamond)

WE HAVE ALWAYS DONE IT THIS WAY

Many organizations, especially granges, provide valuable, useful, profitable, rewarding benefits to their communities. However, resting on past laurels is often a last-ditch effort to remain relevant.

Also, relying on past achievements leads to organizational stagnation. Stagnation leads to the popular saying, "If it ain't broke, don't fix it." Past successes are no guarantee for future success, especially when there are constant changes within local societies. Past successes often encourage members to resist new ideas. If members, especially older members, resist change or new ideas, it is quite frustrating to new members, younger members, or any member who has a new or different idea.

Based upon previous successes, long-time members firmly believe there is no better way to do things. Oftentimes they are correct, but other members become frustrated when brilliant ideas for organizational improvement or change are constantly scoffed at or ignored. When members cannot visualize their future, they become "change blind," which leads to dwindling membership.

I have been asked numerous times, "How can I prevent 'change blindness'?" Ways to prevent change blindness include: Do not pull any surprises. Give a heads-up to the organizational leaders and discuss the significance of your thinking and its importance before presenting it to the group. Be prepared to explain how and why your ideas can benefit the organization. Be prepared to meet some resistance from members.

Even if your organization's past activities have been successful, change could still improve your organization. Change is an important trait of nature. In fact, sometimes change has to happen. It's important to change yet still maintain the mission of the organization.

Sometimes, people do a good job describing a new idea, but it is still shot down. That's incredibly exasperating. When that happens to you, you are allowed to feel a little glum, but if you want to thrive within the group, you need to be positive and bounce back.

Bouncing back within a stagnated group where you don't feel appreciated can deflate your enthusiasm. However, stay positive! Being part of an organization where the members are intolerant to change presents some definite challenges. It's important to be adequately prepared before presenting your new ideas.

Even if your suggestion is rejected, in the long run, you can rest easy knowing that you tried your absolute hardest to get other people's approval.

One of my favorite quotes, which is frequently attributed to Ralph Waldo Emerson but actually was by Muriel Strode, goes like this, "I will not follow where the path may lead, but I will go where there is no path, and I will leave a trail."

Your change process can create and leave a new trail for other people to follow.

PRELUDE: Quilts are patchworks of designed patterns that are sewn together to create an old-fashioned look. They are works of art that can reflect family memories or historical events. The word "quilt" comes from the Latin word *culcita,* which means "stuffed mattress or cushion." Traditionally, a quilt is composed of three layers of natural or artificial fiber (yarn or thread): (1) a woven cloth top (aka patchwork), (2) a layer of batting, and (3) a woven back using a technique called quilting.* Quilting is the process of sewing the three layers of fiber together. One Wednesday morning, after observing a group of women at Plumsteadville Grange sewing a quilt to be raffled off by the grange and won by a fortunate ticketholder, I was inspired to write this narrative titled "Windows of the Past."

WINDOWS OF THE PAST

A quilting* bee is a group of people who quilt together around a wood quilting frame. Pictured here are Plumsteadville Grange members from left to right: Edith Ott, Meg Lomax and Helen Doner. (Photo by Jim Lomax at 2002 Plumsteadville Community Day.)

WINDOWS OF THE PAST

Quilt-making is an art! In the late seventeenth and early eighteenth centuries, Dutch and English settlers introduced quilting* to the United States. Back then, quilting was done out of necessity. Quilts were used for warm bed coverings, room dividers and window coverings to reduce cold drafts.

People can learn quilting by taking classes from experts, but in the past, many children learned to quilt by watching and helping their mothers and grandmothers, then passing the skill down through the generations. While watching and working on the quilts, children would also absorb many words of wisdom from their elders.

During a quilting bee, people get together to sew and quilt around a wood quilting frame, which keeps the quilt taut while its being stitched. Quilting bees are social events where people learn new skills and techniques and chat.

For many years, Plumsteadville Grange members and friends have faithfully met on Wednesday mornings to artfully create magnificent quilts and socialize. The interacting portion of the quilting bee enables participants to learn about impactful communal happenings. For example, one might learn who is recovering from an illness or hospitalization, getting married or divorced, losing their job, building a new home or moving, or even who has died.

When producing a quilt that describes an impactful happening, it is important to following a specific sequence. First a design is chosen from many traditional patterns, including nine patch, pinwheel, Dresden plate, bear's paw and attic windows. Then the material is bought or often found, utilizing accumulated scraps. Of particular concern are colors, and the quiltmakers ask themselves, Will this one blend with that? Is that one too bright or too pale? For who or what is the quilt being made—a wedding present, dowry* chest, a baby, or as a wall hanging? The answers to those questions will help to determine the quilt's size: king, queen, full, twin, or crib.

Next, the fabric is cut into small pieces using templates, a cutting board, and a rotary cutter. The cut pieces are then sewn together in equally sized squares, by hand or machine. Then the squares are checked for size and sewn together in rows, horizontally and vertically. Once all the pieces have been joined to form the large quilt top, the backing is attached, with the batting sandwiched between the front and the back. The quilt is now ready to put in the frame and be either hand-quilted or machine-quilted.

Antique quilts were all hand-sewn, of course. To determine if a quilt was sewn by hand or machine, examine the stitching. If the stitches appear unevenly spaced or of different sizes, the quilt was handmade.

Let me close this narrative with this quote by an unknown author, "In the quilt of life, friends are the stitches that hold it together."

PRELUDE: The world's largest pipeline, the Trans-Alaska Pipeline System, which is commonly known as the Alaska Pipeline, is an 800-mile crude oil transportation system spanning Alaska that includes eleven pump stations and several hundred miles of feeder pipelines. The Trans-Alaska Pipeline System begins in Prudhoe Bay on Alaska's North Slope and stretches through rugged and beautiful topography to Valdez, the northernmost ice-free port in North America. The crude oil pipeline is privately owned by the Alyeska Pipeline Service Company. I was inspired to write this narrative "Alaska Pipeline" because I had a difficult time imagining the immense size of this aboveground pipeline that has the capability to transport more than two million barrels of oil per day.

ALASKA PIPELINE

In March 1975, construction began on the Trans-Alaska Pipeline System, and it was completed in May 1977. Its pipe's forty-eight-inch diameter can transport two million barrels (84,000,000 gallons) of crude oil daily from Prudhoe Bay to Valdez, Alaska. (Photo by Jim Diamond of an aboveground section of Alaska Pipeline between Prudhoe Bay and Valdez, Alaska, in July 2009)

ALASKA PIPELINE

WOW! What a sight! I felt insignificant standing next to a colossal section of the Trans-Alaska Pipeline System, which is commonly known as the Alaska Pipeline. Work began on the Alaska Pipeline in March 1975, and it was completed in May 1977. Its forty-eight-inch diameter pipe can transport two million barrels (84,000,000 gallons) of crude oil each day in Alaska from Prudhoe Bay on Alaska's North Slope to Valdez. Whew! That is a lot of crude oil. The crude oil pipeline is privately owned by the Alyeska Pipeline Service Company.

My neighbor George traveled to Fairbanks, Alaska, to participate in the construction of this massive project. He said thousands of workers were attracted back then to Valdez, Fairbanks, and Anchorage to work under very difficult challenges. George explained extensive complications arose, mainly from the extreme cold and the difficult, isolated terrain. The construction engineers for the pipeline said that it was the first large-scale project that had to deal with complications caused by permafrost, and new science-based construction adroitness had to be developed to work with the frozen ground. Because of Alaska's predominant permafrost landscape, roughly half of the pipeline is above ground.

The pipeline wasn't designed to be a straight line. Its course was planned to protect it against forward-and-backward shocks and to allow for thermal expansion. George told me that while the engineers were building the part of the pipeline that crosses the Denali Fault, they designed Teflon-coated sliders to allow the pipeline to move side-to-side in an earthquake.

In the summer of 1977, the first barrel of oil flowed through the pipeline, and full-scale production was in swing by the end of that year. However, there have been several notable occurrences of oil leakage, including those caused by sabotage, maintenance failure and bullet holes.

When the coronavirus reduced the global demand for oil, the Alaska Pipeline Service Company decreased their North Slope oil production by 15 percent. The international oil price war simultaneously caused a glut of oil on the market. On 19 May 2020, Alaska's Energy Desk Officer in Anchorage Tegan Hanlon reported the "trans-Alaska pipeline requested oil companies to send more crude from the North Slope to Valdez because economic trading was reopening."

I would like to end this narrative by quoting the Governor of Maine and author Paul LePage who wrote, "Everybody looks at the negative effects of global warming, but with the ice melting, the Northern Passage has opened up. So maybe, instead of being at the end of the pipeline, we're now at the beginning of a new crude oil pipeline."

PRELUDE: In 1928, the Future Farmers of America (FFA) was founded by a group of young farmers. Their mission was to teach young boys and men how to feed a growing population by learning that agriculture is more than raising animals and planting crops. The curriculum showed agriculture to be a science, a business and an art. Prior to 1969, only boys were permitted to be members of the FFA,* but in 1969 at the National FFA Convention, a resolution was passed to officially allow girls to become members. Since then, girl FFA members have shaped the future of local, state and national agricultural education and the agricultural industry. I was inspired to write this narrative "Amending the National FFA Constitution" because I attended the 1969 National FFA Convention in Kansas City, Missouri, with one of my students who was the immediate Pennsylvania State FFA president and a delegate who voted to amend the National FFA Constitution to allow girls to become members. This was an important change for me because one of my vocational agriculture students was a young lady who had not been permitted to participate in FFA competitions that led to national competitions back before girls were allowed to be FFA members.

AMENDING THE NATIONAL FFA CONSTITUTION

Congratulations to five members (standing) of the Upper Bucks Tech Future Farmers of America (FFA) chapter who received their Keystone Farmer Degree and two members (kneeling) who received their FFA* jackets during the 1979 mid-winter FFA Convention at the Pennsylvania Farm Show. (Photo provided by the Upper Bucks Tech School in Perkasie, Pennsylvania)

AMENDING THE NATIONAL FFA CONSTITUTION

William E. Hickson, who studied in The Netherlands and Germany, is credited with popularizing this proverb, "Tis a lesson you should heed: If at first you don't succeed, try, try, try again."

The push for female Future Farmers of America (FFA) membership was an effort that tried, tried and tried again.

On 23 October 1935, during the morning session of that year's National FFA* Convention, delegate Alfred Vaughn broached the subject that girls should be allowed full membership at the national level. However, according to the Eighth National Convention Proceedings Report:

> *"That when officially found that any State Association in a Future Farmers of America has girl members on its rolls, such State Associations shall be denied participation in all national Future Farmer of America contests and national FFA awards. And no funds from the national treasury shall be available to such State Associations for the purpose of transporting delegates to the national conventions until such time as the names of the girl members are removed from the official rolls of the State Association and local chapters in accordance with the constitution."*

That was why my student Cynthia Poth Graham, who won the Upper Bucks Tech FFA Chapter, Tri-County, and Regional FFA public speaking contests, could not win the state public speaking contest. If she had won the state contest, she would not have been permitted to participate in the Tri-State competition because to do so, she had to be a member of the National FFA Association.

Back then, even females enrolled in agricultural education classes were not allowed to become FFA members. Some girls got around the rules by applying for membership using only their initials, not revealing their gender. Other girls were allowed to be "social ambassadors" for their FFA chapter. They received a coveted sweetheart jacket.

In 1968, my Upper Bucks Tech student Timothy Ruth, President of the Pennsylvania State FFA, submitted a proposal at the National FFA Convention in Kansas City, Missouri, to amend the State and National FFA Constitution and allow girls to join the FFA. It was defeated.

Then on 15 October 1969, at the National FFA Convention again in Kansas City, Paul Bankhead of California moved and Robert Craig of Michigan seconded once more to strike the word "male" from the FFA constitution. Hurrah! That motion carried! Timothy voted in favor of the motion, and I was with him when the first stanza of this resolution was read, "WHEREAS, we, the delegates to the forty-second annual convention, have voted to allow all students of vocational agriculture to become members of the FFA."

Since 1969, girls have served as convention delegates and national and state officers, and they have been named as American Star Farmers. Today, nearly half of all FFA members are girls, and females hold half of state leadership positions. I would like to close this narrative by quoting Nelson Mandela, who served several years in prison and then became President of South Africa, and said, "Education is the most powerful weapon which you can use to change the world."

In my humble opinion, the FFA and agricultural education in general should always be open to both boys and girls.

PRELUDE: WHEW! The year 2020-2021 was weird, eccentric and atypical—a year without precedent! According to the World Health Organization (WHO) and Centers for Disease Control (CDC), from February 2020 to the end of 2021, the global coronavirus pandemic was worse than ever. Many countries had imposed strict lockdowns because new variants of the virus were infecting people at alarming rates. From the United States to the Portuguese Republic to the Republic of Brazil to the Arab Republic of Egypt, health services struggled like never before. I was inspired to write this narrative titled "A Year of Covid-19" because I personally was impacted negatively by Covid-19, as were hundreds of millions of people around planet Earth. However, I also was impacted positively by certain components of the Covid-19 lockdowns for at least one year.

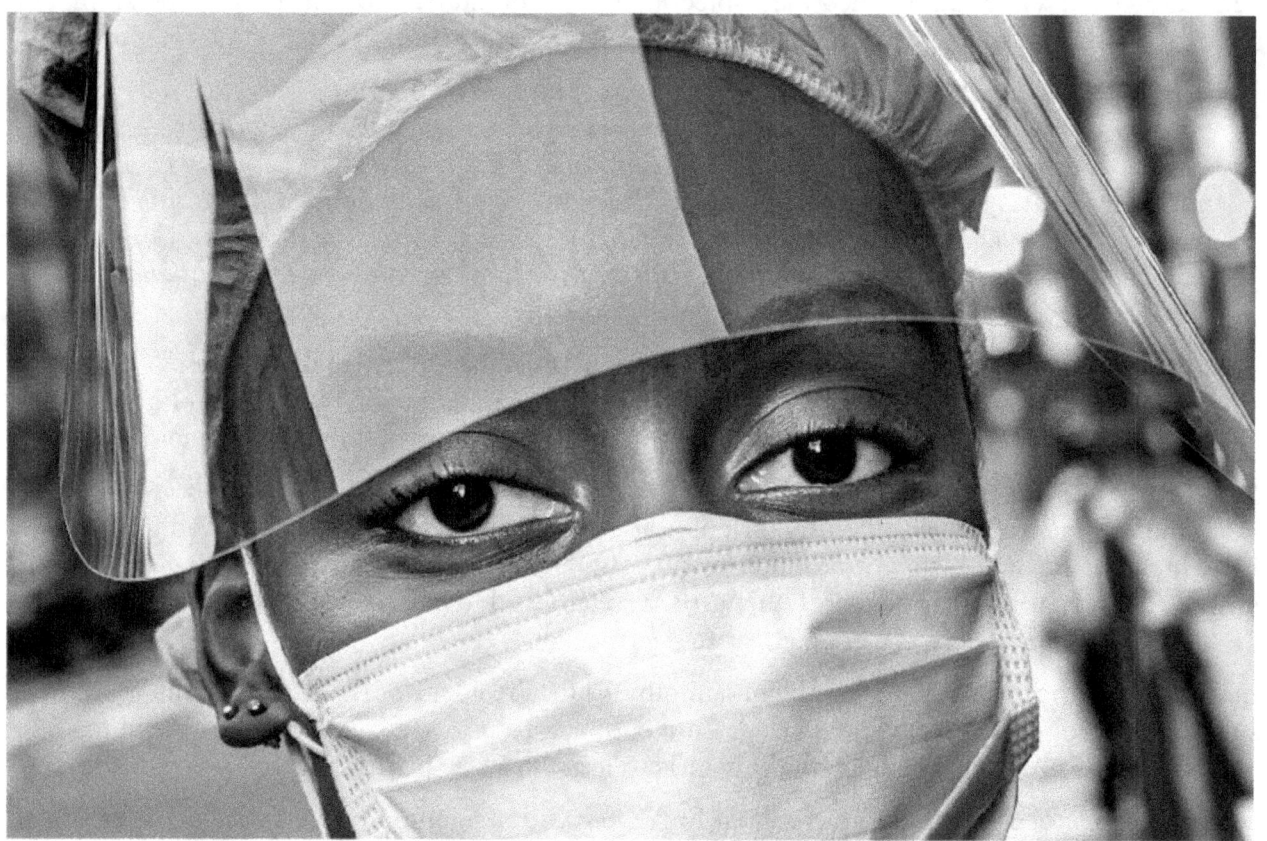

A YEAR OF COVID-19

According to health experts, the best ways to prevent and slow the transmission of the virus was by wearing a mask in public, washing your hands for at least twenty seconds, avoiding close contact with people outside your home, staying at least six feet away from others, avoiding touching your face, and covering your coughs with a tissue or the inside of your elbow. (Photo by Peter Turlley of Shannone, who worked with Covid-19 patients at Lenox Hill Hospital in New York City, in May 2020)

A YEAR OF COVID-19

On 11 February 2020, the World Health Organization (WHO) announced an official name for the disease that was causing the new 2019 coronavirus outbreak, which had been first identified in Wuhan, China. The new name of this disease was coronavirus disease 2019, abbreviated as Covid-19: "Co" corona, "vi" for virus, and "d" for disease. Covid-19 was a new disease that had not previously been seen in humans.

Although most people with Covid-19 had mild symptoms, it could also cause severe illness and death. Older people and those with underlying medical problems such as cardiovascular disease, diabetes, chronic respiratory disease and cancer were more likely to develop severe illness.

The Covid-19 virus spreads primarily through droplets of saliva or discharge from the nose when an infected person coughs or sneezes. Health experts say that the best ways to prevent and slow transmission of Covid-19 are by wearing a mask in public, washing your hands for at least twenty seconds, avoiding close contact with people outside your home, staying at least six feet away from others, avoiding touching your face and covering your coughs with a tissue or the inside of your elbow.

Over the course of the pandemic, Covid-19 has affected different people in different ways. Infected people have had a wide range of symptoms, which may appear two to fourteen days after exposure to the virus. Symptoms include fever or chills, cough, shortness of breath or difficulty breathing, fatigue, muscle or body aches, headache, new loss of taste or smell, sore throat, congestion or runny nose, nausea or vomiting and diarrhea.

I personally stayed home nearly every day for the worst year of the pandemic because I was "ripe" for this horrid virus. I was eighty-two years of age and have a serious case of asthma,* so abiding by the CDC rules contributed to preserving my health during that dangerous time.

Time is a terrible thing to waste while being quarantined, so I used a great deal of my time composing narratives, formulating fifty gallons of homemade 2020 wines, birdwatching and collecting domestic animal bells from around the world. During the pandemic, I acquired a cowbell from a Russian dairy farmer.

In September 2020, I completed and released my book *I Inhale Adventures and Exhale Narratives*, which includes 428 pages of 212 narratives. Then I wrote 404 pages of 202 additional narratives for the book you are currently reading.

I also spent a large chunk of my time on Zoom meetings. During the pandemic, the only time I left my home was to get groceries. Quite frankly, I made the best of being quarantined by focusing on activities I enjoy.

I would like to close this narrative with a quote by American writer Susan Cain, "Spend your free time the way you like, not the way you think you're supposed to."

I truly enjoyed all the free time the pandemic created, which enabled me to do things I like, not what I think I'm supposed to do.

PRELUDE: A slave can be defined as a captured or purchased person who is forced to provide unpaid labor. Slavery has very deep roots! Literature indicates that in Mesopotamia land ownership and various stages of war, enemies were captured and forced to work as slaves. Egyptians captured slaves by sending expeditions up the Nile River. Greeks used 30,000 slaves in silver mines. Roman military captured slaves by the thousands. Anglo-Saxons invaded England and enslaved native Britons. Slavery became a normal practice in rural England's economy after the Black Plague. Europe's slave trade also thrived because of a far-reaching labor shortage. Portuguese traders brought the first large cargo of slaves from West Africa to Europe by sea. Spanish traders brought African slaves to various settlements, including what is now the United States. Massachusetts was the first British Colony to legalize slavery. I was inspired to write this narrative titled "The Bucks County Underground Railroad" because the African-American Museum of Bucks County can reflect lifestyles in Africa before people were captured and shipped abroad. Current and future generations of all races living in the United States should study and be cognizant of slavery's atrocious chapter in American history.

THE BUCKS COUNTY UNDERGROUND RAILROAD

During the Civil War, Harriet Tubman served as a spy and militia leader with the Union forces. Her goals were to defeat and destroy the system of slavery and in doing so, to decisively defeat the Confederacy. (Photo of Harriet Tubman statue provided compliments of the Borough of Bristol, Pennsylvania)

THE BUCKS COUNTY UNDERGROUND RAILROAD

Slavey still exists worldwide. In 2017, a research consortium including the United Nations International Labor Organization, the group Walk Free, and the UN International Organization for Migration released a joint global study indicating that forty million people were trapped in modern forms of slavery worldwide. Their study reported that of those people, 50 percent were enslaved in forced labor in agriculture, manufacturing, construction, mining, fishing, and other physical-labor industries; 37.5 percent in forced marriage slavery; and 12.5 percent in sex slavery.

For years before the Civil War, hundreds of slaves escaped to the North. To help slaves escape north to freedom, anti-slavery advocates organized "underground railroads." The railroad was used as a metaphor to describe the method of moving people efficiently from one place to another. Many Northerners' eyes had been opened to the horrors of slavery, and they intensely desired to help slaves escape slavery in the South.

Before the Civil War, white Southerners were torn between the economic benefits of slavery and the moral and constitutional issues it raised. They grew more and more defensive of slavery and argued that Black people were incapable of caring for themselves and that slavery was a benevolent institution that kept them fed, clothed and occupied and exposed them to Christianity.

The outbreak of the Civil War changed the future of the American nation and most notably the future of African-Americans held in enslavement. (Using the term "enslave" is a way of professing that slavery was forced upon that person, rather than an inherent condition.)

After the South seceded from the United States, President Abraham Lincoln knew that a method to force the renounced states into appeasement was to remove their labor supply: slaves. On 22 September 1862, after a strategic Union victory at Antietam, near Sharpsburg, Maryland, President Lincoln presented his Preliminary Emancipation Proclamation, which decreed that, as of 1 January 1863, all enslaved people in states currently engaged in rebellion against the Union "shall be then, thenceforward and forever free."

For thousands of escaped slaves in the eighteenth and nineteenth centuries, the Underground Railroad offered hope for a new life. This secret network of hidden, safe places relied on abolitionists and taverns, churches, homes and farms to provide respite for runaways on their journey north.

Bucks County, Pennsylvania, was one of several hubs for the underground railroad. The area was home for many stops along the railroad, a small number of which can still be visited today, including the Goldman Law Office at 90 East State Street, Doylestown; Continental Tavern at 2 North Main Street, Yardley; and the Wedgewood Inn, 111 West Bridge Street, New Hope.

I would like to close this narrative by quoting Harriet Tubman, an underground railroad conductor, nurse, spy and leading abolitionist who escaped slavery and led hundreds of enslaved people to freedom, who said, "I was the conductor of the underground railroad for eight years, and I can say what most conductors can't say: I never ran my train off the track, and I never lost a passenger."

PRELUDE: After visiting and working with people within a plethora of societies and cultures and experiencing contrasting schemes of existence in fifty-nine different countries, the only common denominator within humankind I found is "differences." I view civilization as a journey, rather than as a campaign that is not based on circumstances. I was inspired to write this narrative "Civilizations" to reflect my experiences working with people and accepting them for who they were and not being judgmental if their culture contrasted or conflicted with my personal societal traits.

CIVILIZATIONS

This mural titled "Detail of Civilization" by artist George W. Maynard hangs in the Thomas Jefferson Building of the Library of Congress, in Washington, DC. It portrays civilization from 1890 through 1900. (Photographer unknown)

CIVILIZATIONS

A civilization is a complex human society, usually with certain cultural characteristics and technological developments. In many countries of the world, early civilizations formed when people began coming together in settlements.

Even though the concept of "civilization" is difficult to define, it is still helpful to establish a framework to understand how and why humans came together. My viewpoint of civilizations is that they can be a society, culture, and way of life of people in a particular country or in regions within a country.

There are no limitations on differences that exist amongst societies around the world. Some societal differences are quite ancient, other societal differences are in various stages of transition, and still other societal differences are modern and up-to-date. Some of the societal differences I have viewed include customs, religions, gods worshipped, type of agriculture, food produced and consumed, type of housing, economic levels, education levels, indigenous* skills possessed, effect of wars, traditional thinking, climate and climate changes, landscape topography, tribal edicts, past and present plagues and domestic infrastructure, including roads, railroads, telephones and electricity.

Having observed many civilizations, I believe that people of one society must not be judgmental of other societies just because their cultural traits are different. Integrating common societal traits into a harmonious modus operandi within and among groups of people is the birth of peaceful customs, traditions, thinking and beliefs within the bounds of a civilization. In various nations, civilizations have amalgamated over time, like portions of their respective clans. However, to amend certain societal traits affecting the whole of a community, it is critical that the ideas for change evolve from members within the respective clan, not from an outsider. Indigenous knowledge, skills and needs must be the driving force to redesign cultural mores.*

During times of change, a degree of objection by constituents within a clan can be expected. Different points of view can be healthy within a society as long as societal leaders search out amicable solutions with gusto. A change within the mores of a society can become a desirable long-term component of the traits within a civilization.

The late President of the United States Ronald Reagan said, "The history of our civilization, the great advances that made it possible, is not a story of cynics or doom criers. It is a gallant chronicle of optimists, determined people, men and women who dreamed great dreams and dared to try whatever it took to make them come true."

I would like to close this narrative with a quote by William Penn Adair Rogers, an American stage and film actor and a Cherokee citizen born in the Cherokee Nation Indian Territory, who said, "We will never have true civilization until we have learned to recognize the rights of others."

This statement is relevant today to current civilizations around the world, which includes the United States of America.

261

PRELUDE: On 20 January 2021, the day President Joseph R. Biden Jr. and Vice President Kamala Harris were inaugurated, American flags boldly waved on the National Mall in Washington, DC. The flags were from all fifty states, intended to represent more than 200,000 Americans who could not attend mainly because of the Covid-19 pandemic. I was inspired to write this narrative titled "Flags Boldly Waved on National Mall" because I was saddened to realize that those flags represented so many husbands, fathers, wives, mothers, sons, daughters, grandparents, uncles, aunts, neighbors and friends who could not attend and be part of the inauguration excitement because pandemic regulations prevented them from traveling. What a massive disappointment for thousands of American citizens who wanted to be present for the inauguration.

FLAGS BOLDLY WAVED ON NATIONAL MALL

On 20 January 2021 at the National Mall, a field of American flags represented thousands of people who could not attend the inauguration of the forty-sixth U.S. President, Joseph R. Biden Jr., in Washington, DC. (Photographer unknown)

262

FLAGS BOLDLY WAVED ON NATIONAL MALL

At each of the eleven previous inaugurations at the National Mall during my lifetime, thousands and thousands of people traveled from every state in the union, other territories and many from nations around the world to Washington DC to witness the inauguration ceremony.

On 20 January 2021, the day President Joseph R. Biden Jr. and Vice President Kamala Harris were inaugurated, the National Mall was barren of American citizens and international friends. The previous ten months of the Covid-19 pandemic and the civil unrest just two weeks earlier quelled the attendance.

Many peoples' absence was a response to the insurrection at the U.S. Capitol on 6 January, the day pro-Trump rioters stormed the Capitol building, where rioters broke through windows, fought with police, occupied congressional offices, delayed the certification of Electoral College votes cementing Joe Biden's victory, and left five people dead.

Traditionally, inaugurations were joyous occasions filled with celebrating citizens, banquets, dancing, marching bands, and parades, capped off by fireworks. But in 2021, because of two disruptive threats, thousands of supporters cancelled their travel plans to attend the event in Washington DC.

The few people who did show up encountered a scenario much like a military takeover. Because the FBI warned of possible armed protests by Trump supporters who claimed the election was rigged, more than 25,000 National Guard troops were summoned to Washington DC. The soldiers toted assault rifles, military helicopters circled the sky, eight-foot-high concrete barriers were erected, high fences were capped with razor-sharp barbed wire, and police rode in bulletproof vehicles. All government officials wore bulletproof vests.

The scenario was a far cry from the time-honored, peaceful inaugurations of the past.

This inauguration was historic because President Joesph R. Biden, who once stuttered, was the oldest president ever elected. Vice President Kamala Harris was the first female Vice President as well as the first Vice President of South Asian descent as the daughter of an Indian mother and a Jamaican father, who were both immigrants.

Fortunately hundreds of thousands of people in the United States and countries around the world safely watched the inauguration on television in their respective homes.

I would like to end this narrative with a stanza from a poem written by Amanda Gorman who eloquently and persuasively read her poem titled "The Hill We Climb" at the inauguration. It goes like this: "To compose a country, committed to all cultures, colors, characters and conditions of man, and so we lift our gaze, not to what stands between us, but what stands before us. We close the divide because we know to put our future first we must first put our differences aside."

As citizens of the United States, let's all put our differences aside and lift our gaze to what stands before us because we seek harm to none and harmony for all. May God bless Amanda Gorman and the United States of America.

PRELUDE: The desire to support low-income communities in different parts of the world drives retail store owner Maria Loyd to promote her native culture and fashions. Maria opened her first business at the Lehigh Valley Mall in Whitehall, Pennsylvania. Today, as the owner of Artisanal Gifts in Jim Thorpe, Pennsylvania, Maria showcases her native Colombian culture to the world through handcrafted, fashionable clothing and jewelry. Maria said most of her clients come to her store after they met her at trade shows she attended over the years. According to Maria, her clientele are from all over the place, even Europe. Maria said, "I know exactly what it is like not to have anything." I was inspired to write this narrative because most of Maria's handmade products are created from commodities purchased from community farms in other countries, such as coffee beans and red, white and black beans from Colombia.

JIM THORPE'S ONE OF A KIND

Growing up in Colombia, South America, Maria Loyd started her journey in fashion at seven years of age. Little did she know her life's work would be showcasing her native culture to the world. (Photographer unknown)

JIM THORPE'S ONE OF A KIND

Maria Loyd, owner of Artisanal Gifts in Jim Thorpe, Pennsylvania, showcases her native Colombian culture to the world through handcrafted fashionable clothing and jewelry. She recycles materials to produce a mostly Colombian line of products. Her specialty is forging shoes from all-natural products. Maria helps her clientele with aches and pains to find the right shoes to support their back, knees, hips and ankles.

Maria maintains an amazing showroom, exhibiting jewelry made from repurposed items, such as recycled seeds, citrus peels and beans. Most of her items are vegan and natural. She enjoys teaching people about the benefits of recycling.

Maria was born in Colombia, and while she was growing up there, she worked her way into the fashion industry before expatriating to the United States in 2004. When she first came to the United States, Maria worked in New York City, developing fashion products. However, after living for a time and working for other people in the big city, Maria felt it was time to start her own company, and in doing so revisit the fashion roots of her native land.

Maria said, "It was scary since I didn't have the command of the English language, and I didn't have much money."

Maria's best-selling items are jewelry made from the Tagua palm nut, which is grown in Ecuador. Maria sources recycled orange peels here in the United States and she gets her orange seeds from California.

Maria often collaborates with grandsons of Jim Thorpe, Don Wild Eagle and Jon Thorpe, to promote her products and share stories with the local community and beyond.

Maria enjoys teaching clients about indigenous* communities with her handmade items, rather than what people read in books. She especially likes talking with kids, wrapping their purchases, and making their visit to her store an unforgettable experience.

Furthermore, Maria takes pride in honoring the Kuna native communities of Colombia, their ancestors and elders, as well as the Native American communities in the United States. She also takes pride in giving to humanitarian programs.

I would like to end this narrative with a quote from Maria, "I am here, fighting for what I love and want to do. Fashion is my passion. It's in my blood."

PRELUDE: A mass shooting is an incident of violence carried out by one or more deranged individuals at public or private locations, which might have been chosen randomly or targeted for their emblematic set of principles. Numerous injuries and fatalities often result from these attacks. During the July 4th weekend in 2022, while Americans celebrated the birth of our great nation, mass shootings occurred in California, Indiana, Illinois, Missouri, New York, Pennsylvania, Texas, Virginia and Wisconsin. I was inspired to write this narrative titled "Mass Shootings" because it frightens me to attend sporting events, celebrations, holidays, festivities, and other gatherings of large numbers of people. Furthermore, I avoid going into large cities because of my concerns about crimes such as robberies, purse snatching, carjacking and random shootings.

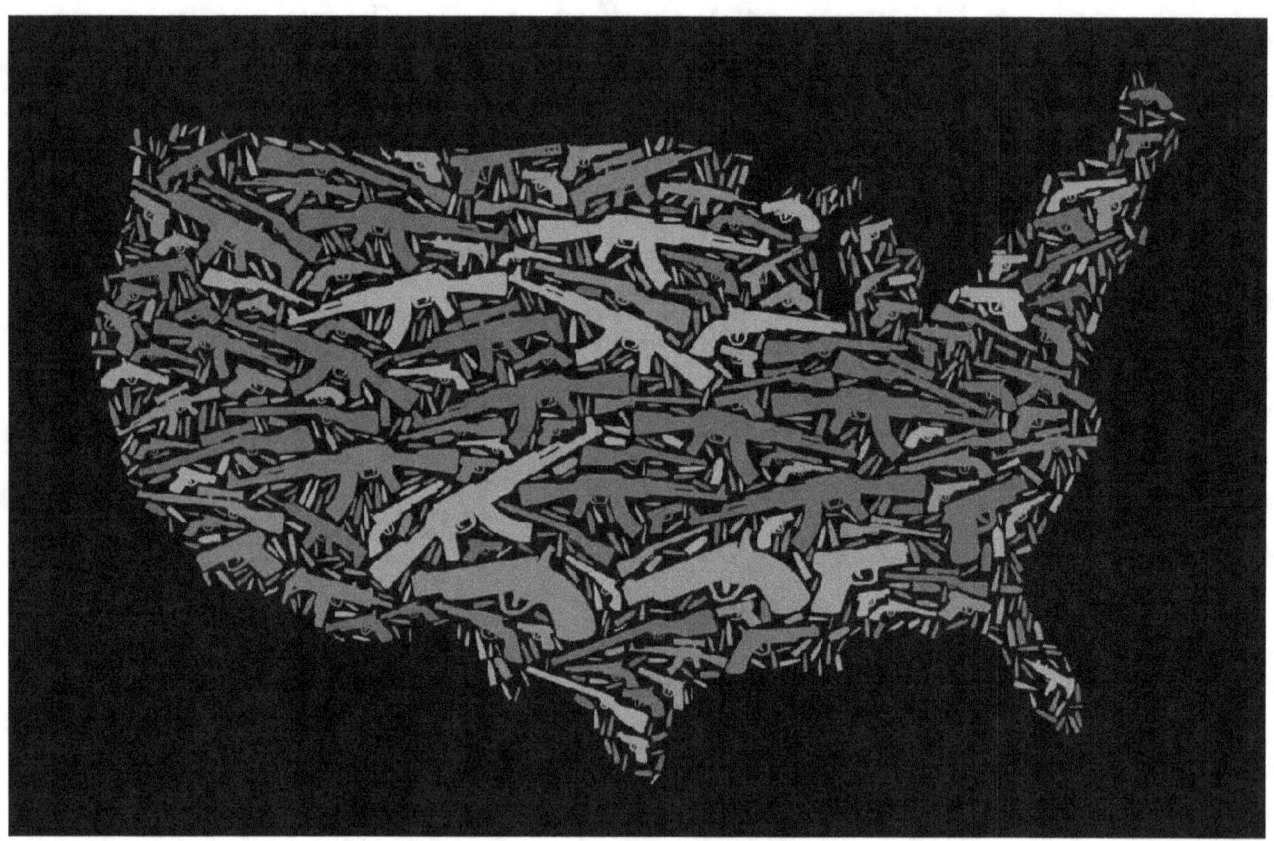

MASS SHOOTINGS

A mass shooting is a violent incident carried out by one or more deranged individuals at a public or private location. Mass shootings across our nation have left many people wounded or killed. (Photo provided by National Public Radio)

MASS SHOOTINGS

In the past twelve years, there has been a drastic increase in the number of mass shootings across the United States of America. The lives of hundreds of innocent children, teenagers, adults, and senior citizens were senselessly destroyed. Between 2009 and 2020, 1,363 people were shot and killed in the United States in mass shootings, and 947 more people were shot and wounded.

The repercussions of a mass shooting impact people far beyond the victims who were wounded or killed. Shootings drastically harm the well-being of survivors and their families, friends and entire communities.

As the number and frequency of mass shootings continues to go up, I ask, "Why? What is happening in our society that causes a driving force within individuals to wound or kill innocent people by shooting them with guns designed to kill the enemy in warfare?"

Mass shootings do not need to be an inevitable element of American life. Experts claim that like all other tragic forms of gun violence, we can prevent mass shootings through commonsense policy solutions.

A bipartisan group of negotiators worked in the Senate and unveiled a legislative bill titled "Bipartisan Safer Communities Act." Just before signing the bill, President Joseph R. Biden Jr. praised the families of gun violence victims with whom he had met. He said their activism in the face of their losses was a difference-maker. President Biden went on to say, "While this bill doesn't do what I want, it does include actions I've long called for that are going to save lives."

In the wake of those horrifying massacres, President Biden signed into law the first major federal gun safety legislation enacted in decades, marking a significant bipartisan breakthrough on one of the most contentious policy issues in Washington, DC. As President Biden finished signing the bill at the White House, he said, "God willing, it's going to save a lot of lives."

This bill included $750 million to assist states in implementing crisis-intervention programs. The money is intended to be used to manage red flag programs, which prevent people in crisis from accessing firearms. It closes a years-old "boyfriend" loophole in domestic violence law, which bars people from having guns who have been convicted of domestic violence crimes against spouses or partners with whom they share children or cohabit. The bill goes after people who sell guns as primary sources of income but have previously evaded registering as federally licensed firearms dealers. The bill also increases funding for mental health programs and school security.

I would like to close this narrative by quoting President Biden who said, "Nothing is going to fill that void left by the victims of numerous families, but they lead the way so other families will not have such horrendous experiences and trauma they've had to live through."

PRELUDE: My late wife, Betty, and I traveled to Rapid City, South Dakota, to visit our longtime friends Bill and Jeanette Keck. From Rapid City, we traveled twenty-five miles northeast to the Black Hills to see Mount Rushmore. Whoa! What an awesome sight! Mount Rushmore is a national memorial that was carved into the mountain by a master carver named Gutzon Borglum to pay homage to the United States of America when it celebrated its first 150 years as a free nation. I was inspired to write this narrative titled "Mount Rushmore" because that fabulous work of art reflects a salute to the founding, growth, development and preservation of this country, the United States of America, that I so dearly love, where I am blessed to be a citizen.

MOUNT RUSHMORE

Betty and I drove into Pennington County to visit Mount Rushmore to observe the famous, colossal artwork carved into the southeastern face of the granite mountain by American master carver Gutzon Borglum. Mount Rushmore features four former presidents of the United States of America. (Photographer unknown)

MOUNT RUSHMORE

While my late wife, Betty, and I were in the Black Hills National Forest of South Dakota, we drove into Pennington County to visit Mount Rushmore to observe the famous, colossal artwork carved into its granite southeastern face by American master carver Gutzon Borglum. Mount Rushmore features four former presidents of the United States of America. Gutzon began carving Mount Rushmore in 1927, and he completed it in 1941.

I learned in grade school that these four former presidents are George Washington, Abraham Lincoln, Thomas Jefferson and Theodore Roosevelt. At Mount Rushmore, a National Parks guide informed us why those four presidents were chosen.

George Washington led European immigrants and settlers in the Revolutionary War to win independence from Great Britain. This is why he is called the "father of the our country." He laid the foundation for American democracy.

Abraham Lincoln was selected because he held America together during the Civil War. He strongly believed his steadfast duty was to preserve the union and that slavery must be abolished.

Thomas Jefferson was the principal author of the Declaration of Independence, which has inspired democracies around the world. He also doubled the size of our country by purchasing the Louisiana Territory from France in 1803.

Theodore Roosevelt led America's rapid economic growth into the twentieth century. He linked the East and the West by negotiating the construction of the Panama Canal. He also worked to end large corporate monopolies and ensure the rights of the common working man.

Betty and I also learned that Mount Rushmore is sometimes known as the "shrine to democracy" because its status has become an American icon both domestically and internationally.

Long before Mount Rushmore was carved, the Native Americans who were the original residents of the Black Hills were displaced by white settlers and gold miners. Mount Rushmore was considered sacred land by the Lakota Sioux.

In 1868, Sioux tribes and the United States government signed the Treaty of Fort Laramie, which assured the Lakota Sioux "undisturbed use and occupation" of the Black Hills, the land now called South Dakota. But the discovery of gold quickly lured thousands of prospectors to the Black Hills to search for gold. The U.S. government began forcing the Sioux to relinquish their claims to the Black Hills. Sioux warriors Sitting Bull and Crazy Horse resisted the U.S. government, which led to the infamous Battle of Little Bighorn in 1876 and the massacre at Wounded Knee in 1890. Ever since those events, Sioux activists have protested the U.S. confiscation of their ancestral lands.

Betty and I then drove to Custer County, South Dakota, to observe the progress of a new colossal work of art of Crazy Horse that was begun by Polish Sculptor Korczak Ziolkowski on 3 June 1968. He was asked by Henry Standing Bear, chief of the Lakota at the time, to carve the monument. The project is still unfinished. The finished art of a Native American warrior with long hair sitting on horseback will be 563 feet high and 641 feet long.

Let me end this narrative with a Sioux proverb, "Speak truth in humility to all people. Only then can you be a true man."

PRELUDE: Since 1961, Peace Corps volunteers have shared trustworthy relationships with people in countries around the world in pursuit of peace and friendship. The transformative impact of the Peace Corps is measured in many ways, such as a shared cup of tea with a host mother that leads to a greater understanding of Americans, a new school library built, a young boy prepared to serve his own community, a young girl who sees herself as equal to her male classmates, and a volunteer who returns home with intercultural enlightenment, magnified career skills, and a lifelong passion for service. This is what the Peace Corps does best for distant unfamiliar societies and its returned volunteers. Peace Corps worldwide personnel are a diverse and far-reaching assortment of host country nationals, American volunteers, families and friends. According to Baha'u'llah, founder of the Baha'i Faith, "The world is but one nation under God, and humankind its citizens." It matters not what deity its citizens adore, worship or obey. In the eyes of their respective god(s), there is neither nationality nor national boundaries. I had to follow a strong, compelling inner desire to do gainful agricultural work overseas. I honestly cannot say why that feeling existed, but I know it was real, and it had to be fulfilled. My late wife, Betty, and I left our safe, secure pastoral life at our Cedar Brook Farm in Ottsville, Pennsylvania, and journeyed to Tchad, Africa, to live in a remote village.

PEACE CORPS VOLUNTEERS

U.S. official Peace Corps logo. (Photo provided by the cordiality of the U.S. Peace Corps)

PEACE CORPS VOLUNTEERS

One of the greatest achievements of President John F. Kennedy was creating the Peace Corps during an unexpected moment and impromptu speech in 1960. The Peace Corps was a new agency that offered opportunities for American citizens to serve both their country and world.

The Peace Corps is an independent agency of the United States government that prepares and deploys volunteers to provide international development assistance. It was established on 1 March 1961 by an executive order of President Kennedy and authorized by Congress the following September by the Peace Corps Act.

The world has always been one body, but humankind through the eons has established surface boundaries that launched so-called citizen homelands. From ancient times through present day, homeland leaders have devised rules and laws that govern supposedly in an orderly fashion. After a long history of conflicts, crusades, campaigns and wars, some homelands have evolved into great, international world powers.

In my opinion, such armed force conflicts are outdated because powerful world nations who are at odds with their neighbors tend to destroy themselves as well. Furthermore, these conflicts cause immeasurable environmental plights, enormous trade gaps and agonizing human suffering.

When my late wife, Betty, and I decided to go to Africa for the first time, my parents could not understand why I would want to do such a thing. We had good-paying, stable employment, had bought our farm, and had a rather bright, unwavering future. From that point of view, they were correct.

However, if financial security, buying a farm, and having an unwavering future was what we were seeking, that is what we had found, but for what reason? What footprint would we leave on this Earth when our Lord calls us home? We knew there was more to life than teaching agriculture to high school students to pay for a farm on which to raise sheep. I felt a strong, compelling inner desire to do agricultural work overseas.

Betty and I joined the Peace Corps as a team. We left our safe, secure pastoral life at Cedar Brook Farm in Ottsville, Pennsylvania, to journey to Tchad, Africa, and live in a remote village for two years with the poorest of the poor. Our new friends in Tchad had no running water, electricity, paved roads, medical resources, gas stations, restaurants, theaters, public transportation, or most of the other niceties found in Ottsville, Pennsylvania. However, Betty and I gained profound, fulfilling peacefulness in knowing that we helped impoverished people help themselves improve their quality of life.

Too many people dream of their future but do nothing to make their desires come true. This French expression best describes my point, *On dois avoir un raison d'etre."* (one must have a reason to be). Dreams cause one to have a reason to be.

Based upon my Peace Corps experiences, I would like to close this narrative by quoting U.S. Senator Ben Cardin (D-MD) who said, "The Peace Corps is one of the most impactful volunteer humanitarian forces in the world. Its volunteers represent the best qualities of American society and reflect the diversity of the United States of America."

PRELUDE: On 6 January 2021, what I witnessed on television was unbelievable! I was born and raised as a citizen of the United States of America! I have a deep feeling and irrefutable love for our democracy, which impacts every citizen from the Arctic Ocean to the Pacific Ocean to the Gulf of Mexico and to the Atlantic Ocean, of which I am proud. I observed an attack on our capitol in Washington DC, the temple of our beloved American democracy. This attack was not by foreign adversaries. It was by a horde of angry American citizens who were skeptical of our institutions and convinced that the 2020 presidential election was stolen by Joseph R. Biden Jr. supporters. I was inspired to write this narrative titled "Unbelievable!" because I still have a hard time believing what happened on 6 January 2021. Yet I know it did happen.

UNBELIEVABLE!

What I witnessed on television on 6 January 2021 was unbelievable—an attack on our capitol in Washington DC, the temple of our beloved American democracy. This attack was not by foreign adversaries. It was by my fellow American citizens. (Photographer unknown)

UNBELIEVABLE!

On 6 January 2021, through an unbelieving eye (I have only one working eye), I witnessed on television a group of American citizens move angrily and forcefully into the capitol of the United States of America in Washington DC in a violent attack against the 227th United States Congress. Blood was shed when five Americans died and several more were injured during the attack. Members of Congress hid in terror as the rotunda was breached before a world watching on TV.

The violence at the capitol was appalling to me because it was an attack on a sacred symbol of American democracy. Furthermore, ambient pressure of surrounding emotions within this rebellious rampage included some of our prominent political and business leaders in an attempt to alter the course of United States history. Because of what happened on 6 January 2021, it is natural that citizens like me feel aggrieved. I do not want to be perceived as being associated with a group of people who have no regard for their political actions. An amendment to the United States Constitution states;

> *"Congress shall make no law respecting an establishment of religion, or prohibiting the free exercise thereof; or abridging the freedom of speech, or of the press; or the right of the people peaceably to assemble, and to petition the government for a redress of grievances."*

I respect the fact that the hooligans who attacked the capitol have the freedom of speech, the press, and to peaceably assemble and to petition the government for a redress of grievances. But not to lawlessly attack our capitol, destroy its contents, risk the lives of our elected legislators, and tarnish our democratic image around the world? How embarrassing!

A portion of the Twelfth Amendment to our Constitution states;

> *"The Electors shall meet in their respective states and vote by ballot for President and Vice-President, one of whom, at least, shall not be an inhabitant of the same state with themselves; they shall name in their ballots the person voted for as President, and in distinct ballots the person voted for as Vice-President, and they shall make distinct lists of all persons voted for as President, and of all persons voted for as Vice-President, and of the number of votes for each, which lists they shall sign and certify, and transmit sealed to the seat of the government of the United States, directed to the President of the Senate; . . . ."*

According to state and federal courts across the nation, the 2020 presidential elections in all fifty states were declared fair and free of fraud and the results were not stolen.

Let me close this narrative with this Buddhist saying, "You cannot hide the sun, the moon, or the truth."

Let us keep the fires of hope and democracy alive in America by widening the circle of patriotic empathy that allows for truth to be told and also for truth to be heard. God bless the United States of America!

PRELUDE: Every morning during my grade school and high school days, the entire class stood, placed our right hands over our hearts, faced the American flag, and in unison said the "Pledge of Allegiance."

"I pledge allegiance to the flag of the United States of America, and to the republic for which it stands, one nation under God, indivisible, with liberty and justice for all."

After we recited the "Pledge of Allegiance," our teacher read a passage from the Bible, then repeated the "Lord's Prayer." This is how we started each school day. No one had the audacity to refuse to state the "Pledge of Allegiance" or the "Lord's Prayer." During my forty-seven-year career using my agricultural, academic and international background, I traveled, worked, and studied in fifty-nine countries on five continents as a farmer, agricultural educator and international consultant. Having experienced the living standards of impecunious people in other nations, this narrative "With Liberty and Justice for All" is my sincere attempt to express my feelings, without shame or inhibition, on the preeminence of our great nation. I proudly repeat the "Pledge of Allegiance," and I dearly repeat the "Lord's Prayer."

WITH LIBERTY AND JUSTICE FOR ALL

The Statue of Liberty was a gift of friendship from the people of France to the United States on 17 June 1885. It is recognized as a symbol of freedom and democracy. (Photographer unknown)

WITH LIBERTY AND JUSTICE FOR ALL

Back in September 1944, I entered first grade at the Woodside Elementary school near Smithfield, Pennsylvania. I was six years old, and beginning that first morning and every morning after, we recited the "Pledge of Allegiance" in our singsong voices.

A common topic I heard older students and adults discussing was World War II. I quickly learned the significance and seriousness of repeating the "Pledge of Allegiance." Even today, more than eighty years later, I am honored and proud to repeat the "Pledge of Allegiance," and I do so with reverence.

My interpretation of "liberty" is a proclamation in what I call a national code of practice. It is the state of being free within American societies from oppressive restrictions imposed by a governmental authority on its citizens' way of life, behavior, religion, or political views.

Sometimes people use the words "liberty" and "freedom" interchangeably. Freedom is more broad than liberty in that it represents the unrestrained ability to fulfill one's desires. However, liberty involves the responsible use of freedom under the rule of law that comes to pass from social systems of ethics, morals, and culture without depriving anyone else of their freedom.

The "Pledge of Allegiance" ends with the words, "With liberty and justice for all." When I learned to recite the pledge, I did not have a clue what the word "justice" meant. However, later in life I learned justice means fairness.

Laws should be applied fairly to all people. That's why the "Lady Justice" statue in Washington DC is blindfolded. The blindfold represents impartial justice when subjecting citizens to the laws of the land. In other words, Lady Justice sees no gender, infirmity, class, age, ethnic group, or color.

That's why I am grateful and proud to be a citizen of the United States of America, which is one nation under God, indivisible, with liberty and justice for all.

PRELUDE: While living and working in several countries on the continent of Africa for nearly ten years, I acquired many indigenous* African objects, which I proudly display in my Pennsylvania home. These objects represent many memories, and at times their number makes my home seem like an African museum. Recently, I reached the age when I felt I needed to seek out an actual museum to display these unique items. I feel that people should have the opportunity to see, study and appreciate the knowledge, talents and skills that African people in rural bush villages use to make their daily lives bearable. The niceties we enjoy in Western nations do not exist in much of Africa. I searched for an appropriate museum to share my African treasures nationwide and came up empty-handed. Then one day, I read an article titled "African-American Museum of Bucks County" in our local newspaper, *The Intelligencer.* I blurted out, "WOW! That's what I have been looking for!" I knew that a local museum would especially appreciate receiving my collection of African objects. I was inspired to write this narrative, "Wow! That's Why I Have Been Looking For!" because I feel that everyone should see these objects African people have used for hundreds of years and continue to use as I write this narrative in 2021.

WOW! THATS WHAT I HAVE BEEN LOOKING FOR

Left: Tchadian tom-tom

Top right: Swazi warrior shields

Bottom right: Tchadian calash

(Photos by Jim Diamond of his artifacts collected in countries in Africa from 1971-1973)

WOW! THAT'S WHAT I HAVE BEEN LOOKING FOR!

Many years ago, a passionate historian, Harvey Spencer of Langhorne, Pennsylvania, and former NAACP president Millard Mitchell of Yardley, Pennsylvania, presented lectures on the Underground Railroad. Together they dreamed of creating a museum in Bucks County, Pennsylvania, to highlight the accomplishments of Black people in our area.

At that time, many people were critical of public school teachers not teaching children about Black history and what their kinfolk accomplished.

In 2014, the African-American Museum of Bucks County was born when it received its designation as a non-profit corporation. Originally, the museum was a traveling show, trekked to schools, libraries, senior centers and other organizations to teach Black historical stories.

Linda Salley was the museum's first president. With a cadre of volunteers, Linda created programs and exhibits of artifacts to tell the stories and experiences of Black people in Bucks County.

One day, the late Harvey Spencer looked across route 413 at the Boone Farm in Core Creek Park near Langhorne, Pennsylvania. He contacted Linda Salley and said, "That building over there is the perfect building for a museum."

Linda agreed, and to make Spencer's idea become a reality, she met with the Bucks County Commissioners and leased the Boone Farm for $1 per year. As of this writing, the Boone Farm is being converted into the African-American Museum of Bucks County (AAMBC), and it is set to open in 2024.

Ironically, many African-Americans worked on the Boone Farm after they fled the South via the underground railroad. The Boone Farm was known to be the only place where Black Americans were paid a fair wage.

The AAMBC will be the only museum dedicated to African-American history in Bucks County. Its goals are for visitors to learn about African history from captivity to escape, their deplorable living conditions, and their contributions to art, culture, policies and sports in Bucks County.

I am donating hundreds of my cherished artifacts to be permanently displayed in the AAMBC to portray lifestyles in African nations before African men and women were captured and shipped to the United States and other nations where they were sold as slaves.

PRELUDE: An academic principle goes like this, "Publish or perish." I was on the threshold of achieving an academic goal of becoming a professor at a major institution of higher learning, the Pennsylvania State University, where I was both a doctoral graduate student and an Instructor of Agricultural Education. After graduation in August 1981, I was promoted to Assistant Professor. That is when I abruptly learned that I was expected to publish the results of my doctoral dissertation as well as other professional topics and present them at professional meetings—or I could look for a different career. The title of my dissertation was "The Effects of Task Instruction Sheets on the Performance of Three Groups of Clientele Studying Sheep Production." The purpose of this post-test-only experimental study was to investigate the effects of using sheep production task instruction sheets in a series of sheep clinics conducted in Pennsylvania. The overall objectives were to develop a package of sheep production task instruction sheets and disseminate them to determine if they were effective on the performance of three different groups of participants: 4-H Club* members, Future Farmers of America members, and part-time adult shepherds. I was inspired to write this narrative, "Writing My Dissertation," because this was my first academic research achievement, and there was much interest in the outcomes.

WRITING MY DISSERTATION

After writing a booklet titled "Sheep Production Task Sheets," composed of thirty-eight competencies, we designed a study to field-test these new instructional materials. (Photo by Jim Diamond, author of "Competency-Based Task Instruction Sheets for Sheep Production," in 1979)

WRITING MY DISSERTATION

For nine years, I was a vocational agriculture teacher at Upper Bucks Technical School (UBTS), then I spent two years as a Peace Corps volunteer before enrolling in a doctoral program at the Pennsylvania State University in 1978. While I was teaching at UBTS, the curriculum coordinator persistently requested I show him my competency-based instruction sheets. What he did not realize was that such sheets did not exist for teaching agriculture. He was perplexed because other vocational education programs were flooded with competency-based instruction materials, and he became aghast that such sheets did not exist for agriculture. Because of the broad scope of topic domains in teaching agriculture, we built our curriculum from textbooks, commodity magazines, Penn State University (PSU) and United States Department of Agriculture research results, and farmer interviews.

Early in my academic program, the chairman of my doctoral committee Dr. James Mortensen told me to start thinking about the topic for my dissertation. I had an idea, so I searched the literature to make sure that topic hadn't already been published. It didn't. One day in November 1978, my former Department Chairman David McClay handed me a publication that excited my thinking. He was the project director of a national study for identifying and validating essential agricultural competencies for fifty-seven major production-agriculture. This is exactly what I needed and what my UBTS Curriculum Coordinator wanted to see. I now had to select a job title with identified competencies and write the competency instructional task sheets.

I had worked my way through undergraduate college as a professional sheep shearer, which gave me practical experience in sheep management, and the McClay study provided me a cluster of sheep occupations to study. I replicated a portion of the McClay study titled "Sheep Ranch Foreman and Sheep Herder" and randomly selected sheep producers in Pennsylvania. I used the following process to select which competencies to delete because many were not applicable to Pennsylvania sheep production: a booklet titled "Sheep Production Task Sheets composed of 38 competencies, we designed a study to field-test the new instructional materials by sponsoring a series of sheep clinics. We randomly selected six counties in Pennsylvania with a sheep population of 500 or more: two counties for 4-H Club* members, two counties for Future Farmers of America (FFA) members, and two counties for adult part-time shepherds. One county was randomly selected and those instructors were given task sheets to use as teaching aides. The instructors in the other counties were not given task sheets.

We planned a demonstration sheep clinic at PSU for the instructors of the clinics so we could teach all of them to teach in the same manner—except for the instructors in the county that was given task sheets. We employed an impartial evaluator to document each instructor's performance scores at the end of each sheep clinic. Two hundred people participated in the clinics: 114 with task sheets and 86 with no task sheets. The 4-H members and part-time adult shepherds with task sheets scored significantly higher than those without task sheets. The FFA* students with task sheets had higher scores, but not significantly.

Therefore, our research showed that using the task sheets to teach skills was effective.

I would like to close this narrative with this saying by an unknown author, "You may see me struggle, but you will never see me quit." After my study, I was able to provide my former curriculum coordinator at UBTS with task sheets because I did not quit.

PRELUDE: Beautiful but rare, the 2024 total solar eclipse was a once-in-a-lifetime event. The sun, moon and Earth aligned perfectly in the rarest of cosmic orders. Watching a sliver of the moon's shadow evolve into a total blackness was astounding. Then suddenly, there was total darkness on Earth because in a total solar eclipse, the moon completely blocks out the sun. When the sun is blocked out, its outer atmosphere, which is called the "corona," can be seen. The final moments before totality include displays of light called Baily's beads. Because of the moon's rugged terrain, sunlight passes through before totality. Eventually, the beads disappear and become a bright spot of sunlight in the corona resembling a giant diamond in the sky, with the sun's atmosphere forming the ring's band. Seeing the diamond ring is an indicator that totality is almost completed. I was inspired to write this narrative, "2024 Total Eclipse" because it was the only time in my life on Earth that I will marvel at such an amazing spectacle of the universe surrounding the planet where I reside.

2024 TOTAL ECLIPSE

The 2024 total solar eclipse was a once-in-a-life-time occurrence to see the sun, moon and Earth align perfectly in the rarest of cosmic orders. I was astonished to see this diamond ring. (Photo by Michelle Sipe of the live image of the total eclipse in Presque Isle State Park, Pennsylvania, on 7 April 2024)

2024 TOTAL ECLIPSE

According to televised NASA maps, a total solar eclipse, the rarest of cosmic alignments, began when the moon's shadow path made landfall on Mexico's Pacific Ocean coast, passed diagonally across the United States from Texas to Maine, then left North America by way of Newfoundland, Canada, and on to the Atlantic Ocean.

Wearing protective glasses, millions of Americans plus thousands of citizens from many nations watched the moon cast its shadow in front of the sun to experience the total eclipse. This was a significant event that was totally out of the control of humankind.

I was profusely impressed how the eclipse pulled humanity together, including all races, religions, skin colors, ages and nationalities. During the total solar eclipse, I heard of no revolutions, demonstrations, robberies, shootings, murders, scams, or protest marches—just jubilation! There were weddings, family reunions, parties and gettogethers to share the experience. I observed much exhilaration, joyousness, delight, glee and excitement. It was so refreshing to see societies blend together and jointly enjoy the event.

I would like to end this narrative with a line from a popular song written by Jill Jackson-Miller and Sy Miller in 1955 titled "Let There Be Peace on Earth." It starts like this, "Let there be peace on Earth, and let it begin with me."

What I observed amongst throngs of enraptured people from around the planet Earth watching the total eclipse on 7 April 2024 was a paramount example of how humankind could have peace on Earth if each would simply say, "Let it begin with me."

PRELUDE: An early chapter of my life contained a lot of unhappiness and confusion. I was a perplexed young man who knew there had to be a better life than what I was experiencing. One day, I sat on a gate that fenced in our large herd of Hereford cattle down in the hollow on my dad's farm, and I prayed for guidance. My prayer was certainly answered when I met Betty Rohrman in the late autumn of 1958 in Doylestown United Methodist Church where she was the organist and choir director. Thanks to my college classmate Gary Fuess, who introduced us. On 25 September 1960, we were married in that same church, and for fifty-five years, we had a blissful marriage. God took Betty away from me on 25 November 2015. Then on 17 August 2022, Susan S. Yeske, a wonderful semi-retired weekly newspaper reporter came into my life, quickly becoming a significant, loyal, staunch component. Susan is an award-winning writer, especially of restaurant reviews. Shortly after we met, a wonderful, meaningful, "bell-ringing" relationship unfolded. I am grateful that was God's way of ending seven years of loneliness and mourning.

YEP! SHE SURE RANG MY BELL

Susan S. Yeske and Jim Diamond. (Photo by Larry Ragan at Plumsteadville Grange, Plumsteadville, Pennsylvania, 12 November 2022)

YEP! SHE SURE RANG MY BELL!

On 25 September 1960, I walked down the aisle,
With a devoted lover who became my wife for a long, long while.
She had been my devoted and loyal mate for more than half a century,
With devotion and loyalty stronger than the sturdiest tree.

However, in 2015 God made preparations to call Betty home.
I was holding her hand when she left to be with God.
A large chunk of my life changed at that very moment.
I was now alone, saddened and perplexed as to what God had in mind for me.

On 17 August 2022, a semi-retired weekly newspaper reporter named Susan S. Yeske
sent me an e-mail memo to make an appointment.
I sensed she was on assignment and hankered to write an article,
featuring my collection of domestic animal bells from around the world.
Whew! She sure rang my bell!
Instead of studying my bells, unknowingly to me, her bells were already ringing upon arrival.
She actually wanted to get to know me.

After our initial appointment, a wonderful and meaningful "bell-ringing" relationship unfolded.
I am now convinced that it was God's way of ending seven years of loneliness and mourning.
Since I met Susan, our affectionate love affair began to grow.

Susan has restored within me inexpressible happiness that once existed.
Even at my age, she caused me to dream,
refreshed and grow a vision of a new chapter of life.
Susan has changed this Aggie's life, when he began to glow.

For whatever reasons, sometimes my emotions needed to be caressed.
With Susan at my side, she recognizes how to best embrace my emotions.
Susan patiently knows when it's time to fashion a cheery mood to redress my stressed wits.

It is now time to put my life back together and move forward with my new beloved admirer.
At the moment, my dreams and visions reflect images whereby we will be very happy,
Secure and alive with aspirations to nurture.

Susan, I am truly much obliged for your seeking me out
And for being the prime mover of this magnificent relationship.
Thank you!
Thank you for ringing my bell.

PRELUDE: No matter at what age, a person needs to love and be loved. In August 2022, my love unfolded for a very lovely and lovable lady. I did not feel such a deep feeling of affection during the first seventeen years of my boyhood. Then the deep feeling of affection dissipated when my happy fifty-five-year marriage ended with the death of my wife. Oh, how I yearned to be loved during the following seven years of melancholy. Single life was no fun. Everything was reduced—enjoyment, cheeriness, gleefulness, laughter and merriment. When I met Susan S. Yeske, and we began dating as senior citizens, I began a new, sensational, exciting chapter of life with a person I now truly love. On 31 March 2023, Sue became my fiancée. Sue and I experience a deep, affectionate love for each other, which inspired me to write this narrative titled, "We Aspire No More."

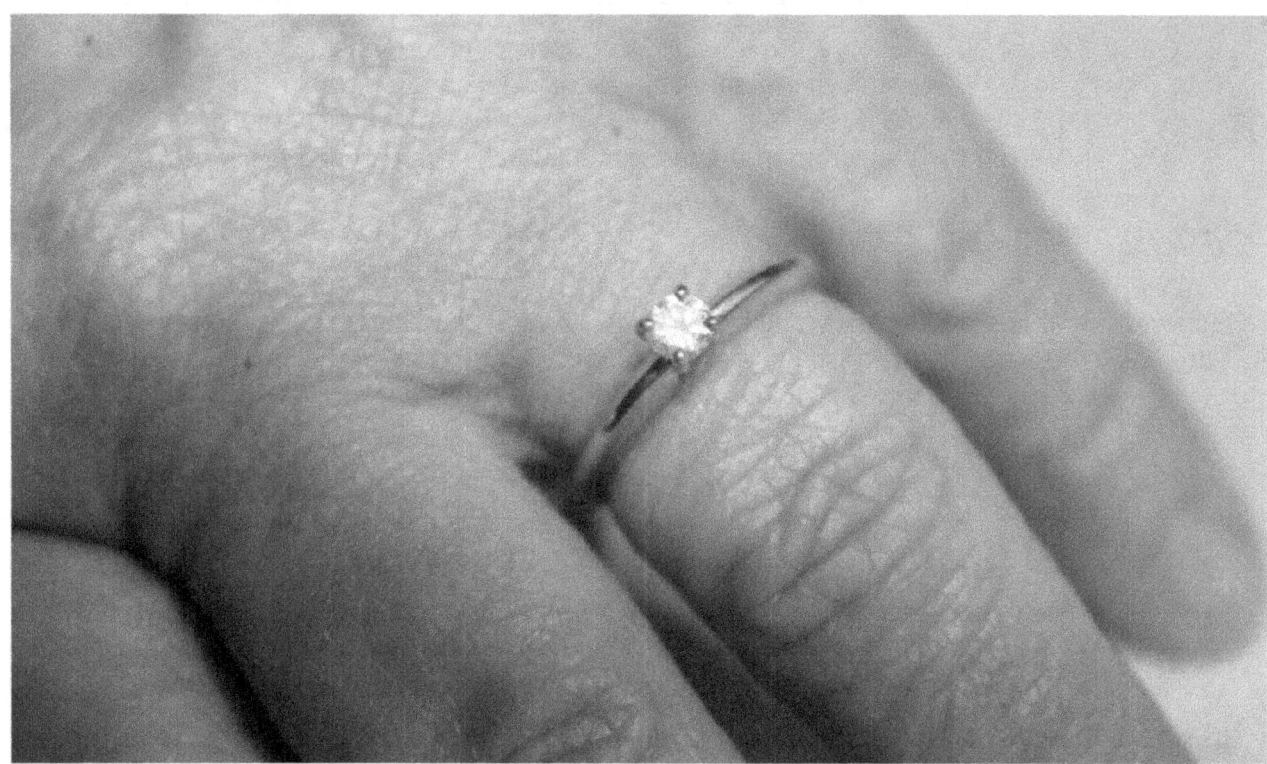

WE ASPIRE NO MORE

I presented this engagement ring to Susan S. Yeske on 31 March 2023, to formalize my deep, affectionate love and wish be married. (Photo by Jim Diamond on 3 April 2023)

WE ASPIRE NO MORE

According to the New Oxford American Dictionary, "Love is a feeling of deep romantic attachment to someone." Love aligns with a plethora of common behaviors and thinking as it relates to human kindness, compassion and affection as unselfish loyalty and benevolent concern for the good of another.

Susan Yeske and I have unfolded a compassionate, affectionate love affair that has enabled us to make plans to formalize our love for each other by getting married.

We look forward to expunging our lonely, solitary lifestyles. Also we look forward to enjoying the happiness, exhilaration, ecstasy and bliss of this exciting new chapter of our lives.

In our past relationships, Susan and I learned that combining lifestyles and households can either strengthen or stress a love relationship—or maybe a little bit of both. To strengthen and harmonize a love relationship, both the husband and wife must be compatible and respectful. Also each must appreciate the other.

At our ages, Susan and I know that blending two senior citizen lifestyles requires calmness, self-restraint, composure, even temper, understanding, kindness, diligence, tolerance and common sense. I distill these traits into three guidelines for myself: Try to maintain patience, persistence and perseverance. These three virtues enable a romantic, happy lifestyle to unfold.

Both Sue and I look forward to a prolonged, loving relationship for the remaining days of our twilight years.

I would like to close this narrative by quoting Sadhguru, a visionary and one of the foremost authorities on yoga, who said, "If you want to know the process of life and its source, the first thing to do is raise your level of aliveness. Being joyfully alive is the only way to truly know life."

Being engaged to Susan Yeske certainly raised aliveness within both of us. That aliveness in turn caused us to truly know life and to be even more joyfully alive.

Whenever I am asked how I am doing, I consistently, habitually respond, "If I were any better, I would not be able to stand it!"

Over the past several decades, I have consciously raised my level of aliveness because I have never known the *good* Lord to make a *bad* day. If I ever do not make a day a good one, I know well who to blame.

PRELUDE: One day in 2022 while sitting in a comfortable chair on my deck, I prayed for guidance to live a better life. That prayer was certainly answered when I met Susan S. Yeske on 17 August 2022. Susan, a wonderful, semi-retired weekly journalist became a significant, loyal, staunch component of my life. Our wonderful, meaningful relationship unfolded, and God ended my seven years of loneliness and mourning. My love for Susan inspired me to write this narrative titled "New Chapter of Life." Love is such a delight! Our love for each other has generated precious memories that hopefully will continue to multiply for our remaining lives together.

NEW CHAPTER OF LIFE

Susan S. Diamond, née Yeske, and I in front of the Block Memorial Chapel on the campus of Delaware Valley University shortly after our wedding on Saturday, 7 October 2023. (Photo by Krystal Knapp)

NEW CHAPTER OF LIFE

Life is short. There is no time to leave important words unsaid or good deeds undone. When a loved one becomes a memory, that memory becomes one of life's most precious treasures. As one grows older, those memories become even more precious.

It was seven years since my late wife died and ten years since Susan's late husband died. Living alone was not been much fun for either of us.

While Sue and I were living alone, we each met several nice people who we could have spent more time with to end our loneliness and mourning. However, I was not yet ready for a courtship. I needed time to heal from mourning before getting serious with another lady friend.

Sometimes a person comes into your life unexpectedly out of nowhere, makes your heart race and changes you forever. On 17 August 2022, a semi-retired newspaper journalist named Susan S. Yeske emailed me to make an appointment. I sensed she was on assignment to write an article about my collection of domestic animal bells from around the world.

After some chitchat, I asked Susan if she wanted to interview me. She immediately said no! I instantly realized she was not interested in studying my domestic animal bells from around the world or writing an animal bell story. She actually was interested in becoming acquainted with *me*. Apparently Susan's bells were already ringing!

We made plans, and Susan came to my home for tea. While we enjoyed our cups of tea on the deck at my log home, known as Clearwater Dell,* I invited Susan to join me for lunch at a local restaurant.

During that lunch, Susan rang my bell! Since that glorious meeting, our affectionate relationship unfolded into a bona fide love affair. Susan changed this Aggie's life, and I began to gleam with contentment.

Sue and I have many corresponding traits that strengthen our personal relationships. We both have a feeling of deep romantic attachment for each other, and we fell in love.

She is one of a kind—tenderhearted, loving, unselfish, good-natured, attentive, friendly, devoted, caring, supportive, and above all, she expresses her fondness for me, which greatly comforts me, having lived so long as a lonely widower on my farm.

Susan has restored my inexpressible happiness. Even at my age, she causes me to dream refreshed, and together we are writing this new, exciting chapter of our lives.

I passionately look forward to having an enchanting life with Sue. Love is such a delight! Thank you, dear Lord, for such a marvelous blessing!

PRELUDE: Aging is usually associated with dynamic changes in a person's biological, psychological, physiological, environmental, behavioral and social processes. All humans experience some or all of these changes over time. They are not all bad. For example, your reaction time might slow with age, but your number of memories and wisdom and accumulated knowledge typically increase. For example, I have written and published more than 600 nonfiction narratives based upon my life experiences. Unfortunately, aging also increases the risk of developing horrid human diseases, such as stroke, cardiovascular disease, cancer and Alzheimer's disease. Roughly two-thirds of the people who die each day around the globe do so from age-related causes. I was inspired to write this narrative titled "Aging with Finesse" because I have reached age eighty-three, having found aging to be interesting and to some extent enjoyable.

AGING WITH FINESSE

I have been blessed to live long enough to have my hair and beard gray and many youthful laugh lines etched into my face. The three people in this photo were always ready for a good laugh, even at the risk of causing wrinkles—from left to right: Arlene Yerkes, Earle Yerkes and Betty Diamond. (Photo by Jim Diamond of three friends aging with finesse near Holiday, Florida, February 2014)

AGING WITH FINESSE

I have had a wonderful forty-seven-year career as an agricultural educator and farmer. I've been blessed with two marvelous marriages. I believe I'm successfully navigating the aging process. Yes, sometimes I am forgetful, but eventually, I remember the important things. More importantly, as time marches on, I've become kinder to myself. Today, I'm my own friend.

As I became older, I became bolder. I care far less what other people might think of who I am and what I do than I used to. Whose business is it if I choose to read a book for hours, devote a whole day writing a narrative, or watch *Perry Mason* on television until 3:00 a.m., and sleep until noon the next day? I don't question myself anymore. I also have earned the right to be wrong.

Over the years, I've suffered many broken hearts, when I've lost a beloved pet or person. But looking back, I know that broken hearts give us strength. They teach us understanding and compassion.

I know now that a heart that has never been broken is pristine and sterile. It has not yet known the comfort of being incompetent, especially during times when one has wept over a lost love.

During the past sixty-five years, I have diligently maintained a positive attitude to spread joy to all of the people around me. My positive attitude has helped me befriend a lot of people. I believe as we age, it gets to be positive because we care less about what other people think. Aging offers this gift of freedom.

Too many of my friends left this world before they understood the immense freedom that comes with aging. American motivational author Louise Lynn Hay said, "Know that you are at the perfect age. Each year is special and precious, for you shall only live it once. Be comfortable with growing older."

English singer and songwriter David Bowie wrote, "Aging is an extraordinary process where you become the person you always should have been."

According to Mark Twain, "Age is an issue of mind over matter. If you don't mind, it does not matter."

I like the person I have become. The aging process sets me free. I do not waste my time lamenting over what should have been and what should be.

Yes, I have some aches and pains in my hips, shoulders and lower back where pills can't reach. My "soothsayer joints" accurately predict when the weather is changing, so I always know when it's going to rain soon. Doctors have said surgery is the only option, but at my age, I can endure the aches and pains—especially if the weather remains clear and dry.

I would like to close thus narrative by quoting American comedian George Burns who said, "You can't help getting older, but you don't have to get old."

Also Will Rogers said, "One of the many things no one tells you about aging is it's such a nice change from being young."

Age is just a state of mind, you are only as old as you allow yourself to get. Do your best to age with finesse!

PRELUDE: Lucille Ball once wrote, "The secret of staying young is to live honestly, eat slowly and lie about your age." What age constitutes "old"? It depends upon who you ask! The Social Security Administration indicates that eligibility for seniors can start at sixty-two, even though sixty-seven is the retirement age. Medicare considers a person to be a senior at sixty-five years of age. Many stores and restaurants offer discounts to customers over age fifth-five. People can join AARP at age fifty! Let's face it, the term "senior citizen" is subjective. I didn't retire until age seventy, and even then it wasn't because of my age. I retired because I needed more free time to do what I wanted to do, go where I wanted to go, and meet people I wanted to meet. I was inspired to write this narrative, "Becoming a Senior Citizen," because I am now eighty-five years old—and still making friends, writing, traveling, splitting firewood, going deer hunting and the list goes on. I have been blessed that I am still able to do what I want to do.

BECOMING A SENIOR CITIZEN

Becoming a senior citizen often means starting a new chapter in life, much like when you became a teenager, got married, had children, or started a new career. Although aging can't be avoided, most senior citizens look in the mirror and wonder, *Where did all the years and youth go?* (Photo by Jim Diamond of Gary and Alma Fuess at a restaurant to celebrate their wedding anniversary)

BECOMING A SENIOR CITIZEN

When I was seventy years old, I retired. I didn't leave the career I dearly loved because of my age. I needed more free time for activities I still had to do, places I still desired to visit and people I still wanted to meet.

I am now eighty-five years of age, and I am still very active traveling, writing books, meeting people, splitting firewood and the list goes on.

Becoming a senior citizen is a new life chapter, similar to other life chapters when we were teenagers, newly married, raising families, or developing careers. It's now time to make new memories by reflecting on your life and saying something like, "I have been blessed with good health, a happy marriage, successful career and a beautiful home, and I am economically secure."

I remember seeing older people through the years and thinking that I was far from their ages and retirement. I could not fathom what it would be like when I reached their age. Yet here it is!

Now most of my friends are retired and getting grey. Many have passed away. Some move slower than they once did. Some of them are in better mental or physical shape than I, and others worse. In them all, I see lifestyle changes. Not like the ones that I remember when I was young and vibrant. Our ages are now like those older folks that we used to see and never thought we'd be. Now one wonders what endeavors will shape our new lifestyles.

Within the past two years, I have begun to see an older person within myself. I walk slower and with a cane. I get sleepy in mid-afternoons. I have aches and pains where a pill can't reach. I tend to forget names, and I avoid responsibilities that I can no longer do.

A French saying I always quote to new retirees goes like this, "*On dois avoir une raison d'etre.*" In English, it means one has to have a reason to be. Senior citizens who are able must have a reason to be or they will grow old quickly. Reasons to be include becoming a member of volunteer organization(s), reading at the library, enrolling in courses, traveling, making new friends, having a hobby, volunteering, and being active in a church, temple, or mosque.

Whatever a new retiree decides to do, they must always remember that it is your health that is the real wealth, not the number of stocks owned, large sums of money in bank accounts, or pieces of gold. The last pair of pants that you put on do not have any pockets. In other words, you can't take your wealth with you. Take care of your well-being because you only get it once.

I would like to close this narrative by quoting my late wife, Betty, who said to me when I retired, "May you be proud of the work you have done, the person who you are, and the differences you have made."

At the age of eighty-five, after eight years as a widower, I began a new chapter of life by marrying my magnificent, affectionate wife, Susan. Together we look forward to spending the rest of our days together as a very, very happy married couple. Life sure is wonderful for this senior citizen!

I hope that after you have read this narrative, you will take time to ponder the essence of the composition and think about your personal future destiny.

PRELUDE: I particularly enjoy classical music, which in my opinion has greater potential for expressiveness and therefore more potential for emotional insight and perceptiveness. Early music was rooted in the sponsorship of churches and royal courts in Western Europe. That's why the early music of ancient Rome and Greece was predominantly religious and vocals accompanied by instruments. I was inspired to write this narrative titled "Classical Music" because of its complex musical form and harmonic organization. Listening to classical music cleanses my mind and enables me to more clearly think about memories, which generate new thoughts, which often evolve into new narratives.

CLASSICAL MUSIC

The Princeton Symphony Orchestra is a cultural centerpiece of the Princeton, New Jersey, community and one of New Jersey's finest music organizations. The orchestra presents orchestral and chamber music programs of the highest artistic quality. In this photo, the Princeton Symphony Orchestra performs at the historic Richardson Auditorium on the campus of Princeton University. The musicians emit sounds rich in overtones that are often used in meditation or guided imagery. (Photographer unknown)

CLASSICAL MUSIC

I do not profess to be an exceptional musician, a profound maestro, or even a knowledgeable classical music expert. However, I take keen delight in listening to beautiful, relaxing classical music. I especially like listening to it on my micro computer while documenting thoughts and works of art. I often sit back, close my eyes, and visualize my thoughts.

I learned that classical music includes rhythm (beat, tempo), melody (pitch, theme), harmony (chord, progression), form, tone and texture. Being able to identify these components helps me to better enjoy the music.

I believe that most people have experienced the power of music to impact their emotions; however, researchers have found that music can impact us even more than we realize. For example, certain vibrations and harmonies can create strong physical, mental, emotional and spiritual reactions.

The intentional application of music to impact health and well-being is called sound healing. Types of music or sounds that are especially beneficial for healing include chanting, singing and harmonizing. Apparently, hearing the human voice is extremely healing.

Singing has been shown to release endorphins, among other benefits. The Gregorian chant has been discovered to be a particularly powerful type of group singing. Harmonic singing is a specific skill and a completely separate branch of sound healing. Singing Bowls (often made in Tibet) are made of metal alloys or from quartz and when played they emit sounds rich in overtones that are often used in meditation.

Researchers also have shown the benefits of classical music, in particular compositions by Mozart and Vivaldi, to help open specific neuronpathways (specialized cells transmitting nerve impulses) of the brain to enhance learning.

Orchestras are made up of different types of instruments that produce music rich in overtones, so attending live orchestral concerts could someday be prescribed just like medicine! Drum circles and Taiko drumming create vibrations that have been shown to improve the overall well-being of participants. Taiko drumming, for example, has been used very effectively for cancer survivors.

I would like to close this narrative by quoting American naturalist and essayist John Burroughs who wrote, "I go to nature to be soothed and healed and have my senses put in order."

This quote interests me because when my late wife, Betty, used to see me going for a walk alone into our woodland, she knew I had an issue that needed to be resolved. Listening to nature's orchestra of sounds during my walks helped soothe and heal my personal concerns.

PRELUDE: Occasional heatwaves have always been expected in the summer in most of the United States. But scientists tell us that over the coming decades, every region of the United States is expected to experience hotter temperatures and more frequent, intense heatwaves. As climate change makes heatwaves more intense and more frequent, people need to be cognizant of the dangers and health risks that come with it. This worsening heat poses serious health risks, especially for the very young and elderly and for construction, agricultural and other outdoor workers, plus people who live in dense urban areas. I was inspired to write this narrative titled "Damn! It's Hot!" because as I wrote this narrative on 9 August 2022 at 9:59 a.m., my outdoor thermometer showed the temperature was already 93 degrees Fahrenheit.

DAMN! IT'S HOT!

A heatwave is when the maximum and minimum temperatures stay unusually high for three or more days. In Australia, heatwaves kill more people than any other natural hazard. Changes to our environment, housing designs and agricultural practices could help reduce the impact of heatwaves on both our communities and economy. (Photographer unknown)

DAMN! IT'S HOT!

Damn! It's hot! The latest science on our climate indicates it's likely to keep changing as global temperatures rise. These climate changes could be curtailed if humankind would take reasonable actions to reduce the heat-trapping emissions flowing into the atmosphere.

Americans and people worldwide in climate-threatened regions, including Pennsylvania, are anxious for solutions. If we don't curb climate change, we will have more wildfires, rising seas, heatwaves, droughts, floods and storms. Flooded beach towns will be abandoned along thousands of miles of coastlines, and islands will be submerged. In some parts of the world these effects are already seen.

Heat will become so oppressive that crops will fail, impacting food availability. Furthermore, agricultural field workers won't be able to endure such oppressive heat. Huge wildfires will scorch millions of acres and spew toxic smoke plumes in broad enshrouds across the planet.

To slow the advance of such catastrophes, scientists insist that citizens of the world must stop gushing greenhouse gases from accumulating in Earth's atmosphere and distorting its climate. Although some of the damage is irreversible, we can halt the advance of climate degradation. It's vital for life as we know it.

Examples and foreshadowing of hostile weather conditions ahead include recent devastating floods in central China and Western Europe, back-to-back hurricanes in the Southeastern United States, out-of-control wildfires in the American West, and sea levels flowing into coastal cities around the world.

Excessive heat fueled by climate change contributes to droughts, wildfires, crop failures and impaired human health. Flooding caused by rising sea levels allows saltwater to intrude into freshwater supplies and causes failures of water treatment systems that spill raw sewage into adjacent waters.

These expensive problems affect the well-being of people and communities. Major cities such as Miami, Fort Lauderdale and Tampa and the Florida Keys fight to hold back rising sea levels. In the next few decades, if carbon emissions continue to grow, most of the country could see 20 to 30 more days annually with temperatures above 90 degrees. These heatwaves could be more frequent, and they will also be hotter than what we experience today. Heat is among the deadliest extreme weather hazards in the United States. Heat exhaustion can cause dizziness, a weak pulse, nausea, cramps, and fainting. The most severe of heat-related illnesses, heat strokes, occur when a person's temperature increases above 103 degrees Fahrenheit. Increased periods of extended high temperatures can increase cardiovascular mortality, respiratory mortality and heart attacks.

I would like to close this narrative by quoting a chemical engineer and congressman who said, "Fighting climate change is a moral vital importance that is driven by love of our children and grandchildren. The only thing that matters in life is whether or not our children and grandchildren are proud of us. The West is on fire, floods are imminent in the South, and glaciers are melting in the North." When looking at the big picture, do you think your children and grandchildren are proud of you?

PRELUDE: One day, I visited my dear friend Oskar Larsson and suggested that we recognize and honor our late wives with a granite bench at Delaware Valley University (DVU). We both felt that would be a lasting remembrance of two devoted wives who had a deep affection for DVU. Betty and Ruby were both strong DVU enthusiasts who cherished their DVU friends, alumni, faculty and staff. The inscription on the bench reads, "Loving memory of Elizabeth R. Diamond & Ruby H. Larsson." Ruby passed away in October 2011 and Betty passed away in November 2015. I was inspired to write this narrative titled "Dedication of Granite Bench" because Oskar and I were so emotionally moved when we presented the lovely granite bench to DVU on 31 January 2017.

DEDICATION OF GRANITE BENCH

At Delaware Valley University, I (DVU class of 1961) and my friend Oskar Larsson (DVU class of 1952) jointly presented a lovely, sturdy granite bench to Delaware Valley University campus in loving memory of our late wives, Elizabeth R. Diamond and Ruby H. Larsson. (Photo by Joseph Gall [DVU class of 1961] of me and Oskar Larsson dedicating the granite bench on 31 January 2017)

DEDICATION OF GRANITE BENCH

Elizabeth R. Diamond and Ruby H. Larsson had been devoted, beloved friends of Reverend Steve McComas of the Rolling Hills United Methodist Church, who officiated at the dedication of a granite bench newly placed at the beginning of the walkway in front of Lasker Hall leading to Ulman Hall. The names of Elizabeth and Ruby etched on the bench honor those two steadfast, loyal advocates who will be perpetually remembered.

All Delaware Valley University (DVU) alumni, faculty, students and friends are invited to sit on that bench to ponder memories that are one of life's most precious treasures and the older they grow, the more precious memories become.

I cohosted the dedication of the bench with my dear friend Oskar Larsson. Ironically, Oskar was the college registrar, and he was the first person I met at DVU in July 1957. Back then it was called the National Agricultural College (NAC). Oskar had interviewed me and accepted me into NAC.

In January 1961, after I completed my studies in large animal science at NAC, I began teaching at NAC. At that time, Oskar and I were both enrolled in a master's degree program at Lehigh University in Bethlehem, Pennsylvania. We became dear friends, and over the years a strong friendship unfolded also between our wives, Betty and Ruby. Many times, Betty and Ruby enjoyed lunch and long "women's talks."

Over the years, Betty truly enjoyed interacting with DVU students. We hosted many DVU students at our home for home-cooked dinners. At times, some undergraduate students even lived in our home, and Betty really enjoyed being a housemother to them. Betty cooked their meals and made special desserts. We had lots of laughter and interesting discussions, and Betty made everyone study—including me. More importantly, Betty was a great listener when students needed to talk.

Betty and I had a very close relationship with the Larssons for more than sixty years. We even babysat their two daughters occasionally.

In May 1990, while Betty and I lived and worked in eSwatini, Africa, Oskar and Ruby visited us for a month. Oh, what a glorious time we had making memories! We hiked three miles into Pine Valley to see ancient Bushman paintings, visited Kruger National Park to see wild animals in South Africa, volunteered to make Extension Worker booklets in the Ministry of Agriculture, visited two wild game parks in Swaziland, and tasted Swazi cuisine in several unique, fascinating restaurants.

A memory is a way of holding onto people, events, travels, personalities, behaviors, characters, events, failures and traditions you never want to lose. I would like to close this narrative with a quote by Helen Keller, "So long as the memory of certain beloved friends lives in my heart, I shall say that life is good."

Life has been good to Oskar and me. Dedicating that beautiful, sturdy granite bench in memory of our late wives made a memory that will live in our hearts forever.

PRELUDE: An award is a symbol of recognition given in honor of an achievement. I was profoundly honored to receive the Distinguished Service to Agriculture Award and to stand amongst other prominent Pennsylvania farmers, legislators and agricultural leaders who preceded me with this prestigious recognition. Sigmund Freud once refused to attend a festival in his honor and said, "When someone abuses me, I can defend myself; against praise, I am defenseless." Like Freud, I was defenseless when Pennsylvania Farm Bureau President Rick Ebert telephoned to inform me that I had been selected to receive this notable recognition. I was inspired to write this narrative, "Distinguished Service to Agriculture Award," in honor of the nine honored guests who accompanied me to experience this once-in-a-lifetime event.

DISTINGUISHED SERVICE TO AGRICULTURE AWARD

Rick Ebert (right) President of the Pennsylvania Farm Bureau, presents Distinguished Service to Agriculture Award to Jim Diamond (left) at the 2021 PA Farm Bureau Annual Meeting at Hershey Convention Center in Hershey, Pennsylvania. As one of many Pennsylvania agricultural educators, we try to do the work we are called to do. (Photo by Bill Zeiders, Pennsylvania Farm Bureau of Distinguished Service to Agriculture Award plaque presentation in Hershey, Pennsylvania, 16 November 2021)

DISTINGUISHED SERVICE TO AGRICULTURE AWARD

I have been blessed with a forty-seven-year career as a farmer and agricultural educator that took me far, far beyond my wildest expectations. Who would have ever thought that this naive farm boy from rural Fayette County in southwestern Pennsylvania who stuttered and despised high school would one day become an Instructor of Animal Science at his alma mater, a Vocational Agriculture Teacher at an area vocational technical school, an agricultural Peace Corps volunteer assigned to the President of Tchad, Africa, a Professor of Agricultural and Extension Education at Penn State University, an International Agricultural Education Consultant for the United Nations, and the Dean for Agricultural and Environmental Sciences at his alma mater, Delaware Valley University. This all became a reality because of the support I received during a glorious fifty-five-year marriage to my late wife, Betty, and a plethora of friends who encouraged and supported me all along the way.

Some of those wonderful supportive friends who were with me when I received the Distinguished Service to Agriculture Award included Dr. Benjamin Rusiloski, President of Delaware Valley University; Dr. David L. Kantner, Retired Cooperative Extension Regional Director; Dr. Kathleen Jones, Professor of Education, Science and Math, Juniata College; George P. Perry, Retired Cooperative Extension Educator, Schuylkill County; Mark Scheetz, president, Bucks County Farm Bureau; and Gary Fuess, Retired Corporate Purchasing Manager, GEO Specialty Chemicals. I was especially pleased that my two sisters, Jane Ross of Smithville, Ohio, and Betsy Diamond, of Kentfield, California, made a special effort to share the joy of this special occasion.

Martin Luther King once said, "I have a dream." I also had a dream that one day in the future I would make myself into someone of prominence who could leave behind a footprint that benefits humankind. Many people have a dream, but they do not make their dreams a reality. Keeping hold of a dream without causing it to convert into a reality idles away the present. In spite of this, everyone should have a dream and aspire to cause it to emerge at some point during his or her life.

Dreams give one a reason to be. As I've mentioned before, a French expression best expresses my point, *On does avoir une raison d'etre*. (One must have a reason to be).

My dreams focused on domestic and international agricultural endeavors that help people help themselves. I hope and pray that my career efforts leave a legacy that in some way will benefit humankind. I hope that I leave our planet a better place for future generations.

During my time as a Commonwealth of Pennsylvania Agricultural Educator, I tried to be a rainbow in people's prosperity because I did the work I was called to do. I was elated to be selected for this distinguished honor and being placed amongst the previous esteemed recipients of the Pennsylvania Farm Bureau's Distinguished Service to Agriculture Award.

PRELUDE: Hatred can mean intense hostility and aversion often derived from fear, anger, feelings of revenge, sense of injury, prejudice, and intensely disliked people. After being released from prison, Nelson Mandela said, "No one is born hating another person because of the color of his skin or his background or religion. People must learn to hate, and if they can learn to hate, they can be taught to love for love comes more naturally to the human heart than its opposite." After the way Mandela was treated for several years in prison, he was very humble to forgive the people who caused him much hardship and distress. Before Martin Luther King Jr. was assassinated, he said, "Hatred paralyzes life; love releases it. Hatred confuses life; love harmonizes it. Hatred darkens life; love illuminates it." I was inspired to write this narrative titled "Hatred" because I am saddened there is so much hatred within our society caused by learned attitudes and feelings toward other people because of their skin color, nationality, religion, and because of one's anger, prejudice, greed and desire for revenge. This narrative is an attempt to express my attitude toward people who for whatever reason learned to hate other people. This photo titled "Last Jew of Vinnitsa" portrays a profound, deep-rooted, entrenched form of hatred.

HATRED

In 1941, a member of Einsatzgruppe D was about to shoot the "Last Jew of Vinnitsa," in Vinnitsa, Ukraine. (Photo from rarehistoricalphotos.com)

HATRED

The revised standard version of the Holy Bible, letter of James, Chapter 3, verse 16, says, "For where jealousy and selfish ambition exists, there you will find disorder and every vile practice."

American evangelist Billy Graham said, "Racial prejudice, anti-Semitism, or hatred of anyone with different beliefs has no place in the human mind or heart."

The well-published poet Will Smith wrote, "Throughout life, people will make you mad, disrespect you, and treat you bad. Let God deal with the things they do because hate in your heart will consume you too."

During everyone's life, they will encounter people who disrespect them and make them mad. Maybe they will be tempted to hate those people. But in the long run, hatred can shape people's lives because of its intense hostility and bitterness derived from fear, anger, prejudice, intense dislike, and the temptation to seek revenge.

Don't let anger sour your heart because it can lead to a learned behavior pattern that can form deep hatred. The ancient Greek philosopher Socrates said, "From the deepest desires often comes the deadliest hate."

Regardless of the depth of hatred, it often can be neutralized when coated with sincere love, genuine concern, unfeigned understanding and unselfish kindness.

People who hate often generate rumors, which are then spread by dimwits and accepted by morons. According to award-winning author Frank Sonnenberg, "Repeating a rumor is as vicious as starting one."

If you wish society to become more affectionate and sympathetic, become more affectionate and sympathetic yourself. If you wish to belittle fearfulness within society, first belittle your own. You can bestow these precious gifts upon your society. I personally don't have time to hate people who despise or dislike me because I'm too involved loving people who love me.

Former First Lady Eleanor Roosevelt said, "Great minds discuss ideas; average minds discuss events; small minds discuss people." This is why I personally surround myself with people who think and talk about visions, dreams, fresh ideas and pleasures to behold, but not about other people negatively.

PRELUDE: While I was attending West Virginia University, I usually went home on weekends to help my father with farm chores. I could not afford to buy a used car nor pay for gasoline, insurance and maintenance, so I got around by hitchhiking—asking strangers for free rides in their cars. Back then, hitchhiking was also called "thumbing." I was inspired to write this narrative titled "Hitchhiking" remembering the time when I traveled weekly from Morgantown, West Virginia, to Woodside, Pennsylvania. I met a lot of kind people and had many interesting conversations while traveling. Once, I also hitchhiked across Pennsylvania to Bucks County for a college interview.

HITCHHIKING

Back when hitchhiking was common in the United States, hitchhikers would stand on the shoulder of the road, face oncoming vehicles, and hold out their right arm with their thumb up and four fingers tucked into the palm of the hand. It was always advantageous to both the hitchhiker and driver to select a site to stand where the driver had a sufficient distance and safe location to stop. (Photo by Jim Diamond of a friend who was hitchhiking in February 1959)

HITCHHIKING

During my fall 1956 and spring 1957 semesters at West Virginia University (WVU), I hitchhiked from Morgantown, West Virginia, all the way home to our farm near Woodside, Pennsylvania, on Friday afternoons. On Sunday evenings, after attending church service, my Aunt Betty would drive me back to the university.

Attending two semesters at WVU taught me that I was not as dumb as I always perceived myself to be. That's when I decided to complete my college education, but at a smaller school.

I learned there was a small agricultural college in Bucks County in Eastern Pennsylvania called National Agricultural College (NAC—now Delaware Valley University). I wrote a letter to inquire about their offerings. In July 1957, I received a packet of NAC admission materials, and my goal at that time was to study large animal science, then return to our farm and raise Hereford cattle.

One of the requirements for acceptance into NAC was a personal interview on campus. NAC was 325 miles from our farm, and I had no car. I decided to hitchhike the 325 miles for my interview. In July 1957, I hitched a ride from Uniontown, Pennsylvania, to the Pennsylvania Turnpike Donegal Interchange. I stood there for twenty minutes, holding up my thumb to oncoming cars, trying to catch my next ride. Finally, a car stopped, and the driver asked, "Which direction are you going?"

"East," I replied.

"Come on in," the driver said. "I'm going to the Harrisburg East Interchange."

At the Harrisburg East Interchange, I stood outside the toll booth for thirty minutes, thumb up. Another car stopped, and the driver asked, "Which direction are you going?"

"East," I replied again.

"Get in, he said. "I'm going to the Norristown Interchange."

Whew! Norristown, Pennsylvania, was the farthest I had traveled so far in my life from Woodside, and I was tired. In Norristown, I found a room in a YMCA for the night. Early Saturday morning, I began hitchhiking the remaining twenty miles on Route 202 north toward Doylestown.

After three short rides, I arrived at NAC. I met registrar Oskar Larsson, who interviewed me; reviewed my credentials, asked me several questions, and gave me an interesting tour of the NAC campus and farms, which convinced me that I wanted to continue my education there. After lunch with some faculty, Oskar informed me that I qualified to be accepted into NAC. WOW! Without any further thoughts, I accepted their offer.

I walked across the NAC campus to Route 202 South, hitchhiked to the turnpike, then caught one ride across Pennsylvania to Donegal, arriving at midnight. There was no way I could hitch a ride to Woodside at that hour of the night, so I asked the man in the toll booth if I could call my father. He said, "Sure!" I telephoned my dad, told him were I was, and asked if he could pick me up. On the way home, I informed my dad where I had been and why. He had mixed emotions about my being accepted into NAC. Nevertheless, that is how my educational and career odyssey commenced.

PRELUDE: Sauerkraut" is a traditional, delicious, moist German dish composed of finely cut raw cabbage that has been fermented. It has a salty, sour flavor. The word "sauerkraut" is also German, meaning "sour cabbage." Some historians claim the Mongol Emperor Genghis Khan brought sauerkraut to Europe. Roman writers mentioned preserving cabbages and turnips with salt. Other people say sauerkraut originally came from China. I was inspired to write this narrative titled "Homemade Sauerkraut" because I enjoy eating homemade sauerkraut on mashed potatoes with pork. But more importantly, I enjoy socializing with the group of Plumsteadville Grange members who annually assemble on a Saturday morning in November to munch hot dogs with sauerkraut, sup some homemade wine and "swap some lies" with each other while making homemade sauerkraut so it will be ready for eating on New Year's Day.

HOMEMADE SAUERKRAUT

Captain James Cook took sauerkraut on his sea voyages after he learned it prevented scurvy. (Photo by Jim Diamond of grange members making homemade sauerkraut at the home of Scott Guiser in November 2019)

HOMEMADE SAUERKRAUT

Once you taste a hearty helping of homemade sauerkraut piled atop a heap of mashed Pennsylvania-grown potatoes, you will never eat canned sauerkraut again.

American writer Mark Kurlansky once wrote, "In nineteenth-century Russia, sauerkraut was valued more than caviar."

According to nutritionists Stacie Hassing and Jessica Beacom of the Real Food Dietitians, "Sauerkraut is good for the gut and tastebuds. Eating just a spoonful or two before a meal increases saliva production, decreases stomach pH, and activates certain digestive enzymes to digest your food better."

Plumsteadville Grange members Scott Guiser and his wife, Betsy, hosted the first annual sauerkraut-making event at their home one Saturday morning in November for grange members and friends. It is desirable to wait until November to make sauerkraut because using cabbage that has experienced a hard frost makes better sauerkraut.

At the sauerkraut-making event, participants worked together to make sauerkraut. Scott brought a triple-blade cabbage slicer, and we sliced the cabbage, then salted it. We placed the cabbage into the wooden handmade African mortar I had brought from eSwatini (Swaziland). We pounded the sliced cabbage with the pestle until the cabbage juice appeared. The crushed salted cabbage and its juices were placed into a crock to ferment.*

We poured in a large plastic bag about two gallons of tap water. Then we placed the bag atop the chopped cabbage. The water pushed the plastic bag against the side of the crock, forming a seal while nature did her job during the fermentation process. Next we placed the crock in a cool cellar to ferment for four to six weeks.

After several weeks, we removed the plastic cover and with two fingers lifted a sample of sauerkraut and tasted it. Sauerkraut should be white and taste salty. During the fermentation process, the sugars in the cabbage leaves are converted into lactic acid, which causes the pleasant sour taste. You can eat sauerkraut uncooked or cooked.

During my boyhood on our family farm, we usually butchered a hog on Thanksgiving Day and grew enough cabbage in our garden to make sauerkraut. It was a local tradition to eat homegrown pork and homemade sauerkraut on New Year's Day to have good luck during the whole year.

Throughout the years, we continued this tradition, and it is even more fun when we have a group of friends who make modern-day sauerkraut. We have added important flavoring ingredients to the sauerkraut to excite the tastebuds: a dash of funny jokes and a sprinkling of uncontrollable howling, guffawing, doubled-up laughter and giggling.

I had always thought one had to believe in good luck to get it. Instead, we can acquire a year's quota of good luck simply by eating a copious serving of homemade pork and sauerkraut on New Year's Day.

PRELUDE: "I don't understand it" is what some people of all ages say about poetry. Many don't understand because they cannot comprehend the meaning of the author's phraseology. They do not have an appreciation of poetry because of its ambiguity. I prefer to write narratives instead of poetry. Poems are written to educate and be enjoyed. However, some people become frustrated or confused while attempting to determine what a poem really means. I was inspired to write this narrative titled "I Understand It" because so many times I have read poetry that causes me to ask myself, *What is the author trying to say?* Such writings exasperate me and make me feel that I'm wasting my time reading a concoction of words that do not make sense in my mind. Hence the reason I prefer to write narratives that describe my undisputed, authentic experiences.

I UNDERSTAND IT!

Narratives make writing more descriptive and easier to understand. Narratives can and should convey to the reader a deeper understanding of the indigenous* language in which it is written.

I UNDERSTAND IT!

After my wonderful forty-seven-year career as an agricultural educator, it became important for me to write narratives to document and express my feelings, emotions and experiences. My narratives reflect on paper my thoughts, experiences, opinions, reactions, lessons and memories without shame.

Writing short narratives publicly expresses the hallmark components of my persona without restraints. I don't write narratives to fill books or create mental exercises. My narratives are written to communicate.

While reading my narratives, a reader should effectively comprehend what the words are portraying. Reading a narrative involves the mind, senses and emotions as the described experience is a reality.

The power of a narrative is that words make one think a thought. A thought makes one feel the words. A narrative makes one feel thoughtful words.

Narratives are a type of literature that is difficult to describe but easy to recognize. In addition to imagery and metaphor, narratives often use repetition, creative punctuation and emotional language.

To be engaged in a narrative, the reader should read it slowly and participate fully with mind and senses. A narrative captures the reader's attention while attempting to understand and analyze it. Once there is enough understanding to analyze the narrative's structure and language, the reader is provisionally empowered to understand the author's purpose. Now the reader is prompted to describe what inspired the author to write with such feeling the beautiful, thoughtful, meaningful words.

All of my narratives are based on actual experiences. In every narrative, I have embedded at least one lesson within the text, and I challenge the reader to identify the lesson(s) and ponder its ramifications.

I wish to conclude this narrative by saying, When I can no longer speak, hear me through my written words.

PRELUDE: Loneliness kills! That was the conclusion of a study by Brigham Young University researchers who are sounding the alarm on what could be the next big public-health issue, on par with obesity and substance abuse. Loneliness is a feeling of social and mental isolation that can negatively impact both mental and physical health. It seems like loneliness is caused by people who experience the uncertainty of negative or challenging life circumstances. I was inspired to write this narrative titled "Loneliness" because I have worked with people who were experiencing loneliness for a period of time.

LONELINESS

Middle-aged and older adults tend to be particularly at risk of loneliness. They exhibit detectable incidences of depression, cardiovascular impairment, chronic pain and prolonged fatigue. (Photographer unknown)

LONELINESS

Social workers have claimed that loneliness causes negative symptoms of various mental and physical health conditions, such as anxiety, cognitive decline, mood disorders, unremitting pain, and even ineradicable cardiovascular issues. Middle-aged and older adults are particularly at risk for loneliness and they exhibit detectable incidences of depression, cardiovascular impairment, chronic pain and prolonged fatigue.

Many people who are living confined alone in a personal home or in a nursing home or assisted living home often experience loneliness and sadness because they have no family or friends who visit and socialize. Recently, the *New York Times* featured a study on loneliness and deemed our society is experiencing a "loneliness epidemic."

In the workplace, loneliness decreases performance and affects creativity, reasoning and decision-making. Moreover, loneliness and weak social connections are associated with a reduced lifespan similar to someone smoking fifteen cigarettes a day or suffering from obesity. Loneliness is also linked to a greater risk of heart disease, dementia, anxiety, mobility loss, and depression. It has been documented that social isolation can increase the risk of premature death by up to 50 percent.

Let's face it, feeling stimulated, motivated and influential can be tough in our modern, hectic lives. Approximately half of U.S. adults sense loneliness and dislocation at various times.

I would like to close this narrative by sharing advice from Ken Wells, an author and a former senior therapist at Psychological Counseling Services in Scottsdale, Arizona, who worked as a leader with pioneers in the field of addiction treatment, wrote, "Make peace with your loneliness. There is a wounded child within each of us that needs to be recognized and embraced. Loneliness is magnified when you busy yourself with activity and neglect the pool of pain that exists within you. People try to minimize this pain by comparing their life experience with others. This only isolates the wounded child and intensifies loneliness. Coming home requires that you focus on healing your wounded child."

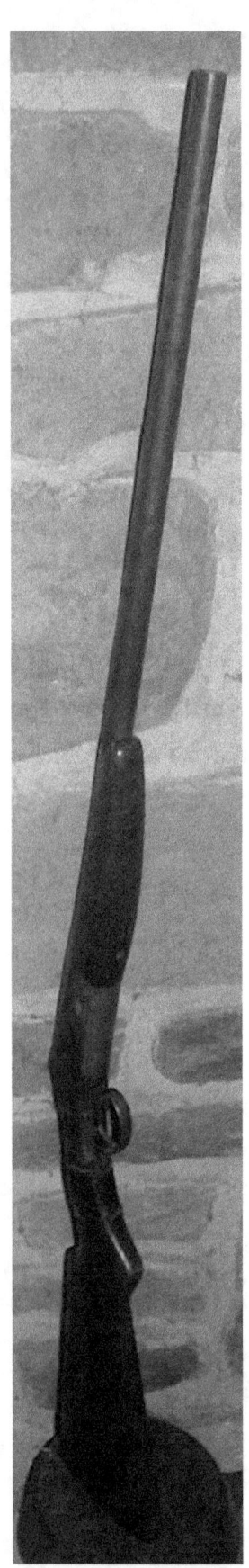

PRELUDE: The Riverside Arms Company of Chickopee, Massachusetts, was in business in the late nineteenth and early twentieth centuries. In 1916, the company was purchased by the J. Stevens Arms and Tool Company, which used the Riverside Arms Company USA name as the brand for an economy line of gun products. This gun was reported to be a variant of the Riverside Model 315, and it was made between 1915 and 1929. (Unfortunately, no records give an exact date when this gun was made.) I was inspired to write this narrative titled "My Single-Barrel Shotgun*" because this single-barrel, 16-gauge shotgun was given to me by my father, and it was the only gun I ever used for hunting small game and shooting on New Year's Eve to celebrate the arrival of a new year.

MY SINGLE-BARREL SHOTGUN

(Photo by James E. Diamond of his 16-gauge single-barrel Riverside Shotgun displayed at his home in January 2021)

310

MY SINGLE-BARREL SHOTGUN

When I was a boy on our farm in Woodside, Pennsylvania, my father was a farmer and also a coal miner. At one time, my father owned a small bituminous coal* mine near Old Frame, Pennsylvania, where he mined and sold custom coal.

Back then, custom coal was sold by the bushel,* and my father delivered it to local customers who had coal-burning stoves in the basements of their homes. My dad had a 1934 Chevrolet flatbed truck with sides that could haul 100 bushels of coal when fully loaded. As a rule, coal customers had a chute they would hook to the truck that reached through a cellar window toward a receptacle near the coal furnace. My dad would shovel the coal onto the coal chute, and it would slide into the cellar. After my dad completed unloading coal from the truck, the customer would pay him.

Occasionally, a customer would be short on money and ask my dad if they could pay him within a couple weeks. My dad was kind and always gave good customers extra time to pay their coal bills. Once a customer owed my dad for two truckloads of coal and did not have money to pay his bills. The customer asked my dad if he could give him his single-barrel shotgun* to hold until he got enough money to pay his bill. My dad would not sell him any more coal until he paid his bill, which he never did. So Dad kept the single-barrel shotgun.

When I was twelve years old, I was old enough to buy a hunting license and go hunting for small game with an adult. Gosh, was I excited. My dad gave me the single-barrel 16-gauge shotgun displayed herein. It was the perfect gun for a twelve-year-old hunter.

My dad and my uncle Wes Gower took me hunting for the first time for rabbits, ring-necked pheasants, and gray squirrels. I remember well the first ring-necked pheasant I shot. My untrained dog flushed it out, and I shot it with one shot. Over the years, I hunted with friends, my brother, and my dad. When I went off to college, I took my shotgun with me. I learned having a firearm in the dormitory was a no-no. So I broke it down into three pieces and hid it under my mattress. I kept it there until I met my girlfriend, who ultimately became my dear wife. I had asked her father if I could keep my shotgun in his house. He was not a hunter and said he never had a gun in his home. However, he said as long as I kept it out of sight it would be okay to keep it there.

During one hunting season, Dick Clark (yes, that Dick Clark!) went hunting with me and two of my hunting buddies Joe Fulcoly and Steve Ferdo on my Ottsville farm. My two buddies were Delaware Valley University professors and friends of Dick Clark, who back then hosted the Philadelphia show *Bandstand*. I also used that shotgun to hunt ringneck pheasants in South Dakota and on my farm to shoot skeet,* hunt ruffed grouse and rabbits, and scare away my neighbors' dog from chasing my sheep. My hunting friends would often poke fun at me about using my old 16-gauge single-barrel shotgun with a cracked stalk wrapped with black tape when they all had much newer, fancy Remington shotguns. Occasionally I would teach them a lesson on hitting a target with my ancient single-barrel Riverside shotgun, especially when we shot skeet.

I would like to close this narrative by saying the caliber or age of the gun used on a hunt isn't important. Hunting teaches the value of being present in the moment, fully immersed in the experience and the environment around you. It is a journey to test your limits and learn to respect the wilderness and its creatures. It allows you to escape the noise of the world and find harmony in the symphony of nature.

PRELUDE: An attractive morning makes one feel it's going to be a wonderful, fulfilling day. Sitting on a bench looking across the landscape admiring the allure of nature reveals something that humans cannot replicate. The day I took this photo, white cumulus clouds pasted to a clear blue sky slowly crept from the east on a gentle breeze. The panoramic view was decorated by the blazing sun peeping over the horizon and beginning to cast its golden haze over the countryside. To me, every day is a good one because I have never known the good Lord to make an unpleasant day. I was inspired to write this narrative titled "Oh, What an Enchanting Morning" because on days like this, if I felt any better, I would not be able to stand it.

OH, WHAT AN ENCHANTING MORNING

Regardless of the season, every day is a beautiful day. One can find beauty in every day—even days with pouring rain, blowing snow, driving sleet, falling hail, frigid temperatures and dark low clouds. (Photo by Jim Diamond of icicles on a cliff bordering Rapp Creek on his farm near Ottsville, Pennsylvania)

OH, WHAT AN ENCHANTING MORNING

One morning, strolling in the thick magnificence of nature, I breathed clean fresh air, listened to unprocessed natural sounds, and felt thankful to experience nature's splendor. I was inspired watching songbirds dart from tree to tree as the leaves on giant oak, sugar maple, and wild cherry trees noiselessly fluttered to the ground. Back at my home, I saw the American flag gently wave on the soft, balmy breeze.

Weather plays an important role in our lives. Personally, I do not allow the weather to decide whether it's a marvelous day or an atrocious one. We can do nothing about the weather. Humankind has no control over the climatic traits that surround us each day.

I enjoy warm, clear, calm days with the sun beaming its rays over the great outdoors, while children run, play ball, skateboard, slide, see-saw, laugh, and have loads of fun. Children know that regardless of the season, every day is beautiful—even days with pouring rain, blowing snow, driving sleet, falling hail, frigid temperatures and dark low clouds.

Sure, inclement weather causes people to wear heavy coats, boots, gloves, earmuffs, waterproof hats and raincoats. But wearing such gear encourages people to slush their way to their place of employment or home to a blazing fireplace to sip a cup of hot chocolate. Children warmly dressed throw snowballs, make snow angels, ride sleds down a slope, or ice skate, all having fun in the cold perilousness of Mother Nature.

Sitting in front of a blazing hot fire on a cold, wintry day, "swapping lies" with dear friends, and sipping a glass of homemade sour cherry wine is what life is about. The more wine we sip, the better the lies get. Such memories are one of life's treasures, and the older we grow the more valuable our memories become.

I would like to close this narrative with a quote from Margaret Wolfe Hungerford's 1878 book titled *Molly,* "Such beauty is in the eye of the beholder."

Oh, how fitting. That expression fits the natural works of nature during winter, spring, summer and autumn. Hungerford's expression reflects the fact that all things in nature are beautiful.

However, what looks beautiful to me might not be beautiful to other people. It depends on the point of view of the person who is viewing the scenery.

PRELUDE: Using jugs as acoustic musical instruments reached its popularity in the 1920s, when jug bands were popular because the jugs were cheap and easy to carry around. Common musical jugs were made of different materials, including ceramic jugs, glass jugs, plastic bleach bottles and tin kerosene cans. Jugs of different materials and sizes produce different sounds. From time to time, jugs have even been used in recordings. One type of musical jug is the Caribbean *botija,* which was a potbellied jug with two openings and was played in early Cuban musical sextets. I was inspired to write this narrative titled "Playing the Jug" because I enjoyed hearing jug bands in my youth and the self-styled bluegrass music played by Briscoe, the widowed father of the six-member Darling family on the *Beverly Hillbillies* television show. His ceramic jug had its own personality and added a deep, characteristic sound to the family's bluegrass music.

PLAYING THE JUG

Jugs can be made of glass, plastic, ceramic, tin or other materials, and they make acoustic music when accompanied by other musical instruments, such as guitars, violins, pianos, accordians, or wind instruments. I always enjoyed listening to the uniqueness of jug music. (Photographer unknown)

314

PLAYING THE JUG

An empty clear glass or stoneware jug can be used as a musical instrument. A jug is played with "buzzed lips" to produce a trombone-like tone. Jug players shape their mouth as they would at the mouthpiece of a brass instrument. Jugs produce a deep, full, reverberating sound as their main resonance frequency, similar to a bass instrument. The characteristic sound of the jug is low and hoarse, below the sound of other musical instruments. The jug is part of a band's rhythm section.

Jug bands originated in the nineteenth century in Louisville, Kentucky, and they were primarily African-Americans. At that time, jug solos were common. Most jug bands used a single jug player, but there are recordings of jug bands that used two or more jug sections.

A larger jug produces a lower musical pitch while smaller jugs produce higher pitches. The pitch of a bottle played in this way can be controlled by adding to or reducing its contents.

The loudness of a jug is a function of the speed of the air blown across the top. The musician holds the mouth of the jug about an inch from their mouth (see photo) and buzzes their lips directly into it. This emits a blast of sound. The jug does not touch the musician's mouth, but instead it serves as a resonating chamber to amplify and enrich the sound made by the musician's lips.

Changes in pitch are controlled by loosening or tightening the lips.

Jugs will also produce sound at their main resonance frequency when air is blown across the top opening. This instrument is normally not used in bands because it is relatively quiet and produces only a single pitch.

I would like to close this narrative by quoting British modernist poet Basil Binting, who once wrote, "Whether you listen to a piece of music, or a poem, or look at a picture or a jug, or a piece of sculpture, what matters about it is not what it has in common with others of its kind, but what is singularly its own."

What Basil was alluding to is that regardless of the art form, excellence is not being the best, it is doing your best. In other words, be your creative self and be your best.

PRELUDE: United Plantation Orange Groves are located on Piggs Peak Road in the Northwestern Kingdom of eSwatini (aka Swaziland) and is the country's largest exporter of oranges. I visited United Plantation Orange Groves numerous times, and the orange trees always appeared to be properly pruned and very well managed. United Plantation has two farms, Ngonini and Tambuti, which grow oranges and grapefruit for export, using the River Gold label, which seems to be well received by several markets. The fruit is shipped from ports located at both Maputo, Mozambique, and Durban, South Africa. I was inspired to write this narrative titled "A Product of eSwatini" because I purchased a bag of oranges labeled "River Gold" at a food market near my small farm in Bucks County, Pennsylvania, My familiarity and visitations of United Plantation Orange Groves made this purchase very special because the plantation's orange trees always seemed to be a well-managed farming operation.

A PRODUCT OF eSWATINI

While shopping for groceries at our local Giant Foods in Plumsteadville, Pennsylvania, I picked up a bag of oranges and placed it into my grocery cart. Then I looked at the small tag attached to each orange to identify its country of origin. Wow! The tag said, "Product of eSwatini." I knew those oranges had been grown at the United Plantation's Orange Groves. (Photo by Jim Diamond of oranges grown in eSwatini at United Plantation Orange Groves.)

A PRODUCT OF eSWATINI

Orange is a happy color. Oranges strengthen and encourage a general feeling of joy, well-being and cheerfulness. I believe that breakfast without orange juice is like a day without sunshine.

One day, the sun shone brightly near my small farm while I was shopping for groceries at our local Giant Foods in Plumsteadville, Pennsylvania. I picked up a bag of oranges and placed it into my grocery cart. When I looked at the small tag attached to each orange to identify its country of origin, I thought, *Wow!* The tag said, "Product of eSwatini." (aka Swaziland).

I knew exactly where they were grown: United Plantation Orange Groves, because I had visited United Plantations in Northwest eSwatini numerous times during the four-and-a-half years I lived in eSwatini and worked at the Ministry of Agriculture.

United Plantation Orange Groves markets their fruit under the brand names River Gold and Swazigold. I remember seeing decent housing and schools and a medical infirmary provided by United Plantations for its employees.

That day, I purchased three bags of oranges and shared them with my friends and colleagues. While munching a Swazi orange, I had a wonderful opportunity to reminisce with friends about my Swatini experiences.

This was an excellent example how international trade impacts our local food markets in Pennsylvania—especially when I am familiar with its origin. It is such a delight that modern transportation and technology enable people in the United States of America and other countries to have access to out-of-season fruits and vegetables grown so far from their country.

Let's close this narrative with a line from a poem titled "Oranges" written by Jean Little, who shows how love and friendship are exemplified through sharing an orange. She wrote, "Citrus and its intimacy are not strictly romantic. It is also a perfect representation of platonic love."

PRELUDE: Quietness can be defined as an absence of noise or clamor. It reflects peacefulness, calmness and stillness. Tranquility and serenity are often the genesis for evolution of thoughts, ideas, contemplation, introspection, reflection, judgement and cogitation. Quietness can release mental and emotional strains or tensions resulting from adverse circumstances. I was inspired to write this narrative titled "Quietness" because challenging, oppressive career duties and responsibilities gave me the need to be alone at times, such as going for a long walk alone in a remote quiet forest to hear the rustling of leaves, singing birds and cracking twigs from squirrels running through the leaves while feeling a gentle breeze. I also enjoy walking along a lonely beach with gentle waves lapping onto the sandy shore with an occasional porpoise jumping from the water. In those two places, I can achieve symmetry for my stressors and command of my emotions.

QUIETNESS

Early one morning, I heard the overwhelming silence of the moon just before sunrise. Dawn quietly and gently lifted the shining sun into the blue sky decorated with puffy clouds. (Photo by Jim Diamond of a full moon from his farm before sunrise near Ottsville, Pennsylvania)

QUIETNESS

A Buddhist proverb says, "There are three things one cannot hide: the moon, the sun and the truth."

The moon and sun both rise and set with deafening silence. Regardless of how peacefully a serene moon or a blazing sun fulfill their deliberate and relentless solar intentions, they enable truth to soothe emotions, which causes contentment.

Early one morning, I heard the overwhelming silence of the moon as it snuffed out its illumination just before sunrise. Dawn quietly and gently lifted the shining sun into the blue sky decorated with white puffy cumulus clouds. As Earth rotates, the sun performs its solar duties by spraying daylight onto portions of the planet at different times of the day.

Dusk sets the sun onto the horizon to blot out the daylight so the moon can fulfill its hushed duty. Regardless which phase the moon portrays, its beauty garnishes the night sky with a variable degree of night-time illumination.

Nighttime skies softly twinkle with faraway stars, planets, galaxies and solar systems with a plethora of unknowns. In a breezy woodland shrouded with leaves or naked trees mutely covered with white snow, a full moon creates imaginative shadows that dance inaudibly among the trees.

Springtime sunshine sprays rays onto trees to discreetly tantalize buds to become a whispering fountainhead of blossoms and leaves. Blossoms are a mass of tree flowers that noiselessly evolve into a fruit. Green leaves are the main organs that soundlessly provide photosynthesis and transpiration.

One evening, I heard quietness and calm after a pounding rainstorm ended. After my dear friends departed and the front door was closed, I was alone. Suddenly, the silence was stupendous. I then went for a walk on our desolate gravel road and heard the shuffle of my footsteps while pondering the blessing of good friends. When one keenly listens, quiet stillness dominates one's intellect, sets aside emotions, and creates a breathing space to relax.

In quietness, I find inner peace.

PRELUDE: While I was living somewhat comfortably in St. Thomas, Virgin Islands, during a three-month Peace Corps French language training program, my late wife, Betty, and I had to climb 100 steps up to our dormitory room. We studied and practiced speaking French from 6 a.m. to 9:30 p.m five-and-a-half days each week. The Peace Corps had a very efficient, effective way of teaching languages. When we arrived at the training camp, I knew two French words: oui (yes) and non (no). After just twelve weeks, Betty and I were both able to comfortably communicate in French. One evening, a fellow Peace Corps trainee and I walked over a mountain to Mandahl Bay for a quick, refreshing swim in the Caribbean Sea. I was inspired to write this narrative titled "Shark!" because we were fortunate to get out of the water before we tangled with a shark.

CARIBBEAN REEF SHARK

One evening, while I was swimming with a colleague in the Caribbean Sea, I heard a fisherman yell, "Shark!" I looked toward the fishermen to see two of them pointing at a shark (*Carcharhinus perezii*) they had caught in their nets. (photographer unknown)

CARIBBEAN REEF SHARK!

During the second week of February 1971, my late wife, Betty, and I needed a break from our intensive French training program. We decided to hike with another Peace Corps volunteer trainee three miles over the mountain in front of our training camp to Mandahl Bay for exercise and a quick, refreshing swim in the Caribbean Sea. Mandahl Bay is located in the north region of U.S. St. Thomas, and it was sparsely populated that day, except for a few people fishing from a rock jetty. The location did not have much of a public beach, but it was very secluded. While we walked barefoot to the water, we stepped carefully around the stones that smothered the little white sand that was available. However, the beach had a relaxing, rustic, rural, natural charm. Its major natural attractions included a ringed mangrove lagoon, rich marine life and birds, and some of the most breathtaking, unspoiled coral reefs. It was a favorite fishing spot for local residents, especially at the rock jetty not far from where we were to swim.

Betty decided to find a comfortable spot on the rocky beach to sit and study her French while my friend and I went swimming in the Caribbean Sea. Oh how wonderfully invigorating and exhilarating that swim felt after a long period of studying French. While we swam, we saw a small group of local fishermen on the stone jetty about 1,000 feet away.

Suddenly, I heard one of the fishermen yell, "Shark!"

I looked toward the fishermen to see two of them pointing at a shark they had caught in their nets.

I called to my friend, "Let's get out of here! There is a shark over there."

We both swam as fast as we could to get out of the water because of the danger of sharks.

We saw a lot of commotion on the jetty, so my friend and I walked toward the jetty. Also we wanted to see the shark they caught. Before we reached the jetty, the shark escaped their nets and swam away. The fishermen told us it was a Caribbean Reef Shark, which often get snagged in their nets.

According to those fishermen, Caribbean Reef Sharks are the most abundant reef shark in Mandahl Bay. Because they are not aggressive, they are not considered dangerous. The fishermen told us the five types of sharks commonly found in and around Mandahl Bay are Caribbean Reef sharks, nurse sharks, black tip sharks, hammerhead sharks and leopard sharks. However they indicated that sharks are seldom seen by people on the beach.

However, this farm boy from Ottsville, Pennsylvania, had never seen a shark in the wild nor did he know anything about sharks other than they sometimes can be dangerous.

What an electrifying worldly experience we had during our break from our French studies. I would like to end this narrative by saying, Salt water heals all wounds, relaxes the mind and rejuvenates life forces.

PRELUDE: Our great country the United States of America has been a land of freedoms and a multitude of rights. Minorities in the United States traditionally have had to endure many hardships. Only when people of all nationalities can come together as equals will the United States assuredly become an eminent nation. Beginning in the sixteenth century, millions of African people were kidnapped, enslaved and shipped across the Atlantic Ocean to many countries, including the Americas, under horrific conditions. I was inspired to write this narrative titled "Skin Color" because on Sunday 24 July 1994 while on a United Nations assignment in Tanzania, my United Nations colleague Harry Burkale and I arrived in the town of Mtwara. It was gloomy, depressing, humbling experience at best. Across from the old German outpost, adjacent to the Indian Ocean beach, were two large, decrepit buildings with bars on their windows. Two Tanzanian leaders informed us that those two buildings were once used to house captured Tanzanians until enough were assembled to fill Portuguese slave ships. We were told that Arab merchants and in some cases tribal chiefs captured Tanzanian men deep in the interior, then walked them in leg chains to Mtwara's prison-like structures where they were sold to sea merchants.

SKIN COLOR

It is important to understand and appreciate one's past heritage, but it is also important not to hinge today's way of life on it. Not even God can change past historical events. (Extended "colored" family from South Africa showing a broad spectrum of human skin coloration)

SKIN COLOR

Internationally, human skin color ranges from the lightest white to the darkest brown, with a plethora of shades in between. As a rule, skin color differences among people results from pigmentation of biological parents.

Whatever the skin color, certain gruff humans exhibit unjustified insulting behavior from unfounded opinions of a class of people having different traits based on spoken language, nationalities, or other affiliated classes of people. For example, in the summer of 1907, when my grandparents immigrated to the United States from Italy, it was bad enough being a foreigner let alone an Italian. My grandfather was called a "Dago" and sometimes a "Wop." To become more acceptable to secure work and discourage discrimination, he changed his last name from Diamanti to Diamond.

During the World War II era, Italian immigrants in America encountered harsh treatment from both citizens and the government. Prejudice magnified by war were directed at the Italian populations, resulting in internment, executions and harassment of hardworking Italian laborers. It is a sad irony that many of those discriminated people had sons fighting overseas in the United States military to save the world from fascism.

It is important to understand and appreciate one's past heritage, but it is also important not to hinge it to today's way of life. I have a difficult time when people identify their skin color or nationality, by saying for example. "I am a Native American," "I'm a black American," "I'm an Asian," or "I'm a Latino," "I'm a person of color." Whatever their birth background, when they become legal citizens of the United States, they are AMERICANS! As a second-generation Italian-American, I don't go around with a chip on my shoulder that says, "I am an Italian-American." I am an American!

The horrible historical backgrounds of immigrants who suffered forced labor and inequalities causes me to think that many people today link their heritage to being a partial cause of racism, racial inequalities, or discrimination. We are living in the twenty-first century, and it is time to put aside our kinfolk lifestyles and inaugurate modern-day lifestyles of acceptance, happiness, economic growth and success. Constantly reminding other people of their discriminated past makes me feel immigrant kinfolk are eliciting pity for their unhappy ancestral lineage. We truly sympathize with their past. However, today people are people, not Hispanic, Black Africans, Italian, Puerto Rican, or any other nationality. To me it matters not their nationality, skin color, shape of their eyes, religion, level of education, or style of dress; they are people and fellow citizens! And if they are legal USA citizens, they are Americans.

It is time people of all shades of color accept and respect each other without unjust and prejudicial treatment. Let's close this narrative by quoting American author Kathryn Stocker who said, "All I'm saying is, kindness doesn't have boundaries."

For the past sixty-five years, regardless of another person's skin color or kinfolk, each day I made sincere efforts to be kind and spread sunshine to people with a positive attitude and without any boundaries regarding their heritage.

PRELUDE: It seems our lifestyle is getting faster and faster. We drive too fast. We eat too fast. We try to get in the shortest line at a bank or in a store. People of all ages in most communities across the United States have gravitated toward living in the fast-paced world of cellphones, computers and social media. Crowds of young, middle-aged and senior people try to keep up with the expectations of others while living with an uneasy feeling that our lifestyles have become overwhelmed with imploring, immediate demands. We're compelled to get and stay on the fast track. We strive to achieve the maximum amount in the shortest possible time. We want not just to succeed, but to be first and the best. Our to-do lists show how busy we are. We are stressed to the maximum. Our fast pace is seen in how people drive. Our blood pressure rises when someone doesn't move the instant a traffic light turns green, or when they are driving too slowly. Many people are addicted to work and a fast-paced lifestyle. Often what suffers most is our health and the quality of our relationships. Sadly, for some people time and money are more important than people and interrelatedness. I was inspired to write this narrative titled "Slow Down" because as I examined the past thirty years of my life, I realized that I also became slowly addicted to a much faster-paced lifestyle. Now that I am retired I ask, "How did I get so addicted to living a faster-paced lifestyle?"

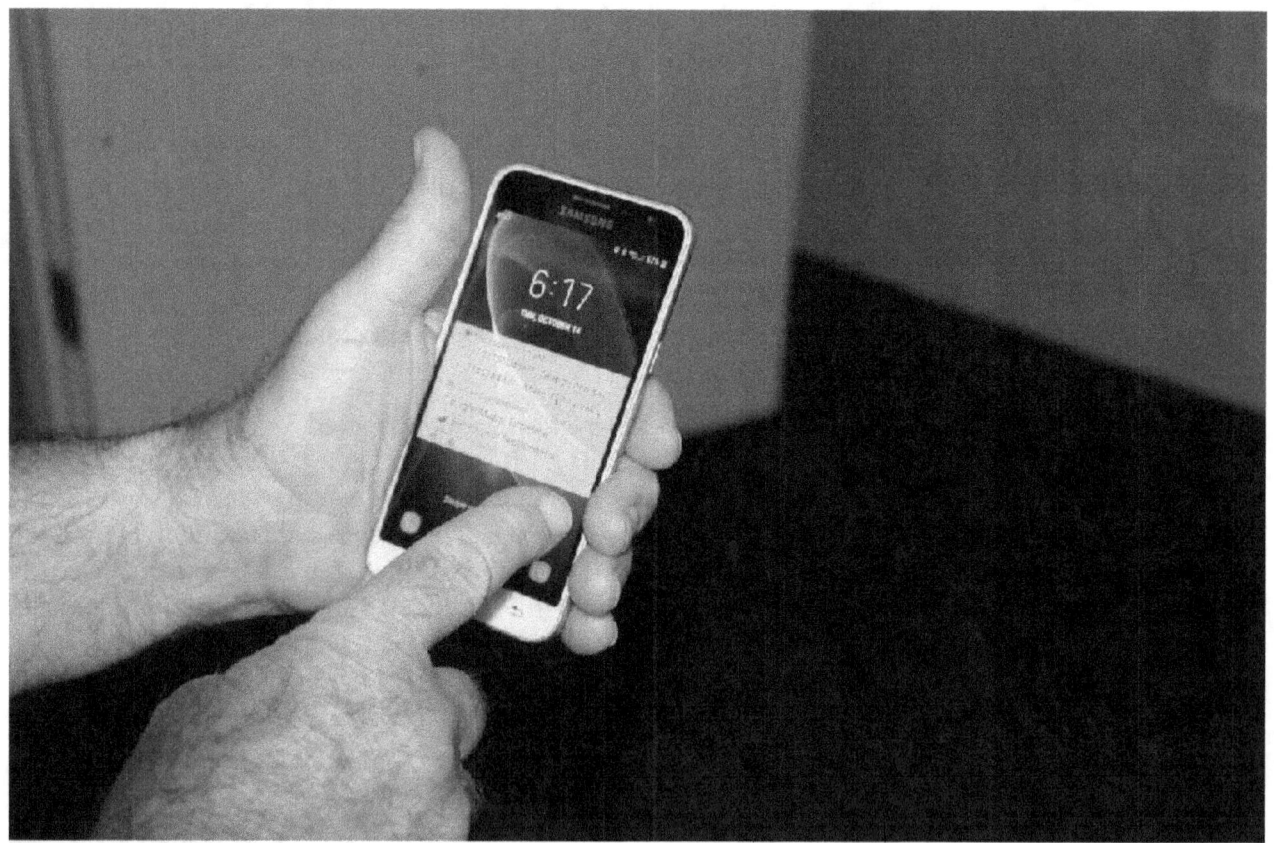

SLOW DOWN

We work, work, work to be able to afford to buy products that we didn't really need to begin with. We are anxious and don't take time to relax. (Photo by Jim Diamond of a fast-living friend who is constantly on his cellphone even when he is supposedly relaxing, October 2021)

SLOW DOWN

Herds of humankind are caught up in an unhealthy cycle of advertising, cyber intelligence, publications, declarations, spending, work and conversation with others. Advertisers tell people they absolutely must buy their new, improved gizmos or featured foodstuffs. Many people spend and spend, buying things not really needed. And then with drudgery people work two jobs to afford to pay for those products or services that were not really needed to begin with. We're anxious and don't take time to relax and think. We think that our job performance is so important that there is no way we can take a day off every once in a while just to relax.

The word "vocation" comes from a Latin word that means "a calling." Your vocation is what God has called you to become. The word "professional" has a similar origin. Originally, a professional referred to someone who understood the intimate connection between faith and work; it was someone who was able to carry faith into the workplace.

Today, when we hear the word "professional," we tend to think of a successful businessperson sitting behind a big desk overseeing the work of hundreds of people. Or maybe we think of a successful surgeon, persuasive professor, competent engineer, creative architect, or famous athlete.

Pause for a moment and think about yourself and grasp the fact that you are experiencing life as it now exists. Recognize the fact that your life is precious and fragile. Ask yourself, *Am I cognizant that I am living my life to its fullest with love and strong feelings of affection in something that gives me pleasure and satisfaction?* Envision previous events in your life that have impacted your journey; is it all as it is supposed to be? Ask yourself, *What do I need to do to establish an error-free style of living? How do I rehabilitate mistaken behavioral traits?*

Answers to such questions can slow down a lifestyle that dictates behavioral and personality patterns brought about by peer pressures and societal expectations.

From my point of view, each person decides for themselves which pace of life they desire. I prefer to live at a reasonable pace, but it can depend on situations. Sometimes I confront unforeseen scenarios when I don't have enough time because of over-scheduling daily tasks, and I am forced to be rushed and do things very quickly.

Technologies alter people's lives, and many people are hooked on social media, the internet, and virtual life. Some have been enslaved by it. Even though technologies simplify our lives, I think a fast-paced life impacts our mental and physical condition, jeopardizes our attention and productivity, erodes our emotional health, and threatens our relationships with family, friends and other people. I would like to close this narrative by quoting Shah-Rae Weaver, a songwriter from Adelaide, Australia, who wrote the words to a song titled "Just Slow Down." It goes like this:

"Just slow down. Slow down your speech. Slow down your breathing. Slow down your eating. And let this slower, steadier pace be the perfume in your mind. Just slow down."

Everyone must understand the whole of life, not just one segment of it. That is why you must slow down, look at the beautiful skies, contemplate the beauty of wildflowers, sing when it rains, listen to growling winds, appreciate the falling snow, enjoy a warm wood fire, and relish the feeling of warmth of a sunny day. Everyone must have a reason to be in this life, and these are some reasons why one must slow down and enjoy your reason for being.

PRELUDE: Time is not an object or substance that one can touch, taste, hear, smell, or see but it possesses three things: what has occurred (past), what is occurring (present), and what will occur (future). It is impossible to keep what has occurred from fading into the present, which is sandwiched between what has occurred and what will occur. Time can be measured by nanoseconds, seconds, minutes, hours, days, weeks, months, years, decades, and eons. I was inspired to write this narrative titled "Time on Earth" because I have reached an age of having lived eighty-six years. I am living in the present and have fewer years that will occur. However, each day while on this Earth, I diligently exert myself to do my best because I only get that day once.

TIME ON EARTH

Time has no sounds to call attention, however, it is the stuff that makes life interesting, fruitful and meaningful. You are what you are because you have used your time in a pragmatic manner. (Photographer unknown)

TIME ON EARTH

Benjamin Franklin once said, "Don't waste time because that's the stuff life is made of." Time quietly, quickly causes people, flora* and fauna* to evolve from simpler to more complex.

Time is characterized by three phases: past, present and future. Yet, in the philosophy of time, presentism is the belief that only the present exists, and both the future and the past are unreal.

Leading modern Buddhist philosopher Stcherbatsky, who wrote extensively on Buddhist presentism, claimed, "Everything past is unreal; everything future is unreal; everything imagined is absent, and mental is unreal."

Based upon Stcherbatsky's postulation, reality is only the present. Hence, it is impossible to keep what has occurred from fading into the present, which is sandwiched between what has occurred and what will occur. Reality is now, today, this very moment, the present time, the here and now, this day, the time being.

Time has no sounds to call your attention, however, time makes life interesting, fruitful and meaningful. Time guides and directs one's dreams, yearnings and desires.

Different people approach time with pessimism, optimism, or hope. Optimists see the world as a positive place, believing that people and events are inherently good. Pessimists tend to view only undesirable outcomes. Hopeful people live with a certain amount of wanting, wishing, perseverance, suffering, or even despair. Hopefulness is an emotional state, whereas optimism and pessimism are conclusions reached through deliberate thoughts that lead to positive or negative attitudes.

Whether you are an optimist, pessimist, or hopeful person depends upon whether your time usage is impractical or pragmatic. A positive attitude generates optimistic attitudes amongst people and makes them smile. Making people smile each day makes my day more meaningful.

Haitian diplomat and journalist Joseph Raymond once stated, "Whoever does not know the past must have little understanding of the present and no vision for the future."

Friends, family and time are three of life's most precious treasures, and the older we grow the more precious they each become. Even though we have numerous ways to communicate, such as visiting, writing a letter, telephoning, emailing, zooming and texting, unfortunately, people's time seems to quietly, quickly dissipate without using a sufficient portion of it to communicate with friends and family. We allow time to slip through the present because we are so involved with our own lives that we overlook the importance of the lives of longtime friends and close family.

I would like to close this narrative by quoting Leo Tolstoy, a Russian writer who is regarded as one of the greatest authors of all time, who once said, "The two most powerful warriors are patience and time."

Don't be afraid of growing older; be afraid only if you are standing still. Time on Earth is the continued sequence of events that occur in an irreversible progression from the past, through the present, and into the future. Think positive thoughts, make people happy, and do not waste time while on this Earth.

PRELUDE: Your personal legacy should reflect who and what have been most important in your life. It should speak from your heart in your own words, thoughts and actions. Determining what legacy you want to leave behind will bring a deeper meaning to your life—both now and in the future. Ideally, you can share your personal legacy with loved ones while you are still alive—rather than it being read at your funeral or memorial celebration. Unfolding a personal legacy must come from the heart, which expresses your love and appreciation for the enlightenment that has enhanced your career and life. I was inspired to write this narrative titled "Unfold Your Personal Legacy" because Delaware Valley University prepared me for a forty-seven-year career that took me far beyond my wildest expectations. I have reached the age when it is time for me to unfold my personal legacy with charitable gifts that are within my financial capability.

UNFOLD YOUR PERSONAL LEGACY

It is the contentment and fulfillment that one experiences during and after giving that matters, not the amount given. The Greek statesman Pericles once said, "What you leave behind is not what is engraved in stone monuments, but what you wove into the lives of others." (Photographer unknown)

UNFOLD YOUR PERSONAL LEGACY

When I was a student at Delaware Valley University (DVU), scholarships and financial aid programs weren't given as they are today. When the former Soviet Union launched the satellite Sputnik on 4 October 1957, under the leadership of President Dwight D. Eisenhower, the U.S. Congress passed the National Defense Education Act, which enabled American institutions of higher learning to enhance student capabilities to learn science and mathematics. Had it not been for the National Defense Education Act, plus my shearing sheep and milking cows, I would not have been able to afford to complete my education at DVU. Because of that assistance, DVU was the Alpha and Omega of my wonderful career.

That's why it is now time for me to give back to DVU and make charitable gifts that are within my financial capability. Hopefully these gifts will assist current and future Aggies in adequately preparing for their respective careers that take them far beyond their wildest expectations.

Anne Frank stated, "No one has ever become poor by giving."

Winston Churchill said, "We make a living by what we get, but we make a life by what we give."

It is the contentment and fulfillment that one experiences during and after giving that matters, not the amount given.

You can use a myriad of methods to make charitable donations. I have created a three-pronged approach to giving. First, my donations must have more than just one use. For instance, I could endow scholarships that help students finance their education while simultaneously growing the DVU endowment.

Second, I give in perpetuity through an estate plan. People should not leave this life without including philanthropy in their estate plan.

Third, I entrust money to Charitable Gift Annuity Funds to enhance monthly personal retirement income.

Each of these three methods is a leg of my charitable triune.

Let me close this narrative by quoting Chinese philosopher Lao Tzu, who said, "Kindness in words creates confidence. Kindness in thinking creates profoundness. Kindness in giving creates love."

With this being said, may your love for your alma mater, church, friends, family and social group(s) be reflected in your personal legacy and giving.

PRELUDE: In the autumn of 1621, the Plymouth colonists and Native Americans named Wampanoag shared an autumn harvest feast that is acknowledged today as one of the first Thanksgiving celebrations in the colonies. The Native Americans joined the celebration by bringing a deer to share. Fowl, fish, eel, shellfish and cranberries were part of the feast. On Thursday, November 26, 1789, President George Washington issued a proclamation for "a day of public thanksgiving and prayer." Beginning in 1863, President Abraham Lincoln encouraged Americans to recognize the last Thursday of November as a day of thanksgiving and prayer. I was inspired to write this narrative titled "What Are You Thankful For?" because Thanksgiving is a time to say thanks for the blessings but also for the challenges of life and how God gets you through those challenges.

WHAT ARE YOU THANKFUL FOR?

During the week before Thanksgiving, I often ask people what they are thankful for. They will generally recite a synopsis of personal events and desirable circumstances (Photographer unknown)

WHAT ARE YOU THANKFUL FOR?

During the week before Thanksgiving, I often ask people what they are thankful for, which usually elicits a synopsis of personal events and desirable circumstances. We all should be thankful for good happenings and events of life. But Thanksgiving is also a time to give thanks for lessons we learned by remembering the negative things that have happened to us as well.

Saying thanks for what we learned is especially important when our world has been turned upside down. It is imperative to express thanks for learning how to best deal with more than our fair share of personal problems. One needs to remember to ask forgiveness for the act of judging people, for failing to carry out an undertaking due to oversight or carelessness, or for deliberately disregarding or avoiding noticing others in need.

Remember what you learned through the difficult times of life and how God was with you, especially how He led you through the wilderness. May we always remember with gratitude those whom God sent to guide us into our respective lifestyles, who offered us advice and prepared us to excel within our careers.

Saying "thank you" is a polite expression used to tell someone that you are grateful because they have given you an object or performed for you a kindhearted task. Saying "I thank you" acknowledges receiving a service, gift, or compliment or accepting or refusing an offer.

Hearing the words "thank you" usually makes the benefactor happy to know that they are giving you a helping hand.

Regardless of your thoughts at Thanksgiving—the time of the year designated to give thanks—acknowledging other people for the kind acts they provided to needy people endorses such positivity. Being appreciative tells people of your awareness and understanding of the significance of something they did for you or for others.

Such gracious acts are in God's favor, and we must express our gratefulness to God.

I would like to close this narrative by quoting American talk show host and author Oprah Winfrey, "Be thankful for what you have; you'll end up having more. If you concentrate on what you don't have, you will never, ever have enough."

Therefore it is important to be thankful for what we have, truthfully knowing that we possess enough to endure life's challenges while living a joyous lifestyle.

PRELUDE: More than sixty years ago, Delaware Valley University (DVU) enrolled three students who became esteemed companions: David Kantner, a member of the DVU class of 1960; me, a member of the DVU class of 1961; and George Perry, a member of the DVU class of 1963. We three had a great deal in common. We were all born in, raised in, and still live in Pennsylvania. We each lived on and worked for our fathers' farms. We each worked as agricultural educators. We all were employed by the Pennsylvania State University, and we were often colleagues and collaborators on various agricultural education programs. We each were undeniably happily married to very supportive wives, who became surrogate sisters. Additionally, we each traveled together with our wives throughout North America and also to Africa, Europe and Oceania. Furthermore, together with our spouses we have bid adieu to forty-three years and welcomed forty-three new years into being, I was inspired to write this narrative titled "When We Are Together" because when we are together, we enjoy a lot of laughter, good-natured chit-chat and in-depth discussions. But more importantly, this narrative is my virtuous, heartfelt attempt to express my sincere longtime respect, appreciation, gratitude and love for these dear longtime friends.

WHEN WE ARE TOGETHER

When my dear longtime friends and I are together, we always have a lot of laughter, good-natured chit-chat and in-depth discussions focused on solving world problems. (Photo of left to right: Connie Kantner, Gamal Mina, Betty Diamond, George Perry, Barbara Perry, Jim Diamond, Nagy Mina Dave Kantner, in Sydney, Australia, 2007)

WHEN WE ARE TOGETHER

Friendship and memories are two of life's most precious treasures. The older we grow, the more precious they both become. My friends and I gather together during holidays, special occasions, during our travels overseas, and sometimes just for the hell of it. When we are together with or without our spouses, we are a surrogate family of dear friends bound together by love and precious memories.

The word "surrogate" comes from the Latin word *surrogae*, which means "to put in another's place" or "to substitute." My friends and I are a surrogate family. Sometimes people's friends became their surrogate family after most of their biological family members are deceased. In our case, we each have biological family members who live far away, have different interests, and some of which are a "pain where a pill cannot reach."

A surrogate family of friends is often inseparable, and they hold each other in high esteem. My surrogate family and I share memories that often rekindle happiness, gratification, amusement, sadness, despair, sorrow, melancholy and other feelings. All these memorable stories together flavor and reflect individual magnetism that pulls us together as a surrogate family.

When we are together, even though we often repeat our favorite stories, trying to relive the past, no matter how hard we try, we cannot bring back the old days. Not even God can retrieve the past. All we can do is remember past events and confabulate about them. It is fun to recall those times that molded our personas.

A Hebrew proverb on friends and foes goes like this, "Who is mighty? He who makes an enemy into a friend."

In 1998, when I was in eSwatini (Swaziland), Africa, a Swazi farmer said to me, "If you make your enemy your friend, you no longer have an enemy."

To make an enemy into a friend, it's usually necessary to do a few things: sincerely apologize for any past wrongdoings, focus on the enemy's desirable traits, forgive, discover what you have in common, express understanding, and offer assistance if there is a bonafide need.

Lucius Annaeus, a Roman philosopher and statesman who was a tutor and advisor to Nero, the last Roman Emperor, wrote, "One of the most beautiful qualities of true friendship is to understand and to be understood."

Understanding and being understood are two virtues that are rapturously evident among me and my dear friends. Because of our common backgrounds, we comprehend and get the drift of nearly everything that is uttered. I am very thankful for and indebted to my family of friends, and I hope that our relationships continue far into the future.

Let me close this narrative by quoting French-Algerian writer Albert Camus, who wrote, "Don't walk behind me; I may not lead. Don't walk in front of me; I may not follow. Just walk beside me and be my friend."

PRELUDE: Soil conservation is the process of protecting the soil from degradation. It involves treating the soil as a living ecosystem,* requiring the continual return of organic matter to the soil. A conservation air tour is an airplane ride to give people a bird's-eye-view of soil conservation practices. During an air tour of farms in Upper Bucks County, our goal was to observe seven best management practices of soil conservation. This was a very, very effective teaching method that students will forever remember. I was inspired to write this narrative, "Conservation Air Tour" because during this tour, my students grasped the importance and purpose of soil conservation practices. The students raised the funds to hire three small four-passenger airplanes by selling seedling trees at the Doylestown Shopping Center for the Pennsylvania Department of Forestry.

CONSERVATION AIR TOUR

Yep! Inside this small airplane are three Upper Bucks Tech Future Farmers of America members observing soil conservation practices in Upper Bucks County, which they had been studying in the classroom for five weeks. (Photo by Jim Diamond at the Pennridge Airport near Perkasie, Pennsylvania)

CONSERVATION AIR TOUR

All organisms that make the soil their home play important roles in producing healthy, fertile soil. These organisms break down organic matter, release nutrients, and open up spaces for air and water to circulate. Organic matter provides good soil structure and water-holding capacity, promotes water infiltration, and protects the soil from erosion and compaction.

Teaching conservation units was challenging because the students were not familiar with the best management practices, and many of them lacked farm experiences. After I taught a soil conservation unit for five weeks, I wanted to bring the topic to life for my students by taking them on a conservation air tour to see what they had studied.

As chairman of the Bucks County Soil Conservation District, it was easy for me to get the resources and personnel to plan the air tour. However, I had to get both the administration and the parents to buy into my idea.

When I told the director about my air tour idea, he responded, "You're going to do what?" I explained to him that conservation air tours are common across Pennsylvania and the United States. I even invited him to participate. He reluctantly approved the air tour—as long as the parents agreed.

When I told the parents about my air tour idea, I was amazed at their support, especially the people who had never ridden in an airplane. Our event was even covered by our local news media.

The day before the scheduled flight, a conservation officer took two of my students with several bags of lime, and they traveled throughout Upper Bucks County by car identifying conservation practices on farms that could be seen from the air. At each site, they made huge white numbers with lime that could easily be seen from the airplane. When this task was completed, we made handouts for students that identified and explained seven best management practices as seen from the airplane: contour strips, cover cropping, waterway, farm pond, bank stabilization, no-till farming and wind breaks.

We also flew over Lake Nockamixon and the three schools of the students: Quakertown High School, Palisades High School and Perkasie High School followed by the Upper Bucks Tech School on our flight back to the airport.

Our conservation air tour lasted more than thirty minutes. The students were astonished at flying in an airplane for the first time and seeing sights and roads they were familiar with from the air. More importantly, they were better able to understand what they had been studying for five weeks.

I would like to close this narrative by quoting Dr. Charles E. Kellogg, soil scientist and Chief of the USDA's Bureau for Chemistry and Soils, who wrote, "Essentially, all life depends upon the soil… There can be no life without soil and no soil without life; they have evolved together."

Furthermore, I would like to quote Henry Ford, entrepreneur and founder of the Ford Motor Company, who said, "The farther we get away from the land, the greater our insecurity will be."

These two famous people understood that understanding, protecting and appreciating best management practices for healthy soil conservation is essential for our happiness and well-being as citizens on planet Earth.

PRELUDE: One day, while I discussed international travel with my neighbor and good friend James A. Michener, who was also a famous American author, he said, "If you reject the food, ignore the customs, fear the religion, and avoid the people, you might as well stay home. You are like a pebble thrown into water. You become wet on the surface, but are never part of the water." My response to Mr. Michener was, "I view a tourist as a person who travels to see things that are different and then complains when they aren't the same." Unfortunately, tourism is a key driver of socio-economic progress around the world. I personally prefer to immerse myself in places where I can learn to appreciate and respect the culture, art, customs, traditions, music and religion while helping people help themselves to deepen their own identity. I was inspired to write this narrative titled "Customs, Traditions, Cultures and Religions" to share some of my knowledge learned during the international endeavors that I was a part of on five continents.

CUSTOMS, TRADITIONS, CULTURES AND RELIGIONS

The Incwala ceremony is held on the fourth day after the full moon nearest the longest day of the year, 21 December 1988, by King Mswati III Kraal in eSwatini. (Photo by Jim Diamond during an Incwala Ceremony in eSwatini, on 21 December 1998)

CUSTOMS, TRADITIONS, CULTURES AND RELIGIONS

Helping people help themselves was the philosophical foundation for the international projects and programs that influenced my work in nations around the world. I have learned that people tend to have, in varying degrees, an interwoven ethnic and national pride, which is characterized by cultural dignity and personal integrity. It is crucial that modern concepts not compete with nor replace traditional practices in a culture, but instead they should add to the culture for consideration, acceptance, then implementation or rejection. Here are some examples of existing customs, traditions, cultures, and religions I observed in various societies.

eSWATINI: The principal Swazi social unit is a traditional beehive hut thatched with dry grass. In a polygamous homestead, each wife has her own hut and yard surrounded by reed fences. The polygamous headman advises his wives on all social affairs. A *sangoma* is a traditional diviner who is consulted for sickness or even death. His diagnosis is based on communication through trance with natural superpowers. The most important cultural event in eSwatini is the *Incwala* ceremony, which is held on the fourth day after the full moon nearest the longest day of the year, 21 December. *Incwala* translates to "first fruits ceremony."

TCHAD: There are twelve main Tchadian holidays, and most of them are religious. Political events, such as Independence Day and the Proclamation of the Republic, are particularly festive, featuring parades and sports: The Feast of the Sacrifice, Ramadan, and Eid-al-Fitr are among the notable Muslim holidays in Tchad. These religious events are celebrated by Muslim communities across the nation and honored by Tchadians.

BULGARIA: According to the Orthodox Christian tradition, during Dance in an Ice Cold River on 6 January, a priest throws a metal cross into the ice cold waters of the local river. The bravest local men run into the water bare-chested, trying to fetch it, seemingly unaffected by the freezing temperatures. Everybody is invited to Wake Up Before Dawn to get Dirty in the Valley of Roses for the Festival of Roses, which is scheduled each May and June in the town of Kazanlak. Flowers are hand-picked and their petals are pressed for oil, which is used in the cosmetic industry in French perfumes: Bulgarian hikers climb Stara Palnina Mountain to attend a summer Blueberry Music Festival at 5,000 feet. Because there is no vehicular access, everyone has to carry their food, tent, and gear up an extremely steep path.

CHINA: Chinese culture is said to have begun with the Yellow Emperor 5,000 years ago. He was a cultivator of the Tao ("the Way") and was said to have great power and wisdom. He taught his subjects how to live in accordance with the Heavenly Way. Taoist thought, considered a source of Chinese culture, was systemized by the sage Lao Zi more than 2,500 years ago, presenting and explaining the mysterious ways of the universe, which he called the Tao. Buddhism reached China from ancient India. Its focus on personal salvation and meditation profoundly affected Chinese culture, and it does so to this day.

It is crucial that foreign travelers respect traditional local customs, traditions, cultures, religions with thoughtfulness and not sneer at them. Visitors should make sincere efforts to study and learn about their importance and significance.

PRELUDE: Social workers claim that when one is disturbed, their normal lifestyle is disrupted, which can result in emotional or mental difficulties. A disturbed lifestyle can create a feeling of social and mental isolation, which can negatively affect mental health. It seems that when one experiences a disturbed lifestyle, uncertain negative or challenging life circumstances evolve. I was inspired to write this narrative titled "Disturbed" because I have worked with several people (especially young people) who were disturbed. Even I experienced a disturbance in my life for a period of time after my late wife, Betty, passed away. Fortunately I was able to successfully cope with the common symptoms of a lifestyle disturbance by making every day a good day.

"Your time is limited, so don't waste it living someone else's life. Don't be trapped by dogma, which is living with the results of other people's thinking. Don't let the noise of others' opinions drown out your own inner voice. And most important, have the courage to follow your heart and intuition."
—Steve Jobs

DISTURBED

Usually an educator who becomes acquainted with students, especially adolescents and young adults, can observe one or more emotional and mental disturbance(s). Adolescents and young adults, and also older adults, are particularly at risk for emotional and mental disturbance. Symptoms include substance abuse, cognitive decline, suicidal thoughts, mood disorders, mental and physical health issues, chronic pain and prolonged fatigue.

If an educator recognizes students with these symptoms, he or she should heed these warnings by carefully and judiciously obeying school policies and or legal responsibilities.

Once one of my high school senior student's grades suddenly plunged. I noticed he was not socializing with his peers, and he also looked depressed and had glassy eyes. My teacher's aide found him in our shop smoking pot. This boy was clever, which told me he wanted to get caught and was ready to talk.

I took him aside to talk about his perceived problem(s). Whew! The boy lived with his middle-class parents and relayed to me a very sad situation in his home.

I said to him, "Please let me know if you would like me to speak to your parents."

His immediate response was, "Yes. Tell them everything."

He was scheduled to go on the senior class trip the next day, but he canceled.

I telephoned his mother and said, "I need to speak with you and your husband as soon as possible." We scheduled a meeting for the following Tuesday evening in my classroom.

My late wife, Betty, was concerned because she feared a negative outcome from the meeting. I met the parents alone in my classroom, and upon their arrival, I greeted them and invited them to sit at a table.

With no small talk, we immediately got to important points for the meeting. As I described what their son told me, the father broke in and angrily denied what I was saying. Twice I had to intervene in a husband-and-wife dispute. Although the teen's mom agreed with what their son told me, his father could not accept there was a problem and denied the points being made. We spoke for more than two hours.

Before the parents departed, I suggested they take their son to a nice restaurant where they could be alone and let him talk. I said, "You are going to hear some things you don't want to hear. However, let him talk and get these issues out." I knew that the teen was ready to face his father.

Fortunately, the parents took my suggestion seriously and scheduled a dinner reservation with their son at a fine dining restaurant. After that, the teen quickly improved his behavior by socializing again with his peers, raising his grades, then graduating from high school.

Shortly after his high school graduation, his parents threw a celebration party for their son, and I was invited. What a glorious time we had. His mother and aunt called me to the side, and in tears, they thanked me profusely for helping their son and nephew. He is now a graduate of a major university and is gainfully employed with a prestigious position.

PRELUDE: I spent nine challenging, innovative, rewarding years of my forty-seven-year career teaching agricultural sciences at Upper Bucks County Area Vocational Technical School (UBCAVTS). The tech school opened in September 1966. Between Christmas and New Year's Day 1966, President of the School Board Penrose Hallowell drove to my farm and informed me that the new tech school should have a vocational agriculture course. He said that the school principal wanted to talk with me about starting that program. After a lengthy discussion at his office, the principal wanted me to begin the next day. For various reasons, I was not able to begin the next day; however, we agreed that I would start on Monday, 27 January 1967. That was the beginning date of the Vocational Agriculture program at UBCAVTS. Over the years, due to changes in career needs and opportunities, the program has evolved into a vast array of units of study within two separate programs: Agricultural Technology and Life Sciences Academy, Animal, and Veterinary Science. I was inspired to write this narrative titled "Final Exam on the First Day of School" because fifty-seven years later, these programs have impacted hundreds of young people during their formative years and careers.

FINAL EXAM ON THE FIRST DAY OF SCHOOL

In this photo, Upper Bucks County Tech College students at Open Gate Farm learn about desirable and undesirable soil traits with students teaching their peers as an integral part of their final examination assigned to them on the first day of school. (Photographer unknown)

FINAL EXAM ON THE FIRST DAY OF SCHOOL

In January 1967, I walked into the small storage room at Upper Bucks County Area Vocational Technical School (UBCAVTS) where I would be teaching my new three-hour-long class. I had thirteen students, six in my morning class and seven in the afternoon. I had no facilities, curriculum, equipment, reference materials, or field trip bus, just fourteen desks, sixteen lockers and a burdizzo.* To this day, I do not have a clue where that burdizzo came from.

Back then, a group of people in the community opposed establishing the agriculture program at UBCAVTS based upon their opinions and emotions. To address their concerns, we conducted a study during the summer of 1967 to gather support and facts for establishing the agriculture program. One of the facts was that in 1967, the three school districts in Upper Bucks County were made of rural agricultural communities. We therefore created my agriculture program.

The late Florence Schaufhausen, owner of nearby Open Gate Farm, strongly supported our agriculture program. We used her farm as an ag laboratory, where we plowed fields, sheared sheep, held our land-judging contest, and made management decisions.

My colleagues thought I was innovative because I used a lot of new teaching methods and taught a plethora of topics with a hands-on modus operandi. For example, on the first day of school in the autumn of 1967, I announced to the students, "I am giving you your final examination today, on the first day of school."

Whoa, this was unthinkable! The students were not accustomed to such an announcement. At that point, they did not have a clue what was going to be taught during class, so for sure they had no idea what could be asked on their final exam at the end of the school year.

I explained this would not to be a written exam. I asked each student to identify a skill they had learned and mastered and could share with the class, such as how to milk a cow, show a hog at a fair, catch snapping turtles, clean a shotgun,* use a chainsaw, or shear sheep. The students needed to obtain my approval for their topic by Thanksgiving. Once they got the approval, they had nearly five months to gather information, describe their skill, learn how to demonstrate it, and then teach their classmates how to perform their skill.

I scheduled one student presentation for each period of each day beginning 1 April. Often in a school bus, the class and I would go to a student's home or farm where the student would speak about and demonstrate his or her skill.

This exercise taught the students how to write a theme, improve their writing skills, speak in front of a group, improve their self-confidence, answer questions about their skill, and develop social acceptance amongst peers. I was amazed how much my students enjoyed teaching their peers a skill they had mastered—and oftentimes teaching me as well. For example, one of my students and his father trapped snapping turtles and sold the meat to restaurants for snapper soup. At the end of that student's presentation, his mother and father brought a kettle full of snapping turtle soup for all the students to sample. That was teaching at its best.

I would like to close this narrative by quoting English author Michael Morpurg, who said, "It's the teacher that makes the difference, not the classroom."

The students teaching students at their homes and/or on their farms helped form my classroom.

PRELUDE: At Upper Bucks County Area Vocational Technical School, I was a vocational agriculture instructor for students in grades ten, eleven and twelve for nine wonderful years. As long as I can remember, the Monday following Thanksgiving Day was always the first day of deer-hunting season in Pennsylvania. Even though school was open, nearly all of the students in my class were absent because they went deer hunting. I never reprimanded a student for spending a couple days deer hunting with their family or friends because my fondest memories of my father were from deer hunting with him when I was their age. Nevertheless, when a student returned to school after deer hunting, I wanted to hear about how their big buck got away when they shot and missed. Many deer hunters in Pennsylvania have a long-time tradition when one misses shooting a buck qualifies them to have their shirttail cut off. Some of the stories were stretched a bit, and others were humorous. I was inspired to write this narrative titled "Shirttail Ceremony" because it was a pleasurable in-school activity that needed to be documented, especially for my former students who still remember it.

SHIRTTAIL CEREMONY

When my students came back to school after hunting deer for two or three days with their family or friends, I always wanted to hear their deer-hunting stories. My class rule for all student deer-hunters was that if a student missed shooting a deer, they qualified to have their shirttail cut off. (Photographer unknown)

SHIRTTAIL CEREMONY

When students came back to school after hunting deer for two or three days with their family and friends, I always asked them to share with me stories from their deer-hunting adventures.

I started a tradition where if a student missed shooting a buck, his or her shirttail was cut off in our shirttail ceremony! Our shirttail ceremony became so well known amongst previous students who missed shooting their buck, information about it was passed on to underclassmen.

Unlucky students fulfilled my instructions and voluntarily brought an old shirt with them to school because they knew the rule. Students who missed their big buck were instructed to go into the men's room and change into an old shirt. When they returned, each had to stand in front of the class and tell their short story describing when, where, how, and why they missed shooting a "huge multi-point buck."

My students who were not able or permitted to go deer hunting were not left out of the ceremony. I got them involved by giving each a pair of scissors.

I would say, "Oh great hunter above, thank you for causing this deer hunter to miss shooting that beautiful big buck in your woods. This prevented your beautiful buck from being sent to buck heaven. Amen!"

Then the students with the scissors would step forward and cut off a chunk of that student's shirttail.

After the shirttail ceremony, I hung the shirttails on the bulletin board with the student's written story and name. On top of the bulletin board was this statement, "I like big bucks, but I cannot lie."

My yearly shirttail ceremony camouflaged learning with excitement. My students learned to overcome fears of speaking before a group. They developed self-confidence. Students who did not go deer hunting still felt accepted by the class because they were involved in the ceremony. Student hunters practiced their writing skills and penmanship by writing a short story. Plus students familiarized themselves with each other, which enhanced their social skills.

Years later, former students still visit my home to update me on their career, marriage, children and parents. We reminisce about memorable experiences they had with me, especially the Shirttail Ceremony, which lives on in our memories more than forty years later.

PRELUDE: At Upper Bucks Area Vocational Technical School, my students studying vocational agriculture expressed great interest in home butchering, especially during the annual Pennsylvania deer hunting season. Many of my students harvested deer during their hunts with their friends or family, but few of them knew how to process those harvested deer. I decided to add a teaching unit called "Butchering and Processing a Deer," including both lectures and hands-on participation. Before adding this unit, I needed permission from my students' parents. They gladly gave me permission because if I taught their teens how to process deer, it could save them the high cost of having their deer processed at local commercial butcher shops. My students could then pass on their knowledge and skills of home butchering and processing harvested deer to future generations. My students and their families benefited from this new teaching unit so much that I was inspired to write this narrative titled "Students Learn How to Butcher a Deer."

STUDENTS LEARN HOW TO BUTCHER A DEER

Whether a student was a hunter, an aspiring hunter, or simply just curious about how the meat they eat goes from animal to plate, they learned how to process harvested deer in my class by observing and doing. (Photographer unknown)

STUDENTS LEARN HOW TO BUTCHER A DEER

My teaching unit at Upper Bucks County Area Vocational Technical School (UBCAVTS) "Butchering and Processing a Deer," began after deer season in Pennsylvania with a short lecture, using an unprocessed deer harvested by the father of one of my students. After a short lecture, I demonstrated how to remove the hide, hang the carcass, split the carcass, identify the wholesale and retail cuts, debone certain cuts, how to use a steel to sharpen knives, and wrap and label the meat before freezing.

Whether a student in my class was a hunter or an aspiring hunter or simply curious about how the meat they eat goes from animal to plate, they learned how to process harvested venison.

Before this deer butchering and processing unit, I asked my UBCAVTS students to tell their parents, friends and neighbors that they were learning how to butcher and process a deer and that we needed harvested deer on which to learn and practice their skills. There was no charge to the student, families, or school for us to process the deer, but I asked the hunter to provide a couple rolls of freezer paper in which we could wrap the meat.

During the deer processing, my student butchers were expected to practice sanitary procedures. They also were required to follow federal and state regulations for the handling and preparation of meat products.

I assigned one student to schedule when the hunters would come to our class with their deer. The program was so popular that we had to stop accepting deer! When a deer arrived, a student was responsible for recording the hunter's name, address, telephone number, kinds of cuts preferred, how many cuts wanted in a package, date when the meat would be available, and whether the hunter wanted the hide. The hunter were welcome to stay for class to watch the students process the deer.

Within six days of this unit, students working in pairs could process a harvested deer and wrap the cuts in just two-and-a-half hours.

Many hunters tipped the students for their efforts. If a hunter did not want the deer hide, students would salt the meat side of the hide, wrap it, and store in a cold, outside building. At the end of hunting season, we sold those hides to a deer hide tannery in Clearfield, Pennsylvania. We invested all of the money received for tips and sale of the hides into the Future Farmers of America chapter treasury to hire a bus for a future field trip.

The grade level of the participants included ten, eleven and twelve. Several of my UBCAVTS graduates were hired by local butcher shops and large meat processing companies because they had learned basic knowledge, which minimized employer on-the-job training.

I would like to end this narrative by quoting American radio and television writer Andy Rooney, who said, "Don't take a butcher's advice on how to cook meat. If he knew, he'd be a chef."

However, butchers do often give customers free advice on how to best prepare certain meat cuts.

PRELUDE: What makes a plant a weed? I define a weed as a plant that's growing where it is not wanted in landscaping, vegetable or flower gardens, or within large agricultural crops, such as corn, soybeans and hay. Weeds are valueless annual or perennial plants not intentionally planted in an area that interfere with the growth of desirable plants. Weeds compete with intentional plantings for water, nutrients, light and growing space. Weeds also attract insects and diseases to desired plants. Some weeds can sting you, and some are poisonous. On the other hand, some weeds are edible. Some prevent erosion, and some make good grazing for wildlife. Some weeds have gorgeous flowers that add beauty along roadsides, mountainsides and uncultivated fields. I was inspired to write this narrative called "Weed Identification" because teaching weed identification to high school students was a dull topic—unless I added some excitement, such as by converting a "contest" into a "test"

WEED IDENTIFICATION

Some weeds (wild species of plants) have gorgeous flowers that add beauty along roadsides, mountainsides and uncultivated fields. Some weeds are edible, and some prevent erosion and some make good grazing for wildlife. The wildflowers in this photo are red common wild poppy *(Papaver somniferum)*. (Photo by Jim Diamond of wild poppy flowers along Ridge Road, two miles east of Upper Bucks County Area Vocational Technical School)

WEED IDENTIFICATION

One problem homeowners, gardeners, and farmers all experience is the constant struggle to control weeds growing in their flower gardens, vegetable gardens, fields and lawns. Weeds have vigorous growth, and they are able to quickly take over lawns, gardens, and fields. Weeds, also known as "wild plants," are simply any plant that is growing where it is not wanted.

Like any type of plant, the two types of weeds are annuals and perennials. Annual plants live for only one growing season, then they die. Perennial plants come up and grow again year after year. How successful a weed is at growing depends upon its environment (such as swamp, clay soil or rocky soil), the steepness of the grade, depth of topsoil, accompanying plants and altitude.

Examples of common perennial weeds that grow in Pennsylvania include skunk cabbage (*Symplocarpus foetidus*), common dandelion (*Taraxacum officinale*), bloodroot (*Sanguinaria canadensis*), crabgrass (*Digitaria spp.*), lambsquarters (*Chenopodium album*), chickweed (*Stellaria sp*) and pigweed (*Amaranthus spp.*).

In my classrooms, I always focused my teaching modus operandi on the belief that what I hear, I forget. What I see, I may remember. But what I do, I know. I find it's important that students listen, watch and actively participate in several different ways.

In my programs, my students needed to identify fifty different weeds that grow in Upper Bucks County. On the way to school, I would stop along the road, at a neighboring farm or local public park and select ten different specimens of weeds.

In my classroom, I had ten containers, such as bottles, jars and vases, each half filled with water. I placed one weed into each container, and I wrote the common name of the weed on an index card that I set next to the container. I gave the students the entire three hours of class to study those weeds and their names. We did that for five days.

After that, we had a "Weed Identification Contest" with fifty weeds to identify. I numbered each plant and removed its index card. I gave each student a handout with the numbers one to fifty on it. Students went through the plants and wrote on their handout the name of the plant with the corresponding number.

The student who correctly identified the most weeds won a blue ribbon and $10. The second-place student won a red ribbon and $5, and the third-place student received a white ribbon and $2. All of the other students were given a yellow ribbon for participation.

Wow! The students were excited. To break a tie score, students were instructed to recommend a herbicide as a control for a designated weed specimen. After all the scores were tabulated and ranked, the ribbons and money distributed, the students were then informed that their scores would be doubled and that would be their "test grade" for the weed identification unit.

I would like to close this narrative by quoting Leonardo da Vinci, painter, engineer, scientist, theorist, sculptor and architect. who wrote, "Learning never exhausts the mind." This was reality, especially when learning programs provide worthwhile, useful content to learners. The teaching methods described here enabled students to learn useful content quickly and easily. This teaching was effective. Forty-eight years later, two of my former students told me they still remembered all of the weed names.

PRELUDE: Ralph Waldo Emerson said, "Do not go where the path may lead; go instead where there is no path and leave a trail." Teachers, guidance counselors, parents, grandparents, aunts and uncles, neighbors and friends often ask immature students, "What do you want to be when you graduate?" As a general rule, the youngster's answer is a job title with lots of syllables. Asking a youngster what they want to be someday is not a fair question because they simply do not know. Furthermore it is likely the career where they will spend the bulk of their working years in all probability is unknown. There are many phases in the collective learning process that young people must pass through to organize their psyche to identify their true life and career interests. The purpose of these lines is an attempt to put into perspective those phases that everyone must pass to be successful in selecting career options that cultivate their individual interests. Thomas Jefferson said, "Honesty is the first chapter in the book of wisdom." The wisdom of young people begins by being honest with themselves and to stop trying to impress others with a long job title. They must focus on identifying their personal interests.

WISDOM OF SEARCHING FOR A CAREER

It's no sin not to achieve desired ambitions that faltered or failed as long as learning was achieved during the process. (Illustrator unknown)

WISDOM OF SEARCHING FOR A CAREER

Merging life experiences and academic studies prepares a young person to encounter career opportunities and to face the challenges of life. During puberty, many youngsters begin to explore interests.

Yet, choosing a career at an early age is not always wise for various reasons. Many adults ask young people, "What do you want to be after finishing school?" The response typically is a job title with many syllables to sound notable and cool.

It's not fair to ask immature people this question because their innate interests have yet to unfold. Truly, they do not yet know what their destiny might hold.

A more fair question to ask is, "What are your interests?" That's because a young person's responses usually reflect their actual likes—and usually leave out their dislikes.

College expands a young person's intellectual potential to deal with life's challenges without fears. Life is full of lessons, and the more education we get, the more uninformed we become because we learn there is yet so much more to learn.

Some life lessons are costly, while other life lessons are free. But regardless of the cost of the lessons, learning grows with interest.

Identifying a person's likes and dislikes is part of learning. As a person passes through life, their knowledge, interests and careers are apt to change. It's no sin not to achieve sincere ambitions that faltered or failed, as long as you learned in the process.

However as one's interests unfold, it can take a long time to find one's true self and to discover one's ambitions. Do not fret or get discouraged or depressed. Your dreams and true self will ultimately emerge and produce happiness and a feeling of well-being.

PRELUDE: Is it condescending to refer to nations as "developing," "third world," "underdeveloped," or "less fortunate?" Can a nation and its people be placed into one of these categories merely based upon economic status, social standards, political system and religious orientation? During my career, I worked and traveled in fifty-nine different nations under the United States Agency for International Development, Food and Agricultural Organization of the United Nations, Peace Corps, Discovery Services Project, and South Eastern Consortium of International Development. During this time, such adjectives were often used to describe other countries of the world, despite their curious and changing histories. I always questioned why professors, government officials, authors, donor agencies, sociologists, economists, intellectuals, consultants and international workers used these derogatory adjectives that portray judgement and negativism upon other nations and societies that could impact future relations. I was inspired to write this narrative titled "You Be the Judge" to describe my questions and feelings about why such terms were used to describe other societies. I challenge you to judge if these unflattering terms are appropriate—or not.

YOU BE THE JUDGE

When opinions within a country are molded by economic levels or political systems, negative connotations often result. Superiority is implied by first-world countries who perceive themselves as being more successful than allegedly third-world countries. (Photo by James E. Diamond of Darling Harbor, Sydney, Australia)

YOU BE THE JUDGE

The words "developing world" and "third world" seem to be on everyone's tongue. We read them in newspapers, and we hear them on television and in lecture halls.

In 1949, President Harry S Truman's Point IV Program was set forth, after which the term "third world" became preeminent. During the 1950s, the United Nations changed the term to "underdeveloped." During the 1960s, many colonies gained independence and seats in the United Nations General Assembly. A need to respect the new U.N. representative's feelings led to a more hopeful-sounding word. The term "underdeveloped countries," was changed to "rapidly developing countries," and adopted by the United Nations.

The older terms "developing world" and "third world" implied an air of negativism and superiority. In this case, negativism is an attitude influenced by skepticism about a country and its people that has been affirmed by opinions of others. In my opinion, varying points of view were needed to impede such stereotypical conclusions.

When opinions within a country are molded by economic levels or political systems, negative connotations often result. First-world countries imply superiority when they perceive themselves as better than other countries they deem "third-world."

I then ask, "When does a country qualify as "developed" or being a "first-world country."

In my opinion, underdevelopment is endorsed by monetary institutions. How do world traders, educators and politicians benefit by labeling countries with an adjective that calls out their economic, political, social, or religious orientations?

Many nations have cultural traits and civilizations that date from distinctive epochs of time, and those traits have both good and bad elements. Can nations retain the basic elements of their culture and still be acknowledged as an equal within the world community of nations? Can nations sustain their individuality and character and still enter into the age of science and technology?

One cannot assume that personal opinions, formed by influences of economic and political factors, can be considered "true" knowledge.

When we make assumptions, two problems occur: lack of authenticity and lack of accuracy of knowledge. Are professional educators and government leaders inclined to base their opinions on mythical knowledge, empirical knowledge, or both?

When citizens of one nation reference another nation with derogatory or judgmental adjectives, is it true that the societal opinion of that nation is a confession of its character? You be the judge!

PRELUDE: Dance conveys the hidden language of the inner self. Ballet is a type of dance that originated during the Italian Renaissance in the fifteenth century. Later in France and Russia, ballet developed into a concert dance form. It has since become a widespread, highly technical form of dance. Ballet dancers practice a strict hierarchy and gender roles. In French, a male ballet dancer is often referred to as a *danseur,* and a female is referred to as a *danseuse.* In English, a female ballet dancer is called "ballerina" and males are referred to as "ballet dancers." Originally the rank of ballerina meant the principal dancer in a ballet company. However, today it's more common to call a female dancer a "ballet dancer" rather than a ballerina. I was inspired to write this narrative titled "Ballet Apprenticeship" because I attended the 2021-2022 Performance and Exhibit Season sponsored by Lehigh Valley Charter High School for the Arts, in Bethlehem, Pennsylvania. I was very impressed by the dancers' extraordinary professionalism, dedication and passion. The students were well supported by their parents, choreographers, directors, instructors, lighting designers, sound operators, stage managers house managers, poster designers and the Charter Arts faculty. Kudos to those stalwart students, especially to the seniors for a phenomenal final production prior to their high school graduation.

BALLET APPRENTICESHIP

It takes roughly eight to ten years of learning to become a professional ballet dancer. Training ideally begins when a student is between seven and ten years of age. (Photographer unknown)

352

BALLET APPRENTICESHIP

The first ballet was *Ballet de Polonaise* performed in 1573. In Italy during the Renaissance, ballet was the entertainment at aristocratic weddings.

One of the first ballet masters was Domenico da Piacenza. A ballet master is the employee of a ballet company who is responsible for the level of dancers' competence in their company. The most famous *ballerina* in the world was Margot Fonteyn, who was born in May 1919 in England and began ballet classes at age four. She had a long career with the Royal Ballet in London and was expecting to retire at age forty-two until Rudolf Nureyev appeared on the scene. He was a Russian-born Austrian ballet dancer, who became the world's first male ballet superstar and known as the "father of ballet and choreography." He defected to the West in 1961 and joined the Royal Ballet, where he began his noted partnership with Margot.

It takes roughly eight to ten years of learning and tutelage to become a professional ballet dancer. Training ideally begins when a student is between seven and ten years of age.

My dearest friend Angelina Moors became interested in ballet dancing at an early age and began taking lessons with Miss Cindy's School of Dance in Quakertown, Pennsylvania. There she learned about the type of work ethic needed during rehearsals and how choreographers communicate. At age fourteen, Angelina enrolled in Lehigh Valley Charter High School for the Arts. Like many ballet students, she began taking technique class once or twice a week. It's normal for a young person to feel overwhelmed at his or her first ballet class. The plethora of poses and positions one needs to learn is stressful, especially because many of the position names are in French. But with practice and time, a student soon becomes fluent in the language of ballet. By the time Angelina was fifteen years of age, she was taking more than ten classes per week. Understanding the five basic positions was a great place to start for Angelina as she was making ballet building blocks.

In classical ballet, the five basic positions involve both the feet and arms. The five basic positions are First Position: The heels are together with the toes of each foot pointed out toward either side, with legs straight and turned out, following the position of the feet; Second Position: Legs are straight and the feet are turned out to each side like in first position, but the difference is that the heels do not touch and are instead about hip-width apart; Third Position: This position is rarely used, since it can be mistaken for a careless and disorganized first or fifth position; nevertheless it is still important to learn. Begin in first position, and then slide the heel of one foot so it lines up with the middle of the other foot, keeping both feet pointing out in opposite directions. Fourth Position: Stand with one foot about a foot's length in front of the other foot. Each foot should be pointing in an opposite direction, and the toes of the back foot should line up with the heel of the front foot. Fifth Position: This position is the most difficult one. It's like fourth position, but there is no gap between the feet. The feet should be together with heel to toe and toe to heel.

I would like to close this narrative by quoting Martha Graham, an influential American dancer, teacher and choreographer of modern dance who stated, "Great dancers are not great because of their technique; they are great because of their passion."

My dear friend Angelina is quite passionate about her ballet dancing, and she is well on her way to become a great ballerina.

PRELUDE: While visiting Badlands National Park in South Dakota, my late wife, Betty, spotted a wild American bison not far from our car. Wow! It was a gigantic animal! American bison are indigenous* to river valleys, plains and prairies in the Central and Western United States. Historically, they were a significant food source for Native Americans and provided them with shelter, fuel, tools and clothing. In efforts to reintroduce bison to tribal lands the Tribal Buffalo Council works cooperatively with the National Park Service to transfer bison from national park lands to tribal lands. On 9 May 2016, the National Bison Legacy Act was signed to name the bison the national animal of the United States. I was inspired to write this narrative titled "American Bison" because of the awesome excitement of seeing our national animal, a wild American bison, for the first time, watching it harmlessly walk in front of our car. Whew! What a stupendous thrill!

AMERICAN BISON

I am indebted to the courageous individuals who made noble efforts to bring the American bison (*Bison bison*), now our national animal, from near extinction to a healthy existence in our national parks and on Native American lands.(Photo by Jim Diamond in Badlands National Park, South Dakota)

AMERICAN BISON

My late wife, Betty's and my mission for traveling to Rapid City, South Dakota, was to visit dear friends Bill and Jeanette Keck. Together we planned to ride to Black Hills National Park to see the southeastern face of Mount Rushmore. There the four gigantic carved sculptures portray four previous presidents of the United States: George Washington, Thomas Jefferson, Abraham Lincoln and Theodore Roosevelt. What an awesome sight!

After a marvelous two-day visit with the Kecks, Betty and I bid adieu to Bill and Jeanette, and we set out alone to look for birds and wildlife and enjoy the beauty of South Dakota.

I particularly wanted to see a wild American bison. We traveled to Badlands National Park to observe the flora* and fauna* in that stunning landscape. As we slowly drove along a dusty gravel road, Betty excitedly shouted, "There's a bison!"

Sure enough, I saw an enormous American bison far from our car, munching on some dried prairie grass and walking lackadaisically toward us. This humongous male beast had no fear of us, nor did it pose any threat to us. However, he did stop to pose for us so I could get this accompanying photograph.

American bison have very poor eyesight that they compensate for with exceptional senses of smell and hearing. A Badlands National Park ranger told us that although bison injure more people than any other animal in the park, almost all bison attacks are preventable.

Hence the reason Betty and I stayed in the car. The park ranger also told us to watch a bison's tail for clues to its mood. If a bison's tail hangs down and switches, the bison is calm. However, if a bison's tail is standing straight up, the bison feels threatened and annoyed, and you should immediately generate plenty of space between you and the bison.

Bison are quite agile and able to jump high fences. They are also strong swimmers.

In Africa, Betty and I saw hundreds of cape buffalo, which are indigenous* to African habitats. However, the cape buffalo is not related to the American bison. The American bison is the largest indigenous wild mammal in North America. Males (bulls) can reach up to one ton in weight. I estimated the bull bison in front of my car weighed close to one ton.

Historically, millions of bison once roamed over all of North America. However, as European settlers pushed west, they reduced the bison habitat and hunted them to near extinction. Today, the bison would be extinct if not for Teddy Roosevelt and a few private individuals collaborating with Native American tribes and the Department of Interior to protect the surviving remnants of bison.

I personally am indebted to those courageous individuals who made noble efforts to bring this now-national animal to a healthy existence in our national parks and on Native American lands. I would like to close this narrative with a Native American proverb, "Listen to the voice of nature for it holds treasures for you."

PRELUDE: The Atlantic bottlenose dolphin is one of the most charismatic critters in the ocean. Bottlenose dolphins are excellent swimming mammals, which enables them to be skillful predators.* Because they adapt well in various habitats, the population of bottlenose dolphins is quite large and not close to being endangered. The bottlenose dolphin is quite familiar to the general public because of the wide exposure they get in captivity in marine parks and dolphinariums across America, plus being in movies and television programs. Bottlenose dolphins are very social animals that live in pods of ten to twenty-five bottlenose dolphins. Some pods have hundreds of bottlenose dolphins. I was inspired to write this narrative titled "Atlantic Bottlenose Dolphins" because when my dear friend Dr. Kathleen Jones and I boarded a ship called "Whale Watching" and sailed along the Cape May Harbor and then the Atlantic Ocean, we saw many Atlantic bottlenose dolphins. I was fascinated by their swimming antics in the Atlantic Ocean.

ATLANTIC BOTTLENOSE DOLPHINS

Bottlenose dolphins (*Tursiops truncatus*) have an interesting behavioral pattern when new calves are born, sometimes allowing "aunties" to help raise their babies. They have outstanding eyesight, and like bats, they use echolocation* to find the location of objects by reflected sound. (Photo by Jim Diamond of bottlenose dolphins off the coast of the Atlantic Ocean near Cape May, New Jersey, 27 July 2022)

ATLANTIC BOTTLENOSE DOLPHINS

Bottlenose dolphins can grow to eight to twelve feet in length, and they really do have bottle-shaped noses for which they are named. Their backs can be different shades of gray such as gray-brown, gray-green, or even plain gray, while their belly is white. Bottlenose dolphins have eighteen to twenty-six small, sharp teeth on their upper and lower jaws.

Male bottlenose dolphins are called "bulls," females are called "cows," and babies are called "calves." The gestation period for a cow is about twelve months, and a newborn calf will be three to four feet in length. A cow will nurse its calf for more than one year.

Bottlenose dolphins have an interesting behavioral pattern when new calves are born. Sometimes another female bottlenose dolphin called an "auntie" will stay close to the cow and calf to help. Usually the auntie is the only other bottlenose dolphin that a cow will let close to her calf. A normal dolphin cow will typically give birth to a calf every two to four years.

Bottlenose dolphins have outstanding eyesight, and they can use echolocation* to find objects by reflected sound. I was amazed to learn that bottlenose dolphins make high pitched clicks, and when these clicks hit an object, some of the sound will come back. Listening to the echo and interpreting the time it took for the echo to come back gives the dolphin information about the structure and size of objects, such as fish. The dolphin will continue clicking and move its head to get more information about the object and its distance away.

Bottlenose dolphins swim by moving their tail flukes up and down through the water. They use their pectoral flippers to steer while swimming, to stroke, or to touch each other. Bottlenose dolphins that are closely bonded sometimes swim turning or twisting or face-to-face touching flippers.

Bottlenose dolphins breathe through a blowhole located on the top of their head. They usually breathe about every two minutes, but they can hold their breath a bit longer when necessary.

The coastal bottlenose dolphins we observed (see photo) eat a wide assortment of fish, including mackerel, herring, cod and squid. Bottlenose dolphins use their teeth to grip their prey. Dolphins do not use their teeth to chew their food. Instead, they swallow fish whole, headfirst, so the spines of the fish do not get caught in their throats.

Together bottlenose dolphins cooperate in hunting and herding fish into a huge group and then taking turns feeding while others keep guard.

In the United States, dolphins are safeguarded by the U.S. Marine Mammal Protection Act. Bottlenose dolphins are top ocean predators.* Dolphins have few predators of their own, including large shark species such as tiger sharks, dusky sharks, bull sharks, great white sharks and orca whales.

I would like to close this narrative by quoting Albert Einstein who said, "There is no question dolphins are smarter than humans as they play more."

Oh how true!

PRELUDE: It has been reported that the California sea lion population is growing steadily and is estimated at around 257,000 individuals. California sea lions are very social animals, and groups often rest closely packed together at favorite sites on land or float together on the ocean's surface in groups called rafts. Sea lions have short, thick hair, a large belly and a rather large chest. They are able to walk on their long front and rear flippers, sometimes reaching eighteen miles per hour. They can be recognized by having small ear flaps. Often sea lions reside on rocky coasts in small groups called colonies. I was inspired to write this narrative titled "California Sea Lions" because I have seen and heard sea lion colonies a few times on the coasts of California. They can be extraordinarily noisy. They bark constantly while establishing a territory.

CALIFORNIA SEA LIONS

California sea lions (*Zalophus californianus*) are the most vocal of all sea mammals. They bark, growl and grunt. During the breeding season, male California sea lions bark incessantly while establishing a territory. Once their turf has been established, the males bark only when maintaining and defending their territories. (Photo of a California sea lion provided by Pittsburgh Zoo, Pittsburgh, Pennsylvania)

CALIFORNIA SEA LIONS

E ven though sea lions and seals are different in many ways, they are often mistaken for each other. Sea lions have small external ears, while seals have tiny ear openings. Sea lions use their powerful forelimbs to propel themselves, while seals use their hind flippers for propulsion.

When sea lions are wet, they appear to be black. However, males range in color from chocolate to dark brown, and females range from light tan to golden blonde. When sea lions are dry, their coarse hair takes on a velvety feel.

It has been reported that the California sea lion population is growing steadily, and as of this writing, their number is estimated at around 257,000 individuals. California sea lions are very social animals. Groups often rest closely packed together at favorite sites on land, or they float together on the ocean's surface in groups called "rafts."

California sea lions are the most vocal of all sea mammals. During the breeding season, male California sea lions bark constantly while they are organizing a territory. Hearing their loud, constant, raucous barking can annoy beachgoers who want to lie in the sun and enjoy the serene, relaxing ocean sounds.

In the wild, sea lions can live between fifteen and twenty years. These self-serving feeders eat whatever is accessible or reachable, including squid, Pacific whiting, herring, northern anchovy, octopus, hake, rockfish, lamprey and other seafood. Each day, a sea lion can eat 5 to 10 percent of its body weight. Sea lions hunting food in a group communicate using barks, grunts and growls. Their ears are able to pick up sounds both above and below water.

Female California sea lions reach sexual maturity around three years of age, and males are sexually mature at five years of age. The females' gestation period is twelve months; however, sea lions delay mating two to three months to allow pups to be born during summer when food is abundant and reachable. Each year, sea lions return to their breeding grounds in Southern and Central California where females give birth to their pups in early summer. Nearly all of the pups are born in May and June each year.

I would like to close this narrative by quoting Australian zookeeper Steve Irwin, who said, "If we can teach people about wildlife, they will be touched. Share my wildlife with me. Because humans want to save things that they love."

I hope and pray that people and future generations will learn about wildlife and protect their existence because of their love, appreciation and fondness for it. Protecting wild habitats and animals is essential to having a far-reaching capability to withstand the throes of human population growth and commercial development.

To practice what I preach, my farm is permanently preserved to protect wildlife habitats, and it is a certified wildlife habitat to enable wild animals to expand their populations.

PRELUDE: The reptile world is filled with chameleon variations. These colorful chameleons are known for their ability to change color, their sticky tongue, and their eyes that can be moved independently of each other. A common chameleon is chiefly arboreal among prehistoric lizards with a prehensile tail, independently movable eyeballs and unusual ability to change the color of their skin. Like snakes, chameleons do not have an outer or a middle ear, so there is neither an ear opening nor an eardrum. However, chameleons are not deaf: they can detect sound frequencies in the range of 200 to 600 tone cycles per second, and they can see in both visible and ultraviolet light. I was inspired to write this narrative titled "Common Chameleon" because I often see them in my woodlot, and I am amazed at their ability to change color so they can blend into their environment.

COMMON CHAMELEON

Common chameleons (*Mediterranean chameleon*) exhibit very little danger to humans. The worst thing that might happen is they bite, and even though the bite is painful, it is nontoxic and usually avoidable. (Photo by Jim Diamond of a chameleon on a tree in his managed woodlot in 2021)

COMMON CHAMELEON

Common chameleons are a group of lizards descended from common ancestors. They are members of the reptile family. Chameleons are a distinctive, highly specialized group of prehistoric lizards. They live mainly in woodlands.

Chameleons are known for their range of colors and their ability to change to different hues and brightness according to their surroundings. They also have stereoscopic mobile eyes (stereoacuity is possible due to binocular disparity), parrot-like feet (two toes pointing forward and two toes pointing backward), long extrudable tongues, prehensile tail and crests on their heads.

Chameleons periodically shed their skin to get rid of old skin cells and to grow into a healthy, adult chameleon. On average, young chameleons shed their skin every three to four weeks, and adult chameleons shed their skin once every eight weeks.

Adult chameleons are greedy eaters, and in the wild they eat often if they can find prey. In the wild, their food can be scarce, so they will eat as much as they can when they find it. If chameleons can't find food, they can survive for several weeks without eating as long as they have access to water. In the wild, chameleons commonly eat grasshoppers, crickets, flies, cicadas, grasshoppers, snails and leaves and other plants. Young chameleons require more food than adults.

Chameleons have excellent eyesight that allows them to see their prey from up to ten yards away. Their eyes move independently of one another, and they have a full 360-degree view of the environment around them, which allows them to search for and locate prey quickly.

Chameleons move very slowly when approaching their prey. Once they are within a tongue's distance, they quickly shoot out their sticky tongues to capture their meal.

I would like to close this narrative with an African proverb that goes like this, "The chameleon changes color to match the Earth; the Earth doesn't change color to match the chameleon."

Like chameleons, humans often change the color of our personality, interests, career goals, desires, dreams, and *raison d'être* ("reason to be") as we go through our careers and lives. These changes impact our persona within our colorful world that colors our lives.

PRELUDE: A cougar and a mountain lion are the same animal. The Penn State University Nittany Lions could also be called Nittany Cougars, Nittany Pumas, Nittany Panthers and more. According to the Guinness World Records, the cougar has the most names of any animal, more than forty. Depending upon the location, it is known to as the puma, panther, mountain cat, mountain lion, mountain screamer, painter and catamount, just to name a few. Even though cougars are wicked predators,* they seldom attack people. When they do, they can be extremely dangerous. Cougars are an endangered species. They live in open areas and in forests in parts of the United States, Canada and South America. The cougar is a carnivore, so it requires meat in its diet. They will eat any animal they can catch, from insects to large hoofed mammals. Its primary prey are mule deer and white-tailed deer, elk, moose, horses, domestic livestock like calves and sheep and rabbits. I was inspired to write this narrative because at 10:15 p.m. 19 October 1992 while my late wife, Betty, and I were returning home on Tabor Road in Upper Bucks County, Pennsylvania, we observed a cougar dash across the road in front of our headlights. We were overwhelmed with excitement at seeing such a rare critter so near our farm!

COUGAR

According to the Pennsylvania Game Commission on 27 May 2021, there have been no wild cougars (*Puma concolor*) sighted in Pennsylvania since their expiration in 1871. Even though cougars are seen in Pennsylvania throughout the year, but the U.S. Fish and Wildlife Service claims that they are officially extinct. (Photo compliments of U.S. Fish and Wildlife Service)

COUGAR

According to the Pennsylvania Game Commission on 27 May 2021, no wild cougars have been sighted in Pennsylvania since their expiration in 1871. However, there have been hundreds of reported cougar sightings throughout the Eastern United States, including Pennsylvania, and in 2011, there was a confirmed mountain lion killed in Connecticut.

The U.S. Fish and Wildlife Service claims that the cougar sightings were young cougars roaming in search of new breeding territories.

On 19 October 1992, after a strenuous, trying day as Dean of Agricultural and Environmental Sciences at Delaware Valley University, my late wife, Betty, and I went to our friends Darvin and Dot Gruver's home to play a lively game of pinochle. For me, that was therapy that prepared me for a good night's sleep.

Dot and Darwin were at an age they could no longer travel, yet they loved to play pinochle. Betty and I spent many evenings playing cards with them because it was merriment entertainment for the Gruvers and emotional therapy for me.

At 10:15 p.m., as Betty and I drove home on Tabor Road, a critter crossed the road in front of our car. I had the high beam headlights on, and both Betty and I got a good look at it. It was fawn tan, with a long tan tail and a roundish head, and it was about the height and length of a full-grown Labrador retriever. We were puzzled what kind of critter we observed.

When I got home, I googled "Pennsylvania wildlife." Voila! There on the screen was a photo of the critter we saw—a cougar. Betty and I were sure it was a cougar, but we did not report seeing it to anyone, including the Pennsylvania Game Commission because we feared that people would think we were imagining what we saw.

Various literature documents that cougars have a powerfully built muscular body, extraordinary eyesight, keen hearing, large paws, retractable claws, sharp carnivorous* teeth and hind legs that are more muscular than the forelegs, enabling them to easily climb trees. Adult cougars can reach a length of five feet with a tail length of two or three feet and can weigh between 115 to 220 pounds. In addition to being fast runners, they are also skilled swimmers.

Three years later, I was traveling on Tabor Road past a dear neighbor who was standing next to the road working on her lawn. She stopped me and asked, "Jim, do we have mountain lions around here?"

I responded by asking, "Why do you ask?"

She said, "There was one in the back of our house sitting on a stump, and I took its picture out of an open kitchen window." I asked to see the photo. She said sure, went into her house, retrieved the photo, and showed it to me. Sure enough, it was a young cougar. I told her about our sighting three years earlier not far from their home. She gave me a copy of her photo for the record.

I would like to close this narrative by quoting Charles H. Hinnant, a University of Michigan author who wrote, "The cougar is an emblem of the dream of absolute power, and as a wild rather than a domestic animal, it belongs to a world outside the realm of societies and culture."

PRELUDE: Chipmunks are small, striped rodents that are common to Pennsylvania woodlands and near my home in Bucks County. They normally dig extensive burrows in lawns, woodlands and stone wall openings with several concealed entrances. Chipmunks find very comfortable living quarters in the stone wall adjacent to our garage. They are reddish-brown with five dark black and white stripes along their backs. During winter months, chipmunks enter torpor.* They do not truly hibernate because they periodically wake up to eat some of their stored food. I was inspired to write this narrative titled "Eastern Chipmunk" because we often see them scampering around our lawn, stone wall, sidewalk and nearby woodlands during the summer.

EASTERN CHIPMUNK

Chipmunks (*Tamias striatus*) are quite talkative with their complex chattering and sounds warning of nearby predators.* Their chattering is a quavering or vibratory sound, which includes chitters, chucks and rapid repeating alarm calls. (Photo by Jim Diamond of an eastern chipmunk in his pasture near Ottsville, Pennsylvania)

EASTERN CHIPMUNK

I see these rodents quite often around my rural home and find them to be a source of enjoyment. However, other people consider chipmunks to be garden and lawn pests. Still other people keep them as pets, but I personally appreciate their presence outdoors and sneer at keeping chipmunks or any wild animal as a pet.

Chipmunks burrow elaborate networks of tunnels with areas for sleeping, food storage and body waste storage. If you see one chipmunk scurrying around, likely several more are nearby because multiple chipmunks often live in the same burrow.

However, when chipmunks scramble around woodlands, gardens and lawns, they are usually alone. Except during the spring mating season, chipmunks usually ignore other nearby chipmunks.

Chipmunks are important prey for local predator* animals, such as foxes, coyotes, racoons, snakes, cats, dogs and birds such as owls and hawks. However, chipmunks are also predators themselves that eat bird eggs and newly hatched birds in their nests.

Chipmunks use their cheek pouches to transport food. They gather food and store it in their burrows usually in late summer and early autumn to prepare for survival during winter torporing.* Chipmunks eat berries, grains, nuts, acorns, some green plants and certain mushrooms. They normally gather food from the ground, but occasionally they will climb a tree for some goodies.

Chipmunks are quite talkative with their complex chattering and sounds warning of nearby predators. Their chattering is a quavering or vibratory sound, which includes chitters, chucks, and rapid repeating alarm calls.

Eastern Chipmunks mark their territory with scent glands in their cheeks and their urine.

Eastern Chipmunks mate in early spring and again in early summer, producing litters of four or five young twice each year. The young emerge from the burrow after about six weeks and strike out on their own within the next two weeks.

Chipmunks are important in forest ecosystems. Harvesting and hoarding tree seeds establishes tree seedlings; they consume several different kinds of fungi, including those involved with symbiotic* mycorrhiza* with trees. They are also a vector for spores of subterranean truffles.

I would like to summarize the essence of this narrative by quoting Mark Twain who wrote, "Plan for the future because that's where you are going to spend the rest of your life."

PRELUDE: Eastern tent caterpillars are among the most social of larvae. They work together to build their tents and keep each other warm at night. Eastern tent caterpillars attack several species of broadleaf trees and shrubs and produce unsightly tents. When their populations become large, the caterpillars can defoliate trees, stunting their growth, especially wild cherry and fruit trees. Tents are resistant to weather, and they will remain in a tree for a long time until they are forcibly removed. I was inspired to write this narrative titled "Eastern Tent Caterpillars" because eastern tent caterpillars were all over my farm on several broadleaf tree species, especially black cherry trees, fruit trees and shrubs. Tent caterpillars cause limited damage to trees or foliage. Removing the tent will eliminate their unsightliness.

EASTERN TENT CATERPILLARS

Eastern tent caterpillars (*Malacosoma americanum*) live in groups within a silken tent. The silk is produced by glands in the caterpillars' heads, and the tent provides protection from many natural enemies. (Photo by Jim Diamond of tent caterpillars and their tent on his farm near Ottsville, Pennsylvania, in August 2022)

EASTERN TENT CATERPILLARS

All eastern tent caterpillars turn into rather nondescript moths, which are a plain reddish-brown color with blurred white stripes across the front. Eastern tent caterpillars create tents, which they use for a sleeping area at night. They live and sleep in close quarters to keep each other warm during chilly days and nights. Furthermore, their tents are used for food storage. They are not harmful to humans or pets, and these caterpillars use pheromones to mark off trails on host trees.

Eastern tent caterpillars move slowly. They are rich in protein, so they have several predators* that assist in keeping their numbers within reason. They are ideal food for predators such as red-eyed vireos, Carolina wrens, American robins, wasps, yellowjackets, ground beetles, flies, toads, skunks, deer mice, beetles, ants, spiders and other fauna,* and in some cases even bears.

Eastern tent caterpillars live in groups within a silken tent. The silk is produced by glands in the caterpillars' heads, and the tent provides protection from many natural enemies. Caterpillars will begin building a tent in the fork of a tree, but as they leave the tent to feed on new leaves, a silken strand follows them and enlarges the tent as the caterpillar eats. The silky tents spun by the caterpillars make trees unsightly, and the caterpillars are annoying when searching for food or a suitable place to spin their tents. Tents are resistant to weather, and they will remain in the tree a long time unless they are removed.

In late spring to early summer, female moths deposit egg masses, often on thin, wild cherry tree bark or twigs. They use spumaline, a sticky, frothy substance, to glue the eggs to bark or twigs. The spumaline also serves as a hard, protective covering around the egg masses. In early April, the eggs will hatch, and the caterpillars will quickly mature. Young eastern tent caterpillars are black. They spin silk tents on the branches near the hatch site, and as the caterpillars mature, the tents get bigger.

I would like to close this narrative by quoting Sara Ginsberg, Nick Perri, and Erin Skallerup of the University of Michigan Biological Station who wrote, "The relationship between tent caterpillars and black cherry trees has led to the caterpillars' complete immunity to the toxic cyanide produced by black cherry trees." This might be the reason why eastern tent caterpillars favor the wild black cherry trees growing in my woodlands.

PRELUDE: My forty-acre farm is surrounded by woodlands, and it is enrolled with the Forest Stewardship Program. It is an approved National Certified Wildlife Habitat. The stream flowing through the farm, Rapp Creek, is an Exceptional Value Watershed. The property is preserved with the Tinicum Conservancy. Also, the farm has a completed conservation plan with the Bucks County Soil Conservation District. Together these agencies provide sound management guidelines for good stewardship of my pastures and woodlot. Anytime I see an unknown animal for the first time on my land it's exciting, educating and thrilling. Sighting an unknown animal challenges me to positively identify it, study its traits, learn its behavior patterns, and determine the status of its existing population. I was inspired to write this narrative titled "Fisher" in an attempt to capture the essence of a once-in-a-lifetime event on the land that I so dearly love.

FISHER

Sighting an unknown animal, like a fisher (*Pekania pennanti*), gives me an educational challenge that causes me to positively identify it, study its traits, learn its behavior patterns, and determine status of its existing population. (Photo of a fisher provided by the Pennsylvania Game Commission.)

FISHER

On 30 August 2021, as I drove my car into the garage, I noticed a critter in front of the woodshed. I wondered whose cat it was or if it was a stray.

It was dark brown, but its tail looked different than a domestic cat. When the animal sensed my presence, it hastily ran into the nearby woods. Hence my sighting was only momentary.

I parked my car in the garage, did a couple minor chores, then went outside to sit on the front deck and read the mail. When I looked over the railing, on my driveway I saw that dark brown critter hunkered down, looking at the house.

That time, I got a prolonged look at it and concluded it definitely was not a stray domestic cat. It looked different. Its beady eyes were intently staring at me. Its ears were smaller and rounder than a housecat's. And its tail looked bushy.

I stood and went inside to get my camera to take its picture, but when I returned the animal had left the driveway and meandered out of sight into the woods.

I kept wondering, *What kind of critter was I looking at?*

I went to my computer and googled "Pennsylvania wild animals." I scrolled down and *voila*! There it was: a photo portraying exactly the critter I observed in front to the woodshed and my driveway.

It was named fisher (*Pekania pennanti*). It is a small, carnivorous mammal native to North America, a forest-dwelling creature, and a member of the weasel family. Fishers prefer to hunt in forests. They are agile climbers, but they spend most of their time on the forest floor where they prefer to forage around fallen trees. Fishers feed on a wide variety of small animals, such as squirrels, rabbits, mice, and voles as well as ground-nesting birds, waterfowl and songbirds. They will occasionally eat fruits and wild mushrooms. Despite the animal's common name, they rarely eat fish.

They sometimes are misleadingly referred to as a "fisher cat," although they are not cats. Fishers have few predators* besides humans. Their pelts were once in high demand, and they became extinct in parts of the United States in the early twentieth century. Conservation and protection programs allowed the species to rejuvenate, but their numbers are still reduced.

After living on my farm for more than 60 years, that was my first sighting of a fisher. Furthermore, six days later, my housekeeper spotted what she called a "stray cat" on the ramp leading to my home. She called to me, and I too saw it. I informed her it was not a stray cat, but a fisher. After a short viewing, I watched where it went. It quickly dashed into an old groundhog hole under the woodshed.

I would like to bring this narrative to a close with a Native American (Lakota) proverb that goes like this, "When a man moves away from nature, his heart becomes hard."

I do not want to move away from nature nor do I want to have a hard heart. Therefore, I declare: I plan not to disturb that old groundhog hole because fishers are still endangered, and I am pleased that there is at least one snuzzled in an old groundhog hole here on my farm.

PRELUDE: Komodo Islands National Park is a volcanic island located in the center of the Indonesian archipelago, between the islands of Sumbawa and Flore. It is composed of three major islands: Rinca, Komodo and Padar. It also has numerous smaller ones, and all of them are of volcanic origin. Komodo dragons are found only on Indonesia's Lesser Sunda Islands, and they have survived harsh climates on these islands for millions of years. Komodo dragons are the largest, heaviest lizards on planet Earth! Fully grown dragons can weigh 300 pounds and grow ten to fifteen feet long. They eat only meat from wild deer, pigs, carrion, water buffalo and humans. They often cannibalize their young dragons. I find these lizards intriguing and have been wanting to see them in the wild by traveling to Komodo Islands National Park. Because of limitations on my time and expenses, I was inspired to write this narrative titled "Komodo Dragon" because of my strong interest in seeing this dangerous critter that is a live remnant from the dinosaur ages.

KOMODO DRAGON

Komodo dragons (*Varanus komodoensis*) are the largest, heaviest lizards on the planet. Fully grown dragons can reach a weight of 300 pounds and grow ten to fifteen feet long. (Photo by Jim Diamond of a Komodo dragon at Reptileland, Lewistown, Pennsylvania, 14 October 2019)

KOMODO DRAGON

From 2017 to 2020, I yearned to travel to Indonesia's Lesser Sunda Islands to observe the Komodo dragons (*Varanus komodoensis*) in the wild and photograph them in their natural habitat. I was prevented from scheduling such a trip because of costs, the requirement to comply with the Covid-19 quarantine regulations on board a ship, and having read an article that beginning in 2020, tourists would be limited from entering the Komodo Islands National Park to observe dragons. It has been reported that poachers have caused a decrease in the number of young dragons on the islands.

Komodo dragons rely on their natural camouflage,* and they lie quietly and patiently waiting for unsuspecting prey to come by. Komodo dragons are predators* that will eat almost any kind of meat including carrion. With pronounced neck muscles, they bite the prey, pull back on its hide, and make a gaping wound.

The dragon's saliva contains five toxic bacteria. They also have venom glands that inject venom that reduces their prey's blood pressure, causes massive bleeding, prevents clotting and fosters shock. Often dragons begin eating their prey before it is completely dead. If an animal escapes the jaws of the dragon, it is followed sometimes for miles until the toxins take effect. Using their long, forked tongues, dragons have a keen sense of smell to find weakened or dead prey.

I learned that ships with their passengers stopped at Komodo Islands for only six hours, and a park ranger would take passengers on a short walk to see wild Komodo dragons. To me, traveling halfway around the world to participate in a short mini tour to see wild Komodo dragons was not the best use of my time. The need to adhere to the tragic Covid-19 quarantine regulations on board a ship was enough for me to reluctantly make the decision not to travel to Komodo Islands.

Subsequently, I learned that there are Komodo dragons right here in Pennsylvania at the Pittsburgh Zoo and Reptileland near Lewistown, Pennsylvania. When I visited Reptileland, I saw two Komoda dragons: a male and a female. I learned much about their behavior, eating habits and danger they pose to animals and people.

During our visit, we learned from one of the caretakers that the morning before, while she was preparing to feed the Komodo dragon in the photo, it attacked her. She showed us the hole its tooth punched into her leather boots. Fortunately it did not puncture her skin, and she successfully got away.

The animal caretakers at Reptileland keep the male and female Komodo dragons in separate enclosures* because if they were together, they would fight.

The Komodo dragons we observed were detained in first-class facilities of clean, brightly lit, spacious enclosures. Seeing two Komodo specimens at Reptileland fulfilled my yearning to see the dragon in the wild.

PRELUDE: The North American raccoon is the most common of seven species of nocturnal mammals found in North America. They are round, furry creatures with bushy ringed tails and eye masks. These animals might look like bandits, but they can be quite terrified when frightened. Raccoons are very adaptable, and they can live in a wide range of climates and habitats. In addition to natural habitats in woodlands, North American raccoons often live in human communities. Raccoons can be vicious when approached by humans. Humans should be particularly cautious of approaching raccoons because they are common carriers of rabies, roundworms and leptospirosis. Certainly, no one should keep a racoon as a pet. I was inspired to write this narrative titled "North American Raccoon" because as I write this story I am currently watching and photographing a raccoon at 6:45 a.m. nibble on a partially baked potato I threw outside of my home last evening. The racoon appears to be very cautious about its surroundings.

NORTH AMERICAN RACCOON

Baby raccoons (*Procyon lotor*) are called "kits" or "cubs." They are usually born in early summer. The gestation period of females is sixty to seventy-three days, and she will have one to seven cubs. Together, a mother and her cubs are called a "nursery." (Photographer unknown)

NORTH AMERICAN RACCOON

North American raccoons are found in North and Central America, Japan and Europe where they live in various climates and habitats. It was a long period of time before they were found in North American mixed forest areas. However, during recent times, raccoons discovered that urban areas offer food and shelter, to the annoyance of homeowners who face unwanted attic dwellers and garbage can raiders.

Early American settlers and Native Americans relied on small game like raccoon to supplement their diets. In the American South, raccoons were once an important food staple for enslaved individuals.

Typically, racoons make dens in dead, hollow trees or caverns, though they will also make themselves at home in attics, barns, abandoned cars and other man-made locations. North American raccoons are nocturnal and sleep during the day. During the winter, they tend to sleep more; however, they do not hibernate in the traditional sense. It has been reported by the University of Michigan's Animal Diversity Web that they lose about half of their body weight during the winter by sleeping as their bodies live off stored fat.

As omnivores,* North American raccoons eat both vegetation and meat. The vegetation in their diet consists of cherries, apples, acorns, berries, peaches, citrus fruits, plums, wild grapes, figs, watermelons, beech nuts, corn and walnuts. Some of the raccoon's favorite animal treats are frogs, fish, crayfish, insects, rodents and bird eggs. When food is scarce, raccoons will scavenge human trash or eat roadkill. Raccoons are one of the primary carriers of the dreaded rabies virus in Pennsylvania and the United States.

The gestation period of females is sixty to seventy-three days, and she will have one to seven cubs. Baby raccoons are called "kits" or "cubs," and they are usually born in early summer. Together, a mother and her cubs are called a "nursery." For the first two months of their lives, babies live in their den and are weaned somewhere between seven to sixteen weeks. At twelve weeks, the cubs will begin to roam away from their mothers for whole nights at a time. Cubs will become completely independent at eight to twelve months of age. In the wild, raccoons can live two to three years.

Raccoons have five toes on their front paws and use them like a human hand. Chief Powhatan of the Algonquin Tribe and the father of Pocahontas, called the raccoon "*ah-coon-em*" which means "scratches with his hands." Raccoons can easily climb trees, can fall up to forty feet without injury, and run up to fifteen miles per hour. Furthermore, it has been said that the black mask around a raccoon's eyes helps deflect glare and improve their night vision.

I would like to close this narrative by indicating that Native Americans were well-acquainted with the raccoon. The Sioux believed the clever raccoon embodied wisdom or spirit powers, allowing it to outwit larger predators* such as coyotes, foxes and wolves. I believe the Sioux's cognizance of raccoons was correct because raccoons are certainly clever, and they can easily outwit larger predator animals.

PRELUDE: As I wrote this narrative in June 2021, thousands upon thousands of seventeen-year cicadas were singing their love songs around my farm in the woodlands and pastures and on farm buildings. They are called Brood X (one of fifteen broods of periodical cicadas) currently in Pennsylvania, Ohio, Maryland, New Jersey, Indiana, West Virginia and Virginia. Brood X was the 2021 brood of cicadas that was singing, mating, and dying on my property. The next generation of nymphs burrowed underground and will feed on tree roots for seventeen years before performing an encore in 2038. I was inspired to write this narrative because at my age, I probably will never again hear such huge choirs of Brood X sing or see them flying around my farm.

SEVENTEEN-YEAR CICADA

Natural traits of brood X cicadas (*Magicicada septendecim*) involve four governing happenings according to the literature: emergence from the soil, singing, mating and dying. (Photo by Jim Diamond of a seventeen-year cicada at his home near Ottsville, Pennsylvania, early July 2021)

SEVENTEEN-YEAR CICADA

Entomologists have identified at least fifteen dissimilar broods of periodical cicadas that appear at various times throughout the United States. They are found only in North America, and they are different from the annual cicada, which emerges once a year. After seventeen-year cicadas emerge from the ground, they climb the nearest vertical surface and shed their exoskeleton. When free from the old skin, their wings will inflate with fluid, and their adult skin will harden.

According to entomologists, the brood I heard as I wrote this narrative on my farm is brood X. Entomologists have documented enormous numbers of cicadas loudly "singing" (up to ninety decibels) by rubbing their wings together. In the mid-afternoon during ten days here around my home, in woodlands and pastures, the volume of enormous numbers of brood X cicadas singing can be gratifying and pleasurable or annoying and exasperating. I personally find their singing enjoyable because it is much different compared to other natural sounds normally heard on the farm. Natural traits of brood X cicadas involve four managerial episodes according to the literature: emergence from the soil, singing, mating and dying.

Female cicadas make tiny holes in branches of trees and shrubs where they lay 200 to 400 eggs. Nymphs hatch in six to ten weeks from the eggs in the tiny holes. Newly hatched cicadas expeditiously fall to the ground where they will burrow into the soil and spend much of their next seventeen years. They feed off plant roots as their bodies increase in size and go through the process of metamorphosis into the body portrayed in the accompanying photograph.

To close this narrative, I would like to quote science journalist Catherine Price from her book *101 Places Not to See Before You Die,* "If locusts are ravenous sociopaths, cicadas are more like frat boys, clumsy, loud and obsessed with sex."

In my opinion, seventeen-year cicadas are mostly beneficial. Yes, they are clumsy, and they are loud and obsessed with sex; however, they are not lunatics or ferocious. They harm nothing, and they exist only for a couple weeks.

Cicadas are mostly beneficial. They prune mature trees and aerate the soil, and when they die, their bodies serve as an important source of nitrogen for growing trees. They do not bite or sting, and they provide quick snacks for raptors, fish, spiders, lizards, snakes and turtles. Most cicadas are essential critters who are benevolent to their habitats and environments.

PRELUDE: Common garter snakes are native to North America. The garter snake is the Massachusetts state reptile. Chances are most people have been startled after seeing a garter snake slithering in the grass or sunning itself on a rock. As a rule, they are the most common, harmless snake in the neighborhood. However, if you pick one up, it might try to defend itself with a nontoxic nip. But rest assured, it is not harmful. Garter snakes are benevolent and approachable. They eat the pests that munch your garden crops. They are a medium-sized snake of eighteen to fifty-five inches in length. I was inspired to write this narrative titled "There Is a Snake in the Grass" because I often see garter snakes around my home. In addition, within a rocky creek bed across from my home, one can on occasion spot a slightly poisonous copperhead snake.

THERE IS A SNAKE IN THE GRASS

If you spot a garter snake (*Thamnophis sirtalis*), do not be frightened! Leave it alone or shoo it away. If you try to pick it up, even though it is harmless, it will try to defend itself with a relatively harmless nip. (Photo by Jim Diamond of a garter snake outside his home, August 2019)

THERE IS A SNAKE IN THE GRASS

Snakes play an important role by sharing the environment we live in. They eat insects and mice and shoo away pesky house sparrows, European starlings, grey squirrels, voles and moles. Certain species of snakeskins (not garter snakes) are used to manufacture belts, handbags and wallets. Once while staying in a hotel in Bamako, the capital of The Republic of Mali, West Africa, I noticed the four walls and ceiling of an elevator were lined with tanned boa constrictor skins.

If you see a garter snake in the grass, leave it alone or shoo it away. If you have the intestinal fortitude and desire to pick it up, even though it is harmless, it will struggle and try to defend itself with a harmless nip. Do not kill it. Consider it your friend.

Some people keep snakes as pets, but snakes were intended to be wild reptiles, not pets. Often pet snakes grow to a size whereby they need to be euthanized* or turned loose in the wild.

A good example is found in the Florida Everglades. Many pet boa constrictors that have grown to a size where they are expensive to feed and become dangerous are released in the wild within the Everglades. A female boa constrictor can hatch sixty to seventy eggs annually. These snakes camouflage themselves so well they are virtually impossible to see with the naked eye. Even professional snake hunters in the Everglades cannot easily spot them. In Everglades National Park, boa constrictors are taking a serious toll on indigenous* populations of raccoons, squirrels, alligators, rabbits, birds, white-tailed deer, possums and other wildlife.

According to Alice K. Turner in her book *The History of Hell*, "Snakes were in the ancient world, because of their skin-shedding ability. Often they symbolized immortality or eternal youth."

If Turner's postulation has any semblance of truth, why is it an automatic response for most people to fear a garter snake in the grass? Why do many people go to great lengths to kill a snake, not knowing if it is poisonous, nonpoisonous, beneficial, or indigenous to the surrounding environment?

Throughout history, inquisitive children have entered their homes holding a common wiggly garter snake they enthusiastically caught to show Mom or Grandmom. With a lack of enthusiastic cheerfulness, mothers and grandmothers have yelled, "Get that thing out of my house!"

PRELUDE: Costa Rica has three species of anteaters: lesser, giant and silky. In all probability, the tree-dwelling lesser anteater, which is also called the collared anteater, is the most common. Anteaters can be found in grasslands, tropical dry areas and rainforests. In the wild, lesser anteaters eat termites, ants, soft fruits, grubs and bird eggs. Lesser anteaters do not have teeth. Their tongues are two feet long but only a half-inch wide. Their tongue is attached to their sternum, which enables it to flicker nearly 150 times per minute. When an anteater is feeding, their salivary glands secrete a sticky saliva that coats the tongue, making it easier to gather insects. I was inspired to write this narrative titled "Lesser Anteater" because of my excitement at seeing this critter for the first time in the wild. This animal was unique, different, unusual, exotic, colorful and eye-catching. I felt I needed to identify this critter and document some of my thoughts about it.

LESSER ANTEATER

In the wild, jaguars and other large cats kill lesser anteaters (*Tamandua tetradactyl*) for food. But humans are their greatest threat for extermination. Some are run over by cars on highways, while others are killed for their pelts. But the biggest problem is the destruction of their habitat by logging. (Photo by Jim Diamond in Costa Rica, February 2018)

LESSER ANTEATER

While on an evening hike on a mountain trail in Arenal Volcano National Park, an uncanny-looking animal came running on the trail behind us. I grabbed my camera and quickly aimed and took its picture. After I was able to see the photograph on my camera that evening in my room, I was able to identify it using a wildlife reference book and determined it was a lesser anteater, which is also called a collared anteater.

Lesser anteaters are solitary and nocturnal, and they spend much of their time in trees. In the wild, jaguars, cougars, ocelots, and other similar big cats kill lesser anteaters for food. However, humans are their worst predators.* People use and sell the lesser anteater pelts, and some are run over by automobiles, but the worst problem facing the lesser anteater is destruction of its habitat by logging.

When lesser anteaters are attacked by a predator, they defend themselves with their sharp claws.

I learned that lesser anteaters were named "anteater" because their diet consists largely of ants, termites and some soft-bodied grubs. It was interesting to learn that the lesser anteater does not have teeth. When they eat, the chewing is aided by pebbles they swallow with insects. The bugs are swallowed into the anteater's stomach, where strong muscles grind them up.

Anteaters use their long, sharp claws to agitate ants and termites in their homes. As the ants or termites come out of their home to protect it, the anteater collects the ants or termites with its two-foot-long sticky tongue and has a Costa Rican gourmet insect lunch.

As the lesser anteater sauntered past us (see photo), it paid no attention to us hikers and meandered on the trail until it was out of sight. The lesser anteater is considered the most pungent-smelling critter in the animal kingdom. Their loathsome odor is four to seven times more intense than a skunk. Nevertheless, we did not smell such an odor as the lesser anteater ambled before or after us.

The interior of a termite hill is a very complex structure created to house a society of termites. When a lesser anteater views an anthill as an obstacle, they use their sharp claws to agitate termites or ants. With their two-foot long sticky tongue, they slurp the attacking termite inhabitants from the termite mound for a tasty, nutritious termite meal.

I would like to conclude this narrative with a quote by Norman Vincent Peal from his book *The Power of Positive Thinking*, "Stand up to your obstacles and do something about them. You will find that they haven't half the strength you think they have."

Also, I'd like to share a saying I always liked, "Assumptions are the termites of relationships."

PRELUDE: In September 2018, with my dear friends Dave and Connie Kantner, I cruised from Miami, Florida, to the Republic of Cuba to visit a neighboring island that once was our friend, then our foe, and now desires to renew our friendship. I vividly remember 31 December 1958 when Fidel Castro finally ousted Fulgencio Batista and replaced his government with a revolutionary socialist state. Fifty-seven years later, it was reported that in the evening of 25 November 2016, Fidel Castro died of natural causes. Castro's body was cremated, and on 4 December 2016, his ashes were placed in a cedar box entombed by his brother Raul into a small niche on a boulder from *Sierra Maestra* Mountains near Santiago de Cuba, followed by a military band ceremony and a twenty-one-gun salute. Thousands of Cuban citizens commemorated the historic leader of Cuba's Revolution Sunday. I was inspired to write this narrative titled "Cuba Bids Farewell to Fidel Castro" to document my memories of Fidel Castro and his revolution.

CUBA BIDS FAREWELL TO FIDEL CASTRO

Being able to see the boulder with "Fidel" inscribed on it created an unconventional sensation within me about a person's death. It was a bittersweet moment because I had a mixture of self-gratification and sadness as I looked at that boulder. (Photo by Jim Diamond of Castro's Tomb near Santiago de Cuba in September 2018)

CUBA BIDS FAREWELLTO FIDEL CASTRO

Fidel Castro died of natural causes on the evening of 25 November 2016 at the age of 90. Being able to see that enormous solid boulder with "Fidel" inscribed on it created an unconventional sensation within me about a person's death. It was a bittersweet moment because concurrently I had a mixture of self-gratification and sadness as I looked at that boulder. According to *Granma*, Cuba's Communist Party Newspaper, the boulder containing Fidel Castro's ashes was from the *Sierra Maestra* mountain range, which was a stronghold for Fidel Castro and his rebels during their efforts to overthrow Fulgencio Batista. The *Sierra Maestra* mountain range was very prominent in the Cuban Revolution; it can be seen on the horizon from Castro's tomb (see photo).

Fidel Castro was the son of a wealthy Spanish farmer, who grew up to be a Cuban revolutionary and politician, then the leader of Cuba from 1959 to 2008, serving as the prime minister and president of Cuba.

The shape of his tomb was inspired by a line from a poem written by José Martí, "All the glory of the world fits in a single kernel of corn." For centuries corn, has been an integral component of mesa-American cultures, and many Latin American indigenous* groups who adjudged corn to be sacred. Yet truth be told, Cubans and visitors struggled to see a resemblance of a corn kernel in the boulder.

Following Fidel Castro's retirement, his health deteriorated, but he continued to interact with the Cuban people, published an opinion column titled "Reflections" in *Granma*, used a Twitter account, and gave occasional public lectures.

Although Fidel Castro was disliked by Americans, he did some good things for the Cuban people. He converted most of the Cuban military bases built by Fulgencio Batista's regime into schools. Fidel required all children to attend school. In talking with Cuban citizens in Santiago de Cuba, San Juan and Havana, they seemed to love him dearly. On the other hand, Cuban citizens who escaped to Florida despised Fidel Castro. Following the botched invasion at the Bay of Pigs, the Cuban Missile Crisis, and Cuba's alignment with the Marxist-Leninist doctrines in the former Soviet Union, the longtime camaraderie between American and Cuban leaders disintegrated.

The London *Observer* stated that Castro proved to be "as divisive in death as he was in life," and that the only thing that his "enemies and admirers" agreed upon was that he was "a towering figure" in the world who "transformed a small Caribbean island into a major force in world affairs."

Let's end this narrative with a Cuban proverb that goes like this, "A lie runs until it is overtaken by the truth."

During my Cuban visit, I sensed its people were beginning to be overtaken by truth.

PRELUDE: In 2020, I was fortunate to qualify for the People to People Educational travel through Oceania Cruises to Cuba. The category titled agricultural education qualified me to visit farmers in Cuba. After we arrived in Havana, we were scheduled to visit a farm for one day some twenty miles east of Havana. My first impression of the farm was it reminded me of a farm in southwestern Pennsylvania during the early 1940s. Our host farmer owned sheep, cattle, horses, hogs, goats, poultry, rabbits, fruit trees and vegetable garden. I was inspired to write this narrative titled "I Didn't Know That" because our Cuban friend could not purchase dewormers for his livestock due to the sanctions placed upon Cuba by United States. Because of the sanctions, animal dewormers simply were not available, such as Cydectin Oral Drench or Generic Ivermectin for sheep and Quest Plus Gel or Panacea Suspension for horses.

I DIDN'T KNOW THAT

Tobacco plants (*Nicotiana tabacum*) come from the nightshade family and contain a type of nicotine in their leaves. In 1828, doctor Wilhelm Heinrich Posselt and chemist Karl Ludwig Reinmann, both from Germany, first isolated nicotine from the tobacco plant and identified it as a poison. (Photographer unknown)

I DIDN'T KNOW THAT!

Our amicable Cuban host was very proud of his farmstead—even though he did not own the land. He enthusiastically showed us his small herd of Angus cattle, a few Suffolk sheep, some Nubian goats, six horses, and eleven black sows with several young piglets (breed unknown), a pen full of white New Zealand rabbits, and local chickens roaming around the farmstead. Also I counted six Toulouse geese at various places, a large vegetable garden, and a few fruit trees sprinkled around the farmstead. I recognized mango, avocado, guava and papaya trees. After observing the livestock, I concluded that improvement in management practices and updated facilities would increase his farm income.

While observing the livestock, I noticed the sheep, goats and horses exhibited indications that something was wrong with their physical well-being. When animals are heavily burdened with internal parasites, there are a variety of symptoms that can be observed to identify if they are infected. Some general symptoms typical of parasite infections cause anemia, loss of weight, poor condition, glassy eyes, tight hide and not thrifty. The sheep, goats and horses showed all of these symptoms. With my livestock background, these symptoms caused me to suspect intestinal parasites were the problem.

I did not want to embarrass our host by bringing my suspicion to his attention in front of the group. I diplomatically waited until I was able to get him alone away from his other guests. I privately asked him, "When was the last time you dewormed your sheep, goats and horses?" He responded, "Never!" I asked, "Why?" His response was, "I am not able to get the dewormer because of the sanctions placed against Cuba." I said, "Oh!" Then I asked, "Do you have a veterinarian nearby?" He responded by saying, "Yes, we have a veterinarian but he cannot get the dewormer as well because of the sanctions!" I responded, "Oh!" I thought about his plight for a few minutes, then approached this issue with a practical solution. I said to him, "I know tobacco is grown here in Cuba because Cuban cigars are very popular and expensive. What I want you to do is get 15-20 fully grown tobacco plants. Hang them upside-down from your barn rafters and let them get "bone" dry. Remove five or six plants from the rafters, break the dried leaves off the stalk and crush them with your hands over a five-gallon bucket. Then mix the crushed tobacco leaves into the feed and let the animals eat the tobacco in the feed. I want you to do this three times with two days in between feeding them tobacco. The nicotine in the tobacco will eliminate the worms from the intestinal tract of the animal, especially round worms."

My host said, "I didn't know that! I can easily get some tobacco plants to try this method of deworming my animals." This was a non-scientific method of deworming livestock, but in most cases it is effective. My father used to give chewing tobacco to his team of horses and I used to feed cigarettes to my sheep for this very reason. For my new Cuban farmer friend, this was an inexpensive and practical deworming method that could contribute to improving the management of his livestock and improve the general health of his animals until hopefully someday soon he may be able to purchase an approved dewormer for all of his animals.

PRELUDE: Diplomatic relations between the Republic of Cuba and the United States of America was severed in 1961, but on 20 July 2015 diplomatic representation was hinted at with the establishment of a Cuban Embassy in Washington, D.C. and a United States Embassy in Havana. I was inspired to write this narrative describing my trip to Cuba because my credentials fell into one of 20 licensed categories for authorized travel there. It was my first opportunity to visit this island country as an "agricultural educator" to observe and study Cuban agricultural and production practices. My first impression of the farm we visited in 2019 was like visiting a farm in Pennsylvania in 1940. However, it seemed to me that local organic farming was a noteworthy food production system for food security, environmental and sustainability on an island nation that imports 70 to 80 percent of its food consumed by the Cuban population. Small organic farms can be an important source of food for the residents throughout Cuba.

ORGANIC FARMING IN CUBA

Teams of oxen pull plows to prepare the red Cuban soil to grow organic food products for Cuban residents. Cuban farmers and their workers hand-weed row crops, and on occasion they spray biological products to control insects. (Photo by Jim Patrico of DTN/The Progressive Farmer)

ORGANIC FARMING IN CUBA

When the When the Soviet Union collapsed in 1991, Cuba lost its major source for fuel, fertilizer and pesticides. As an island nation, local organic farming was a notable food production system for food security, the environment and sustainability on an island nation that imports 70 to 80 percent of the food consumed by the Cuban population. Organic farming, also known as ecological farming or biological farming, is an agricultural system that uses fertilizers of organic origin such as compost, animal manure, green manure and bone meal plus placing emphasis on practicing crop rotation and companion planting. It originated in Europe early in the 20th century in reaction to rapidly changing farming practices. Small organic farms could be an important source of food for the residents throughout Cuba.

Cuban farmers have been hampered by a lack of access to modern farm equipment and supplies because of the US embargo. Organic farming typically requires more human labor, so it leads to higher levels of employment. Without fuel, fertilizer and pesticides, organic farming is a method of agriculture that is based on modeling agricultural practices of natural systems. Because organic techniques depend on microbial health of the soil, many farming practices are geared toward ameliorating soil health, for example, planting legumes to fix nitrogen in the soil, while certain flowering plants will attract pollinators. Tillage of other native plants provides "green" manure to improve soil nutrients. Additional soil-building techniques range from companion planting to rotational grazing of animals, to rotational planting of plants, to applying compost to soils and leaving fields fallow* for a season.

In some areas of Cuba, local organic farming has played a critical role in partial food availability for the Cuban people. Organic standards are designed to allow the use of naturally occurring substances prohibiting synthetic substances. Even though my Cuban friend did not own the land, he raised a small herd of cattle, a few sheep, draft horses, turkeys, chickens, hogs, vegetables and tropical fruits all without modern equipment or fertilizer, and he was very proud of his farming operation.

PRELUDE: The Republic of Cuba is the seventeenth largest island in the world, the second largest island in the Caribbean Sea and the ninth-most-populous island in the world. It is the largest country by land area in the Caribbean Sea and is located between the Atlantic Ocean and the Caribbean Sea. Diplomatic relations between Cuba and the United States were severed in 1961, however, on 20 July 2015 notable diplomatic relations were restored. United States diplomatic representation in Cuba is handled by the United States Embassy in Havana and a similar Cuban Embassy in Washington, D.C. Tourist travel in Cuba must fall into one of 20 licensed categories. I was inspired to write this narrative because it was my first opportunity to visit this island country where I vividly remember the revolution unfolding in 1959 led by Fidel Castro. Inasmuch, Cuban people and Fidel Castro despised the dictator regime of Fulgencio Batista in view of the fact that he allowed wealthy USA tycoons to exploit and control Cuba. Fidel Castro deemed it necessary to begin a revolution for change by attacking the Moncada Barracks in *Santiago de Cuba* on 26 July 1953. We were informed Castro's purpose for the attack was to snitch Batista's ammunition and arms for storage near Castro's hideout for future use.

THE REPUBLIC OF CUBA: FRIEND OR FOE?

Confident, optimistic and committed Cuban people are the entryway into Cuba's soul! Cuba's diversified people, whose ancestors hailed from Africa, Asia and Europe, have an inherent hope for their future and devoted love for their homeland. (Photo by Jim Diamond of Cuban Flag proudly flying in Havana, Cuba on 23 September 2018)

THE REPUBLIC OF CUBA: FRIEND OR FOE?

Cuba is more than just walking in Ernest Hemingway's footsteps or touring his cream-colored Havana home. Hopeful, optimistic and committed Cuban people are the entryway into Cuba's soul! Cuba's diversified people, whose ancestors hailed from Africa, Asia and Europe, have an inherent optimism for their future and devoted love for their homeland on the Caribbean Sea's second largest island.

Since Cuba's revolution in 1959, led by Fidel Castro, a massive reduction of ship traffic into and out of the Port of Havana occurred, especially in 1960 after the United States placed an embargo on imported goods. With Cuba's alignment with the former Soviet Union and its Communist principles, cargo ship traffic slightly increased in regular shipments from Eastern Europe. However, with the demise of the Soviet Union in 1991, shipping traffic into Havana's harbor was drastically reduced. When Fidel Castro alienated his hard-fought revolution by retrenching relations with the United States, it seriously impacted the Cuban lifestyles and economy, prevented thousands of American tourists from visiting the unique island while American businesses simultaneously withdrew.

On 3 February 1962 President John F. Kennedy signed Proclamation 3447 which established the embargo against Cuba to reduce "the threat posed by its alignment with Communist powers." Now 62 years later, in gentle Atlantic breezes, there may be some changes on the horizon. Efforts are being made to amend and update the Cuban Constitution which may enable the Cuban government and its citizens to be more free-enterprise oriented. President Bill Clinton in 1998 modified the embargo by authorizing the sale of certain foods and agricultural products to Cuba. However, President George W. Bush in 2004 tightened the embargo to include restrictions on travel and remittances to Cuba. President Barack Obama in 2015 announced a series of processes intended to normalize Cuban relations with the United States. American entrepreneurs immediately launched the process of establishing plans to schedule tourist ship services to the Republic of Cuba, even though trade embargoes were still in place.

I was fortunate to qualify as an agricultural educator for a general license titled group People-to-People through Oceania Cruises which authorized me to travel to Cuba. On 24 September 2018, on a private veranda outside my elegant stateroom on Sirena, an Oceania cruise ship, I sat writing this narrative as we peacefully sailed back to the United States from the Republic of Cuba. Long live the Republic of Cuba: hopefully as a dear friend and not as a despised foe.

PRELUDE: Life is complex in Honduras and especially problematical in slums, particularly when children do not have a "mum." It has been reported that single moms have been raped and abused. Often women gave birth to a child who inherited its "mum's" horrid drug addiction. Many more horrid, morbid examples exist. While visiting an artisan marketplace, we discovered a trove of handcrafted jewelry made by local Honduran people. Honduran jewelry production was a cottage industry whereby artisans expressed their personal solitude, compassion, tolerance and empathy for others to revere. As we explored and studied the various forms of jewelry, we learned that much of the jewelry reflected unwritten mor*ès* of Spanish influences or personal lifestyle stories. Jewelry such as earrings, necklaces, lockets, bracelets, rings and an assortment of men's jewelry were inexhaustible. Honduran families formed units made up of family members who worked together to make jewelry to sell. Even though the jewelry income was minimal, it was a means to generate some funds to support their respective family needs.

TAKE CARE OF MY "LAMBS"

Latin American Missionary and Bible (LAMB) Institute at San Buenaventura, Honduras is a refuge to care for little "lambs" that have suffered strife. It is a place committed to giving youngsters hope, a future and a purpose for their life. (Photo by Jim Diamond of a missionary with God's little "lambs" near San Buenaventura, Honduras)

TAKE CARE OF MY "LAMBS"

Latin American Missionary and Bible Institute (LAMB) is a place where the Lord accumulated a "flock" of little "lambs" that were so cuddly and cute. At San Buenaventura, Honduras is a LAMB refuge to care for little "lambs" that have suffered strife. A place committed to giving youngsters hope, a future and a purpose for their life.

Now for more than 80 of God's littlest "lambs" it's a Christ-centered residence for those who were rescued from poverty, abuse and violence. It's a place where youngsters learn about the love of Jesus and His devotion, an abode where little "lambs" can feel affection for Jesus and to love Him in spite of their location.

How can God's cute little "lambs" evolve to have a meaningful lifestyle? When a stranger sexually assaulted its young mother dressed only in a towel? How can God's cute little "lambs" grow to be a respectable young Honduran dweller while living with a single, unemployed mother without a husband in a dingy cellar?

Each of these "lambs" have a name like Sally, Jean, John or Kyle and each named lamb is being prepared and disciplined in His sight for a Christian lifestyle. Their lives are precious to Jesus and a plethora of volunteer missionaries are committed to carry out God's wish that these "lambs" evolve into Christian visionaries.

Pray for each of God's "lamb's" success! And that they do not have to again encounter duress. I profusely thank God for the opportunity to do His Will and to function as a volunteer who yearns that God's "lambs" will one day use their learned knowledge and skills with gumption.

PRELUDE: A wind turbine is an apparatus that converts kinetic energy from the wind into electricity. The blades of a wind turbine turn between 13 and 20 revolutions per minute, depending on their technology, at a constant or variable wind velocity. The wind turbine is automatically oriented to take maximum advantage of the kinetic energy of the wind. The wind makes the blades turn, which start to move with wind speeds of around 3.5 m/s (m/s means meters per second) and provide maximum power with a wind speed 11 m/s. For very strong winds (25 m/s), the blades are feathered and the wind turbine slows down to prevent excessive voltages. Wind turbines have an average life of over 25 years. I was inspired to write this narrative titled "Wind Turbines In Honduras" because I perceive this alternative source of energy has an important future role in eliminating carbon from the atmosphere to reduce global warming and provide a dependable and less expensive form of electricity. Wind turbine technology can yield lower maintenance costs, less downtime, increased energy production and a no-failure-prone gearbox.

WIND TURBINES IN HONDURAS

During a follow-up mission trip to Honduras I was astounded at the number of newly constructed wind turbines observed on mountainous areas surrounding the capitol Tegucigalpa. (Photo by Jim Diamond of newly constructed wind turbines near Tegucigalpa, Honduras)

WIND TURBINES IN HONDURAS

Many times we have been able to observe wind turbines dominating the landscape, but we do not always know how these colossal "fans" work or whether or not the wind turbines will assist unemployed people in paying electric bills with large extended families and low wages. During a recent follow-up mission trip to Honduras, I was astounded at the number of newly constructed wind turbines we observed on Cerro de Hula and Izopo Mountains surrounding the capitol Tegucigalpa. Honduran President Porfirio Lobo inaugurated "Cerro de Hula," Central America's largest wind farm, built by Gamesa and Iberdrola Engineering and outfitted with 51 of Gamesa's G87-2.0 MW turbines, The site's owner is Globeleq Mesoamerica Energy, a developer of renewable energy projects in Central America, operating through its local subsidiary Energía Eólica de Honduras.

Many times, here in Pennsylvania, observing wind turbines has become somewhat of a common and engrossing sight in mountainous regions. But in slum-dominated Tegucigalpa, Honduras and surrounding poverty-stricken communities, one normally asks, how do Honduran residents afford to hook into a wind-powered electricity distribution system?

A wind turbine will meet the needs of a home requiring 300 kilowatt hours per month in a location with a 14-mile-per-hour (6.26 meters-per-second) annual average wind speed. A small wind energy system can be connected to the electricity distribution system (called grid-connected system). A grid-connected wind turbine can reduce consumption of electricity for lighting, appliances, electric heating, cooling and vehicle charging. If the turbine cannot deliver the amount of energy needed the utility makes up the difference. However, when the wind system produces more electricity than a household requires, the excess is an electric credit. My question still remains: how will wind turbines assist unemployed people in paying electric bills with large extended families and low wages ?

Wind turbines cannot work without wind or when there is too little wind or as the blades are moving too slowly because the wind turbine no longer produces electricity. The turbine starts to create power at what is known as the cut-in speed. Power output continues to grow as the wind speed increases, but at a slower rate than it does right after the cut-in point. All of the critical functions of the wind turbine are monitored and supervised from the substation and the control center to detect and resolve any incidents. A wind turbine system should be installed by a professional installer who is a licensed electrician. These issues are associated with installing the wind system: a professional installer should find the most suitable location for a wind system, estimate the annual energy output and choose the proper size turbine and tower and decide whether to connect the system to the electric grid. The energy generated runs through the inside of the tower to the base. From there, the energy goes to an underground line to a substation where its voltage is raised to inject it into the electrical grid and distribute it to points of consumption.

I would like to close this narrative with this Chinese proverb, "When the wind of change blows, some people build walls, some build windmills." With that being said, my pastor once said to me, "When life brings big winds of change that almost blow you over, close your eyes, hang on tight and believe."

PRELUDE: The highlight of our Regent Seven Seas Cruise aboard the Seven Seas Marineri to Rio de Janeiro, Brazil on Monday 3 October 2014 was visiting the Christ the Redeemer Statue. This phenomenal statue on top of Corcovado Mountain (2,297 feet) in Tijuca National Park was nearly 100 feet high, weighing 700 tons and overlooks Rio De Janeiro. The statue of Christ the Redeemer was constructed between 1922 and 1931 and since its dedication on 12 October 1931 it has become a symbolic protector of people living in Rio De Janeiro's urban environment. I was inspired to write this narrative titled "Christ the Redeemer" because of the awesome personal feelings that unfolded within me as I looked up at Brazil's magnificent National Historic Heritage.

CHRIST THE REDEEMER STATUE

We purchased tickets to take the cog train most of the way up to the statue. During this event we got a wheelchair for Betty because she was unsteady in her walking. (Photo by Jim Diamond of the escalator from where we disembarked the cog train on 10 March 2014)

CHRIST THE REDEEMER STATUE

With dear friends Dave and Connie Kantner we decided to visit the phenomenal Christ the Redeemer Statue on top of Corcovado Mountain (2,297 feet) in Tijuca National Park overlooking Rio De Janeiro, Brazil. We purchased tickets to take the cog train most of the way up to the statue. We boarded the cog train by pushing Betty safely in her wheelchair and we had an enjoyable trip up that steep mountain. When the cog train reached its end we disembarked the train and walked a short distance to an escalator to take us to the top (see photo). A young man wearing a yellow vest with a badge to indicate he was an employee saw Betty was in a wheelchair and said to us, "It is my duty to safely take her up the escalator." When we got to the viewing deck, he said to call him when we were ready to descend down the escalator. We profusely thanked him for his kindness and concern. We respectfully stared at and photographed that awesome statue for nearly an hour at different angles and places because it captivated our basic knowledge of Christ. This statue of Christ has become a symbol of Christianity around the world in addition to being a cultural icon of Brazil.

It was time to be on our way from that wonderful, reverent visit to begin our odyssey back down the escalator to board the cog train. I searched and searched for that young man with the yellow vest and he was nowhere to be found. I told Betty I could hold her wheelchair with no problem going down the escalator. I pushed Betty in the wheelchair to the escalator and we slowly began to descend. As we were about halfway down, Betty's wheelchair started to roll and I could not hold it back. The wheelchair went backward toward me and I held Bettys head so she would not bang it against the step behind her. Whoa! What a predicament! No one offered to help, but someone down front hit a button to stop the escalator. Betty was holding a cane and somehow it got lost amongst the crowd. We were able to get Betty to stand up even though she was physically and emotionally injured. With her head bleeding a bit, she was able to walk down the remaining steps on the idled escalator and we boarded the next cog train to the entrance portal. There a nurse came to treat Betty's head and we got a taxi to take us back to our hotel. We were able to get a hotel driver to take us to a local hospital to get Betty's head wound treated. What a frustrating experience we had getting someone to treat Betty. We waited nearly one hour to get a nurse to clean and bandage her small wound. We were instructed to wait until a doctor came to look at Betty. We waited two additional hours but he never came, so we telephoned the hotel and asked them to send their driver to pick us up. We were able to meet up with the Kantners and together we had a nice dinner at the restaurant in the hotel and reflected on the day's experiences. Whew! What a horrifying and exhilarating Brazilian incident that will be forever remembered.

I would like to close this narrative with a note by an unknown poet who wrote, "Sadness is when the reality is contrary to what you expected." When I could no longer control that wheelchair I was petrified for Betty's safety; I was disheartened because the happiness Betty experienced on that observation deck was impaired; I was personally embarrassed that I could not control that wheelchair; I was saddened that the reality of this disheartened incident was not what I expected. I thanked God over and over that Betty successfully recovered from her distress and that we could happily continue our voyage through South America.

PRELUDE: Some of the most popular coffee in the world originates in South America, and perhaps no country in the region does it better than Brazil. Brazil's geography within the tropical zone is ideal for growing coffee. Brazil has an estimated 300,000 coffee plantations spread across 13 of its states. Even though harvest season runs from May to August, like most people I drink coffee all year. I was inspired to write this narrative titled "Brazil Coffee" because I drink one cup of coffee each morning with my breakfast, but I was not aware that Brazil was the largest exporter in the international coffee trade. While in Sao Paulo, Brazil with dear friends Dave and Connie Kantner, my wife Betty and I visited a warehouse stacked high with hundreds of sacks filled with coffee waiting to be exported from the Port of Santos, Brazil's primary coffee exporting port. The Port of Santos is also home to two regions where high-quality coffee is grown.

BRAZILIAN COFFEE

Brazilian farmers produce 40 to 60 million bags annually, and is also known for being the world's largest exporter of instant coffee. Brazil produces some 25 percent of the world's coffee supply. (Photo by Jim Diamond of bagged coffee in Sao Paulo, Brazil during October 2014)

BRAZILIAN COFFEE

Coffee grown in Brazil is predominantly of the arabica variety, which is approximately 80% of the total Brazilian crop. In recent years, Brazilian farmers have produced 40 to 60 million bags annually, and the country also is known for being the world's largest exporter of instant coffee. Brazil produces some 25% of the world's coffee supply. The largest international buyers of Brazilian coffee (in descending order) are Belgium, Japan, Italy, the United States and Germany. Not only is Brazil the largest exporter of coffee, it is also among the countries that drink the most coffee.

Brazilian coffee is usually exported in these forms: green coffee, ground & roasted coffee, instant coffee (aka: soluble coffee), concentrate essential extracts, and coffee residues (aka: coffee grounds). Coffee first came to Brazil in the early 18th century when in 1727, Lieutenant Colonel Francisco de Mello Palheta was commissioned by Portugal to steal a coffee plant from French Guiana. Supposedly after smuggling the coffee plant into Brazil, Palheta began to cultivate it in the state of Pará. Stimulated by European and American market demands, by the 1840s, Brazil dominated the world coffee market.

The state of Minas Gerais is by far Brazil's most important coffee-producing state; nearly half of the entire country's coffee production is based there. Higher elevations and rich soils in this state make it perfect for growing the country's famous specialty coffees.

Brazilian specialty coffee is sun-dried with natural processing. After its 17 varieties are produced at elevations of 3,300 to 3,500 feet on red mineral soils, it is selectively harvested, electronically sorted, sun-dried naturally and is sustainable-certified directly by the farmer.

I would like to close this narrative by citing Nanu Hoffman, founder of Sweatpants & Coffee, an online magazine, who wrote, "With enough coffee, I feel as though all things are possible. Many of them are highly unlikely, but they are possible." With this all being said, it is possible that today's good mood was prompted by reading this narrative titled Brazilian Coffee while supping a cup of hot, steaming Brazilian java with a dear friend.

Glossary

ACACIA - A tropical tree that has narrow leaves and dark fruit pod.

ACID RAIN - Any form of precipitation with acidic components, such as sulfuric or nitric acid that fall to the ground from the atmosphere in wet or dry forms.

A-DAY - A three-day activities event at Delaware Valley College. It is a family friendly event organized and run by the students to benefit campus activities, clubs and brings the campus and surrounding community together for educational exhibits, competitions, entertainment, fun and great food.

AGRICULTURAL EXTENSION OFFICER - A government employee who offers a non-formal agricultural education programs to rural people.

AGRICULTURAL EXTENSION SYSTEM - A nonformal agricultural education programs to rural people.

AGRONOMIST - An expert in the science of soil management and crop production.

AGONAL BREATHING - Serious medical sign requiring immediate medical attention that generally progresses to apnea and death.

AGRARIAN - Relating to the ownership and use of land, especially farmland.

AKA - Also Known As.

AMISH - Members of a strict Mennonite sect that established major settlements in Pennsylvania.

ANGALIO - Saramajingaye word - African throwing knife.

ANIMAL UNIT – 1,000-pound beef cow.

ANIMISTIC - Belief in the existence of spirits separable from bodies.

ARTIC CRAWLER - A slow-moving tundra vehicle that can travel on ice, over snow, in water and deep mud.

ASTHMA - A disease that affects the lungs and causes coughing, tight feelings in the chest and abrupt difficulty in breathing.

BAKELITE - A hard, infusible and chemically resistant plastic.

BALAFON - A tuned West African percussion instrument.

BALEEN – A horny substance that grows as fringed plates from the upper jaws of certain whales to strain food, especially small crustaceans from the water.

B AYA RITES - Girls that reach maturity and are initiated into tribal restricted traditions.

BBC - British Broadcasting Corporation.

B.C. - Before Christ.

BEEHIVES – Manmade structures meant to house bees.

BIALY - A flat bread roll topped with chopped onions.

BIRDER - A person who likes to watch birds.

BITUMINOUS COAL - A solid carbonaceous residue derived from low-ash, low-sulfur bituminous coal from which the volatile constituents are driven off by burning in coke oven at temperatures as high as 2,000 degrees Fahrenheit.

BLACK LUNG - Coal workers' pneumoconiosis (CWP), commonly known as "black lung disease," occurs when coal dust is inhaled. Continued exposure to the coal dust causes scarring in the lungs, impairing your ability to breathe.

BREAM – A common fish found in the Zambezi River, Zimbabwe and Zambia.

BREACH - A leap out of the water by a whale.

BOVINE An animal of the cattle group, which also includes buffaloes and bisons.

BOB - Move the head up and down. - The front of a ship.

BTU - British Thermal Units.

BUGLE A loud bugle-like mating sound of a bull elk, moose, wapiti and other species of deer.

BURDIZZO - Name brand of a company that makes a castration device which employs a large clamp designed to break the blood vessels leading into the testicles.

BUSH - Uncultivated and sparsely populated wild areas of land covered with unaffected vegetation, especially in Africa.

BUSHEL - A measure of capacity used to measure custom coal sales.

CABRITA - Meat from a young goat.

CALLER - In American, a form of square dancing, dancers are prompted through a sequence of steps by a caller to the beat of music.

CALVE - Act of a cow giving birth to a calf. - To release a mass of ice that breaks away.

CALVING - When giant pieces of ice fall from the glacier into the bay to form huge chunks of floating ice and icebergs.

CAMOUFLAGE - Coloration, size, movements, body shape, time of day and other methods wildlife use to blend into their respective environment to avoid being seen by predators.

CANTON - A subdivision of a country established for political or administrative purposes.

CARNIVOROUS - Animals with a digestive system that digests meat of prey animals.

CARDING WOOL - An operation that converts loose, cleaned scoured wool into continuous, untwisted strands.

CASTRATE – To remove the testicles of an animal.

CAY - A low bank or reef of coral, rock or sand.

CENTIMETER - A metric unit of length = 0.3937 inch.

CFA - A currency used by fourteen African countries.

CHEVON - Meat from a mature goat.

CHUNCE – A mud brick structure with openings at the end of each brick to allow dry winds to pass through the chamber to dry hanging grapes.

CHU CHU - A Mongolian reindeer half wild from fending for themselves on the steppe. They respond to the nomadic herder command "chu, chu."

CINNAMON FLOP - A a moist breakfast cake with a brown sugar and cinnamon crumble topping.

CLAPPER - A free-swinging piece of metal or wood or horn suspended on the inside of a bell that when jostled strikes the side of the vessel and causes a distinct sound.

CLEARWATER DELL - Name of the author's home.

COAL MINING PATCH - Small villages with a few dozen to a hundred frame houses, with a coal company store and perhaps a chapel.

COKE - A substance made from coal; it consists of around 70 percent carbon and 30 percent hydrogen and can be used in blast furnaces for smelting and purifying iron ore.

COLACA – The final anatomical section of a bird.

CONEY – Common name for rabbit meat.

CORD - A pile of wood with a volume of 128 cubic feet, measured as a pile of wood eight feet long, four feet high and four feet wide.

CORIOLIS – Water going down in a drain in the Southern Hemisphere spins clockwise. Scientists claim this motion is caused by the Earth's rotation.

COVERT - Bird feathers covering the bases of the main flight or tail feathers.

COUTE DE JETE – French word - African throwing knife.

CRESHE – A group of young impalas.

CRIMP - The wave effect of wool fibers. Usually the fiber wools show the most crimp. Uniformity of desired crimp generally indicates superior wool.

CRIMPER - A piece of tractor pulled equipment attached to a mowing machine with two rollers that crushes the stems to decrease the drying process time.

CHRYSALIS – The inactive state of butterflies.

DEAD FURROW - Last open groove in a plowed field made by a moldboard plow.

DECIDUOUS – A tree or shrub that sheds its leaves annually.

DECONSECRATED - Transfer a building from sacred to secular use.

DESERTIFICATION - Dry Harmetin winds blow Sahara Desert sand in Southerly directions towards where people live and farm.

DETRITUS - Usually, refers to waste some kind, but it can actually mean any accumulation of material such as piles of dead leaves.

DIABASE - A solidified rock with fine or medium-size grain formed by intense volcanic heat underground.

DIRECT CURRENT ELECTRICITY - One-directional flow of electric charge. An electrochemical cell is a prime example of DC power.

DISC HARROW - An agricultural implement that is used to chop up unwanted weeds or crop residue and is used to till the soil where crops are to be planted.

DIURNAL CYCLE - Variations in meteorological parameters such as temperature and relative humidity over the course of a day that result from the rotation of the Earth about its axis and the resulting change in incoming and outgoing radiation.

DOO DOO - Slang for solid excrement of Greater Kudu.

DOWRY - Money or property paid by the bride's family to the groom or his family at the time of marriage.

DRIVER - A person piloting a light, two-wheeled horse-drawn vehicle in harness racing

DUTCH DOORS - Two half doors on top of each other. The top door can be opened with the bottom door closed. The bottom door can be opened with the top door closed.; or both doors can be opened or closed.

ECHOLOCATION - Locating prey and objects by reflected sound used by animals such as dolphins and bats.

ECOSYSTEM - An environment that local groups of interdependent organisms inhabit and depend on for continued existence.

ENCLOSURE - An archaeological term that refers to a wide wall or fence that surrounds a designated area(s).

EPHEMERIS - A table giving calculated positions of a celestial object at regular intervals throughout a period of time.

EUSOCIAL - Insects that exhibit advanced social organization where one queen produces offspring and nonproductive bees care for the young.

EUTHANIZE – To put to death an animal that is suffering from an incurable illness or serious injury.

EWE – A female sheep.

FALLOW - Arable land left without sowing for one or more years to allow it to recover and store organic matter while retaining moisture and disrupting pest life cycles.

FAO - Food and Agriculture Organizasstion of United Nations

FARMING SYSTEMS RESEARCH - A system of doing agricultural research on African farms without previous research based knowledge or information as guidelines. This style of doing research assumed that the farmer would more readily adapt changes.

FARRIER - A specialist in equine hoof care, including the trimming and balancing of horses' hooves and placing of shoes on their hooves if necessary.

FAUNA - Animal life of a particular region, considered as a whole.

FERMENT - The chemical breakdown of sugars converted to ethyl alcohol by bacteria, yeasts or other microorganisms as a process involved in making wine or beer.

FERROMAGNETISM - A property of certain materials such as iron that results in a significant, observable magnetic permeability.

FFA – Future Farmers of America. An organization of, for and by high school students interested in agricultural sciences and leadership. The organization is now for any student to explore a broader spectrum of careers.

FJORD - A narrow inlet from the sea between cliffs.

FIORDLAND - A geographic region in the Southwestern corner of New Zealand's South Island dominated by steep mountains with it's valleys flooded by ocean water.

FLEECE - Total amount of wool on a sheep before or after it has been sheared.

FLORA - Systematic descriptions of plants found in a region at a particular time and/or place.

FORB OR PHORB - An herbaceous flowering plant that is not a graminoid (grasses, sedges and rushes), examples of which include sunflowers and milkweed.

4-H CLUB - The youth development program of the Cooperative Extension System and USDA, maintained by National 4-H Council and America's largest youth development organization—empowering nearly six million young people with the skills to lead for a lifetime.

FRAGMENT BREED - Selective breeding of the Icelandic sheep began in the 19th century but it led to diseases that the Icelandic sheep was very sensitive to and therefore it was stopped. Today it is forbidden to import sheep to Iceland, so it has remained very isolated in Iceland and is therefore one of the purest breeds of sheep in the world.

FSR - Farming Systems Research

FUMAROLE - An opening in or near a volcano, through which hot sulfurous gases emerge.

GEE - A command for an animal (dogs, horses) to go to the right.

GEOTHERMAL ENERGY - Heat energy from the Earth.

GILDING – To cover with gold paint.

GILT – An immature female pig that has not yet given birth to a litter.

GLEANER - An annual literary and artistic journal that features poetry, short stories, creative nonfiction, drawings, paintings and photos submitted by students, faculty and staff at Delaware Valley University.

GOD'S WINDOW - One the Blyde River Canyon Nature Reserve's most astonishing views over South Africa's lowveld with majestic cliffs that plunge down 700 meters.

GREASE WOOL - Wool that has been sheared from a sheep but not yet scoured (cleaned).

GREENHAND DEGREE - The first of four degrees in the FFA (Greenhand, Chapter, State Farmer and American Farmer).

GROWTH RING - A casing of cell forming concentric rings in the cross-section of a woody tree trunk and each ring represent a year's growth that begins in the spring.

GRUEL - (aka *boulle*) A dish similar to a porridge, made by boiling sorghum or corn meal in water until firm that is consumed by using the fingers, breaking off a morsel and dipping it into the gravy-like sauce with pieces of venison.

HALAL - Meat butchered as prescribe by Muslim law.

HERBIVORES - Animals that eats only plants.

HOT HOUSE LAMBS - Lambs that weigh 35 to 50 pounds and are harvested and sold to ethnic groups who consider lamb an important dish for Easter Sunday dinner.

HAND - A measurement of four inches to measure the height of a horse from the ground to the withers (top of the shoulders).

HARVEST FOR ALL PROGRAMS – Program where American Farm Bureau's young farmers and ranchers work to help provide food to those in need around our country. Throughout the year, farmers and ranchers across the nation donate food, funds and people power to create a hunger-free America.

HAW - A command for an animal (dogs, horses) to go to the left.

HEATHER - A purple-flowered Eurasian heath that grows abundantly on Moorland and Heathland.

HECTARE - A unit of land measure: 2.47 acres = one hectare.

HEMATITE – Heavy and relatively hard oxide mineral, ferric oxide that constitutes the most import ant iron ore because of its high iron content (70 percent) and abundance.

HERMAPHRODITE - An animal or plant that has both female and male organs for reproduction and secondary sexual traits.

HIDE - A structure where people can safely be concealed to observe wild animals and birds unnoticed.

HOAR FROST - In the early morning when the dew freezes, a white frost is formed onto grass and trees.

HOLLOW – Term used by local people in western Pennsylvania, parts of West Virginia and Southern Ohio for a valley within the hills.

HOMOGENIZE - A process used to mix and disperse milk fat globules to prevent milk from separating and give it a more homogeneous texture.

HORTICURALIST - A person on whose work involves growing fruits vegetables, flowers or ornamental plants.

HUTCH - A type of cage used primarily for housing domestic rabbits.

INDIGENOUS - Originating in and typical of a region or country.

INSECTIVORES - Animals or birds that eat insets as a major portion of their diets.

IRON AGE - Depending upon the region, it is a period of time that falls between 1200 BC and 600 BC.

JERRY-RIGGING - Something made or formed in a particular place or by a particular process or alter a thing so that it is formed into something different to replace a needed automobile part.

JOCKEY - A professional person who rides a horse in.a horse race.

KAPOCK - A fibrous, cottonlike substance that grows around the seeds of the ceiba tree and is used as a stuffing in bed mattresses in several African countries.

KAREX - An underground channel in the Gobi Desert to transport water from the mountain to an oasis called Turpan in the middle of the desert to irrigate grapes and other minor crops.

KEFIR- A sour Irish drink made from goat milk fermented with certain bacteria.

KEMP - Courseness of wool fibers.

KERATINOUS - Main component in hair and horns.

KEYSTONE SPECIES - A species that plays a critical role in maintaining the structure of an ecological community.

KINDLE - The act of a rabbit giving birth.

KIWI - Nickname for New Zealand citizens.

KNOBKERRY - A large club with a job at one end and can be used for throwing at animals in hunting or for clubbing an enemy's head.

KOB DE BUFFOON - An antelope found in the northern savannas across sub-Saharan Africa from Senegal to South Sudan.

KRAAL - In many African societies, an enclosure constructed near village huts where cattle and other livestock are confined.

LATENT NEEDS - Needs not currently met by existing products or services that are generally not known to be needed by consumers.

LEA - Grassland or meadows.

LETHORA - A material made from the skin of an animal by tanning or a similar processing.

LICHENS - A complex symbiosis of algae and fungi that appear green or gray or yellow and are usually found on rocks and trees.

LIFER - The first time a birdwatcher sees a new bird and adds it to his/her bird list.

LITTORAL - Of or relating to the shore of a lake, sea, or ocean.

LOAM - A fertile soil of clay and sand containing humus.

LODE - A vein of metal ore in the Earth.

LOLOLA – Local term in Swaziland used for the practice of paying for a bride price in the form of cattle.

MAIZE - Field corn.

MAGNETOCEPTION - The premise that an influence of a magnetic field as it relates to the brain of an organism.

MARCHE - French word – Market.

MARSUPIAL - A mammal whose young who are incompletely born but carried and suckled in a pouch on the mother's belly.

MASTITIS - Inflammation in a cow's udder as a result of staphylococci and/or streptococci infection, a symptom of which is long, stringy milk stripped from the teat.

MELANISM - An unusual darkening of body tissues caused by excessive production of melanin, a dark brown to black pigment occurring in the hair or skin.

METER - A unit of measure. 1 meter = 39.3700 inches.

MOHAIR - The long, silky hair of the angora goat.

MOLT - A loss of skin especially as a regular feature of a tick's life cycle. The adult ticks shed their third molt before they lay eggs.

MOONBOW - Rare natural atmospheric phenomena that occur when moonlight is reflected and refracted off water droplets in the air from Victoria Falls.

MORES - Norms that are widely observed and have great moral significance.

MULLIONED - Vertical bar between the panes of glass in a window.

MUSHER - Driver of a dog sled team.

MYCORRHIZA – A fungal root.

NANO-INDENTATION - A powerful, quantitative method for obtaining mechanical properties from very small volumes.

NIPPERS - A tool used for nipping a horse hoof to the white line during the hoof trimming process.

OLIVINE - An important rock-forming mineral group.

OMNIVORE – An animal that eats food of both plant and animal origin.

ORT - A morsel of food: leftovers.

ORI - Indigenous Polynesian people of New Zealand.

OSCYPEK *(os-TSEH-peck)* - A smoked cheese made from salted sheep's milk in the Tatra Mountains in the Southern region of the Republic of Poland.

PACE - When a horse moves in a lateral gait where both legs on the same side are lifted together.

PASTEURIZE – A process where milk is treated with mild heat, usually to less than 100°C (212°F), to eliminate pathogens and extend shelf life.

PINNACLED - A natural peak, especially a distinctively pointed one on a glacier.

PIROQUE – French word - A long, narrow canoe made from a single tree trunk.

PISTE - Two commonly traveled wheel tracks that enable one to drive their vehicle in and through the bush that are commonly found in Africa's undeveloped national parks.

PLACE - When one bets on a horse to place, they win money if the horse finished the race first or second.

POD - A group of whales or hippos.

POINT - The end of a mountainous summit.

POLLED - Cattle having the horns cut off or being naturally hornless.

POLLINATION - Transfer of pollen to an ovule in a flower to allow fertilization - Flower nectar provides bees with the sugar to fuel their flights. The proteins and amino acids in pollen are vital nutrients needed by young bee larvae back in the hive.

PORT - Left side of a ship when looking toward the ships front (bow).

POTABLE - Drinking water that is safe to consume.

PREDATOR - A carnivorous animal that hunts, kills and eats other animals to survive.

PROSE POETRY - A body of work that appears as prose but reads like poetry, lacking the line breaks associated with poetry while maintaining a poetic quality.

QUILTING - The process of joining a minimum of three layers of fabric together either through stitching manually using a needle and thread.

RACK WINE - Siphoning wine off the sediment at the bottom off wine cask or carboy.

RAM – A male sheep.

REBAR – A rigid steel rod reinforcing concrete.

RENNET – A substance made of enzymes that are found in the lining of unweaned calf, lamb or kid. Young mammals' main source of food is milk. The enzymes slow down the digestions of the liquid milk by turning it to a solid in the mammal's stomach, young animals, typically veal. A lot of rennet can be made from each animal.

REPARIAN - Relating to or living or located on the bank of a natural watercourse (such as a river. creek) or sometimes of a lake or a tidewater.

RESTITUTION - To restore to a former state or position or to give back.

RINDERPEST - A viral disease mainly affecting cattle, sheep, goats, cape buffalo and some species of antelope in Central Africa.

ROE - Fish eggs.

ROOST - A place where birds settle to rest at night.

ROSIN - Used as internal reinforcement for very thin skinned metal objects - things like silver, copper or tin plate candlesticks where it is simply melted, poured into a hollow thin-skinned object, and left to harden.

ROUND – Large muscles found on the hind leg of a cow or bull.

RUMINANT - Animals that are able to acquire nutrients from plants by fermenting it in a specialized stomach prior to digestion through microbial actions. The process takes place in the front part of the digestive system.

RUT - An annual time of the year when male deer fight other males for access to mate female deer.

SAN - Bushmen, are the members of any of the indigenous hunter-gatherer cultures of southern Africa, and the oldest surviving cultures.

SAVANNA - Flat grassland, sometimes with scattered trees in tropical regions.

SCRAPPIE - A fatal prion disease of sheep and goats characterized by twitching, excitability, intense itching and excessive thirst.

SECOND CUTS - When a sheep shearer makes a second stroke over sheared area cutting off short pieces of wool that is too small to spin.

SERACS - A pinnacle or block of ice in the crevasses or slope of a glacier.

SETTLE - A cow that has been bred by a bull, or other domestic animals that have been mated with a male of that species.

SHAMAN - A person regarded as having access to, and influence in, the world of good and evil spirits.

SHOCK - (aka stook) A group of twelve sheaves of grain placed upright and supporting each other to allow the grain to dry and ripen.

SHOTGUN - A long-barreled firearm designed to shoot a straight-walled cartridge known as a shotshell.

SHOW - When one bets on a horse to show, they win money if the horse finished the race first, second or third.

SILVICULTURE - Science and practice of growing a forest, which includes soil preparation, planting seedlings, seeding, tending, management, marking timber and harvesting timber.

SILICOSIS - A form of occupational lung disease caused by inhalation of crystalline silica dust.

SKEET - A shooting sport in which a clay target is thrown from a trap to simulate the flight of a bird.

SPENT - Crop residue after being harvested such as dried corn stalks, straw and husks.

SPERMATHECA - A sac in a honeybee queen to store sperm.

SPINDLE – The traditional shape of Oscypek, smoked sheep's cheese from the Podhale region.

SPINNERS - Persons who spin cleaned wool into yarn using a spinning wheel.

SPINNING WHEEL - A wheel mounted on a frame and operated by a treadle that twists wool fibers into yarn.

SPINNING - The process of drawing out and twisting wool fibers into yarn.

STOCK – Part of a shotgun that is composed of two parts: the butt-stock and the fore-end or forearm. The butt-stock is the piece of the shotgun that marries to your shoulder and cheek, and allows the trigger-hand a grip.

STRIP MINING - Removal of soil from top of a bituminous coal seam to be stripped with draglines and hauled away to steel mills, power plants and home heating.

STOMATA - A pore found in the epidermis of leaves, stems and other organs that controls the rate of gas exchange between the internal air spaces of the leaf and the atmosphere.

STRIP A MILK COW – A process by which milk is squirted into a strip cup. Stringy milk on the cup's screen is a symptom of mastitis. Also stripping each teat stimulates the cow to begin dropping her milk from the four-teat cistern.

STICK SLIP PHENOMENON - A type of motion exhibited by objects in contact sliding over one another. The movement of a bow across a string to create musical tones in a bowed string instrument.

SUINT – Dried perspiration in oil form deposited in wool from sheep. Contains potassium salts.

SULKY - A light two-wheeled horse-drawn vehicle for one person, used in harness racing.

SWIDDEN – A field created by slash-and-burn agriculture, a farming method that involves the cutting and burning of plants in a forest or woodland.

SYMBIOTIC – A mutually beneficial relationship.

SYMBOLOGY - The art of expression by symbols.

TEDDER - A piece of equipment pulled by a tractor that takes the hay out of windrows and spreads it flat across the field allowing it to dry faster.

TEFF - Cultivated for its edible seeds. It is one of the most important staple crops in Ethiopia and Eritrea.

TERMINAL LAKE - Lakes where water flows in but not out that are fed by streams and water leaves by evaporation or by seeping into the ground.

THRESHING MACHINE - A huge labor intensive machine powered with a pulley and wide belt from a stationary tractor. Sheaves of wheat are placed into the thresher where grain is separated from the straw. Straw is blown onto a straw stack and grain falls into burlap sacks.

TOPOR - A state of physical or mental inactivity.

TRANSHUMANCE – A seasonal type of nomadism in Africa whereby people and cattle are moved over huge areas of land regardless of international boundaries to find grass and water.

TREKKING - A long arduous journey, especially one made on foot.

TRIBUTARY – A river or stream flowing into a larger river.

TROT – When a horse proceeds at a pace faster than a walk, lifting each diagonal pair of legs alternately.

TUNDRA - The nearly level treeless plain between the ice cap and the timber line of North America that has permanently frozen subsoil.

TUYA - A flat-topped, steep-sided volcano formed when lava erupts through a thick glacier or ice sheet in Iceland.

TWITCHER - A person who goes to great lengths to view new bird species, usually to add to their life list.

UNHARROWED - Unplowed.

UP LAND PARK - Upland areas are high above sea level. They usually experience lower temperatures, higher rainfall and higher wind.

VELD – In Southern Africa, expansive grasslands in higher altitudes.

WARP - In weaving, the threads on a loom over and under which other threads (the weft) are passed to make cloth.

WEAN - When an animal reaches an age when it no longer suckles milk from its mother.

WHORL - An individual circle, oval, volution or equivalent in a whorled pattern, which consists of a spiral or multiple concentric objects (including circles, ovals and arcs).

WIN - When one bets on a horse to win, they win money if the horse finished the race first.

WINDROW - A long line of hay across the field made by tripping the hay rake in line with previous raked hay.

WITHERS - The highest part of a horse's back, at the base of the neck above the shoulders. The height of a horse is measured to the withers.

WOODEN SOUND BOARD - The surface of a string instrument that the strings vibrate against, usually via some sort of bridge.

WOOL POOL - A cooperative managed by members who own small flocks of sheep that brings their small lots of wool to a central location (pool) and creates a sizeable volume of wool preferred by large wool companies.

YARN - A tale that relates to a personal experience or event.

www.ingramcontent.com/pod-product-compliance
Lightning Source LLC
Chambersburg PA
CBHW081527120626

46550CB00009B/2643